OF **DIVINE**
ECONOMY

OF DIVINE ECONOMY
REFINANCING REDEMPTION

MARION GRAU

T&T CLARK INTERNATIONAL
A Continuum imprint
NEW YORK • LONDON

Copyright © 2004 by Marion Grau

All rights reserved. No part of this book may be reproduced, stored in a retrieval system, or transmitted in any form or by any means, electronic, mechanical, including photocopying, recording, or otherwise, without the written permission of the publisher, T & T Clark International.

T & T Clark International, Madison Square Park, 15 East 26th Street, New York, NY 10010
T & T Clark International, The Tower Building, 11 York Road, London SE1 7NX
T & T Clark International is a Continuum imprint.

Unless otherwise indicated, biblical quotations are from the New Revised Standard Version Bible, copyright 1989, Division of Christian Education of the National Council of the Churches of Christ in the United States of America. Used by permission. All rights reserved.

Cover art: *One Window* by Robert Delaunay, Musee National d'Art Moderne, Centre Georges Pompidou, Paris/SuperStock

Cover design: Jim Booth

Library of Congress Cataloging-in-Publication Data

Grau, Marion.
  Of divine economy : refinancing redemption / Marion Grau.
      p. cm.
  Includes bibliographical references and index.
  ISBN 0-567-02730-9 (hardcover)—ISBN 0-567-02740-6 (pbk.)
  1. Redemption—Christianity. 2. Feminist theology. 3. Economy of God. I. Title.
  BT775.G69 2004
  234—dc22
                          2004010714

Printed in the United States of America

04 05 06 07 08 09   10 9 8 7 6 5 4 3 2 1

Contents

Acknowledgments — vii

Introduction — 1

Chapter 1—Of Divine Currencies in Postmodernity — 23

Chapter 2—Found Lacking: Masculine Hysteria and the Economics of Redemption — 41

Chapter 3—Ms.Appropriating Properties: Hysterical Women and the Gendering of Redemption — 91

Chapter 4—Divine Commerce: A Countereconomic Reading of Redemption — 135

Chapter 5—Divine Economy Refinanced — 173

Works Cited — 227

Index — 243

Acknowledgments

This book has been blessed by many gifts and investments into the life of its author. Günter and Heidi, my parents, have ceaselessly supported my ongoing quest for wisdom, even when that quest has led me far away from native German turf and from the family bakery. My sister, Ines, and my brother, Axel, have continued in the family business, which has allowed their older sister to squander her inheritance elsewhere.

In a gesture that reminded me of its (somewhat ironic) gospel motto "freely you have received, freely give," Drew University allotted me a generous scholarship. But far beyond the gift of financial support, I owe thanks to the extraordinary, incomparable powerhouse that the Drew Theological School faculty is. Among them, first and foremost to my committee, whose contributions to my life and quest are only poorly expressed here: Catherine Keller, brilliant writer, inspiring teacher, patient mentor, and supportive friend, for the trust she invested in me, for her gentle, yet firm guidance and sound advice. Virginia Burrus, extraordinary teacher, purveyor of intricately and finely argued prose on ancient Christian texts and bodies, challenging mentor and friend, whose cutting edge engagements with patristic literature and sharp reader's eye and writer's skills are dazzling; and to Stephen Moore, for his creative, evocative, and provocative work on New Testament texts. I thank them for continuing to open their door when this often, I am sure, maddeningly persistent graduate student was more than they had bargained for. They gave exorbitantly, and I remain exceedingly grateful for their contributions to my work and development as a scholar. A shoutout to the splendid crowd of fellow Drewids, especially Sharon Betcher, Tom Buchan, Anne Daniell, Morrey Davis, Antonia Gorman, Sigríður Guðmarsdóttir, Won He Joh, Michael Nausner, Mayra Rivera, Rob Seesengood, and Eric Thurman for fun, challenges, conversations, and support.

From my growing connections in the Bay Area and the Graduate Theological Union: Naomi Seidman's interest in my work has been a great gift; Marty Stortz gave generous feedback; Rebecca Lyman, Arthur Holder,

Judith Berling, and Rita Nakashima Brock have been invaluable mentors; Rosemary Radford Ruether gave time generously at the GTU and offered scholarly co-operation.

Liz Cunningham helped diminish my fears by giving generous advice about editing and publishing. Bud Bynack provided a round of most excellent editing. Thanks for kind words and support go to Cheryl Anderson, Nancy Bedford, Daniel Boyarin, Mary McClintock Fulkerson, and Kathryn Tanner. I am grateful to the faculty at the Church Divinity School of the Pacific, who graciously allowed me to fumble my way through being a new faculty, and who generously embraced me as a new colleague. Thanks especially for allowing me to attempt a resurrection of the "Feast of Fools" within the liturgical calendar of the seminary. I am immensely grateful to be here.

I would like to thank those who have commented upon the manuscript in part or even in its entirety: Hanna Smidt, a Danish exchange student, generously offered support and excellent editorial skills in person and per e-mail. Others were Caro Hall, Kevin Jones, and the students in a class with the title "Of Divine Economy" (which ended up being the title for this book) whose excitement facilitated new insight into the texts. Kathryn Rickert's mentoring and support helped preserve my sanity throughout graduate school and the first three years of professorhood.

I am indebted to all wisdom-seeking communities I belong to, who both keep me from writing and inspire me to think, research, and write to students and staff at CDSP and around the exciting and complex inter-denominational, inter-faith, and inter-disciplinary co-operations of the Graduate Theological Union and the University of Berkeley.

At T&T Clark/Continuum, Henry Carrigan generously supported this new author, Amy Wagner graciously responded to e-mails during that last week of editing marathon, and Don Parker-Burgard sifted through the manuscript for errors. Any remaining mistakes are likely my own.

For these and many other miraculous exchanges, comprising only a tiny part of the divine economy, I remain indebted.

Marion Grau
Berkeley, California
June 14, 2004

Introduction

Think of us in this way, as servants of Christ and stewards of God's mysteries [*oikonomous musterion theou*]. (1 Cor 4:1)

The consequences . . . are vast because economics like theology is the old science of human relationships.

> Marcella Althaus-Reid, *Indecent Theology: Theological Perversions in Sex, Gender, and Politics*

There was a time when the advertising industry could claim that its purpose and justification was to inform consumers about the choices they had. But how much choice, how much agency—political, social, economic—is actually accessible to us? Increasingly it may seem as if brand choice is one of the few choices we have left to make. Yet, even there, we have little knowledge or control of how materials are grown, fed, mined, produced, assembled, packaged, transported, sold, and—once discarded—disposed of. Discouraged with the ironies of political processes on either side of the political spectrum, cynical about motives and actions of corporate executives as well as consumers and citizens, many feel at a loss over how to bring about the changes needed to cease the exploitation of the earth and of animal and human life on this planet. In the words of feminist economist Julie Nelson, the danger is to believe that "the system is locked up. No one has agency, and there is . . . no potential for actual relationship with the structure. The only hope is to step outside the structure, to burn it down, to take it over from the top, or to break it apart."[1] Instead, Nelson argues, the economy is "part of an ongoing creation. Even corporations are part of an ongoing creation. When we see this, we can recognize that such grand powers given names like 'market forces' or 'global capitalism' do not have

---

1. Julie A. Nelson, "Breaking the Dynamic of Control: A Feminist Approach to Economic Ethics," *Journal of Feminist Studies in Religion* 19 (Spring 2003): 33.

an independent existence outside the flux of experience and historical time." Rather, they are relationships in the world we "individually and collectively inherit and can seek to pass on or transform." Thus, she argues that both the conservative thinkers who idealize the "free market" and those on the left who demonize "capitalism" join in assuming that "they are talking about some substance or essence, some structure or machine, that exists somewhere beyond or above us and our history."[2] It is in this spirit that I would like to challenge some of the Whiteheadian "fallacies of misplaced concreteness"[3] in economic and theological reasoning and think beyond the danger of paralysis to transformative faith in action.

This book is an attempt to map spaces for theological thinking and practical agency in a culture that appears strikingly effective at commodifying dissent, where protest and resistance are being branded, packaged, and sold back to us as products.[4] What images of agency do biblical texts and theological tradition offer to us today? It is my contention that the figure of the sacred trickster, a denizen of the ambivalent borderlands of religion and culture, shows one particular form of agency that can break through, interrupt, even shift the terms of the status quo. I do not claim that this form of agency is the only one possible, but it does strike me as a figure complex enough to track the many layers of meaning that mark the contemporary experience of reality for many in a globalizing economic scenario. The trickster is a figure with many possibilities and hence is paradigmatic for our own web of relations. Trickster energy can be destructive or productive, effective or ineffective, complicit or resistant. There are tricksters who swear quixotically at windmills, and there are wise fools (such as those in some of Shakespeare's plays) who speak truth to power, claiming space to enunciate what needs to be said.

Can tricksters and fools be agents of real transformative power, or do they serve only as amusement for the powerful? It depends. In a relational universe, where power flows in multiple directions and at times in unpredictable ways, the particular context of a situation or text—where and when and how challenges to truth regimes are enunciated—matters deeply. As chaos and complexity theories would suggest, the initial conditions of an event flow into it, but they do not determine its outcome. I propose the

---

2. Ibid., 34.
3. Alfred North Whitehead defines this fallacy as "the accidental error of mistaking the abstract for the concrete" and uses it as a tool to challenge seemingly rational scientific abstractions that erase important distinctions while making great truth claims. Alfred North Whitehead, *Science and the Modern World* (New York: Free Press, 1925), 51.
4. On the commodification of dissent, see Naomi Klein, *No Logo: Taking Aim at the Brand Bullies* (New York: Picador, 1999); and Thomas Frank, *The Conquest of Cool: Business Culture, Counterculture, and the Rise of Hip Consumerism* (Chicago: University of Chicago Press, 1997).

sacred trickster as one of the shapes an "economist of God's mysteries" can take on, and I offer three particular figures—rich young man, poor widow and divine slave—as the narrative concretion of such agency. This trickster is a bit of a holy fool, since tricksters engage in hopeful thoughts and practices, transgressing even their own cynicism and disillusionment. Their experience of the divine does not let them rest in their quest to live more closely to its elusive lure. And they know that the line between quixotic insignificance and humble yet persistent and often seemingly foolish interventions on behalf of a sacred vision can be thin and fluid. They know that even their own visions can at times betray the hoped for outcome. Yet they maintain the need to be foolish—not stupid, which indicates a lack of intelligence—in the sense that they engage in practices of persistent hope against the odds.

How can we make sure to identify the problems and propose creative and effective approaches rather than wasting time stabbing at windmills? In the fluid borderlands of individual and communal agency, sacred and secular, divine and mundane, the trickster becomes a point of concretion at which we can explore, imagine, and incarnate what it would mean to become more effective "economists of God's mysteries."

In the nineteenth century, the Gospels became contested territory among economic thinkers. They were appropriated for their alleged endorsement of both capitalist and anticapitalist potential. Some writers have pointed out that early urban Christians lived in an essentially communist church where all goods were shared, while others claimed Jesus as an exemplary capitalist.[5] Contemporary prosperity evangelists, such as Kenneth and Gloria Copeland, Kenneth Hagin, and other neo-pentecostal "health and wealth" preachers, claim that prosperity will follow a commitment to Jesus Christ.[6] Conversely, although later generations of liberation theologians have developed sophisticated and modified responses in the face of the ongoing success of global capitalism, many of the early representatives of liberation theology were fundamentally critical of capitalism as a system.

However, it is questionable whether capitalism and the critiques it has inspired, most notably Marxism, are indeed polar opposites. History would suggest a more complex picture, challenging assumptions of differences

---

5. Among the more prominent supporters of the communist thesis was Friedrich Engels. See L. William Countryman, *The Rich Christian in the Church of the Early Empire: Contradictions and Accommodations* (New York: Edwin Mellen Press, 1980), 4. Countryman's introduction provides a helpful overview of modern exegetes' tug-of-war around the meaning of early Christian attitudes toward work and money.

6. See, for example, Paul Gifford, "Prosperity: A New and Foreign Element in African Christianity," *Religion* 20 (1990): 373–88; and Simon Coleman, "Charismatic Christianity and the Dilemmas of Globalization," *Religion* 29 (1998): 245–56.

and similarities alike.[7] Notwithstanding the increasingly widespread protests against Western economic policies and American-style capitalism since the end of the Cold War and what looks to many like a triumph of capitalism worldwide, the value of simply continuing to rehearse stale oppositions is open to dispute. This is true not just in the economic realm but in theology, which remains engaged with the issues, practices, and discourses of economy and exchange. Proponents of liberation theology and radical orthodoxy have identified neoclassical economics as another problematic outgrowth of modernity, while some North American constructive theologians[8] retrieve the ancient concepts of *oikos* (house) and *oikonomia* (household management) to propose Christian alternatives to the increasing dominance of neoclassical economic reasoning and practices in many areas of contemporary life.

This particular text, however, goes a somewhat different route. It stands loosely in the tradition of Max Weber's *The Protestant Work Ethic and the Spirit of Capitalism,* which explored the ambivalence of Calvinist asceticism in relation to a specific economic system. Beyond Weber, *Of Divine Economy* traces the interaction between theologies of redemption and concerns of gender and social status in Western culture and capitalism, beginning its inquiry with ancient Christian texts. The text explores spaces in Western Christianity's ambivalent relationship to capitalist and Marxist theories of economy and highlights possible alternatives beyond the increasingly stale reiterations of neoliberal capitalist economics and their neo-Marxist critiques.

What follows draws upon the proliferation of economic terminology in contemporary critical theory, rereading ancient Christian traditions of divine economy in an effort to map a "third space" beyond the bipolar positions regarding neoclassical economics as they have structured theological discourse. I search, then, for an opening, for a "triton genos," as Jacques Derrida writes, which "would trouble the very order of polarity, of polarity

---

7. Robert Young has thus commented on the variety of forms of "postcolonial Marxism" that "does not necessarily come in recognizable universal western forms." He argues that the "west itself has always generated its own self-critique (above all in Marxism)" but also feels that the "notion that postcolonialism is merely a western invention" needs to be critically investigated. Young, *Postcolonialism: An Historical Introduction* (Oxford: Blackwell, 2001), 6ff., 63, 66. Some have seen basic commonalities between capitalism and its Marxist critique, asking whether they are not based on the same basic neoclassical analysis of economic exchange. Marcella Althaus-Reid suggests such similarities when she describes Marxist-based liberation theologians as "somehow Hegelians, and right-wing Hegelians at that," belonging to an "idealist theological market," in which "sexual idealism pervades theology, including Theology of Liberation." Marcella Althaus-Reid, *Indecent Theology: Theological Perversions in Sex, Gender, and Politics* (London: Routledge, 2001), 22.

8. For a collection of writing by a group of constructive theologians see Rebecca Chopp and Mark Lewis Taylor, *Reconstructing Christian Theology* (Minneapolis: Fortress, 1994).

in general."⁹ In that "third space," I propose to reconstruct a theology of divine economy that embodies "miraculous" exchanges that challenge the capitalist/anticapitalist polarities that so powerfully pervade and structure Western and, increasingly, global societies. In a spacetime in which many feel that resistance is futile, that we are already assimilated into overt and covert structures of oppression and exploitation, this book looks for ways in which we might refuse to act within the narrowness of polar extremes and instead attempt to counteract the matrix of co-optation. Thus, proposing and exposing moments of redemptive agency, I propose a *status confessionis*, a stance of witnessing that is neither hopeless nor utopian but that attempts to live in a space that resembles Antonio Gramsci's "pessimism of the intelligence and optimism of the will."¹⁰ It is a space of divine-human action within creation in which humans participate, where salvific energies merge beyond the distinctions of divine and human realms. In this space, conceptions of divine and human power are reconceived in the encounter with the sciences of chaos and complexity. The vision of divine economy here proposed does not resemble a "template of omnipotent-total-order," but finds kinship with what Catherine Keller locates in the biblical beginnings of creation: the chaos that is "*always already* there, that is now being recognized as an alternative order that had been so long mistaken for disorder."¹¹

Rather than trying to enunciate purist idealizations of what a Christian economics should look like, I propose that the messiness of Christian tradition, the untamable power of its jarring images and visions, helps us live more honestly within our own contested locations. At the same time, it reminds us that behind the use of the oracular term "the economy" in popular political rhetoric stands the ancient theological term *oikonomia theou*, describing divine agency within the cosmos, the way in which the universe functions and develops throughout the course of human history, specifically as it relates to redemptive agency.

In ancient philosophical and early Christian writings, *oikonomia* refers to the rules or management of a household. We find the term *oikonomia* in only a few biblical texts, such as 1 Corinthians, Ephesians, and other apostolic letters. The most important biblical passages for patristic interpretation (1 Cor 1:2; Eph 1:10, 3:2, 3:9) describe *oikonomia* as divine householding or plan of creation. Within patristic literature, the concepts

---

9. Jacques Derrida, *On the Name* (trans. David Wood et al.; Stanford, Calif.: Stanford University Press, 1995), 89, 92.
10. Quintin Hoare and Geoffrey Nowell Smith, eds. and trans., *Selections from the Prison Notebooks of Antonio Gramsci* (New York: International Publishers, 1971), 175n.75.
11. Catherine Keller, *Face of the Deep* (New York: Routledge, 2003), 28.

of God's ordering of creation and history are often expressed with the Greek term *oikonomia* ("the plan, the order") or the Latin term *dispensatio*.[12] The patristic use of *oikonomia theou* covers various theological conceptions of divine agency within creation, one of them slanted toward the incarnation, death, and resurrection of Christ, the other more specifically toward divine pedagogy and salvific action throughout the history of the cosmos. This second understanding came to be known as *Heilsgeschichte*, or "salvation history."

To reconstruct the uses of this term in a third space beyond the often pervasive capitalist/Marxist dichotomies poses a constant methodological challenge—avoiding the retroactive "transmutation" of present-day economics into prior economic circumstances.[13] By contrast, in this book I try not to impose the restricted contemporary meaning of economic discourse on the past but to allow the discourses of the past to challenge and open up contemporary understanding and uses of such economic terminology. I explore the ancient complex of meanings not in an attempt to reclaim some purportedly original meaning and thereby achieve some sort of ideal interpretation, but to demonstrate the problematic narrowing of the term "economy" in recent times and the range of its potential uses. In this way, the intertextual layers of meaning and the play between them become available for the theological reconstruction of a divine economy.

By tracing how economic energies have scripted Christian soteriology and asking how these economic soteriologies—in all their ambivalence—can contribute to a contemporary understanding of a coredemptive *soteria*, I want to propose new ways of making economic symbols of redemption alive and meaningful in a postmodern context. Uncovering the interactions between asceticism and economies of salvation in the Gospels and other early Christian texts may allow contemporary Christians to reinvent ascetic practices within a decidedly nonascetic "free-market" orthodoxy of economic globalism under Western leadership. To that end, I employ poststructuralist, feminist, and postcolonial texts, despite their manifold differences and tensions, as tools to read ancient Christian texts. Such a strategy means to encourage theological practitioners to remain honest, to repent of hidden tendencies to dominate, to counteract pervasive temptations to increase consumption, and invest in redemptive economic subjectivities and figures for multiple genders, races, and classes. The construction of what might be called a theology of countereconomy thus

---

12. Irenaeus uses the term *oikonomia theou* frequently in *Adversus haereses*.
13. Compare Pierre Bourdieu's warning against reading the texts of ancient and non-Western societies through the lenses of capitalist/Marxist dichotomies. See Bourdieu, *Outline of a Theory of Practice* (Cambridge: Cambridge University Press, 1977), 177.

strives to inhabit modest, but strategically decisive, points of resistance in a complex contemporary economic space.

An Exorbitant "Economy"

The pervasiveness of economic terminology and concepts in Western public and academic discourse contributes to the prospects and the challenges of this project. The flexibility of economic metaphors and terms, the proliferation and dissemination of terms such as "economy" and "economics" in noneconomic realms, is simultaneously a problem and an opportunity. "Economy" can serve as a "shorthand for the contracted and institutionalized economic processes of Western civilization as embedded in the commodity market,"[14] but the term has also migrated into literary and psychoanalytic theory, where we find uses such as the notion of a "rhetorical economy" to denote the ways in which a text structures and orders its themes. We find Jean-François Lyotard writing about "libidinal economy,"[15] Jacques Derrida about the "economy of différance,"[16] and Luce Irigaray about the "economy of relationships," the "economy of sex," the "economy of representation," a "signifying economy," and an "exchange economy."[17]

The multiple uses to which the term has been put may seem to have threatened its determinate meaning in the same way that, in the discourses of modernity, metaphors were said to undermine clear and distinct ideas. And yet the manifold connotations of "economy" serve to disrupt the strict separation of academic disciplines, linking such diverse fields as biblical, historical, and theological studies, economics, literary studies, feminist, post-Marxist, and post-Freudian critiques. The proliferation of the use and application of the term "economy" in Western philosophy and theory has

---

14. Kurt Heinzelman, *The Economics of the Imagination* (Amherst: University of Massachusetts Press, 1980), 37.
15. Jean-François Lyotard, *Libidinal Economy* (trans. Iain Hamilton Grant; Bloomington: University of Indiana Press, 1993).
16. Jacques Derrida, *Margins of Philosophy* (trans. Alan Bass; Chicago: University of Chicago Press, 1981), 22.
17. Luce Irigaray, *Speculum of the Other Woman* (trans. Gillian C. Gill; Ithaca, N.Y.: Cornell University Press, 1985), 18ff., 33, 41, 50, 115. Regarding the frequent use of *économie* by Irigaray and Hélène Cixous in their "critique of market economy," Judith Still remarks, "This slippage from the production and distribution of goods and services within society to the psychic organization of individuals (the phallic economy driven by castration anxiety) is perhaps easier to achieve in French, where the term *économie* is more happily used in a metaphorical sense, to refer to the way in which something is organised, than it is in English." Judith Still, *Feminine Economies: Thinking against the Market in the Enlightenment and the Late Twentieth Century* (Manchester: Manchester University Press, 1997), 150.

stretched this "notoriously flexible metaphor"[18] so far "that in its largest sense the word denotes our capacity for creating intellectual structures and for imaginatively regulating them."[19] The fertility of "economy" and related terms as metaphors thus points to the fruitful connections between all realms of life. As Donna Haraway observes, "the one fundamental thing about the world [is] relationality."[20] The productive metonymy[21] of the semantic field of *oikonomia* offers a way to widen and complicate the context of theological engagements with economic issues, to explore the extent of their relations. That is the opportunity offered by the broader, more metaphorical uses of the term. The use of "economy" in modern and postmodern discourses occurs in the long shadow cast by Adam Smith, the father of so-called neoclassical or neoliberal economics, the academic discipline still dominant in the vast majority of Western business schools and economics departments.

Smith's theory of the "invisible hand" that appears to regulate productivity and demand in the market with near miraculous infallibility remains one of the foremost orthodoxies of contemporary scientific economics. Arkady Plotnitsky has argued that the expansive use of "economy" in the broader venues of post-Hegelian intellectual history can be linked to the effect of Adam Smith's work on Hegel: "Adam Smith's political economy was a major influence on Hegel during his work on *The Phenomenology of the Spirit*. . . . From the *Phenomenology* on, economic thematics never left the horizon of Hegel's thought, the emergence of which also coincides with the rise of economics as a science, which conjunction is, of course, hardly a coincidence."[22]

From Hegel onward, a specific branching in the dissemination of economic metaphoricity can be discerned. Thus, Plotnitsky posits:

> Economics thematics have had central significance in a number of key developments in modern and postmodern, in a word post-Hegelian, intellectual history—in Marx, Nietzsche, Freud, Heidegger, Bataille, Lacan,

---

18. Heinzelman, *Economics of the Imagination*, ix.
19. Ibid., x.
20. Donna J. Haraway, *Modest_Witness@Second_Millennium. FemaleMan©_Meets_OncoMouse*™ (New York: Routledge, 1997), 37.
21. My use of this term is related to Homi Bhabha's notion of it as a "figure of contiguity that substitutes a part for a whole" in a "rhetoric of repetition or doubling," exposing an "uncanny sameness-in-difference." Homi Bhabha, *The Location of Culture* (London: Routledge, 1994), 54.
22. Arkady Plotnitsky, "Re-: Re-Flecting, Re-Membering, Re-Collecting, Re-Selecting, Re-Warding, Re-Wording, Re-Iterating, Re-et-Cetra-Ing . . . (in) Hegel," *Postmodern Culture* 5, no. 2 (1995): 1. Other critics date the ascendance of "economy" differently. Heinzelman cites the publication of William Stanley Jevons' *The Theory of Political Economy* in 1871 as the crucial document that "heralded the marginalist revolution" which in turn led to the development of neoclassical

Althusser, Deleuze, Derrida, Irigaray, and others. From this perspective, one could even suggest that all post-Hegelian criticism and theory is fundamentally "economic"—post-Smithian. They are profoundly related to economic models, metaphors, and modes of inquiry; or conversely, and often interactively, to dislocations or deconstructions (here understood as **constructive** dislocations) of such "economies" as traditionally or classically conceived.[23]

Thus, we see in Derrida's early text "From Restricted to General Economy: A Hegelianism without Reserve" his own version of Bataille's "general economy" (identified with political economy), which is a deconstruction and dislocation of the "restricted economy" (restricted to commercial value).[24] This expansive, exorbitant "general economy" bursts the "restricted economy," and Derrida's infamous *différance* emerges as a profoundly economic concept, an "economic detour" that explodes the confines of a narrowed *"circuit of reproductive consumption."*[25] Here I will be extending Derrida's and Plotnitsky's reading, interpreting the proliferation of the term "economy" as protest against a "restricted economy" that would claim to limit its deliberations to purely financial exchanges.

Theology and *Oikonomia*

The Western Christian economic "habit" that such a movement seeks to "interrupt" is that of "profiting from" a colonizing metanarrative of Christian salvation history by exploiting and oppressing others.[26] In theology, similar movements can be found in the convergence of Marxist discourses with political and liberation theologies in the 1960s. Theological engagements with the issues of wealth and faith drew on early Christian texts that thematize the tensions between God and Mammon. Yet only a handful of U.S. theologians have worked with an explicit focus on the relationship between contemporary economics and theology. The work of

---

economics, which remains the dominant mode of economic reasoning even today. Martha Woodmansee and Mark Osteen suggest the emergence of two related discourses, in the science of economics and the birth of the novel. Compare Martha Woodmansee and Mark Osteen, eds., *The New Economic Criticism: Studies at the Intersection of Literature and Economics* (Economics as Social Theory; London: Routledge, 1999), 5.

23. Plotnitsky, "Re-," 1; emphasis in the original.
24. Jacques Derrida, *Writing and Difference* (trans. Alan Bass; London: Routledge, 1978), 270.
25. Derrida, *Writing and Difference*, 271.
26. While some may not, as Haraway suggests to her readers, wish to live entirely outside the "bracing discourses of salvation history," even if it were possible, we might at least hope to read them alongside other stories, rather than blotting them out. See Haraway, *Modest_Witness@Second_Millennium*, 45.

John Cobb, Douglas Meeks, Mark C. Taylor, Stephen Long, and Sallie McFague has been crucial in formulating a theological—or in the case of Taylor, an *a/theological*—response to the issues and problems of postwar Western economics.[27] Cobb, Meeks, and McFague have employed *oikonomia (theou)* as a metaphor for the theological reconstruction of divine agency within creation, a reconstruction that stands in critical dialogue with neoclassical economics. Thus, in their own ways, they have pushed toward a broadening of the term "economy," while Taylor has effectively unveiled the danger of the collapse of traditional theological language into capitalist phraseologies. In the face of a modern economic reasoning that ignores the problematic consequences of economic action on human and natural environments, Cobb's, Meeks's and McFague's retrieval of *oikonomia* points toward the inseparability and irreducibility of creation beyond any binary opposition between the human and the natural in which nature would be designated as an "environment." All three describe God's creation as an interrelated whole. Long, in connection with the project of constructing a radical orthodoxy, aims to inhabit a space beyond the binaries of procapitalist and anticapitalist theologies and positions himself alongside a "residual tradition" exemplified by John Milbank's call for a religious socialism.

Whereas Cobb, Meeks, McFague, Taylor, and Long have used the ancient theological texts to perform a theological reading or critique of modern economics, however, I have reread ancient theological texts that deal with economic matters to recover neglected economic images of salvation using a reconstructed typological hermeneutics. Deconstructing imaginary notions of pure Christian economic origins, what comes into view are biblical and patristic traditions that formulate embodied "economic desires" as they "walk hand in hand with erotic desires and theological needs." Early Christian attitudes toward wealth, structures enforcing power over women and slaves are economic models that express relationships "based on erotic considerations concerning the economy of bodies in society, their intimacy and distance and the patterns of accepted and unaccepted needs in the market."[28] These sexual and economic stories are often written on the body of Christian figures then and now. Typology, or

---

27. See John B. Cobb Jr., *For the Common Good: Redirecting the Economy toward Community, the Environment, and a Sustainable Future* (2d ed.; Boston: Beacon, 1989); M. Douglas Meeks, *God the Economist: The Doctrine of God and Political Economy* (Minneapolis: Fortress, 1989); Mark C. Taylor, *About Religion: Economies of Faith in Virtual Culture* (Religion and Postmodernism; Chicago: University of Chicago Press, 1999); D. Stephen Long, *Divine Economy: Theology and the Market* (New York: Routledge, 2000); Sallie McFague, *Life Abundant: Rethinking Theology and Economy for a Planet in Peril* (Minneapolis: Fortress, 2000).

28. Althaus-Reid, *Indecent Theology*, 166.

figurative reading, one of the major hermeneutical tools of constructing the concept of a divine economy as a Christian hermeneutic of history, is a way of theologically constructing temporality and relationality. Often a *typos* denotes a specific relationship to God, a specific link in the divine economy: Moses, Elijah, and David in Jewish traditions; Adam and Christ, David and Christ, Eve and Mary, Hagar and Sarah in early Christian material. Through the creative appropriation of narratives that have shaped the hermeneutic community, using a technique involving difference and repetition, these figures are read as milestones and markers in the progression of the godly *oikonomia*. Some forms of typology can be found in the Hebrew traditions, while others represent the creative, enhancing, increasingly supersessionist and exclusivist Christian form of typological interpretation. The reconstruction of any hermeneutic that has served to erect boundaries of exclusion and a logic supporting the destruction of other communities can only be undertaken in a spirit of repentance and with considerable trepidation. The task at hand therefore is to live watchfully in the presence of the risk of reconstruction: the reinscription of prior oppressions in a new guise.

Living in the presence of these risks, this particular exercise in figural reading produces three "theological genealogies." Resembling Foucaultian genealogies in that they try to "dispel the chimeras of origin" of a past before a fall into capitalist relations, these examine "the hazardous play of subjection" involved in the economies of power and redemption, where financial and spiritual investments interact to form faithful subjects.[29] Out of these genealogies emerge what I will call "figures," or "figurations," which track and reconstruct ancient theological economies of lack and plenitude, and of power, sex, and gender to suggest redemptive exchanges that can help transform the structures of economics and of theology. I employ this strategy because "figuration is about resetting the stage for possible pasts and futures." It is "the mode of theory" best suited to a time "when the more 'normal' rhetorics of systematic critical analysis seem only to repeat and sustain our entrapment in the stories of the established disorders."[30] In these figures, which resemble (though they are hardly identical with) the typological hermeneutic found in some biblical texts and patristic sources, potential forms of subversive-constructive theological and practical agency appear. These figures or types represent, but never fully, never wholly so. A

---

29. Michel Foucault, "Nietzsche, Genealogy, History," in *The Foucault Reader* (ed. Paul Rabinow; New York: Pantheon, 1984), 80, 83.

30. Donna J. Haraway, "Ecce Homo, Ain't (Ar'n't) I a Woman, and Inappropriate/d Others: The Human in a Post-Humanist Landscape," in *Feminists Theorize the Political* (ed. Judith Butler and Joan Scott; New York: Routledge, 1992), 86.

"figure collects up the people; a figure embodies shared meaning in stories that inhabit their audiences."[31] They always approximate, however, serving as a tool for hermeneutic imagination that becomes dangerous when reified and that when read reductively can become flat, unproductive, stifling, and destructive.

The figure/*typos* here is meant to serve as a "modest witness" (Haraway), a body that becomes host to ancient-new sacred subjectivities, resistantly, productively, and creatively so. A "modest witness" inhabits the ambivalences of a "dirty ontology," working toward a "situated knowledge" that can take a decisive stand informed by many different knowledges available to its epistemology.[32] Her figures try to break away from images of the same, from homogeneity, from notions of property and authority to escape to a multiply located, diverse, and yet reliable witnessing at a time when historical and theological narratives are in crisis. Such witnessing means "seeing; attesting; standing publicly accountable for, and psychically vulnerable to, one's visions and representations."[33] In this way, the three trickster figures developed in this book witness modestly to possibilities of divine and human redemptive economic agency. They are the descendants of ancient typological figures whose similarities and differences unfold in genealogies and midrash-like pieces, bridging the stretches of the millennia of salvation history. As prophetic, foolishly wise trickster figures, they unveil the monetary, relational, and physical exchanges of theological constructs of divine economy and help shape a hermeneutic discipline of nonconclusive readings. They also incarnate a variety of "tactics" as well as "strategies" to expose, prod, and shift human action toward more divinely economic patterns.[34]

Catherine Keller's analysis of apocalyptic patterns and her ambivalent yet hopeful reconstruction of a counterapocalyptic theology attempting to

---

31. Haraway, *Modest_Witness@Second_Millennium*, 23.

32. The modest witness strives to avoid the "soft and flaccid swamps of ordinary technoscientific objectivity," instead locating himself or herself in a position of "strong objectivity" through "the production of difference patterns in the world" that break down the now proverbial view from nowhere or "the culture of no culture." Haraway, *Modest_Witness@Second_Millennium*, 142, 268.

33. Haraway, *Modest_Witness@Second_Millennium*, 9, 40, 45. Salvation history and the refigurative dynamics of "Western Christian realism" and its narratives incite both Haraway's respect and suspicion. She reads the Isaianic Suffering Servant as a figure representing "a broken and suffering humanity, signifying . . . a possible hope." Haraway, "Ecce Homo," 87. Haraway is fascinated by that servant's metamorphoses, oddities, and the tricksterlike character of the figure of Jesus, and is concerned about its refiguration as the "Sacred Image of the Same" that marks also the "Second Millennium." Like Haraway's own tricksterlike figures, Christ transgresses the boundaries of the nature/culture divide, of pure and impure, sacred and secular, creator and creature.

34. Vincent Miller's adoption of Bourdieu's distinction between tactics as more sporadic actions compared to the institutional, organizational reshaping of structures by way of strategies

search spaces beyond ingrained binary oppositions and crystallized reading patterns has proved salutary in the undertaking of this task.[35] By tracking and reconstructing theological renditions of divine investment strategies, I hope to construct a divine countereconomic space by devising something akin to Keller's "healing strategy," which "return[s] to the source, to repeat it mournfully, playfully, to gently dislodge the causal links between habituated, tormented expectations and present possibilities."[36] Unlike Keller's counterapocalyptic reading of the text of Revelation, however, the present approach cannot rely on a single, contained biblical text or tradition as the one major source for a theology of economy. Rather, theological meditations on the relationship between poverty and wealth, faith and money, rich and poor, giving and getting are found in a great variety of biblical narratives that permeate literature and culture. Biblical texts express divine salvific agency through economic images such as debt, forgiveness, treasure, inheritance, wealth, gift, slavery, ransom, and redemption.[37] *Of Divine Economy* investigates how traditional images of *soteria*—as *oikonomia*—can become newly relevant in Western capitalist societies in which the almost magical power of "economy," as described by Adam Smith's metaphor of the "invisible hand," continues to claim omnipresence, if not omnipotence.

As some have observed, it can seem as if theology and economics have long since traded places in the cultural discourse of power, with economics having taken on the proclamation of the terms and conditions of salvation and damnation in contemporary society. Capitalist and consumerist practices advertise products via "secular technoscientific salvation stories."[38] John Cobb has termed "economistic" the cultural paradigm in which neoclassical economic reasoning determines public and private action to a point where humans, animals, and the earth become mere resources or commodities and has called on religious communities to

---

is helpful here. However, to effect true and deep changes in mindset and action, both forms of action are needed. See Vincent J. Miller, *Consuming Religion: Christian Faith and Practice in a Consumer Culture* (New York: Continuum, 2003), 183.

35. Keller has stressed the profound effects of the metaphor of revelation (or apocalypse) on Western and especially American ideas of history, hope, catastrophe, and the future. Whether we are aware of it or not, and whether we want it or not, so Keller insists, the shape of Western Christian cultures and societies is unthinkable without John of Patmos's text. This end-time narrative, says Keller, continues to engender various versions of an *"apocalypse habit,"* each constructing its own performance, its *"apocalypse pattern."* Her counterapocalyptic stance holds in tension her admiration for the text's "intensity, its drive for justice, its courage in the face of impossible odds," and her rejection of its misogynist, bloodthirsty calls for revenge. Catherine Keller, *Apocalypse Now and Then: A Feminist Guide to the End of the World* (Boston: Beacon, 1996), 11, 19–20.

36. Ibid., 20.
37. Meeks, *God the Economist*, 29.
38. Haraway, *Modest_Witness@Second_Millennium*, 8.

develop viable economic and ecological alternatives.[39] The exploitation of the semantic overlap between salvation and *oikonomia* in ancient texts offers an effective tool for reconstructing a theology for a time and place in which a narrowly structured "economistic" discourse appears to dominate public understanding, formation of identity and agency.[40]

What follows then is an interdisciplinary theological text that engages a variety of postmodern discourses in a dialogue across time and place.[41] In rereading ancient Christian texts along with poststructuralist, feminist, and postcolonial works, I employ these critical theories not as a trendy plot to discredit tradition but as a valuable tool for the critical investigation of material that rarely has been critically engaged. As we will see, rereading Christian texts in this manner reveals the potential of imagining a trickster-like "God the economist"[42]: a gambler and a courageous, hopeful investor in unpredictabilities, involved in subversive divine economic deals. Thus, divine economy emerges as less predictable, as it renegotiates "the dominant *oikonomia*—the economics, the ecology, the ecumenism of order."[43] It deconstructs simplistic characterizations of God as "capitalist" or "communist" and instead delights in uncovering multiplicities of economic relationality that resist tyranny, stasis, and oppression by envisioning strategies of flexible, miraculous exchanges. Aware that "theology has not outgrown the subjection of the *oikos* to the *dominus*,"[44] it points toward the redemption and release of those women and slaves expropriated by the domination of the profit-driven deified economies of late, or extreme, capitalism.

---

39. See John B. Cobb Jr., *The Earthist Challenge to Economism: A Theological Critique of the World Bank* (New York: Macmillan Press, 1999).

40. Cobb has observed that for many contemporary Christians, traditional ecclesial conceptions of salvation have become "vague and diverse"—perhaps even bankrupt—as "the doctrines of atonement that were long central to Christian teaching have lost persuasive power," failing to convince or satisfy inquiring minds among mainstream churchgoers. Thus, he argues, "When the Christian movement is clear both about the salvation for which it hopes and its role in relation to that salvation, it is vital and vigorous. When that is not the case, its energies are difficult to mobilize." John B. Cobb Jr., *Postmodernism and Public Policy: Reframing Religion, Culture, Education, Sexuality, Class, Race, and the Economy* (Albany, N.Y.: SUNY Press, 2002), 24, 25.

41. Cobb's critique of the still dominant "disciplinolatry," as well as his call for an enhanced interdisciplinarity (the cooperation between a variety of academic disciplines) or even a possible nondisciplinarity (an advanced breaking down of boundaries between disciplines), suggests that only thinking within a wide web of relation, aspects, and perspectives can create workable economic alternatives motivated by religious convictions and visions. See Cobb, *For the Common Good*, 125, 127, 161.

42. This term is from Meeks's book of the same name.

43. Keller, *Face of the Deep*, 6.

44. Ibid.

The Plan of the Book

Chapter 1 positions the "third space" I attempt to construct by charting a variety of discursive spaces where theology and economy have intersected since the 1960s. By gaining a greater understanding of how people are invested in the economic structures they find objectionable, we must begin to understand that the line between economic justice and exploitation is not comfortably located outside ourselves but goes right through our own investments, theological, relational, and financial. The chapter further traces the outlines of a countereconomic theology that is less involved in a critique of contemporary economics than in a genealogy of the interactions between theological and material economies, ancient and postmodern.

At the core of the proposed reconstructive figuration in a contemporary feminist and postcolonial third space, chapters 2 through 4 each portray a figure that forms part of ancient and contemporary rhetorical and actual economies. Each of these figures represents an iteration of an ancient image of redemptive divine economy. They are feminist figures in the sense that, as Haraway suggests, "feminist figures of humanity . . . cannot be man or woman; they cannot be the human as historical narrative has staged that generic universal. Feminist figures cannot, finally, have a name; they cannot be native. Feminist humanity must, somehow, both resist representation, resist literal figuration, and still erupt in powerful new tropes, new figures of speech, new turns of historical possibility."[45]

Attempting thus to "resist representation" while exploring "new tropes, new figures" from among our histories, these central chapters, which are structured as a discursive triptych, explore three textually embodied figures that not only blur the boundaries between man and woman, master and slave, but also question the binary opposition of lack and abundance, capitalism and Marxism, divine and earthly economies. Resisting the tendency of "feminist theology . . . to leave biblical interpretation to feminist exegetical and historical scholars,"[46] the approach to an interdisciplinary constructive theology in these chapters consciously engages the texts of the tradition as well as the texts of biblical and historical scholars. Thus, the three figural genealogies are situated in contemporary theological and historical discussions as the descendants of Christian typologies of salvation history. These soteriological genealogies can help us to inhabit a third space

---

45. Haraway, "Ecce Homo," 86.
46. Keller, *Apocalypse Now and Then*, 25.

beyond theological and economic dichotomies only if we hold these figures lightly. They do not mean to represent persons but rather function as textual incarnations, as hermeneutical products of textual economies that have shaped our theological past and present.

These three genealogies trace the literary lives of members in an ancient household: *kurios* (master), *kuria* (mistress), and *doulos* (slave), and their descendants who resemble us uncannily (*unheimlich*). Uncannily, in a sense that points to the ambiguity of our being at home with (*heimisch*) as well as *unheimlich*—estranged and spooked by the spectre of the hierarchies of gender and class written into the divine economy. The power-knowledge constructions of the human household have contributed to images of divine *oikonomia* that reaffirmed the patriarchal shape of the *oikos* at the same time as they called into question the conventions of class and gender among humans. The first figure resembles the rich young man (Matt 19:16–30) in his wealth and corresponding lack of spiritual abundance; the second figure emerges from images of female givers such as the poor widow (Mk 12:43–44), whose lack of material wealth nevertheless counts as abundance with God; the third figure is the slave-liberator found in the christological topos of divine commerce, a sacred trickster mediating between divine abundance and human destitution.

All of these figures share some of the characteristics of the trickster figures Haraway evokes and are formed by modes of textual production akin to what Bhabha has described as hybridity, the "problematic of colonial representation and individuation that reverses the effects of the colonialist disavowal, so that other 'denied' knowledges enter upon the dominant discourse and estrange the basis of its authority—its rules of recognition."[47] Thus, these figures are not untroubled and contain great hermeneutical and incarnational complexity. Chapter 5 further elucidates the trickster qualities that emerge in the central chapters, and rethinks the way they trouble the categories of gender and class. Then it begins to portray contemporary trickster figures as they embody miraculous exchanges.

Ambivalence remains a constant companion, an inspiration and challenge for this exploration. The figural reading proposed in these pages aims to deconstruct the proliferation of polarities as expressed in stereotypes of economic and theological genders, classes, and races and in the locations of various other forms of colonial and postcolonial embodiment. With Gayatri Spivak, they refuse to "continue to celebrate" essentializing moralisms such as those of colonizer/colonized and white/black in which "the migrant

---

47. Bhabha, *Location of Culture*, 114.

is all good" and "the whites are all bad."[48] Instead, they embody a theological response that gives witness to the complexities and complicities of the relations between oppressor and oppressed.[49] They also resist the salvific proclamation of a "mighty mongrel" whose hybrid, mestizo characteristics are elevated as a new superbreed of human that can solve the problems of the past by embodying a variety of pasts and traditions. Such romantic displacements spawn new dangers if hybridity develops into another form of orthodoxy, reinscribing rather than challenging the divisions of the past.

The first two figures show symptoms of hysteria, a notoriously puzzling condition in which the hysteric's body discloses through linguistic and physical symptoms a larger condition transferred onto the sufferer by his or her societal context. Chapters 1 and 3 thus offer a hermeneutic with which to read this trickster among diseases, this "mimetic disorder," as it performs "culturally permissible expressions of distress"[50] in men and discloses unforeseen subversive potencies in women. Hysteria emerges as a disorder that closely maps the gendered economic conditions of lack and plenitude as they are assigned and reassigned in the Christian *oikonomia* of redemption. Although ancient rhetorical economies have endowed male bodies with an abundance of administrative and reproductive power while linking the reproductive cavities of female bodies with the appearance of both physical and mental lack, men too can be marked by hysteria, deficiency, or lack.

In chapter 2, we see how almsgiving and asceticism are theologically negotiated as male investments in an economy of salvation that informs the interpretation of the exemplary narrative of the rich young man in Matthew 19. Ascesis and almsgiving emerge as two modes of divine and earthly resource management for the wealthy males who interpreted Matthew's text. In Matthew 19, wealth becomes poverty, while ascesis and almsgiving, although they represent renunciation, eventually pay off as a

---

48. Gayatri Spivak, *A Critique of Postcolonial Reason: Toward a History of the Vanishing Present* (Cambridge: Harvard University Press, 1999), 377.
49. Chicano theorist Chela Sandoval finds that, at least in a U.S. context, after a necessary and painful process of "differentiation" between white feminists, womanists, mujeristas, feminist poststructuralists, and others, a coalition between a variety of groups and agendas might again be possible and should be explored. For her, "differential coalitional consciousness" is a location wherein "the aims of feminism, race, ethnicity, sex, and marginality studies, and historical, aesthetic, and global studies can crosscut and join together in new relations through the recognition of a shared theory and method of oppositional consciousness." Sandoval, *Methodology of the Oppressed* (Minneapolis: University of Minnesota Press, 2000), 64. Though Sandoval does not mention theology or even religion as one differential consciousness, a countereconomic theology engages in a similar multidisciplinary approach, bridging so-called secular theory and theological and religious studies.
50. Elaine Showalter, *Hystories: Hysterical Epidemics and Modern Culture* (New York: Columbia University Press, 1997), 15.

smart investment in the heavenly economy. Thus, like the seemingly unisex but rather effectively masculine *homo economicus* of the British enlightenment, these readers operate and make economic decisions on the basis of a notion related to hysteria and lack while continually striving for abundance.

Hélène Cixous and Luce Irigaray have shown that in the gendered economies of phallocentric cultures, women are traded as inferior, marked as a hollow "lack," but also signify the place where future abundance and the growth of male descendants (and hence, wealth) occurs. Women's ambivalent position between lack and abundance is similarly reflected in the rhetorical and material economies of gender and salvation in biblical and patristic texts. Chapter 3 traces the figure of the "giving woman" through several such texts. In them, we find the continued reinscription of women as the economically impoverished gender via the stereotypical ascription of lack to the bodies of women. In the overall economy of most early Christian texts, women are rarely "of substance." And even if women appear as significant figures, their images are disciplined and managed through various rhetorical topoi and societal constructs. At the same time, we find figures such as the poor widow presented as the epitome of a wealth of grace in Jesus' *basileia* ("reign" or "kingdom"). At times women emerge endowed with unexpected subversive powers within the constraints of the economies of gender and church structures.

The figure of the "slave" and the "trickster" involves another set of rhetorical economies that have disciplined human and divine economies: the redemptive exchange of a price to redeem—to buy back—the body of a slave. Chapter 4 then reconstructs divine commerce using the soteriological motif of ransom from slavery. Ransom thus becomes the *admirabile commercium*, the divine commerce and miraculous exchange between God, humanity, and the devil. A critical reconstruction of this motif brings the soteriological motif of the *commercium* into the twenty-first century, mimicking the dynamics of ancient slave management even as it changes and modifies them. The ambivalence of the "wonderful exchange" allows for a reconstruction of the topos as the redemptive trickery of a God who, while preserving wisdom and justice, is not above "deceiving the devil" for the redemption of creation. The image of divine commerce thus offers a sacred trickster's scheme as one incarnation of divine countereconomy.[51]

The figures represent textual incarnations of early Christian notions of redemption and salvation as their salvific and material economies

---

51. Jürgen Moltmann suggests that in Hebrew scriptures and early Christian soteriology, God alone can atone for human transgressions and heal the wounds of the afflicted. Moltmann,

(almsgiving, asceticism, gender and class dynamics) become the site where constructions of human and divine economy stand in a close but tenuous relationship to each other. From these genealogies, chapter 5 develops creative possibilities for contemporary theological and economic subjects, for inhabiting various locations in a subversive, prophetic divine economy that imagines exchanges of coredemption, of "consensual salvation" in an ongoing process of mutually transformed relations.[52]

All three trickster figures live in the borderlands of heaven and earth, wealth and poverty, sincerity and deception. They embody forms of theological, sexual, and social hybridity. As genealogies of our contemporary theological and economic context, they help us to inhabit that elusive third space between theological and economic dichotomies. In chapter 5, I imagine what the contemporary incarnations of these sacred tricksters might look like. Holy Fool, Saint Mysteria, and the Counterfeit(ing) Christ are introduced as possible descendants of the figures whose genealogies are represented in chapters 2 through 4. These trickster figures, their similarities and differences, unfold as midrash-like pieces, bridging the stretches of the millennia of salvation history. As revelatory figures, tricksters unveil the monetary, relational, and physical exchanges that become theological expressions of divine economy. Chapter 5 offers a discussion of the possibilities of a tricksterish economics in a world where con men appear to win the day. The sacred trickster's redemptive trickery, in contrast, is inspired by Christ's divine commerce and the tricksterlike "economist" of Luke 16, an ambivalent figure that yet inspires divinely clever trades. A post-Weberian reassessment of ascetic practices suggests that birth control and simplified living on an overpopulated planet is a form of cultural protest, and another possible strategy. A reconstruction of the time-honored motif of the Holy Fool is followed by a call to recognize gender differences among male and female trickster figures and tactics and further to assess the gendered diversity of tricksterisms. Gendering the trickster is crucial if the concept is to be inclusive of women's particular strategies. Beyond the recognition of gender difference, it will be necessary to more deeply que(e)ry divine commerce. The voluntarily enslaved male Christ of tradition is recast (with a little help from Jean-François Lyotard) as Jesus, the calculating female prostitute who barters salvation in return for his/her body. Such tricky trades

---

Der Geist des Lebens: Eine ganzheitliche Pneumatologie (Gütersloh: Chr. Kaiser/Gütersloher Verlagshaus, 1991), 147. Though his reading stresses the singular agency of God in the redemptive process, there are other possible interpretations of the Christian notion of redemption. Moltmann himself does not argue for absolute and singular divine agency; in the end, his theology of hope relies on (divinely inspired) human activity.

52. Althaus-Reid, *Indecent Theology,* 154.

do not promise purity of motive or predictable profit. Rather, they always take place in a matrix of ambivalent relations and resemble the complexity of the created universe, or divine economy, which periodically returns to the creative and unpredictable edge of chaos.

In traditional constructions of redemption, not all models juxtapose the singular activity of God with the complete passivity of humanity. Rather, numerous apostolic and patristic texts central to the Christian tradition's notion of divine salvific activity retain the coredemptive character of divine salvific agency resident in many biblical texts. Eastern theologies likewise have preserved the notion of *theosis* as the human participation in salvation, and a sizable number of feminist theologians emphasize the synergic character of salvific relations between God and humanity.[53] Imagining redemption as a similarly cooperative process involves a soteriology of "modest witnesses" striving to heal and be healed, yet knowing they exist in the fragile space of Paul's old predicament—the turmoil within the redeemed, the ambivalence at the intersection of the "already" and the "not yet." This modest soteriology resonates with "polyglossic"[54] relations and does not easily figure as purely divine or merely human.

In the process of reconstructing redemption, we are working in dangerous and murky zones, as Moltmann reminds us: "For where this way of perceiving history is concerned, Hölderlin's saying is true: 'Where there is danger, the salutary also grows'—as is also its reverse: where the salutary grows, there danger also grows (E. Bloch)."[55] Combining Hölderlin's more optimistic statement with Bloch's more sober observation, Moltmann reaffirms that the *kairos* of a moment in space remains open for many possibilities and includes potential for both dangerous and redemptive moments. In this respect, at least, the theology to be reconstructed here might represent an instance of *theologia viatorum* (theology on the way) suggested by

---

53. See Peter C. Phan, *Culture and Eschatology: The Iconographic Vision of Paul Evdokimov* (American University Studies, series 7; Theology and Religion, vol. 1; New York: Peter Lang, 1985), 124–29. Lucia Scherzberg's survey distinguishes between ethically and aesthetically oriented strands of feminist theology. She counts the work of Plaskow, Moltmann-Wendel, Heyward, Radford Ruether, Schüssler Fiorenza, Sölle, and Halkes among the ethical interpretations of sin and grace. Though it has many historical precedents, Scherzberg does warn against this interpretation's potentially moralist tendencies and recommends a constant, accompanying "Lutheran corrective." Scherzberg, *Sünde und Gnade in der feministischen Theologie* (Mainz: Matthias Grünewald Verlag, 1992), 117, 238. Other traditions that employ images of coredemption are the Eastern Christian traditions, which use the notion of *theosis*.
54. Keller, *Apocalypse Now and Then*, 266; and Catherine Keller, *Face of the Deep*.
55. Jürgen Moltmann, *Theology of Hope: On the Grounds and the Implications of a Christian Eschatology* (New York: Harper & Row, 1964), 263.

Moltmann, a practice that looks at Scripture not as a "closed organism" but as a text open toward future instances of divine economy unfurling in each moment of space-time.[56]

---

56. Ibid., 282.

CHAPTER 1

Of Divine Currencies in Postmodernity

"There is an economy of faith that mirrors and is mirrored by faith in economics," observes Mark C. Taylor, in a comment on the problematic relationship between God and Mammon.[1] This mirroring goes beyond mere similarity and extends to a vital interrelation between the discourses of economy and theology.[2] Identifying the global Western market system as "the first truly world religion," David Loy remarks that the discourses of economics fuel the "aggressive proselytizing of market capitalism" on a global missionary scale, winning "more converts more quickly than any previous belief system."[3] The market, abuzz with religious dispensations and invested with godlike near omnipotent powers, appears "to offer a secular salvation," as theologian Harvey Cox puts it. Economic discourse, he argues, often resembles religious texts: "there lies embedded in the business pages an entire theology" that, consciously or unconsciously, assigns traditional divine attributes to features of "market" or "economy."[4] More recently,

---

1. Mark C. Taylor, *About Religion: Economies of Faith in Virtual Culture* (Religion and Postmodernism; Chicago: University of Chicago Press, 1999), 7.

2. M. C. Taylor, *About Religion*, 7. God and capitalism, the sacred and culture, are intimately connected in Taylor's view. He speaks of an "economy of speculative theology" in which "everything is always already redeemed" and where "postmodernism involves a realized eschatology in which God dies and is reborn in the Magic Kingdom where we enjoy Tomorrowland today" (26). In the logic of Taylor's texts, the "death of God" caused by the disbanding of the gold standard brings about the "birth of the divine [or sacred]." Taylor, *Erring: A Postmodern A/Theology* (Chicago: University of Chicago Press, 1984), 106.

3. David R. Loy, "The Religion of the Market," *Journal of the American Academy of Religion* 65, no. 2 (1996): 275–76.

4. Harvey Cox, "The Market as God: Living in the New Dispensation," *The Atlantic*, March 1999, http://www.TheAtlantic.com/issues/99mar/marketgod.htm.

Dell deChant has read contemporary consumer culture as a religious system that resembles ancient Babylonian or Hellenistic cultures in that it sacralizes a "meta-myth," a "sacred narrative of success and affluence, gained through a proper relationship with the economy, and revealed in the ever-expanding material prosperity of society and through the ever-increasing acquisition and consumption of products by individuals."[5]

Because the powerful rhetoric and financial structures of capitalism penetrate our culture and theology so deeply, these uncanny links between theology and the economic system cannot easily be escaped. Too often, in an effort to reclaim an original or pure conception of economy that can serve as a safely defined antidote to the market economy, theologians have called upon biblical texts and traditions. At the same time, they have overlooked the complexity and ambivalence of Christian traditions when it comes to the relations between God and Mammon, confidently announcing a "social justice Jesus" or devising a redemptive "God the economist" from a selective reading of Christian traditions that reinscribes contemporary capitalist and anticapitalist discourses in our understanding of God's dispensation.[6]

Instead, I suggest that if we hope to contest effectively the manifold destructive effects of capitalist structures of power, we need to begin by taking an inventory of the location and embodiment of the formations of knowledge and faith that shape theological economies. The first step toward the reconstruction of a divine economy that is not encompassed, controlled, or structured by current or past economic systems, no matter how totalitarian, persuasive, and powerful they may seem, is to achieve a better understanding of the ways in which "concepts of God ... which belong to older social formations such as feudal, imperial, and tributary systems still appear in market ideology as a necessary element by which the dominant class explains to itself why it is and should be dominant."[7] Understanding in what ways contemporary theology and neoclassical economics have mutually informed each other will allow us to move beyond mere critiques of contemporary economics. A mournful, playful countereconomic genealogy of the interactions between ancient and postmodern

---

5. Dell deChant, *The Sacred Santa: Religious Dimensions of Consumer Culture* (Cleveland: Pilgrim, 2002), 53.

6. Here I refer largely to Meeks's and in part also McFague's readings. I partly agree with their readings but find myself uncomfortable with their interpretation and application of early Christian texts, which lack a detailed account and reconstruction of the texts' resident ambivalence and complicity with structures of domination. I suspect that this is due in part to their reliance on exegetes with a somewhat strained liberationist reading of the circumstances of early Christianity that can lead to instances of theological idealism.

7. M. Douglas Meeks, *God the Economist: The Doctrine of God and Political Economy* (Minneapolis: Fortress, 1989), 55.

theological and material economies dislodges unchallenged assumptions and unnecessary conclusions and maps the ambivalence of our position within the divine economy, opening up new ways of understanding both the divine "dispensation" and our place in it.

God and Mammon in the Third Millennium

Mark C. Taylor has demonstrated how the communal language and rituals involving God and the market can be mapped onto each other. God and gold each function as a "transcendental signified" that provides the base of the value systems of theology and economy.[8] According to Taylor, not only is "the market" a religious symbol, but theology mimics the structure of economics. In both discourses, he argues, a superior value functions as an underlying benchmark, grounding theological and economic terms of trade. Thus, God and gold, divine and monetary currency, are structurally homologous and mutually reinforcing.

> Throughout human history, gold is not so much a sign as the transcendental signified that is supposed to ground the meaning and value of other signs. Gold, in other words, is a sign constructed to erase its status as a sign. When understood in this way, the reasons for the intersection of economic and theological interests become obvious. God functions in a semiotic system in the same way that gold functions in the economic system. The go(l)d standard is the base on which everything rests.[9]

Since monetary economies are founded on trust in a currency that replaces the "transcendental signified,"[10] the loss of credit, or faith, in a monetary sign has reverberations beyond mere economics. Connecting deconstructive semiotics with post–World War II economic history, Taylor sees a causal relationship between the delinking of monetary currency from the material gold to which its value is correlated and a crisis in "theological currency," such as the 1960s "death of God" theology. The death of God, so he argues, becomes "historically enacted and embodied in society and

---

8. See Taylor's two most relevant books for this context: *About Religion* and *Erring*.
9. M. C. Taylor, *About Religion*, 11. By calling himself an "a/theologian" rather than a theologian, Taylor aims to distinguish himself from more traditional conceptions of theology and to align himself more closely with atheistic theology and "death of God" theology.
10. Derrida's notion of the "transcendental signified" refers to a concept that signifies "*in and of itself*, a concept simply present for thought, independent of a relationship to . . . a system of signifiers." It does then no longer itself function as a signifier. Quoted in Stephen D. Moore, *Poststructuralism and the New Testament: Derrida and Foucault at the Foot of the Cross* (Minneapolis: Fortress, 1994), 17, 18.

culture," a process ending in "postmodernism and its extension in virtual cultures."[11] The specific forms of economy and God Taylor refers to are located squarely in what Fredric Jameson has described as postmodernism and has linked to "the cultural logic of late capitalism."[12] Jameson characterizes late capitalism as the unchained fluctuation of value, the rising and falling of currencies devoid of a benchmark index to give credit to, or against which to gauge one's faithful engagement.

Taylor's radical a/theological accounting of God and gold suggests that theology has been struggling to reconstruct its fundamentally bankrupt "currency" in late capitalism ever since the 1960s. Yet the principal efforts to do so, whether from a conservative or radical theological point of view, have tended to repeat only a cursory analysis of the link between theology and economics in "late capitalism."

Worldwide, one of the most energetic responses to the expansion of global capitalism has been formulated in the liberation theologies of Latin America. Liberation theologians have valiantly denounced exploitative economic practices. Their rhetoric has been powerful and effective. Liberation theology, formulated outside the European and Euro-American centers of theology, emerged at a historical *kairos,* a point of crisis and chance. It responded to the signs of the time—the impoverishment and exploitation of the Latin American poor—based on biblical responses to poverty. Liberation theology places a strong emphasis on the preferential option for the poor, arguing that salvation in Christ becomes incarnate through liberation.[13] For Gustavo Gutierrez, whose seminal *Theology of Liberation* provided a Marxist reading and theological critique of industrial capitalism in the sixties,[14] liberation theology comes close to a "theology of salvation" wherein "the struggle for a just society . . . is very much a part of salvation history."[15] Gutierrez contrasted God's preferential option for the liberation of the poor with Western capitalist economics and its collusion with the dominant theologies of the wealthy. Gutierrez further distinguished liberation from development, arguing that the latter's "timid" reformism is ineffectual because it is ingratiated to institutions with great influence on the

---

11. M. C. Taylor, *About Religion,* 21.
12. Fredric Jameson, *Postmodernism, or The Cultural Logic of Late Capitalism* (Durham, N.C.: Duke University Press, 1991).
13. Gustavo Gutierrez, *A Theology of Liberation: History, Politics, and Salvation* (Maryknoll, N.Y.: Orbis, 1973), xxv.
14. Franz Hinkelammert has pointed out that the liberation theologians' use of key Marxist concepts departs from Marxist orthodoxy early on. Hinkelammert, "Liberation Theology in the Economic and Social Context of Latin America: Economy and Theology, or the Irrationality of the Rationalized," in *Liberation Theologies, Postmodernity, and the Americas* (ed. David Batstone, Eduardo Mendieta, Lois Ann Lorentzen, and Dwight N. Hopkins; London: Routledge, 1997), 36.
15. Gutierrez, *Theology of Liberation,* xxxix, 97.

world economy. Liberation, on the other hand, includes a radical break from the status quo, a transformation of private property and access to political power for the powerless. Thus, Gutierrez argued, the "true meaning and possibilities" of development emerge only within the framework of liberation that puts the "aspirations of oppressed peoples and social classes at odds . . . with wealthy nations and oppressive classes."[16]

With the help of Marxist and socialist theories, liberation theologians have explored the extent to which the framework of colonialism has shaped Latin American societies. Liberation means the cessation of the domination of Latin America by the "great capitalist countries," especially the United States.[17] The church contributes to liberation by engaging in a prophetic task both constructive and critical, through "conscienticizing evangelization," the subversive witness of priests and bishops, and theological reflection preceded by "orthopraxis"—the right action that precedes orthodoxy, right faith.[18] However, the analytic schemes of its early years, with starkly crystallized binaries, oppositions between rich and poor, exploiters and exploited have proved too reductionist to trace the nuances of agency and subversion in resistance to economic structures marked by a rhetoric of dominance and an ethos of wealth acquisition.

As economic globalism spreads across the world, large numbers of Christians around the world have become attracted to the gospel of prosperity that is often propagated along with the neocolonial seeds of globalization. Thus, a variety of related yet distinct prosperity theologies have become influential in charismatic and evangelical circles worldwide. Though not without hermeneutical precedents, the specific hermeneutic and practice that informs many varieties of prosperity theology emerged in the southern United States through the churches and ministries of Kenneth Hagin in Tulsa, Oklahoma, and Kenneth and Gloria Copeland in Fort Worth, Texas. Biblical passages are used to bolster the claim that "prosperity of all kinds is the right of every Christian" and that "God wants a Christian to be wealthy." Since true Christianity "necessarily means wealth; it inevitably brings wealth."[19] Thus, by way of a highly selective biblicist hermeneutic, prosperity theology links God's love and blessings with the benefits of capitalism.

Prosperity theology often arises out of a context in which economic disenfranchisement merges with a particular kind of spirituality. It is deeply

---

16. Ibid., 17, 24.
17. Ibid., 54.
18. Ibid., 68–69.
19. Paul Gifford, "Prosperity: A New and Foreign Element in African Christianity," *Religion* 20 (1990): 375.

connected with the charismatic, pentecostal movements that emerged out of a "lower-class, bi-racial" milieu.[20] Paul Gifford points out that since many Africans interpret wealth and success as signs of the blessing of God, prosperity theologies are potentially even more effective in Africa's independent churches. Thus, "whereas Western churches have tended to restrict salvation to the things of the next world, independent churches to a far greater degree have included in the concept of salvation realities of everyday life like health, fertility, success, and material goods."[21]

In addition, in the context of a spirituality that responds to economic disenfranchisement, the gospel of prosperity sometimes can be preached in the name of liberationist ends. While the gospel of prosperity is most often discussed in the context of white charismatic, neo-pentecostalist circles in the United States, some of the more complex incarnations of this type of hermeneutic can be found among certain black preachers who have used prosperity theology in the process of helping to enfranchise the black urban poor. Pastor and former congressman Floyd Flake's Allen African Methodist Episcopal Church in Jamaica, New York, and Acts Full Gospel Church of God in Christ in Oakland, California, under the leadership of Bob Jackson, have instituted programs and ministries that have taught many parishioners basic life and financial skills. Through such ministries and a rising economic tide, many African Americans in the Bay area have been able to enter the middle class and move to the suburbs.[22] Multidimensional developments such as these suggest that binary oppositions such as liberation theology versus prosperity theology do not map the full complexities of the links between economy and theology well enough.

Having emerged in the 1960s from a coalition of fundamentalist, pentecostal, and charismatic evangelicals, the message of a gospel of prosperity was spread by American evangelists to Sweden, Africa, and Latin America. It is no coincidence that, as Simon Coleman has argued, prosperity theologies "display expansionist tendencies," that the "worldwide revival of conservative Protestantism [comes] at a time when capitalism has apparently been experiencing a global resurgence."[23] Likewise, it would seem more than a coincidence that theologies of prosperity have grown substantially

---

20. Ibid., 373.
21. Ibid., 383.
22. Chris Thompson, "Preaching Prosperity: Acts Full Gospel Became Oakland's Largest Church by Helping Its Parishioners Leave Town for the Suburbs," *East Bay Express* 24 April 2002, 12–21.
23. Simon M. Coleman, "America Loves Sweden: Prosperity Theology and the Cultures of Capitalism," in *Religion and the Transformation of Capitalism* (ed. Richard Roberts; London: Routledge, 1995), 161. Rosalind I. J. Hackett sees a "close affinity between the type of religious multi-nationalism, religious enterprise, values and competitive pluralism engendered by the

during the 1980s in Latin America at a time these countries were under pressure from the IMF and WTO to adopt neoliberal economic policies.[24]

For the new generation of Latin American liberation theologians who have encountered the resistance of neoclassical economics to opposition, "the need for liberation . . . continues to be acute" as "structural injustice in Latin America not only continues, but is even more pronounced." However, the "exhilarating sense of impending revolutionary change is long since gone," as liberation theologian Nancy Bedford observed.[25] In response, liberation theologians have begun to employ some of the tools of postmodern analysis that disturb simple oppositions in order to reopen the way toward the goals that liberation theology has valued.

Faced with the complex reality of the globalization process, Bedford argues, liberation theology has begun to deconstruct some of its binaries, as well as the metanarrative upon which it has consistently relied: "that of liberation attained in history and in fact to be attained soon."[26] It has become tricky to find what particular practice will best satisfy a continued emphasis on orthopraxis. There is no longer a sense of clarity about what practices should be outlawed and opposed, as the "provisional nature of all discourse and practice has begun to be felt more strongly."[27] Attempting to negotiate the reality of globalization while resisting tendencies toward parochialism and isolationism, Néstor Míguez has argued that theological constructions must find ways to better account for the multiple causes and

---

charismatic revival in Africa and global, particularly Western, capitalist forces." Hackett, "The Gospel of Prosperity in West Africa," in *Religion and the Transformation of Capitalism* (ed. Richard Roberts; London: Routledge, 1995), 199.

24. Though some describe prosperity theologies imprecisely as fundamentalist, some prominent fundamentalist voices have condemned prosperity theology as "secular humanism in disguise," through which "sacrificial living and compassion for others have given way to an unbridled quest for self-actualization and self-gratification," as a "slot-machine religion" that "totally distorts the glorious gospel to the unsaved," that "condemns and unfairly judges all godly believers who struggle in financial poverty." Edward G. Dobson, "Prosperity Theology: Secular Humanism in Disguise," *Fundamentalist Journal* (October 1987): 12; and Harold Willmington, "Prosperity Theology: A Slot-Machine Religion," *Fundamentalist Journal* (November 1987): 15, 18. Thus, even Willmington, vice president at Jerry Falwell's Liberty University, could condemn Copeland's and Hagin's hermeneutics and spirituality.

25. Nancy Bedford, "Little Moves against Destructiveness: Theology and the Practice of Discernment," in *Practicing Theology: Beliefs and Practices in Christian Life* (ed. Miroslav Volf and Dorothy C. Bass; Grand Rapids: Eerdmans, 2002), 160.

26. Ibid., 161.

27. From the previously dominant event-centered metaphor of exodus, images have shifted to more process-oriented texts. Jeremiah's investment in land (Jer 32–33), for example, is a "very long-term project" whose humble commitment of hope could outlast the despair to come. These "small moves" and "small stories" contribute to the "imperative to look for ways to be faithful and persevere," thus tying into faith in a salvific process even as the hope for "positive and substantial structural changes has waned in society at large." Bedford, "Little Moves against Destructiveness," 161–64.

effects of economic policies. They must preserve the best of the theories of the past, while incorporating the best fruits of new social studies, anthropology, and other developments in theory, such as discourse analysis and deconstructions of discursive power.[28]

Postmodernity and Postcolonialism: Hybridity and Ambivalence

Poststructuralism and postmodern theory have been central to the effort to open up a third space not annexed by binary oppositions. However, efforts to open such a space have come from several angles serving a variety of ends. In an attempt to inhabit a third space where options exceed the binaries of "capitalist *or* socialist," "liberal *or* conservative,"[29] D. Stephen Long has surveyed a broad range of theological engagements with economic theory in order to recover the "residual tradition" of a "radical orthodoxy." This normative creedal formation, so he claims, bears

> traces of a time prior to that in which the useful has been predominant. It does not seek to be relevant to the modern world through Kant, or Weber, or Marx, but seeks instead to present a rationality rooted in the thirteenth-century work of Thomas Aquinas. It assumes . . . that modernity and secularity are mistakes that must be undone. . . . A capitalist political economy is the "fruit" (or the "weed," according to one's viewpoint) of the modern era.[30]

For this radical orthodoxy, capitalism is "heresy," a side effect of the disintegration of Christian virtues and of creedal orthodoxy in modernity.

---

28. Míguez assesses the situation of Latin America in the new millennium as the "aftermath of a frustrated revolution." A mood of resignation and despair among the sufferers has often turned self-destructive, so that even ancient networks of solidarity in Latin America have eroded. Míguez reports that liberation theology has been weakened, as Roman Catholic authorities have contributed to isolating and silencing prominent liberation theologians and as the growth of conservative charismatic Protestants has muted prophetic voices, eroding the possibility for the church to function as an alternative social paradigm. Néstor Míguez, "Globalization: A Challenge to Hear the Victim's Voice," *Jeevadhara* 1 (2000): 107–9, 112–13.

29. D. Stephen Long, *Divine Economy: Theology and the Market* (New York: Routledge, 2000), 6.

30. Ibid., 178. Long's radically orthodox theology attempts the recovery of a theology *ex machina* from premodern sources. Dismissing what he identifies as "*analogia libertatis*"—the foundationalist assumption of both "dominant" (namely, liberal theologies of economy) and "emergent theologies" (liberation theological accounts of economy) predicated on a modern, liberal notion of human freedom to choose—Long dates the origin of the notion of freedom in modernity and subsequently attempts to delegitimate the *analogia libertatis* by claiming its artificiality and historicity. In Long's critique of liberal theology, liberation theology is reduced to a version of modernist liberalism that radical orthodoxy seems to aim to overcome.

By way of a retrieval of premodern virtues, a postmodern radical orthodoxy aims to reenthrone theology as the queen of sciences and to implement a religious socialism.[31] In this analysis, modernism and capitalism are seen as identical twins. Thus, John Milbank's rejection of "secular episteme," which he denounces as "post-Christian paganism[,] . . . a refusal of Christianity and the invention of 'Anti-Christianity,'" is related to his denunciation of capitalism as "heresy."[32]

Although he elsewhere dismisses Derrida,[33] Long employs Derrida's critique of the metaphysics of presence to claim that both liberal and liberation theologies have an affinity for a "metaphysics of being."[34] For example, Long argues that the black theologian James Cone "identifies all works of liberation with . . . God."[35] It remains unclear, however, what kind of third theological space Long or other proponents of the "residual tradition" such as Milbank, Bernard Dempsey, and Alistair MacIntyre have opened up when it comes to (divine) economics. Long claims to have unrestricted and unpolluted access to an oddly transcendental set of neo-Thomist virtues.[36] It would seem peculiar then for Long, who indicts his interlocutors for operating under a "metaphysics of being,"[37] to have recourse to a neo-Thomist version of Aristotelian virtues as "the good, the true and the beautiful," as if metaphysics was a modern invention and not largely derived from the writings of Aristotle himself.[38] Despite the claim that "theology

---

31. This approach is formulated by John Milbank and other proponents of radical orthodoxy, such as Stephen Long. In what Paul Lakeland identifies as Milbankian "countermodernity," a reestablishment of theology as the "queen of sciences" will insist "that Christian orthodoxy demands the abolition of capitalism and the production of a socialist market." See Paul Lakeland, *Postmodernity: Christian Identity in an Age of Fragmentation* (Guides to Theological Inquiry; Minneapolis: Fortress, 1997), 68; and Long, *Divine Economy*, 242, 260.

32. Quoted in Long, *Divine Economy*, 258.

33. In Derrida, Long claims to find a mere repetition of capitalist logic, concluding that "Derrida's responsibility is no radical account of the ethical life: it is nothing other than the capitalist's opportunity cost." Long, *Divine Economy*, 145.

34. Ibid., 172.

35. Cited in Long, *Divine Economy*, 161. As a critique of one specific writer, Long's critique of Cone remains too facile in its reduction of the theological discourse of liberation to a sacrifice of "the gospel of metaphysics."

36. Long gets tripped up in the attempt both to locate his theology historically and at the same time to declare null and void the past five hundred years of modernity. Problematically locating modernity as the singular culprit for the dominance of economics, Long launches what he hopes to be an outright opposition to a capitalism billed as "heresy" and to the liberalism he sees as operative in the "emerging tradition" of liberation theologies, but not in a "residual tradition" represented by Dempsey, MacIntyre, and Milbank. Long, *Divine Economy*, 178.

37. Long, following Milbank, charges Rahner, Tillich, Cone, and Ruether with the subordination of theological production under metaphysics. See Long, *Divine Economy*, 117, 145, 161, esp. 172.

38. Long furthermore hopes to reconcile Barth's rejection of natural theology with Thomas Aquinas, who is, again unacknowledged by Long, the father of natural theology.

[does not try] to uncover some original event 'behind' history through critical methods," radical orthodoxy in general and Long in particular exhibit a strong nostalgia for a premodern, prehumanistic universe, refusing to acknowledge, or appropriate positively, their own dependence on either modernity or metaphysics.[39]

Ironically, what radical orthodoxy claims differentiates it from liberation theologies—radical orthodoxy's rejection of scarcity, of metaphysics, of liberalism—creeps back in before long. Radical orthodoxy, too, affirms the plenitude—and thus the final omnipotence—of God and strikes a strongly oppositional attitude to capitalism by demanding the "recovery of a Christian socialism destroyed by Marx's and Engels's scientific socialism." Indeed, Long states that Milbank ends up, surprisingly, arguing for "the abolition of capitalism and the production of a socialist market"![40] While the recovery of religious socialism as a third economic space is an important contribution to a countereconomic theology, its announcement in the writings of radical orthodoxy seems primarily polemic and utopian while based upon a unilateral and in the end unsatisfying rejection of modernity *in toto*.

More helpful in exploring the gaps and spaces of a third space, poststructuralist and, in particular, postcolonial thought helps to map spaces of hybridity and ambivalence, beyond the impasse of stolid dualisms and romanticization. A variety of poststructuralist and postcolonial texts effectively have unveiled the ambivalent relations between oppressor and oppressed, countering common suspicions regarding the "toothlessness" of postmodernism "in the face of oppression." Rather, these texts can become tools to unveil, demystify, and counteract the discourse of colonial neoclassical economics and their theological doubles.[41] Thus, Mark McClain Taylor argues that the "deconstructionist writings of Jacques Derrida are a prominent example of the way postmodern thinkers implicitly acknowledge the need to struggle for liberation of oppressed peoples."[42] Taylor further observes that "identifying the co-optive feature of postmodern discourse is not a precursor to rejecting the discourse. On the contrary, the identification helps to clarify the primary condition under which postmodernists' ludic play might actually serve liberating

---

39. On this matter, see Lakeland, *Postmodernity*, 64–76.
40. Long, *Divine Economy*, 260.
41. David Batstone, Eduardo Mendieta, Lois Ann Lorentzen, and Dwight N. Hopkins, introduction to *Liberation Theologies, Postmodernity, and the Americas*, ed. Batstone, Mendieta, Lorentzen, and Hopkins, 16.
42. Mark McClain Taylor, "Vodou Resistance/Vodou Hope: Forging a Postmodernism That Liberates," in *Liberation Theologies, Postmodernity, and the Americas*, ed. Batstone, Mendieta, Lorentzen, and Hopkins, 179.

struggle."[43] Writers such as Edward Said, Homi Bhabha, and Gayatri Spivak have challenged some of the allegedly clear distinctions between colonizer and colonized. Often inspired by poststructuralist writings, these texts elaborate the quandaries of hybridity beyond the less and less useful binaries of "the master and the slave, the mercantilist and the Marxist."[44] "Hybridity" is perhaps best defined by Homi Bhabha as the "interstitial passage between fixed identifications" in power configurations both political and economic.[45] Gayatri Spivak in particular has challenged those who live in these hybrid spaces with her insistence that "the economic be kept visible under erasure" since it is "irreducible as it inscribes the social text."[46] Spivak herself has applied a post–Cold War and postcolonial Marxist reading of capitalism to her own hybrid situation, which both profits from and is exploited by imperialism and capitalism.

Postcolonial analyses of colonial and neocolonial discourse offer the possibility to intricately and carefully map the shifts in the production of power/knowledge and to formulate an equally intricate response to those shifts. While some may dismiss postcolonial thought as the obfuscation of real power imbalances between economic elites and those forced to live on the margins, I welcome its contribution as a necessary complication of problematic oppositions that have prevented solidarity and communication. These theoretical lenses help to analyze and reconstruct the theological expressions of divine economy. As we have seen in the unexpected complexities of the preaching and reception of the gospel of prosperity, and as the protests against the World Trade Organization meeting in Seattle and other demonstrations have shown in the political realm, binary divisions can collapse in surprising ways. Solidarity and mutual recognition between people from different sides of the neoclassical economic divide can form unlikely alliances between North and South, "developed" and "developing," rich and poor, promoters of environmentally sustainable industry and steelworkers.

Marcella Althaus-Reid, an Argentinean liberation theologian, has found postcolonial considerations helpful in her walk, her *caminata*, through the city of Buenos Aires as she reflects "on economic and theological oppression with passion and imprudence."[47] Her theological discourse, theologically and economically "indecent" as it questions the "traditional Latin American

---

43. Ibid.
44. Homi Bhabha, *The Location of Culture* (London: Routledge, 1994), 25.
45. Ibid., 4.
46. Gayatri Spivak, *A Critique of Postcolonial Reason: Toward a History of the Vanishing Present* (Cambridge: Harvard University Press, 1999), 358, 310.
47. Marcella Althaus-Reid, *Indecent Theology: Theological Perversions in Sex, Gender, and Politics* (London: Routledge, 2001), 2.

field of decency and order," pushes the boundaries of orthodoxy. As a continuation of liberation theology that takes its inspiration "from the poor" (rather than writing a theology *for* the poor), hers is also a "sexual theology, a theology of economics and desires," that shifts its context from the rural poor of earlier liberation theology to that of poor urban women.[48] Thus shifting the context of her theological inquiry, she challenges liberation theology to engage in a "continuing process of re-contextualization, a permanent exercise of serious doubting in theology," continually adding "new contextual perspectives."[49]

Constructive Theological Approaches to *Oikonomia*: Toward a Countereconomic Theology

Other steps toward a third space have been taken by constructive theologians in the United States. Process theologian John Cobb, Trinitarian theologian Douglas Meeks, and ecofeminist theologian Sallie McFague have provided substantial theological critiques of current Western economic practices. Though their approaches obviously differ, as do the texts they examine, Cobb, Meeks, and McFague all share a critique of neoclassical economics and call for a fully inclusive, relational, egalitarian *oikonomia*, "God's economy," and "new household rules," as divine alternatives to current exploitative capitalist and consumerist globalizing economic rationales.[50] In different ways, each advocates the inclusion of human values and environmental integrity into the study of economics to further the abundance of what is necessary for human and planetary life on a global scale. Cobb's and McFague's theological critiques, for example, each call for significant reforms and changes within the science of economics, challenging it to become more interdisciplinary and more inclusive of previous "externalities" such as women's unpaid work and the environment.

Building on the work of liberation theologies but foregoing a class analysis, Cobb focused his early theological work on a critical assessment of the shape of neoclassical economy and on its academic institutionalization in the discipline of economics. A pioneer among a group of theologians who have made the relationship between theology and economy or economics their topic, Cobb has laid the foundation for subsequent theological work through his application of process thought and theology to

---

48. Ibid., 4.
49. Ibid., 5.
50. See also Christian ethicist Larry Rasmussen's *Earth Community, Earth Ethics* (Maryknoll, N.Y.: Orbis, 1996).

questions of economics. His most important and incisive work in that regard, *For the Common Good,* is a joint venture with Herman Daly, a former economist at the World Bank. Their critique of the structures of the dominant academic discipline of economics unveils a number of instances of the "fallacy of misplaced concreteness" as it applies to issues such as the market, economic measurement and statistics, economic anthropology, and land use. This "fallacy" becomes a deconstructive tool used by Cobb and Daly to dismantle seemingly rational and scientific economic abstractions that erase important distinctions while making major truth claims.[51]

For the Common Good calls for alternative approaches to economics, arguing that economic research needs to be conducted in the broad context of the social, economic, and cultural aspects of life, and that economic policies need to privilege the "common good" over short-term profits for the few.

In *God the Economist,* Meeks offers a theology of "political economy." A student and early translator of Jürgen Moltmann, whose Trinitarian theology underlies Meeks's perichoretic "economic" trinity, Meeks sees economic discourse infused with divine attributes that propagate problematic and outdated concepts of God, such as omnipotence, omniscience, and immutability. By naming God an "economist," a householder concerned with all of creation, Meeks in effect undertakes a reconstruction of the doctrine of God that is also a reconstruction of political economy. Meeks's work exhibits a singular awareness of the complex meanings of the term *oikonomia,* which he distinguishes from the modern term "economy." In *oikonomia,* he identifies an "egalitarian thrust" that frees the "households of Israel and the church, the household of the nations, and the household of creation from domination."[52] Meeks's Trinitarian ecclesiology represents a visionary account of an alternative economy in which theology can provide alternative perspectives on key economic concepts such as work, property, and needs. To date, Meeks's account still represents the most thorough and wide-ranging assessment of the connections and tensions between theology and economy. Further investigation is needed, however, on many themes Meeks can only touch on within the wide scope of his work.

Sallie McFague's reconstruction of theology in *Life Abundant: Rethinking Theology and Economy for a Planet in Peril* (2000) incorporates insights from the recently developed field of ecological economics. "For the purposes of right action," she proposes a "North American Liberation Theology" for North American, "mostly white, middle-class" mainline

---

51. Alfred North Whitehead, *Science and the Modern World* (New York: Free Press, 1925), 51.
52. Meeks, *God the Economist,* 11.

Christians.[53] McFague argues that the dominant neoclassical approach to economics and ecological economics conceive of human subjectivity differently and, as a result, that each formulates different theological conceptions of divine agency and salvation. Whereas neoclassical economics stresses the independence and sovereignty of human beings by conceiving of them as subjects with inalienable rights and duties, ecological economics, informed by postmodern forms of scientific reasoning, instead maps the interrelatedness of human existence with planetary life. Furthermore, she argues, neoclassical economics neglects the suffering and despair of the poor by prioritizing desires and wants over human or ecological well-being. Since "God cannot do all the work of salvation," she argues, humans must become "auxiliary agents in and for the body of the world," where "our life work is to further the divine purpose of planetary prosperity."[54] To that end, she hopes to create "ecologically literate" Christian spiritualities and life practices.[55]

These efforts to configure a third space beyond the paradigm of neoclassical economics by a reconceptualization of *oikonomia* are not without their problems. First, Cobb, Meeks, and McFague are insufficiently critical of gender, class, and racial domination within the Christian traditions. Cobb's and Daly's application of the Aristotelian distinction between *oikonomia* and *chrematistics*, from which they launch their critique and reconstruction of an economy for the common good, underestimates the roles of gender and class, which do not figure centrally in their oeuvre.[56] Likewise, despite Meeks's insightful warning that "the main problem of all economy"—as opposed to *oikonomia*—is the past and continued use of God as "an agency of domination in economy as well as in politics," he

---

53. Sallie McFague, *Life Abundant: Rethinking Theology and Economy for a Planet in Peril* (Minneapolis: Fortress, 2000), ix, 14, 15, 33. Ecological economics is an emerging strand of economics that addresses the modernist fragmentation of the natural sciences by thinking economics and ecology together. One should remember, however, that ecological economics does not represent the only attempt at stretching current economics to include other categories or to find new foundations for economics through principles such as "sustainable growth" or "natural capitalism." Particularly useful in this respect is the work of converts from economism such as Herman Daly, David Korten, and, within feminist economics, Julie Nelson. See Herman E. Daly, *Ecological Economics and the Ecology of Economics: Essays in Criticism* (Cheltenham, England, and Northampton, Mass.: E. Elgar, 1999); David C. Korten, *The Post-Corporate World: Life after Capitalism* (San Francisco: Berrett-Koehler; West Hartford, Conn.: Kumarian Press, 1999); and Julie A. Nelson, "Feminism, Ecology, and the Philosophy of Economics," *Ecological Economics* 20 (1997): 155–62.

54. McFague, *Life Abundant*, 146, 151.

55. Ibid., 209.

56. Herman E. Daly and John B. Cobb Jr., *For the Common Good: Redirecting the Economy toward Community, the Environment, and a Sustainable Future* (2d ed; Boston: Beacon, 1994), 138–58.

neglects to take into account how misogynist and plutocratic patterns of systemic violence may impair the reconstruction of a doctrine of God as economist.[57] McFague's announcement of a "different kind of economy, one of surprising abundance and sacrificial generosity[,] . . . the *oikos,* the household, in which we are all called to live" likewise problematically assumes *oikonomia* as an ideal category.[58]

Cobb, Meeks, and McFague call for a broadening of the concept of *oikonomia* into a fully inclusive, relational, egalitarian *oikonomia* without a concrete analysis of the biblical metaphor upon which they rest so much of their construction. They thus neglect Christian textual traditions that do not fit into a vision of an ideal, egalitarian *oikonomia.* Althaus-Reid has said of Latin American liberation theology, "While not disagreeing in principle with this rhetoric of prophetism and justice, one may ask what justice, what equality and what liberty are at the core of the theological reflection on globalisation processes?"[59] The same goes, so Althaus-Reid suggests, for the structures of power and gender in economics and theology, as "the dislocation of sexual constructions goes hand in hand with strategies for the dislocation of hegemonic political and economic agendas."[60] Theological critiques of economic systems remain incomplete if they simply replace one grand narrative of omnipotence with another, a theological for an economic dominology. Attempting thus to address both economic and theological oppressions, we must ask what kind of *oikonomia* serves as the basis for a reconstruction of economic theology. Until we begin to address that question, our position as contemporary interpreters of Christian "economic" traditions may be dangerously compromised.

Remaining committed to the articulation of such structures prevents us from being able to recognize and address more complex discursive and economic mechanics and potentially preserves the complicity of theology with oppressive economic systems. Univocally possessive constructions such as "God's household" and "God's economy" proclaim a "household of freedom" or an "entirely different kind of economy"[61] without taking seriously enough the lingering hierarchical and patriarchal dynamics of cultural conceptions of *oikonomia* that continue to shape ancient and

---

57. Meeks, *God the Economist,* 10–11. A similar oversight coupled with a rhetoric of pure, egalitarian Christian origins can be found in the writings of other constructive theologians, such as in Susan Brooks Thistlethwaite and Peter C. Hodgson, "The Church, Classism, and Ecclesial Community," in *Reconstructing Christian Theology,* (ed. Rebecca Chopp and Mark Lewis Taylor; Minneapolis: Fortress, 1994), 307–8.
58. McFague, *Life Abundant,* 182.
59. Althaus-Reid, *Indecent Theology,* 180.
60. Ibid., 6.
61. Meeks, *God the Economist,* 23; McFague, *Life Abundant,* 197.

postmodern Christian discourse on householding, economics, and doctrinal formation. It is perhaps partly for this reason that they turn a blind eye to the lingering tendency within the Christian tradition to reinscribe the inferiority of women and slaves within the Christian *oikonomia*.[62]

The immediate challenge is to move beyond prophetic denunciation, on the one hand, and visionary proclamation, on the other, to a different way of reading biblical images of economy. It does not suffice to stress the egalitarian strands of biblical literature such as the invitational structure of the divine economic banquets in Jesus' parables or the upending of patriarchal familial structures, or to call for a new intentional community by casting children as exemplary recipients of the *basileia*, or to promote ministry rather than domination as the alternative leadership structure of the new community. The romanticization of itinerants, women, ethnic others, and the poor—a problematic tendency in liberation theologies and other progressive theologies—may ultimately be in danger of marking women, natives, and the environment exclusively as victims and innocents through a patronizing gesture that deprives them of agency and responsibility. No doubt we need to be reminded that "*oikos* underwent extreme truncation: *oikos* became market" and to hear the subsequent call for a reexpansion of *oikonomia*, perhaps to include all ecosystems or the entire cosmos.[63] Yet it is equally crucial to examine in more depth what Homi Bhabha has described as the "resemblance" of even a subversive move to what it mimics—that is, to examine the resemblance of ancient as well as postmodern theological constructs of *oikonomia* to colonizing economic structures.[64]

Though more critical of the tradition than other feminist scholars of her day, Elisabeth Schüssler Fiorenza—on whose research Meeks in part depends—proudly claims women as patrons of the early church and elaborates at length the importance of their contribution to church leadership.[65] Her account remains positive throughout, however. The next generation of feminist scholars of antiquity, represented by Karen Torjesen and Virginia Burrus, stresses that while ancient women were able to function as heads of households, early Christian women largely remained involved in structures of patronage and slaveholding.[66] A romanticizing view of the fact that some

---

62. Of course, none of this is new or surprising. I am merely reminding the reader of the explicit Pauline and pastoral insistence that man be the head of woman and that slaves remain obedient to their masters.

63. Meeks, *God the Economist*, 48.

64. Bhabha uses the term to describe the similarity of a subversive discourse to the colonial discourse it mimics. Bhabha, *Location of Culture*, 86.

65. Elisabeth Schüssler Fiorenza, *In Memory of Her: A Feminist Theological Reconstruction of Christian Origins* (New York: Crossroad, 1994), 174–85 and passim.

66. Karen Jo Torjesen, *When Women Were Priests: Women's Leadership in the Early Church*

women, such as Lydia (Acts 16:11–15), had access to positions of power in the *oikos* easily overlooks their entanglement with exploitative structures. Althaus-Reid echoes related but inverse concerns with her challenge of the conventional liberation theological gesture of portraying the poor "as in any old-fashioned moralizing Victorian tale . . . as the deserving and asexual poor." She exposes the "theological representation of absolutes" in liberation theology as they perform the "farce of a simplistic confrontation between oppressive and liberative aspects of our lives."[67]

If constructive theology wants to move beyond what Pierre Bourdieu has called "the lachrymose moralism of the churches" as they bemoan the vicissitudes of the market, it must show more methodological awareness of its own textual and presuppositional anatomy.[68] Acknowledging the mere facts of oppression does not suffice. What appear to be the liabilities of biblical texts, intertexts, and Christian *Wirkungsgeschichte* (effective history) do not merely remain debts to pay but also function as the down payment for a reconstruction of divine economy. A reconstruction of divine *oikonomia* thus critically interrogates its conceptual precedents as they simultaneously reenact their resemblance to dominant economic discourses and menace those discourses.[69] Without such an investigation, this reconstruction would neglect the complex economic dynamics in which contemporary Christians find themselves involved. This includes admitting how much theology is itself part of a larger Western economic mindset by theorizing and theologizing its complex relationship to the economics of academia, including the influence of corporate donors as well as the economic heritage of colonialism and exploitation upon which academia is founded.[70] Ultimately, constructive theologians must remain committed to a dynamic interaction with a multiplicity of conversations, theories, and discourses.

Unlike radical orthodoxy, what follows does not seek to reenthrone theology as "queen of sciences"[71] or uncover a "particular form of the

---

and the Scandal of Their Subordination in the Rise of Christianity (San Francisco: HarperSanFrancisco, 1995), 65, 71.

67. Althaus-Reid, *Indecent Theology*, 149.

68. Pierre Bourdieu, *Acts of Resistance: Against the Tyranny of the Market* (New York: New Press, 1998), 76.

69. Bhabha, *Location of Culture*, 86.

70. John Cobb has addressed these issues in his later work, but not necessarily within the setting of a reconstructive theology of economy. See also Donna J. Haraway, *Simians, Cyborgs, and Women: The Reinvention of Nature* (New York: Routledge, 1991), 97; and Amitava Kumar, *Passport Photos* (Berkeley: University of California Press, 2000), 61.

71. Rebecca Chopp and Mark Lewis Taylor, *Reconstructing Christian Theology* (Minneapolis: Fortress, 1994), 17; John Milbank, *Theology and Social Theory: Beyond Secular Reason* (Oxford: Blackwell, 1990), 380.

Christian narrative that functions as a 'metanarrative'" that "positions all other discourses within its own *logos*, rather than being itself positioned by those other *logoi*."[72] Instead, it "appropriates and reconfigures" the gains of modern thought—such as freedom, rationality, human rights, and subjectivity—to meet new circumstances, positioning itself squarely to face and address "a world in crisis" through theological analyses situated in the contested fields of postmodernity.[73] It proposes a theology of countereconomy that stresses the commitment to liberative action, but claims traditions of exodus and liberation as arising out of the Hebrew and Christian traditions, rather than from modern ideas of personhood and enlightenment conceptions of liberty. While such a theology takes into account the shortcomings of modernity, it attempts to find ways to live in a "constructive ambivalence" toward it.[74] It finds the possibility of a theology inspired by the parabolic metaphoricity of what is "openended, tentative, indirect, tensive, iconoclastic, transformative."[75]

The following chapter begins the construction of this theology by charting an "economics of redemption" as it traces how the biblical figure of the Rich Young Man and its postbiblical reception in antiquity reveal a genealogy of lingering masculine hysteria still visible in contemporary constructions of economics, redemption, and masculinity.

---

72. Long, *Divine Economy*, 242.
73. Peter C. Hodgson, *Winds of the Spirit: A Constructive Christian Theology* (Louisville, Ky.: Westminster John Knox, 1994), 55; Chopp and Taylor, *Reconstructing Christian Theology*, 1, 7–8.
74. Catherine Keller, *Apocalypse Now And Then: A Feminist Guide to the End of the World* (Boston: Beacon, 1996), 24, 27.
75. McFague, *Life Abundant*, 19.

CHAPTER 2

Found Lacking: Masculine Hysteria and the Economics of Redemption

Legei auto ho neaniskos: Panta tauta ephulaxa. Ti eti hustero?
The young man said to him, "I have kept all these; what do I still lack?"
(Matt 19:20)

Whence the characteristic hysteria of our time: the hysteria of production and reproduction of the real.... What society seeks through production, and overproduction, is the restoration of the real which escapes it. That is why *contemporary "material" production is itself hyperreal.*

      Jean Baudrillard, *Jean Baudrillard: Selected Writings* (emphasis in original)

As distant as they are from each other in time and context, the above inquiries into the phenomenon of lack, or hysteria, share more than is obvious at first glance. In the narrative of Jesus' conversation with the rich young man, we encounter an ancient text powerfully formative of male Christian subjectivity, while Baudrillard's diagnosis of postmodern hysteria represents a later intertextual iteration of ancient concepts of hysteria within the context of a critique of the *homo economicus,* that stereotypical figure of Western capitalist subjectivity.[1] True, "real" wealth escapes the

---

1. Following Bakhtin, Daniel Boyarin has argued the intertextuality of all literature: "Since Adam, then, all discourse is dialogue with the past and all literature is therefore intertextual and double-voiced. Even those texts which most insistently claim to be the voice of the subjectivity of

desiring investor and produces hysteria, a symptom of lack that hides as much as it exposes. In the quest for "treasures in heaven," writers inquire into substance and material goods, the relationship between wealth and salvation, gender, empire, and power—in short, the economics of redemption. Visible despite the intertextual transformations of cultural expressions of distress, the phenomenon of hysteria is a surprisingly persistent indicator of how faithful men have negotiated the conflicting claims of God and Mammon. Thus, the frantic search for wealth and power in earthly economies has tended to tragically mirror economic oppression in earthly and divine household structures.

Chapters 2 and 3 explore how gendered concepts of economic and theological substance have negotiated notions of lack/hysteria, abundance, and redemption. They investigate sexed stories of divine economy by looking at an interpretive instance—hysteria—at which hierarchical economic and theological gender constructions and ideologies of decency and property break down and unveil the chaotic instability of the seemingly stable, penetrating omnipotent orders of gendered power.[2] Though theological narratives tend to reinforce rather than transform images of God and the Christian male as a property owner and "economist," they also unveil men's abject, unstable relationship to economic and theological power constructions. This productive instability opens a way to reconstruct divine and human economic agency so as to transform the oppressions of past and present with redemptive potentialities.[3] A critical genealogy of the *homo economicus* postulates a possible ancestor, namely, the Gospels' figure of the rich young man (Matt 19:16–30 and Mark 10:17–31), a figure upon whose literary body a variety of intertextual meditations are inscribed. This genealogy, while fictional, traces uncanny economies of faith, linking the youth in conversation with Jesus with the modern construct of *homo*

---

the author recording his or her personal experience and vision are socially and historically conditioned. The literary text in its intertextuality both continues and breaches the literary tradition of the culture; it preserves the signifying practices of a culture precisely by transforming them." Boyarin, *Intertextuality and the Reading of Midrash* (Bloomington: Indiana University Press, 1990), 23–24.

2. I use here a methodical move that resembles Catherine Keller's deconstruction of the pretensions at *ex nihilo* omnipotence in Gen 1:1 and Western theological traditions that result in a "vicious circle" where "the nothingness invariably returns with the face of the feared chaos—to be nihilated all the more violently." Keller, *Face of the Deep* (New York: Routledge, 2003), xvi. I attempt to deconstruct assumptions about the theological and sexual properties of economic man, showing how hysteria, feared and gendered female, functions as a version of such lack, such nothingness, such abject poverty that keeps returning, despite ever greater attempts at appropriation.

3. Catherine Keller describes the abject, following Kristeva, as that which disturbs identity, system, and order. See Keller, *Face of the Deep*, 55.

economicus and its postmodern critics. Although economic agency is no longer resident predominantly in (white) male subjects, the *homo* of orthodox economic theory remains an abstraction deduced from this concrete subjectivity, and thus remains invested with traits often described as Western and masculine.[4] The rich young man emerges as a male hysteric whose vulnerable masculinity exposes lack even where we observe a material wealth of substance. His "lack" becomes a motif replayed in the texts of later interpreters and commentators, which constitute a partial map of economies of masculine lack and abundance that go on to shape economies of redemption in the formative ascetic texts of the Christian tradition.[5] Contemporary discussions about the economic connotations of voluntary asceticism, feminist economic critiques of the figure of the *homo economicus,* theological critiques of the neoclassical concept of "scarcity," and postcolonial critiques of Western efforts to spread Christianity and forms of capitalism into colonial and neocolonial contexts interact with ancient texts to produce a sustained meditation on the economic connotations of redemption, asceticism, gender, ancient empire, and neocolonial capitalism.

The experience of lack, or hysteria, exposes part of a theological, sexual, and material economy of desire for salvation or redemption. According to most antique medical writers a condition assumed to befall exclusively women, hysteria renders the composite figure of the rich young man and his subsequent textual incarnations a feminized and thus potentially feminist figure. Chapters 2 and 3 and the figures they explore represent an effort that contributes to the "hermeneutic task" involved in "reading the hysteric's body."[6] Donna Haraway's vision of such a model or figure suggests that it "cannot be man or woman"[7] but rather that it exhibits a certain queerness of gender and of economy. The figure of the rich young man

---

4. Feminist economists such as Julie Nelson, Marianne Ferber, and others have unveiled the gender bias of economic man. See Marianne Ferber and Julie A. Nelson, eds., *Beyond Economic Man: Feminist Theory and Economics* (Chicago: University of Chicago Press, 1993).

5. It may be that voluntary asceticism as we encounter it in many ancient texts is a double discourse that both escapes and reinscribes economic structures. While voluntary asceticism can constitute a form of rebellion, an attempt to escape the forces of patriarchy and patrimony, it also reinforces God as the ultimate, omnipotent (male) owner of the cosmos and faith as the ultimate substance of wealth. For the distinction between voluntary and involuntary asceticism, see Susan R. Holman, *The Hungry Are Dying* (Oxford: Oxford University Press, 2001), 4.

6. Elizabeth Bronfen, *The Knotted Subject: Hysteria and Its Discontents* (Princeton, N.J.: Princeton University Press, 1998), xi. For a discussion of ancient and contemporary hermeneutics of hysteria, see Elaine Showalter, *Hystories: Hysterical Epidemics and Modern Culture* (New York: Columbia University Press, 1997); Daniel Boyarin, *Unheroic Conduct: The Rise of Heterosexuality and the Invention of the Jewish Man* (Berkeley: University of California Press, 1997), 192–94.

7. Donna J. Haraway, "Ecce Homo, Ain't (Ar'n't) I a Woman, and Inappropriate/d Others: The Human in a Post-Humanist Landscape," in *Feminists Theorize the Political* (ed. Judith Butler and Joan Scott; New York: Routledge, 1992), 85.

exhibits lack as well as desire for that which he lacks. This desire becomes incarnate in the ambivalent practices of asceticism, where the desire for God and the simple life in which it finds expression resembles capitalist investment structures that can lead—*nolens volens* (against all professed intentions)—to the ascetic accumulation of wealth. Torn between the desire for God and the desire for the security that comes with capital, we observe how he and his interpreters negotiate the temptations of wealth and the call to invest in the divine economy.

The genealogy reveals that the ancient texts already exhibit glimpses of queer theological economies that can help construct more complex, miraculous, redemptive exchanges between men and women, between humans and God. One facet of redemption in the divine economy will lie in que(e)rying the properties and im/proprieties of male economic agency, human and divine.[8] How can our young men move toward a countereconomic third space of desire, of giving, taking, and keeping that transgresses economic orthodoxies and can flourish in creative reciprocity? From this critical genealogy, a Holy Fool of divine madness, a countereconomic trickster begins to emerge. This figure becomes invested in reconstructing a divine economy that makes conscious a web of economic and ecological relationality about which most of us remain in habitual denial. This ascetic resembles Leontius's "Holy Fool," whose antics and tricks expose the greed and exploitation around him and who provides inspiration for contemporary Holy Fools and their satirically mocking, yet hopeful, practices.

What Do I Still Lack?

> Then someone came to him and said, "Teacher, what good deed must I do to have eternal life?" And he said to him, "Why do you ask me about what is good? There is only one who is good. If you wish to enter into life, keep the commandments." He said to him, "Which ones?" And Jesus said, "You shall not murder; You shall not commit adultery; You shall not steal; You shall not bear false witness; Honor your father and mother; also, You shall love your neighbor as yourself." The young man said to him, "I have kept all these; what do I still lack?" Jesus said to him, "If you wish to be perfect, go,

---

8. For present purposes, we note that the psychological experience of lack and the modern neoclassical economic notion of scarcity, while not identical with each other, exhibit significant connotations and similarities. Douglas Meeks has warned of a simple identification of these notions in *God the Economist: The Doctrine of God and Political Economy* (Minneapolis: Fortress, 1989), 171.

sell your possessions, and give the money to the poor, and you will have treasure in heaven; then come, follow me." When the young man heard this word, he went away grieving, for he had many possessions. (Matt 19:16–23)

Contemporary feminist and liberationist interpreters seem to find that the rich young man lacks critical importance for the empowerment of women and the disenfranchised, and so they hasten on to analyze texts that appear to be more central to the effort of liberation.[9] Yet the rich young man seems to have held a special attraction for ancient interpreters, no doubt in part because he provided a text with which socially privileged men could identify. The narrative concretely demonstrates "the impossibility of serving both God and Mammon (6:24),"[10] perched as it is within the tensions of both powers. The young man approaches Jesus with a desire that knows no limits.[11] He longs for *zoon aionon* (life eternal), convinced that he has lived his life according to the divine rules, and thus has a reasonable expectation to gain access to limitless life. Then why does he sense that there is something he lacks? And why, we might ask, does an inscrutable Jesus brush him off, as an impatient teacher referring a student to the basics might do? "Keep the commandments!" And what's more, why does this Jesus refuse to be considered an authority on what is good? His clever answer slightly shifts the terms of the young man's desire; it does not promise the ultimate payoff of life as an unlimited resource and possession, but simply explains how to "enter into life." Asked whether he could specify which commandments he considers to be crucial, Jesus recites the second set of the Mosaic tablets, stressing a man's commitment to his neighbors.[12] The young man seems to know that this is not enough, that something is still missing. *Ti eti hustero*—what did I miss, what did I fail to obtain, what do I lack?—he asks, knowingly.

---

9. See the lack of attention given to Matt 19:16–30 in Elisabeth Schüssler Fiorenza, *In Memory of Her: A Feminist Theological Reconstruction of Christian Origins* (New York: Crossroad, 1994); Amy-Jill Levine, *The Social and Ethnic Dimensions of Matthean Salvation History* (Lewiston, N.Y.: Edwin Mellen Press, 1988); Elaine M. Wainwright, *Shall We Look for Another? A Feminist Rereading of the Matthean Jesus* (Maryknoll, N.Y.: Orbis, 1998).

10. W. D. Davies and Dale C. Allison, *A Critical and Exegetical Commentary on the Gospel according to Matthew* (International Critical Commentary on the Holy Scriptures of the Old and New Testaments; Edinburgh: T&T Clark, 1997), 39.

11. Similarly, Karmen MacKendrick notes that ascetic desire lacks respect for limits. MacKendrick, *Counterpleasures* (Albany, N.Y.: SUNY Press, 1999), 149ff.

12. Judith Plaskow has argued that women as persons were not the addressees of the commandments. The Exodus text mentions that no women were present at the promulgation at Sinai. Several of the Ten Commandments also appear to consider women the property of men. Plaskow, *Standing Again at Sinai: Judaism from a Feminist Perspective* (San Francisco: HarperCollins, 1990), 25.

If the young man kept all the commandments, what might he possibly be lacking? A number of contemporary exegetical commentaries pass by this paradoxical scarcity.[13] Other commentators find the persistence of lack remarkable, if not perplexing, to such a degree that it limits the applicability of the parable. Even so, the young man is met with the ultimate challenge: to give up his *ousia,* his property, the patrimony that he, as a male descendant of his family, was due. Does he lack a self apart from this phallic, patrilineal *ousia* (that which is one's own: property, being, wealth, money), and is Jesus relentlessly pointing to the Viagra of wealth preventing the deconstruction of this *Gestell,* this patriarchal scaffolding?

Davies and Allison fumble and then conclude that "it is better to follow Calvin: 'Our Lord is not proclaiming a general statement that is applicable to everyone, but only to the person with whom he is speaking.'" Others, especially patristic interpreters, applied the challenge spoken to the rich young man to themselves and their communities, reading riches at least potentially as a similar kind of lack. The young man lacks everything by lacking the one thing; his partial lack is excessive and becomes complete lack and barrenness.[14] One might argue that the young man ultimately lacks the desire that would compel him to give up all that secures his position in society and invest it in the poor of the land, and then—sold out, as it were—to follow the rabbi. Is there a hidden lack, a hysteria that expresses the deep mental distress, the deep emptiness, the "barrenness" and deprivation that belies superficial wealth? Cyprian of Carthage, in his *Works and Almsgiving,* compares this "barren rich man" who knows not how to make his wealth fertile to the widow with the two mites who, though "needy in means, is found rich in works."[15] His genitivity,[16] his ownership, and his ability to produce seed (i.e., pass on his *ousia*/property/being) is converted into feminized lack: he becomes the infertile woman, void of fecundity. In *The Gift of Death,* Derrida probes whether it can be possible that "God

---

13. Ulrich Luz, for example, treats this issue only in passing, and is far more interested in plumbing what *Vollkommenheit* (perfection) might mean, while Eduard Schweizer ignores it entirely. See Luz, *Das Evangelium nach Matthäus: Mt 18–25* (Evangelisch-Katholischer Kommentar Zum Neuen Testament; Zürich: Benziger Verlag; Düsseldorf: Neukirchener Verlag, 1997), 124; and Schweizer, *The Good News according to Matthew* (Atlanta: John Knox, 1975), 388.

14. Davies and Allison are referring to Luther's interpretation. See Davies and Allison, *Gospel according to Matthew,* 46, 47.

15. Cyprian of Carthage, *Works and Almsgiving,* 15. The English translation of Cyprian's text follows Alexander Roberts and James Donaldson, eds. *The Apostolic Fathers, Justin Martyr, Irenaeus* (vol. 1 of *Ante-Nicene Fathers*; Peabody, Mass.: Hendrickson, 1994).

16. The grammatical case of the genitive marks ownership. Genitivity, as defined by Stephen Ross, marks also the power to bring forth, to create, to own, appropriate, define, reproduce, etc. See the fascinating analysis of genitivity as property in Stephen David Ross, *The Gift of Property: Having the Good: Betraying Genitivity, Economy and Ecology: An Ethic of the Earth* (Albany, N.Y.: SUNY, 2001), 1ff.

ask[s] . . . that one give without knowing, without calculating, reckoning, or hoping, for one must give without counting."[17] Can the young man "renounce all sense and all property," as Derrida writes of Kierkegaard's Abraham? Can the investment into the divine economy become a "place of true riches, a place of treasures, the placement of the greatest thesaurization or laying up of treasures"?[18]

Clutching his purse, and symbolically his phallus, the young man slips away instead. The disciples remain behind to ponder this strange occurrence. Matthew tacks on an interpretive discussion between Jesus and the Twelve. As the young man departs, Matthew's Jesus remarks, "Truly I tell you, it will be hard for a rich person to enter the kingdom of heaven. Again I tell you, it is easier for a camel to go through the eye of a needle than for someone who is rich to enter the kingdom of God" (Matt 19:23–24).

The camel, unable to penetrate an orifice too narrow for an inflated phallic object, trots away quickly.[19] Size does matter here! The Twelve, much perplexed, or, more euphemistically, "greatly astounded," throw up their hands. "Then who can be saved?" they ask. Jesus follows up with another cryptic remark, the sort of answer that troubles the question, always already frustrating the disciples' desire for answers, for perfection, for eternal *pleroma,* eternal swelling, filling, fulfillment: "For mortals it is impossible, but for God all things are possible" (19:26). Yet Peter continues to try to cajole answers out of Jesus: "Look, we have left everything and followed you. What then will we have?" Indeed, they have renounced the potency of the *pater familias* and have let go of power in the *oikos* (putting their wives in charge of their families?). Matthew's Jesus finally assures them of future riches, of plenty of "pie in the sky":

> Truly I tell you, at the renewal of all things, when the Son of Man is seated on the throne of his glory, you who have followed me will also sit on twelve thrones, judging the twelve tribes of Israel. And everyone who has left houses or brothers or sisters or father or mother or children or fields, for my name's sake, will receive a hundredfold, and will inherit eternal life. But many who are first will be last, and the last will be first. (19:28–30)[20]

---

17. Jacques Derrida, *The Gift of Death* (trans. David Wills; Chicago: University of Chicago Press, 1992), 97.
18. Ibid.
19. Compare Marcella Althaus-Reid's comments on the need to shrink the penile erections of masculine theologies. Althaus-Reid, *Indecent Theology,* 182.
20. Some of these *apophtegmata* seem to have been collected thematically by Mark, on whom Matthew is dependent.

The pericope concludes with a final repression of life lack, announcing a deferred swelling of eternal wealth, a final prosperity found in "eternal life." These hysteric negotiations of lack point to the "resemblance" as well as the "menace" that the divine *oikonomia* of God represents to an empire in which the emperor was considered divine.[21] The figure of the unhappy youth reveals the instability of the patriarchally managed *oikonomia*. Poverty and wealth flip easily; quick turnarounds abound as treasures become reallocated among investors.

Masculine Hysteria, Ancient and Modern

> Freud recounts that when he was having trouble gaining acceptance for the possibility of masculine hysteria, he encountered, among those primary sorts of resistance which do not reveal mere foolishness or lack of culture, the resistance of a surgeon who *expressly* told him: "But my dear colleague, how can you pronounce such absurdities? *Hysteron [sic]* signifies 'uterus.' How then can a man be hysterical?"[22]
>
> Jacques Derrida, *Dissemination* (emphasis in original)

Hysteria is a cognate of *hustera,* a term that signifies a woman's womb. The adjectival form of the root from which the word derives carries with it notions of that which is "following, next," or "later, subsequent." The verb *hustereo* literally means "to be behind, come late," "to come later than, come too late for," or in its metaphorical use, "to lag behind, be inferior to," "to fall below, fail to do justice to," "to fail to obtain, lack," "to fall short," "to be wanting."[23] In a woman, this womb-related lack was thought to be caused by the lack of insemination in a young virgin or a widow and believed to result in the dislocation of the womb. The womb was thought to wander around the body in search of moisture, where it might lodge itself to various organs.

---

21. Homi Bhabha, *The Location of Culture* (London: Routledge, 1994), 86.
22. The correct form is *hystera:* Freud's interlocutor unconsciously neutralized the grammatical gender of the feminine uterus as if to make the point he is so indignantly contesting.
23. See Henry George Liddell and Robert Scott, *A Greek-English Lexicon* (Oxford: Clarendon Press, 1996), 747. See also G. W. H. Lampe, *A Patristic Greek Lexicon* (Oxford: Clarendon Press, 1961), 1466. Many discussions of hysteria or the wandering womb do not list the connotation of lack and deficiency. See Ilza Veith, *Hysteria: The History of a Disease* (Chicago: University of Chicago Press, 1965), ix; Mary R. Lefkovitz, *Heroines and Hysterics* (New York: St. Martin's Press, 1981), 13; and Aline Rousselot, *Porneia: On Desire and the Body in Antiquity* (Cambridge, Mass.: Blackwell, 1983), 69. Since Aristotle, the hysteric's lack has been linked to women's lack of a penis, thus a monster. This reading is repeated, yet with different context and intentions, by Freud's postulation of penis envy. Cf. Catherine Keller, *From A Broken Web: Separation, Sexism, and Self* (Boston: Beacon, 1986), 48–50.

One possible result was suffocation, if it moved to the throat. Hysteria was considered a serious disease that, if left untreated, could lead to death.[24] Ancient commentators often personified this "wandering womb." Plato described the *hustera* as an "animal," an animated being with its own desires and aims, a big mouth with a desire for intercourse with a penis that would result in the acquisition of seed.[25] These organs—seemingly invisible and intractable—appeared to be nothing but black holes that would suck a man's seed into them, acquiring and claiming it. Though the notion of male hysteria experienced a bout of attention in modernity primarily through Freud's work, Ilza Veith describes one rare doctor in antiquity, Aretaeus of Cappadocia, who believed "that there was a form of hysteria unconnected with the uterus which could also affect men. This statement, as well as a similar one in the writings of Galen of Pergamon, was ignored by his contemporaries and did not reappear for nearly a millennium and a half, at which time it was again disregarded."[26]

Sigmund Freud virtually reinvented the concept of hysteria in modernity. Regarding the cause of hysteria, Freud first attempted to explain "all hysteria . . . by child abuse, whether remembered or not."[27] Though he soon abandoned hysteria as a major psychological disorder, and instead continued to develop the notion of neurosis as a major tool of analysis, Freud, as Daniel Boyarin argues, diagnosed male hysteria as "the sexual passivity of the male that feminizes (and paradoxically homosexualizes)," rather than the "gender of the active subject."[28] This passivity of desire, or feminization, can also occur in nonsexual relations that do, however, frustrate a man's sense of masculinity, give him a sense of being acted upon, by men or women, sexually or nonsexually, without being able or willing to resist. Thus, Boyarin argues that "hysteria, in short, while gendered as paradigmatically feminine, is not exclusively about women, but involves both women and 'feminized' men."[29] Whereas female hysteria was thought to be caused by the lack of insemination by a male penis, male hysteria appears to have to do with a lack of masculinity, and remains thus in a sense, a "feminine" problem, since it occurs in "effeminate" or "feminized" men. Thus, even being diagnosed with hysteria was considered emasculating,

---

24. Rousselle, *Porneia*, 67–69.
25. Mark J. Adair, "Plato's View of the Wandering Uterus," *Classical Journal* 91, no. 2 (1996): 153.
26. Veith, *Hysteria*, 22.
27. Daniel Boyarin, "Freud's Baby, Fliess's Maybe: Homophobia, Anti-Semitism, and the Invention of Oedipus," *Gay Lesbian Quarterly: A Journal of Lesbian and Gay Studies* 2 (1995): 122.
28. Ibid., 117.
29. Ibid.

with the result that male hysterics often remained mysterious and anonymous in physicians' records. Thus, Charcot's records of at least sixty male hysterics he treated remained obscure and were only translated into English in the 1990s. Elaine Showalter is one of the "New Hysterians," a group of scholars who have attempted to revive interest in hysteria as a phenomenon that "cuts across historical periods and national boundaries, poses fundamental questions about gender and culture, and offers insights into language, narrative, and representation." She argues that hysteria is a "universal human response to emotional conflict," much of which revolves around gender roles in culture and society.[30] Regarding the lack of data and awareness of hysteria in men, she observes that the

> cultural denial of male hysteria is no accident: it's the result of avoidance, suppression, and disguise. Although male hysteria has been clinically identified at least since the seventeenth century, physicians have hidden it under such euphemistic terms as neurasthenia, hypochondria, . . . shell shock, or post-traumatic stress disorder. . . . For centuries, doctors denied that hysteria was also a male malady.[31]

Under various names, then, male hysteria was thought to be found often in upper-class males burdened with great responsibilities, something like an "executive hysteria" that was observed in men who were graduates of the Parisian universities and who intended to become "heads of factories and rack their brains over mathematical calculations."[32] Showalter observes, however, that records exist that suggest male hysteria existed also, and perhaps especially, in lower-class men who felt great anxiety over their fragile economic situation or their place in the culture.[33] Jean Baudrillard provides a similar reading of male hysteria, unveiling the abject feminine side of the *homo economicus* in capitalist modernity. Thus, as Roy Porter argues, "Baudrillard's account of the hysteria of late capitalism would, in many respects, have made perfect sense to Freud and all the other eminent *fin de siècle* diagnosticians of civilization and its discontents."[34] Porter highlights Baudrillard's account of the resemblance between hysteria and capitalism, as both evoke "an intense, slippery, baffling network of fleeting, volatile manifestations . . . which possibly serves as teasing surrogates for

---

30. Showalter, *Hystories*, 7, 17, 63–64.
31. Ibid., 64.
32. Ibid., 65.
33. Ibid., 66–72.
34. Roy Porter, "Baudrillard: History, Hysteria, and Consumption," in *Forget Baudrillard?* (ed. Chris Rojek and Bryan Turner; New York: Routledge, 1993), 4.

the underlying reality, or more likely mask an absence, a void, beneath and within."[35]

The frenzied, hectic life in consumer capitalism covers up a void of emptiness that claims rationality, the cool calculations, the pretense of precision, predictability, and security. Thus, the dense phallic masculinity claimed for scientific economics falls apart, unfolds the void, the lack of rationality as hysteria, that most stereotypically feminine of all disorders. Porter further argues that for Baudrillard, "hysteria was the sly imp that thumbed its nose and poked out its tongue at the neat Cartesian mind-body dualism; hysteria mocked the formally clear-cut boundaries delineating soma from psyche, the physical from the moral, malady from malevolence."[36]

This mimic hysteria, or "mysteria," is the trickster that unravels the gendered, rationalist pretenses of deified Western capitalism regarding the world of objects and needs. The hysterical male can be read as a trickster mimicking, if not mocking, the supposed masculine rationality of scarcity by unveiling it, if involuntarily, as irrational and as queerly gendered, psychological economy.

Be Thou My Inheritance . . .

> And everyone who has left houses or brothers or sisters or father or mother or children or fields, for my name's sake, will receive a hundredfold, and will inherit eternal life. (Matt 19:29)

Gloria Copeland, a contemporary purveyor of a prosperity gospel, is not alone in suggesting that the above passage constitutes a clever investment strategy. While we might not initially think of the rich young man's story as a self-help guide to financial freedom, Warren Carter has suggested reading Matthew 19–20 as an extended version of a household code or an economic tractate, as a collection of texts that might function as investment guides or management advice.[37] Others have located a "household management topos" in various apostolic writings, predominantly in the Pastoral Letters. As variations on the political philosophy of writers such as Plato, Aristotle, Philodemus, Arius Didymus, Hierocles, and numerous others, this topos became a tool for the internal disciplining of marginal

---

35. Ibid., 2.
36. Ibid., 3.
37. Warren Carter, *Households and Discipleship: A Study of Matthew 19–20* (Supplement to the Journal of the Study of the New Testament; Sheffield: Sheffield Academic Press, 1994), 9.

developing church communities attempting to enforce androcentric, hierarchical authority structures, or at least pose as a textual mimicry of the status quo to appease the Roman authorities regarding the suspect activities and morals of the new household-based cult.[38] Torjesen and Burrus have mapped the complex function of ancient economic tractates with attention to distinctions between public and private, male and female, and orthodoxy and heresy.[39] "Tensions of gender and authority," they find, structure the fabric of apostolic writings as well as patristic sources.[40] Whereas contemporary checkout counter magazines such as *Good Housekeeping* are aimed at female homemakers, the target audience of ancient treatises about household management was more ambiguous. Most, like Aristotle's classic *Politeia,* were aimed at the man in the house, the *kurios*—husband, father, and master. Ancient authors strove rhetorically to inscribe the power of the *kurios* as uncontested, so that "the figure of the male householder stood at the center of the spotlight" over his dependents: women, children, and slaves.[41] Thus, the *kurios* and his heirs were identified and defined largely through access to property.[42] The phallus thus comes to stand close to economic property. If a man is what he owns—if *ousia* describes both his essence or substance and his wealth—giving up wealth includes canceling a part of his self, his masculinity, while paradoxically gaining treasures in heaven. Absence replaces the *par-ousia,* or presence, of wealth, and functions similarly, perhaps, to Derrida's supplement as the semiotic replacement of a presence or value that allows deferred desire to remain suspended in the tease between *hustera* (lack, deficiency) and *pleroma* (perfection, fulfillment, swelling).[43]

The rhetoric and content of the economic treatises reveals how fragile the male foothold on power in the household was. Within a patriarchal *oikos,* the treatises would advise a man how to retain the respect of the

---

38. Ulrike Wagener, *Die Ordnung des "Hauses Gottes": Der Ort von Frauen in der Ekklesiologie und Ethik der Pastoralbriefe* (Wissenschaftliche Untersuchungen zum Neuen Testament 2, series 65; Tübingen: J.C.B. Mohr, 1994), 19–20.
39. See the second chapter in Karen Jo Torjesen, *When Women Were Priests: Women's Leadership in the Early Church and the Scandal of Their Subordination in the Rise of Christianity* (New York: HarperSanFrancisco, 1995); and, more specifically on the politics of public-private, male-female, and orthodoxy-heresy, Virginia Burrus, *The Making of a Heretic: Gender, Authority, and the Pricillianist Controversy* (Transformation of the Classical Heritage; Berkeley: University of California Press, 1995), 7–8, 114, 121–25.
40. Burrus, *Making of a Heretic,* 128.
41. Torjesen, *When Women Were Priests,* 60.
42. S. C. Humphreys, *The Family, Women, and Death: Comparative Studies* (London: Routledge & Kegan Paul, 1983), 1, 10, 13.
43. Cf. Jacques Derrida, *Given Time: I. Counterfeit Money* (trans. Peggy Kamuf; Chicago: University of Chicago Press, 1992).

members of his household and how to construct a unified front even when his power was shaky and constantly contested by women, slaves and children.[44] Elite male authors of economic tracts often inscribed an idealized image of "family values" aimed at reinforcing the clear separation of the hierarchical shape of the Hellenistic household that assigned the strictly separate gendered spheres of public and private to men and women, reiterating gender and power differentials in other stacked hierarchies such as parent-child and owner-slave.[45] Yet views on the proper household management varied, and the actual distribution of household power and duties depended on the context and specific situation.

The *oikos* has thus functioned as a contested, gender-ambivalent space, a space in which hysteria can erupt. It is in and around the power relations between the inhabitants of the house that hysteria is experienced, where women's power can appear to threaten proper male relations to property and patrimony. While men were publicly and legally recognized as *kurioi*, feminist scholars have suggested that at least some wealthy women were invested with the same functions and duties in the absence of males. Thus, historians have identified other ancient texts that portray "women as domestic matriarchs," stressing the realm of the *oikos* as the sole domain of the woman and advocating a strong separation of the male public and the female private spheres.[46] Gender roles within the ancient household were at times flexible, and women did in fact function as householders[47] in day-to-day interaction, even though women's legal subordination was maintained.[48]

Christian writers used the metaphor of the householder often to express the "authority of one who oversees and cares for people's welfare," whether in parables or metaphorical uses of God as a householder.[49] Though we see only the rare woman in Acts in the functional position of a householder, the metaphorical, theological image of a female *oikonomos* or *oikonome* appears to be missing. Even though Burrus and Torjesen make as strong an argument as they can that the householder can appear as a female figure in apocryphal texts—such as Pronoia in the *Apocryphon of*

---

44. Moses Finley, *The Ancient Economy* (Berkeley: University of California Press, 1973), 17–18.

45. *Oikos* and *oikonomia* emerged, says Humphreys, as highly loaded terms in ancient Greek and Roman literature, ideologically embattled in the cultural space of the public, male-dominated *polis*. Equally contested among historians of early Christianity are the status and textual representations of women within the patriarchal households of Rome and the house church communities of early Christianity. Humphreys, *Family, Women, and Death*, 1, 3.

46. Torjesen, *When Women Were Priests*, 92.

47. An ancient household did not merely consist of living quarters but often was more like a small family business.

48. Torjesen, *When Women Were Priests*, 58, 62.

49. Ibid., 56–57.

John, or in a real-life context as the textile merchant Lydia in *Acts*—the textual evidence within the canonical Christian tradition does not suggest that the term "householder" was used to describe women. The *oikonomoi* in parables are males, often slaves with managerial functions, acting as proxies for absentee landlords. God, when described or identified as *oikonomos,* is imbued with an implied masculine characterization.[50] As we see the topos of the *oikonomikos*—the household tractate—adopted and emended by the early Christian communities, divine household management is primarily characterized as a male domain.[51]

From the vantage point of Jesus' divine economy, the rich young man does not make for a particularly good example of a male householder. In fact, his refusal to shrink his gendered financial power is considered bad housekeeping. And what is more, he turns down the possibility for exorbitant future profits. The Matthean version of Jesus' encounter with the rich young man is surrounded by pericopes that suggest seemingly contradictory images of and approaches to the coming of the heavenly *basileia*. Hospitality, food, drink, and shelter are set within the boundaries of the ancient *oikos,* portraying God's hospitality to the poor as the kindness of a landowner who invites indiscriminately to a great banquet (Matt 22:2–14 par.). Other texts invite the listener/reader to leave behind the security of the *oikos* and all its comforts for the unsheltered road. Beginning with the difficulty of whether to mark Jesus either as the resident "glutton and drunkard" (Matt 11:19), or a freewheeling hobo without "hole" or "nest" (Matt 8:20), what Jesus required in terms of discipleship remains contested. The lingering tension between "itinerants" and "householders" (in John Dominic Crossan's terminology),[52] mediated by a church that felt an increasing need to manage and contain itinerants, may have provided the economic and theological background to a variety of readings of the story of the rich young man.[53]

---

50. See, for example, Luke 12:41–48; 16:1–8; 1 Cor 4:1–2; Gal 4:2 (here the term is used to describe a legal guardian, who could only be a male); Titus 1:7; 1 Pet 4:10. Other parables of the *basileia* use the word *doulos* more or less as having the functions of an *oikonomos*. Those slaves are also portrayed as male.

51. Thus Paul, for example, orders the Christian household in a hierarchy of power and gender that mimics the relationship of God to Christ and Christ to the believer: "But I want you to understand that Christ is the head of every man, and the husband is the head of his wife, and God is the head of Christ" (1 Cor 11:3).

52. See for example Parts VII and VIII in John Dominic Crossan, *The Birth of Christianity: Discovering What Happened in the Years Immediately After the Execution of Jesus* (San Francisco: Harper San Francisco, 1998).

53. Warren Carter has held that the coherence of the puzzling sequence of pericopes in Matt 19–21 might consist in the audience's cultural knowledge of the discourses of household management as they concern marriage and divorce, children, slavery, and wealth. Carter, *Households and Discipleship*, 18.

Beginning with the third century, many wealthy Christians, both men and women, felt called to renounce the goods of the *oikos*, to defer gratification to an eschatological future and became voluntary ascetics. For many of them, conversion did not include a change of beliefs as much as it did a conversion of tangible funds into the less tangible investments of the divine economy. Thus, shedding large parts of their possessions, they converted earthly currency into heavenly currency. But this heavenly currency often jarred with the claims of earthly currencies. Not only did it not function according to the rules of material economies, but it even mimicked and at times menaced dominant hegemonies.

An Expanding Economy: Divine and/or Imperial?

> Not only is there no kingdom of *différance*, but *différance* instigates the subversion of every kingdom. Which makes it obviously threatening and infallibly dreaded by everything within us that desires a kingdom, the past or future presence of a kingdom.
>
> Jacques Derrida, *Margins of Philosophy*

What indeed could subvert the notion of kingdom, of phallic, unilateral power? Most of us know all too well that though the invitation to Jesus' kingdom includes a call to give up the powers and treasures of the *oikos*, later textual representations of divine economy often function as a reinscription rather than a subversive mimicry of power brokering. They function as tools to establish and to maintain structures of hierarchy, dominance, and exclusion. While Derrida's text does not directly comment on Jesus' *basileia* as discussed above, his allusion to the *différance*, as a lag in time and meaning that always already threatens to destabilize hierarchical structures, unveiling and contesting them, is a helpful exposé of power within hierarchical structures. If meaning cannot ultimately be controlled, then power cannot rely on language or writing to simply inscribe only one possible reading. The uncontrollable qualities of language always already destabilize hierarchical systems of power. Yet it would seem shortsighted to forget that the disseminating powers of writing can function to effectively narrow the range of interpretation of a tradition's texts and to bolster its rhetorical economies of power. Our Matthean text and its intertexts have spawned and structured subsequent discourses on redemption, economic investment, gender, class, and generational relations within the household. The patristic writers Irenaeus, Clement, Origen, Cyprian, Athanasius, and Augustine have formulated their own notions of "good housekeeping," and their rhetorical economizing of the rich young man exemplifies their theological structuring of the divine economy of salvation. The household of God began as the threatened and martyred body of the church and slowly turned into threat and martyrdom for others, administering salvation through its licensed clerical brokers alone. By Augustine's time, the subversive potential of the heavenly *basileia* Jesus knew ever more closely resembled the power structures of the terrestrial Roman Empire.

Irenaeus of Lyon expanded the scope of the divine economy to include the history of the entire cosmos—long before the Christianization of the empire. His concept of divine economy as salvation history—as a history of divine purpose and structuring woven throughout the cosmos and history of a very specific group of people—is, for better and worse, available in Augustine's time, and becomes lodged into place in the merging of empire and church. Irenaeus wove a fairly fragile notion of narrative coherence in Hebrew and Christian scriptures into the semblance of a flawless, unified, divinely mastered plot, and shaped a well-defined, distinct body of teachings and traditions of one true church that witnessed to the one, true, divine *oikonomia* (Irenaeus, *Against Heresies* 2.25.3). It is in his texts that *Heilsgeschichte* (salvation history) is woven for the first time, as "heresiology becomes historiography."[54] For Irenaeus, the term *oikonomia* forms the frame of reference for all of God's actions within the cosmos, inscribed as a soteriological event within history indivisible from time and its divinely planned *kairoi*.[55] In this anthropocentrically focused narrative, cosmos and creation do not have existence apart from their role as the "arena of salvation—as the eschatological theater of patristic Christianity."[56] The church is part of this metanarrative of *oikonomia*, as well as its keeper and container, defined by and defining its unity of origin, faith, canon, morals, love, martyrdom, hierarchy, and structure, regardless of location.[57] Irenaeus's narrative distinguishes itself from what Rebecca Lyman calls the "dynamic argument" of Justin's apologetic approach, who still "demonstrated infinite possibilities for assimilation and alienation," as his dialogues with philosophy still allow for an "indeterminacy at the boundary which encourages both resistance to and acceptance of surrounding cultures."[58] For Irenaeus,

---

54. Keller, *Face of the Deep*, 50.
55. Alfred Bengsch, *Heilsgeschichte und Heilswissen: Eine Untersuchung zur Struktur und Entfaltung des theologischen Denkens im Werk "Adversus Haereses" des Heiligen Irenaeus von Lyon* (Leipzig: St. Benno, 1957), 82.
56. Keller, *Face of the Deep*, 44.
57. Roch Kereszty, "The Unity of the Church in the Theology of Irenaeus," *Second Century* 4, no. 4 (1984): 202–7.
58. Justin's more brusque approach to Jews and Jewish readings of the Bible does, however, seem quite determinate, even though his attitude toward the (fictional) Jew Trypho appears

as well as Lyman, this dialogical liminality is no longer a viable strategy. Rather, Irenaeus's text demonstrates an "acute need for ongoing distinction, discernment, and exegesis within the community of the one Logos" that takes the shape of a "stark confrontation between Christianity and Hellenism and orthodoxy and heresy."[59] Irenaeus's divine *oikonomia* of salvation history provided the theological foundations for later alliances of divine and imperial powers. The notion of the *oikonomia theou*, first systematically developed by the Lyonnese presbyter in an "age of martyrs," theologically transformed in an "age of Christian rulers," later becomes a colonizing narrative of the *tempora christiana* that occasioned the "legal repression of paganism" as the empire and its phallic swelling appears to be its instrument and incarnation.[60] The new account of a *creatio ex nihilo* also establishes beyond a doubt the power and property structures in this *oikonomia*. Irenaeus hysterically covers up the deep gaps of power by frantically reasserting that his God is the only all-powerful and all-propertied one.[61] Ironically, Irenaeus's confidence in the possibility of keeping what he considers an orthodox church free of heretics with the help of a rule of faith is later replaced by Augustine's admission that it is impossible to keep the *civitas Dei* and the *civitas terrena* separate.

Along with the doctrine of *creatio ex nihilo*, typology is one of Irenaeus's most prominent theological tools. What Paul had rudimentarily suggested in Rom 5:12–15, that there was a first and a second Adam (Christ), and that Adam was "a type of the one who was to come," Irenaeus expanded and elaborated into a typological scheme of couples: Adam and Eve, the young, inexperienced children who had lost access to salvation, and Jesus and Mary, who sweep the entire human history symbolized by the first couple into a recapitulation of redemption, constitutes one of the major arcs of Irenaeus's divine economy. As a narrative device of inclusion as well as exclusion into the narrative sweep, these *typoi* are meant to stand for the entire people of God, and in Irenaeus's mind, for the church. In the opulent scope of Irenaeus's rhetorical management of history, Matthew's wealthy youngster figures as a potential investor in a truly ecumenical divine economy, if at this stage only a metaphorical and not yet imperial Christian

---

friendly and perhaps does represent a certain indeterminacy, since Justin is still in a "Dialogue" with Trypho rather than Irenaeus, who writes "Against Heresies." Rebecca Lyman, "The Politics of Passing: Justin Martyr's Conversion as a Problem of 'Hellenization,'" in *Conversion in Late Antiquity and the Middle Ages: Seeing and Believing*, (ed. Kenneth Mills and Anthony Grafton; Rochester, N.Y.: University of Rochester Press, 2003), 46–47.

59. Lyman, "Politics of Passing," 19.

60. Robert A. Markus, *Saeculum: History and Society in the Theology of St. Augustine* (Cambridge: Cambridge University Press, 1970), 35.

61. Keller, *Face of the Deep*, 50–51.

household. Positioning the rich young man as an example to show the consistency of the heavenly company's growth patterns, Irenaeus works hard throughout *Adversus haereses* to show that "the precepts of an absolutely perfect life ... are the same in each Testament" and point to "the same God." Thus, he relates that regarding "the more prominent and the greatest [commandments,] without which salvation cannot [be attained,] He has exhorted [us to observe] the same in both" (*Haer.* 4.12.3). Irenaeus opens the line of early church interpreters of this Matthean text who see perfection as attainable, as salvation depends on the possible fulfillment of the commandments: "Now, that the law did beforehand teach mankind the necessity of following Christ, He does Himself make manifest, when He replied as follows to him who asked Him what he should do that he might inherit eternal life: 'If thou wilt enter into life, keep the commandments'" (4.12.5). Consistent with his pedagogic interpretation of history, the commandments resemble lessons of increasing difficulty, like steps on a ladder: "setting as an ascending series (*velut gradus*) before those who wished to follow Him, the precepts of the law, as the entrance to life" (4.12.5).

Irenaeus is suspicious of the youth's assertion that he has fulfilled all commandments, and comments in an aside to the reader that "most likely he had not kept them" (4.12.5), thus explaining why "the Lord" stated the obvious. Convinced that the fellow's problem is his greed, the presbyter interprets the Lord's challenge to achieve perfection by shedding property as a device for decloaking the young man's true intentions that might, however, if taken to heart, get the man a bigger share in the future growth of the divine economy, namely, *apostolorum partem*. "If we compare the charts from previous cycles, we will see that growth-earning rates remain consistent," Irenaeus, putting on his investment analyst cap, explains to the reader. "The conditions, terms, and liabilities are the same as before. Hold on to your shares, and eventually your investment will pay off. Don't listen to the advice of other, unorthodox brokers who will tell you that the management has changed during this new phase of expansion" (paraphrasing 4.12.5). Irenaeus thus asserts that the Son "did not preach to His followers another God the Father, besides Him who was proclaimed by the law from the beginning; nor another; nor the Mother" or any other "fable invented by the heretics" (4.12.5). Casting the faithful as investors, in his five-book-long market watch, Irenaeus's readers may find an in-depth assessment of other possible investment options, all to be strictly avoided, of course. Irenaeus's divine economy dwarfs the young man, who is merely a case in point for the consistency of divine householding. His rhetorical ordering and economizing of the divine economy includes a definition of heresy that is in part determined by the heretic's relationship to the Christian tradition and the church.

We have learned from none others the plan of our salvation, than from those through whom the Gospel has come down to us. Thus, those who do not believe the teaching of the apostles as defined by Irenaeus are considered heretics, counterfeiters in the investments of the divine economy. Heretics—literally, "those who think differently"—for Irenaeus are those who lack the true doctrine and *traditio*, who claim multiple legitimate ways to understand the Scriptures or who hold that some of its parts are not divinely inspired (3.2.1). These hermeneutical actions prove to Irenaeus that heretics are putting themselves as authorities over the texts (3.2.2), something Irenaeus himself denies doing, or is unconscious of. Irenaeus's rhetorical economy attempts to control definitions of truth and power in a controlled patrilineal succession of hand-me-down texts and dogmas. For him, the church is the guardian of the apostolic *depositum* (3.5.1) and truth ends with the church borders. While the church holds on to the tradition, heretics constantly seek new teachings (3.24.1) and remain perturbed by conflicting opinions, never able to make up their minds (3.24.2). Against heretical knowledge, Irenaeus holds that the "truth" is accessible for everybody (3.3.1), yet only through the mediation of the church as outlined by Irenaeus (3.4.1; 3.5.1). Heretics, on the other hand, have no insight into the divine *oikonomia* for the salvation of humanity and remain excluded from it (5.29.2). In his defense against various gnostic and other divergent teachings, little complexity to the notion of heresy remains, and almost no room between "heresy" and "orthodoxy." Through the "historical work of simultaneous uprooting and stabilizing,"[62] the presbyter both cites and changes the context of the scriptural intertexts he bases his authority on, as does every writer to some extent. Yet what gets lost, who is excluded, and what form of orthodoxy is preserved and will be proliferated by his mimic work? One might argue with Lyman that Irenaeus's economic work, despite his efforts to the contrary, continues to provoke "endless negotiation of authority and boundary" and continues to resemble a mimic rhetoric much like the one Homi Bhabha describes.[63]

Derrida's texts engage the effects of the Western Christian domestication enabled by such rhetorical economies as Irenaeus's strategic definition of kinship relations in the divine household. His use of the Hebrew term *shibboleth*, as a linguistic currency of sorts, might serve as an interpretive category resembling Irenaeus's *regula fidei* (1.10.1). The *regula*, something

---

62. Boyarin, *Intertextuality and the Reading of Midrash*, 22.
63. Lyman, "Politics of Passing," 22.

akin to a code word or a code phrase, helps Irenaeus to distinguish the Christian from the heretic and the Jew. In this *oikonomia*, the *regula* functions like a "shibboleth, a secret formula" in itself untranslatable, like a "so-called natural or mother tongue" of the *traditio*, of the church. Far from regretting such a "limiting function," Irenaeus "takes pride in it."[64] This *regula fidei* becomes the "*Geheimnis* of language that ties it to the home, to the motherland[,] . . . to economy, to the law of the *oikos*."[65] Irenaeus's "orthodox myth of origin," his typological construction of the *oikonomia theou*, is also a "myth of the origin of orthodoxy" that covers up a void that underlies the theologian's hysterical struggle to regain control of the fluctuations in the divine economy. What does the rich young man lack, according to Irenaeus? Sincerity, orthodoxy? Irenaeus appears to want to ferret out the heretic in him, even as he presses the man's story into the service of promoting the one, true divine economy, found only in fullness of orthodoxy in the context of the church. What forms of lack does Irenaeus fear? Lack of power, lack of "authenticity"? In the urge to shield the divine phallus from his own castration anxiety, he attempts to swell divine power, to control doctrine. As self-pronounced guardian, he hysterically watches over the doors of the divine *oikos*, encouraging the swelling of divine power so that God as pleroma becomes the ultimate environment. Thus, preexistent matter, the mutual investment of the cosmos itself in created matter, a communication of creative powers, is bought out by a unilateral investment in the divine economy.[66]

Lack and Wealth in Alexandria

> Castration—always at stake—and the self-presence of the present. The pure present would be the untouched fullness, the virgin territory of the nonscission, the volume that, not having exposed the roll of its writing to the reader's letter-opener, would therefore not yet be written on the eve of the start of the game. But the pen, when you have followed it to the end, will have turned into a knife.
>
> Jacques Derrida, *Dissemination*

Perhaps not as anxious about his physical masculinity but rather as a "eunuch for the kingdom," Origen is suspected of having turned the disciplining pen

---

64. Derrida, *Gift of Death*, 88.
65. Ibid.
66. Thus, this orthodoxy depends upon the heretical other that can be assigned blame for its own hysterical symptoms. See Keller, *Face of the Deep*, 47.

of the logos into a castrating knife cutting away at his own masculinity. What if this ascetic had inscribed the rich young man's effeminate lack into the literally hysterical—potentially lacking masculinity—text of his own body? As a reader of our Matthean text, Origen proves fascinated with biblical passages of all shades and proveniences, well educated and with financial support to indulge in extended hermeneutical stints. Origen slices to and fro in Scripture, with an intellect sharp as a knife (or pen) producing a heavily intertextual, almost midrashic, reading of the rich young man. On the disturbing question of what the young man might be lacking, despite having allegedly fulfilled the commandments inscribed on the second tablet, Origen provides two different interpretations. We can almost see him opening the Hexapla (showing variants in different manuscripts of the Gospel of Matthew) on his table along with parallel transmissions such as Mark's version, Luke's, and, more obscurely, a rendering found in the *Gospel of the Hebrews*. Comparing Matthew's version with Mark's and Luke's, he notices that the latter two do not preserve the commandment to love one's neighbor.[67] Considering that the various manuscripts of Matthew show bits and pieces missing here and there, he ventures that the commandment to love one's neighbor (19b) was added by a careless scribe or in some other way: "Ponder thus, whether one can answer the present question in a manner that assumes that the commandment: *Love your neighbor as yourself!* might not have been included by the Savior, but was added by somebody who did not understand the meaning of the words."[68]

If the commandment was not original, Origen argues, the question about a continued lack is justified, since the highest level of perfection to be reached, the love of neighbors as oneself, had not been part of the original conversation but was added during the textual transmission. Origen's own standpoint emerges in the second argument: he assumes that the commandment belongs in the original context. As evidence, he cites an apocryphal parallel from the *Gospel of the Hebrews*, a midrashic amendment that preserves an extension to the dialogue between Jesus and the young man: "Thus the rich man has not fulfilled the commandment: You shall love your neighbor as yourself; since he despised many poor people and did not share his wealth with them. It is thus impossible to keep the commandment to love one's neighbor as oneself and to be rich at the same time."[69]

---

67. The edition of the work used here is Origen's *Commentarium in evangelium Matthaei X-XVII* in Origenes, "Mattäus," in *Der Kommentar Zum Evangelium Nach Mattäus. Zweiter Teil* (trans. Herman J. Vogt; Bibliothek der Griechischen Literatur; Stuttgart: Anton Hiersemann, 1990), 109. Translation from the German is mine.
68. Ibid., 107.
69. Ibid., 109–10.

This textual splinter erases Origen's doubts about what the Savior intended: the law is not fulfilled as long as a great number of the young man's brothers can be found in rags, dying of hunger while his own house is full of goods. Origen concludes that as long as there are rich and poor, justice, the concern of the law, has not been fulfilled, and the rich young man lacks true love of neighbor. This interpretation contests Clement of Alexandria's treatise *Salvation of the Rich*,[70] a text which likely formed part of Origen's own Alexandrian context. Without ever referring to his predecessor, perhaps even teacher, the younger man appears to be in conversation with Clement's text, if cautiously.[71] Origen, a voluntary ascetic, not lacking the wealth of education and leisure to meditate on these issues at length, strongly discourages an allegorical interpretation of our story, which Clement, arguing "we must not understand [the Savior's] words literally," has explicitly performed (Clement, *Quis div.* 5). Here we have an instance of Origen's more literal interpretations of Scripture, though only relatively speaking, considering his liberal use of intertextual jumps and midrashic fillers. The younger Alexandrian does indeed appear far more concerned with the careful distinction between textual varieties, as if to chide Clement, who brushes such concerns away by contending that the parallels in all the Gospels have the "same general sense, though perhaps here and there a little of the wording changes" (*Quis div.* 5). Where Clement, living in Alexandria during a time of booming trade,[72] exhibits great concern for the "true salvation" of the rich men in his congregation who have despaired of their chances at redemption, a more strictly ascetic Origen will have none of this kind of wimpy chit-chat. Clement's use of the Markan version, which excludes any mention of the commandment to love one's neighbor but includes comments on Jesus' favorable thought about the young man, who "looking upon him loved him" (Mark 10:21), might

---

70. The translation of Clement's *Quis dives salvetur?* follows Clement of Alexandria, *Salvation of the Rich* (Loeb's Classical Library; New York: Putnam, 1919).

71. The issue of wealth was often experienced as a problem both in antique Christian and philosophical texts. Origen disagrees with Clement on the nature of a human contribution to salvation, writing clearly from a different context, perhaps one that was less sensitive to "the problems of everyday life and unruly passions," as stated in Rebecca Lyman, *Christology and Cosmology: Models of Divine Activity in Origen, Eusebius, and Athanasius* (Oxford: Clarendon, 1993), 46. Clement's tractate appears to be written to address a specific issue of import at a certain time, while Origen's interpretation occurs within the context of a larger project, namely, that of a commentary on Matthew. Peter Brown stresses the difference in context between the two Alexandrians: "With Clement, we had been encouraged to look around us, at every detail of the life of a Christian in a great city; with Origen that busy world has vanished: we already breathe the changeless air of the desert." Brown, *The Body and Society: Men, Women, and Sexual Renunciation in Early Christianity* (New York: Columbia University Press, 1988), 161. Each of these approaches manages the relation between salvation and wealth in specific ways.

72. Brown, *Body and Society*, 162.

not be altogether incidental. Clement perceives a Savior more favorably disposed toward the rich young man than does Matthew, who omits emotive gestures.[73] Thus he maps a divine economy in which rich and poor need each other: thus, "*we* share the burden of their life and work out salvation for them by every possible means; first by begging them from God[,] . . . by healing their souls with reason[,] . . . and leading them on to the possession of the truth" (*Quis div.* 1; emphasis mine). A poor person's investment in intercessory prayer will thus guarantee the salvation of those rich persons who have detached themselves inwardly from their riches by returning the favor of alms with prayers that will reach the ears of heaven. Clement utters a rather general encouragement that the rich "keep the commandments," neglecting to specify when or how they should do so. For Clement, owning riches and keeping commandments are not at odds. Origen, as we have seen, strongly disagrees with Clement's insistence that the continued possession of wealth is necessary to fulfill the commandments. Perhaps he echoes Justin's nostalgic vision of a *koinonia* where people "bring what we have in common stock and share with everyone in need" (*Apol.* 1.13–15), envisioning an ascetic church community modeled on Acts 5 (*In Matt.* 15.15).

Even so, Origen does not argue for complete divestment but for a form of church-based asceticism that should be supported by church officials:[74]

> It would be, I think, the business of genuine (bishops), those who have all the marks of a bishop, to encourage those people who are able (to follow this word of Jesus) and can obey this exhortation, by making an allowance to them for their living out of the common fund; thus there would be produced an image of harmony that distinguished the life of the faithful at the time of the apostles.[75]

Clement and Origen strongly support an active human contribution to salvation by either almsgiving or ascetic divestment. Clement's poor replace supplementary supplication for the lacking salvation of the rich. The rich,

---

73. Davies and Allison, *Gospel according to Matthew*, 40.
74. Cyprian of Carthage, who does not directly engage the rich young man in his *Works and Almsgiving*, exhibits a theory of redemptive almsgiving similar to that of Clement. The salvific powers of baptism are retroactive. Any trespasses incurred after baptism need to be cycled through the coin-launderette of "redemptive almsgiving" that functions to wash out the filthiness of postbaptismal sin. Whether redemptive almsgiving functioned as a means to address increasing tensions and divides between rich and poor in congregations is unclear. Yet, obviously the rich struggle to enter the kingdom, while the problem of the postbaptismal sin of the poor seems irrelevant to the context. Lyman, *Christology and Cosmology*, 46.
75. Origenes, "Mattäus," 112.

spiritually deficient, can thus only be saved by the poor. In Origen's "passionate defence of the self-determination of the individual souls,"[76] divestment is the participatory supplement toward salvation that the rich themselves can add. In his optimistic emphasis on *autexousia*, the human power to self-determination and responsibility of free action is reaffirmed in the context of a third-century fatalism. Origen's deficiency assumes a different shape of *oikonomia*, where deification can supplement for lack by way of a "slow transformation through discipline and instruction."[77]

Both Alexandrians express diverging conceptions of perfection or salvation. They agree that human participation in salvation is pertinent. Yet while in Clement the poor function as agents of salvation for the rich, Origen describes the rich as possible agents of their own salvation through the divestment of their riches, including a church-funded safety net. Rather than identifying two widely oppositional approaches to coredemptive economies in almsgiving (retaining the conventional *oikos*) and asceticism (involving some kind of dissolution of the conventional and the creation of an alternative *oikos*), as one might be tempted to do regarding their rather oppositional theses, both approaches function as two solutions often coexisting within documents.[78]

Clement's solution, often marked as the beginning of accommodation to the increasing presence of wealth in the church,[79] should perhaps be seen as in relative consistency, or at least in connection, with what we might name a "householding tradition" threading through the Gospels, the *Didache*, the *Shepherd of Hermas*, and Cyprian's *Works and Almsgiving*. Origen's reading seems more in line with an ascetic tradition that runs strongly in parts of the Gospels and still more strongly later, stating the urgency of severing the bonds of genetic households and the possessions attached to them. In Origen's case, though, the loss is buffered when the newly divested soon become part of a new, far larger family in which the divine promise of future wealth for those who give up their past wealth is set:

> Receiving many times more brothers and sisters is easy to interpret from the text, already in this world; the brothers in faith are more numerous than

---

76. Lyman, *Christology and Cosmology*, 46.
77. Ibid., 47, 63–64, 81.
78. Compare, for example, the *Shepherd of Hermas*, a text exposing concern both for the poor and for the wealthy. See also Roman Garrison, *Redemptive Almsgiving in Early Christianity* (Journal for the Study of the New Testament Supplement Series; Sheffield: Sheffield Academic Press, 1993), 17.
79. Ernst Troeltsch reads Clement's *Quis. div.* as the ancient church text most favorable to wealth as well as the economically smartest. Troeltsch, *Die Soziallehren der christlichen Kirchen und Gruppen* (Tübingen: J.C.B. Mohr, 1912), 113. Luz stresses Clement's continuation and enhancement of a previously existent line of argument. Luz, *Matthäus*, 133.

those left behind for faith's sake by those who have become faithful. Thus one receives as parents all the righteous bishops and all presbyters of good reputation, also as children all those who have a childlike age.[80]

Thus, ascetic church members, like the disciples who have left house and family behind, receive several times over what they have given up already during their lifetime. They undergo the proliferation of many new siblings found in other church members and of parents in the form of church elders. Only the matter of the increase of new material riches such as real estate makes Origen hesitate in advertising the excellent immediate gratification economy of church asceticism. Though he is tempted to read the houses and fields allegorically, he reasons that consequently the previous more "literal" readings would have to be allegorized as well. In the end, he defers his interpretation by referring to the *eschaton:*

> How somebody will inherit the manifold of fields and houses that he has left, we cannot explain in the same way. . . . And once we begin interpreting fields and houses allegorically, we will be forced to do the same with the previously mentioned things. . . . The many fields and houses . . . I explain to myself by placing them in the quiet of the divine paradise and the city of God.[81]

Clement advocates the sufficiency of almsgiving for the divine economy, while Origen insists on pushing toward—if never quite attaining—complete ascetic divestiture of terrestrial goods. In Clement, the rich are unveiled as lacking in salvation, but their lack can be overcome by the gift of alms to the poor, which in turn make up for the painful, effeminate lack of those rich men who despair of their salvation. Both sides lack something; the rich lack salvation, the poor material goods, and this scarcity results in an economic exchange, human-divine and human-human. In order to guarantee this exchange—as well as its continuation—the rich must not become poor themselves but must detach themselves inwardly from their riches. Origen, however, advocates a different trade-off. For him, there is no alternative but to experience the utter depth of the lack of salvation even among substantial riches and to divest all of them in order to fulfill the commandments as pointed out by the Savior.[82] Clement's text voices

---

80. Origenes, "Mattäus," 124.
81. Ibid., 124–25.
82. Though he advocates the temporal acquisition of the celestial treasures acquired by financial divestment, Origen's view is far from that of contemporary prosperity theology, which would claim that the promise of wealth is owed to believers by God in the here and now.

the desperate hysteria of the wealthy in his congregation who have despaired of being saved. Yet he does not argue for abolishing class divisions between rich and poor, but rather for an economy of exchange where each is in need of the other, supplying what the other does not have access to. Detachment from wealth remains a purely spiritual matter and does not require actual giving up of possessions. Origen's moderate and yet transgressive version of urban voluntary asceticism is still set in a time of martyrs, conceived in a church setting that provides its frame. Some immediate gratification is in place, while Origen ventures that other parts of the dominical promise will not materialize until the *eschaton*. His church-centered asceticism would function as a safety net designed to protect the ascetics from poverty and homelessness, retaining a measure of control that contains the fear of loss of security and allows a certain continuity of comfort.

Just Deserts: Ascetic Investments among the Sand Dunes

> Everything in the world is sold for what it is worth, and someone trades an item for its equivalent. But the promise of eternal life is purchased for very little.
>
> Athanasius, *Life of Antony*

Let us now wander for a moment in the desert where the "strange cleavage" of an economy of *différance* deconstructs ascetic economic speculations in the hollow void of an eremite's cave.[83] In addition to scholars from the field of late antiquity and early Christianity, Athanasius's highly influential hagiography, the *Life of Antony*, has attracted the attentions of several poststructuralist thinkers, theorists, and other scholars interested in how this formative text of the West negotiates economies of power, salvation, pleasure, and desire.[84] As a tool in the fight to gain control over Arian Christians, Athanasius employs the text to inscribe his sense of orthodoxy, while he advocates ascetic life as a means for wealthy *kurioi* attempting to establish econo-theological control over the economies of their bodies and their salvation. Derrida's *différantial* circumlocutions resemble certain aspects of the dynamics of asceticism. *Différance* has an

---

[83]. Jacques Derrida, *Margins of Philosophy* (trans. Alan Bass; Chicago: University of Chicago Press, 1981), 19.

[84]. See, for example, Geoffrey Galt Harpham, *The Ascetic Imperative in Culture and Criticism* (Chicago: University of Chicago Press, 1987); and MacKendrick, *Counterpleasures*.

economic twist to it, and appears similarly suspended between presence *(parousia)* and absence *(apousia)*, negotiating abundance and lack, as the "*différance* that can make a profit on its investment and a *différance* that misses its profit." The supplementary deferral between investment and profit, both materially and ascetically, constitute a "play in which whoever loses wins, and in which one loses and wins on every turn."[85] The desire for perfection and the experience of a lack of perfection can become economic incentives for the investment in the heavenly economy. Thereby, asceticism's regulatory practices, as Geoffrey Harpham has extended Weber, resemble the investment strategies of capitalism. If "asceticism is a self-forming activity" not unlike the capitalist notion of self-interest in trading, then, says Harpham, "asceticism is capitalism without money."[86] Renunciation of immediate gratification holds the promise of a great final reward. In an ideal scenario, a small investment creates great gains—that is, if the trader is lucky, of course. Perhaps, then, as Harpham ventures, "this self-cancellation is the essence of asceticism."[87]

Yet while ascetics may seem to cancel or shatter their selves through a discipline intended to break their wills, they often expose a strength of will and self that suggests the opposite. This ascetic countereconomy of the self might then be similar to the nonteleological economies of desire and pleasure Karmen MacKendrick calls "counterpleasures."[88] MacKendrick writes that "only a vast immodesty can lead one to undertake the discipline of asceticism." Thus, "ascetic arrogance" and "ascetic humility" coexist and paradoxically reinforce each other: "The arrogance of overcoming [a sense of] unworthiness is as evident to the ascetic as it is to us—hence the insistent need to drive oneself to further humility."[89] MacKendrick's ascetic counterpleasures, however, "tend away from all sorts of teleologies." They are pleasures that "don't come within the economy of gratification, the gratifying economy of work and production."[90] They "refuse the sturdy subjective center, defying one's own survival."[91]

---

85. Derrida, *Margins of Philosophy*, 19–20.
86. Harpham, *Ascetic Imperative*, 27, 30.
87. Ibid., 18.
88. "Counterpleasures" are ascetic economies that "tend away from all sorts of teleologies" and "defy pleasure as we have come to understand it." As "strategies against the simple gratification of desire," they inhabit an uncomfortable border, remain ambivalent, are neither normal nor pathological, but remain transgressive in their liminality. In their third space of ambivalence, subversion and co-option are possible, even simultaneously. MacKendrick, *Counterpleasures*, 12, 14, 20. Yet MacKendrick's version of economy is distinct from Derrida's economy of *différance*, which stresses the possibility of simultaneous profit and loss.
89. Ibid., 80–81.
90. Ibid., 12, 19.
91. Ibid., 19.

MacKendrick's counterpleasures thus seem perhaps less "accountable" than Harpham's ascetic "capitalism," which assumes an equal payback between pleasure and pain. Athanasius's *Life of Antony*, in Harpham's reading at least, displays a redemptive ascetic economy that resembles later notions of capitalism. Is then this "master text of Western asceticism," which "holds a position of extraordinary prominence in Western ethics and spirituality," perhaps also a master text formative of patterns of Western economics?[92]

Early in his biography of the Egyptian hermit, the author, who intends this text to transmit a selection of theological and political issues close to his own heart, has Antony emerge as a better version of the rich young man:

> Six months had not passed since the death of his parents when, going to the Lord's house as usual and gathering his thoughts, he considered while he walked how the apostles, forsaking everything, followed the Savior, and how in Acts some sold what they possessed and took the proceeds and placed them at the feet of the apostles for distribution among those in need, and what great hope is stored up for such people in heaven. He went into the church pondering these things, and just then it happened that the Gospel was being read, and he heard the Lord saying to the rich man, *If you would be perfect, go, sell what you possess and give to the poor, and you will have treasure in heaven* (*Vit. Ant.* 2).[93]

The reader learns little about Antony's motivation for an ascetic life, though reasons might be pieced together when we learn that, after the death of his parents, he quickly tires of the duties and tasks of a *kurios*. What at first might seem like the indifference of a young introvert to household affairs could very well have a strong economic undercurrent, as David Brakke argues. The ascetic life as described in Acts might have appeared as the economic and spiritual solution Antony has been waiting for. In addition to a sense of lack and a desire for perfection, Athanasius's Antony and his intended readers may have been more than eager to rid themselves of the troubles and concerns of their abundance. Antony, presumably one of many village landowners facing "increasing financial pressures during the third and fourth centuries," incurred further responsibilities for additional financial duties and liturgies, such as "compulsory public services and offices."[94] Antony's retreat from the uncomfortable

---

92. Harpham, *Ascetic Imperative*, 3.
93. Athanasius here cites Matt 19:21, yet without the call to follow Jesus.
94. David Brakke, *Athanasius and Asceticism* (Baltimore: Johns Hopkins University Press, 1998), 233–34.

claims of society occurs in a two-step program. He "immediately... gave to the townspeople the possessions he had from his forebears... so that they would not disturb him or his sister in the least," but he retains a few possessions for both him and his sister until, during another trip to church, he is moved to give "those remaining possessions also to the needy" (*Vit. Ant.* 2).[95] Opting for a "gradual withdrawal," he nonetheless appears eager to shed the entangled hassles of possessions and to avoid financial losses and hardship.[96] It seems that the spiritual gain involved in divestiture serves Antony's quest for control over his own life, rather than being an expression of a desire to give, an experience of lack, or a concern for the needy. Brakke notes that "wealth, unlike sex, does not disappear from Antony's spiritual life" but remains a constant threat to it. Among the temptations of sex, food, and wealth, "it is wealth that represents the greatest danger for Antony, and, presumably, for the audience that Athanasius addresses."[97] The readers of Athanasius's text, namely, Brakke's householding male ascetics (among them Augustine of Hippo), might be found among the "prosperous citizens who made up the middle ranks of the larger cities and the elite of the country villages."[98] Athanasius's economically saturated description of asceticism and its capitalistic gains thus functions, at least in the logic of his text, as a gender-coded version of asceticism, consistent with other instances of "the holy aspirations of this particular, meticulously cultivated version of manhood."[99] As if to mark his ascetic economics even more clearly as masculine, his alternative commonwealth is not a *basileia*, nor an *oikonomia*, but a *politeia*.[100] The latter traditionally signifies the public realm in which only men moved without restraint and impropriety. Throughout the *Life*, Athanasius threads an "ascetic economics,"[101] describing life in the desert in terms of profit and loss, investment and gain. His rhetoric, like that of Clement before him, and hearkening back eventually to the Gospels, is driven by a mimetic modality in which Athanasius "does not condemn the acquisitive aspect" but rather seeks to "redirect" his prospective holy man's keen business sense toward the acquisition of the superior profits of heaven. Thus, while "everything in the world is sold for

---

95. Note that, while in the quoted text from Acts possessions are given to the church elders, Antony gives his to the "townspeople," perhaps hinting at the financial expectations of his civic, rather than Christian, community.
96. Brakke, *Athanasius and Asceticism*, 234.
97. Ibid., 227.
98. Ibid., 238.
99. Virginia Burrus, *Begotten, Not Made: Conceiving Manhood in Late Antiquity* (Stanford, Calif.: Stanford University Press, 2000), 69.
100. Ibid., 38.
101. Brakke, *Athanasius and Asceticism*, 237.

what it is worth, and someone trades an item for its equivalent[,] ... the promise of eternal life is purchased for very little" (*Vit. Ant.* 16).[102] The earthly economy offers only equity, while the heavenly deal brings in larger gains. Profit, at least for Athanasius's Antony, functions as one of the trademarks of heavenly investments. Where the gospel's anonymous young man sees too much risk of loss or a usurious price for "entry into life," our hopeful ascetic heroes buy into delayed economic gratification in a heavenly capitalism.

Economic divestment here represents an investment of one's desires for gain, spiritual or otherwise, converting terrestrial funds into heavenly currency. But these ascetics are hardly cut off from the bonds of the closed circulation of earthly economies. Rather, the ongoing relationship of exchange between householders and itinerants indicates otherwise.[103] If early "asceticism is capitalism without money," as Harpham suggests, replacing financial profits with the deferred but sweet hopes of heavenly gains, then there is always loss, and at the same time, always gain.[104] Lack of earthly riches promises an abundance of heavenly ones. Harpham suggests that this kind of ambivalence is operative in asceticism and functions neither to simply condemn nor simply endorse culture: "For renunciation ... always cancels itself by turning out to be an affirmation,"[105] and loss is unveiled as profit in tidy reciprocity resembling in its rhetoric a version of unrestrained capitalism. An asceticism of counterpleasures, as described by MacKendrick rather than Harpham, attempts, however, to break through the neat reciprocity of exchanges and might thus function as an illustration—one incarnation—of countereconomy.

The *Life of Antony* thus represents an economic tractate for the divine economy of the incarnation, in which Athanasius attempts to harness the ascetic Antony for an anti-Arian ousianic Christology and soteriology that de-emphasizes human participation. Though the *Life of Antony* was written during one of Athanasius's periods of exile, the actual location of the theological battles of the text is again urban Alexandria. Positioning the desert

---

102. Ibid., 236.
103. Redemptive almsgiving is a point in case, as is Antony's continued, if decreasing, dependence on society. The problem may not reside as much in the circular movements of exchange but in the lack of challenge to the dynamics of political power, which continue to largely be solidified. The addictive quality of almsgiving is perhaps similar to patronage. Both sides profit from the exchange while the status quo remains unchallenged. Cf. Justo Gonzalez, *Faith and Wealth: A History of Early Christian Ideas on the Origin, Significance, and Use of Money* (San Francisco: Harper & Row, 1990); and postcolonial texts that identify the addictive tendency of patterns of domination. See for example Frantz Fanon, *Black Skin, White Masks* (New York: Grove Press, 1967).
104. Harpham, *Ascetic Imperative*, 30.
105. Ibid., 18.

anchorite in tension with the soteriology of Arius and his followers, Athanasius develops the multiply enhanced memory of Antony as a veritable "major offensive in that battle which occupied most of the Alexandrian bishop's whole career."[106] The Arian theological economy of ascesis and soteriology, as interpreted by Gregg and Groh's controversial study, is based on "the axiomatic identification of Christ with creatures" in which humans can, by means of discipline, like Christ be adopted as "sons" of God. Arian Christology thus would seem to propose a different divine economy, one which Athanasius discredits. Athanasian soteriology, on the other hand, asserts a savior "divine by nature" who redeems humans by a grace that enables them to live lives of obedience.[107] Though Athanasius's Christ is the central agent of salvation, humans must still be zealous and aspire to an imitation of Christ that leads to mythical ascent.[108] The *Life of Antony* remains opaque as to whether Athanasian soteriology has to wrestle down Antony's enormous miraculous powers, or whether the Alexandrian bishop has produced them as effects of his ousianic soteriology. Yet Antony remains a strongly ascetic character, and even though Athanasius asserts that Antony was orthodox and friendly toward Athanasius, the connections between the Arians and Antony seem more than purely coincidental.[109] In Athanasius, more theological texts, a "sacred blood transfusion," implies "not simple human passivity but rather a complex responsiveness."[110] Thus, for Athanasius, a human contribution to salvation, if markedly restricted and economized, remains in place. The divestment of riches is crucial but does not register as sufficient. Emphasis shifts toward the magnitude of temptations and Antony's idealized battle with demonic powers and the achievement of a stasis-like slowdown of life energy to emulate divine immutability.[111] Thus, we find here, in the form of the *Life of Antony,* another, admittedly odd, version of a household tractate, an investment guide, a broker's advice, resembling the economic parables of the divine *oikonomia* and the *Haustafeln* encountered in the Pastoral Letters, addressing most likely the *kurios* of the household. The mimicry of hierarchical power dynamics, while partially disruptive, equally cites and reinscribes structures of dominance,[112] while some of the most insidious

---

106. Robert C. Gregg and Dennis E. Groh, *Early Arianism—A View of Salvation* (Philadelphia: Fortress, 1981), 134.
107. Ibid., 144, 143.
108. Brakke, *Athanasius and Asceticism,* 201, 219.
109. Gregg and Groh, *Early Arianism,* 137.
110. Burrus, *Begotten, Not Made,* 42.
111. Ibid., 73.
112. Judith Butler, *Gender Trouble: Feminism and the Subversion of Identity* (Thinking Gender; New York: Routledge, 1990), 146.

oppressions—toward women, children, and slaves—remain largely unrecognized and unaddressed, confined to the margins of the ancient texts. Antony rebels against the constraints of the *oikos*. Yet his figure is employed by Athanasius as the desert guarantor of the embattled urban Alexandrian "orthodoxy" that, paradoxically, gains popularity also through the spread of the desert monk's domestication by way of hagiography.

Masculine hysteria in Athanasius's text emerges as the fear of a lack of control over body, substance, and doctrine.[113] This fear of feminizing powerlessness, of loss of control, is compensated by an increase in spiritual powers in control over body functions demonstrated by raucous fights with demons, whom Antony courageously defeats, and the divesting of one's body of comfort and riches, as well as food. Thus, in Athanasius's text "materiality's chaotic default femaleness must be stabilized, simplified, and sublimated in ascetic production of the divinized self as a virtual—though never quite 'real'—man."[114] The management of food intake and sleep deprivation results, as Athanasius reports, in Antony's surprising control of mind over body, which renders him near divine.[115] Yet the attempt to master one's own body and mind is often ambiguously linked to the orthodox pursuit of mastery over the minds and bodies of others.

Imperial Economies of Power

> Thus, when the nature of the work here undertaken requires us to say something of it, and as occasion arises, we must not pass over in silence, the earthly city also: that city which, when it seeks mastery, is itself mastered by the lust for mastery even though all the nations serve it.
>
> Augustine, *City of God*, Book 1, Preface

> If the project of Imperialism is violently to put together the episteme that will "mean" (for others) and "know" (for the self) the colonial subject as history's nearly-selved other, the example of these deletions indicate explicitly what is always implicit: that meaning/knowledge intersects power.
>
> Gayatri Chakravorty Spivak, *Critique of Postcolonial Reason*

---

113. If the standard of power is to "make something from nothing," any other form of power can seem deficient, or effeminate. Keller, *Face of the Deep*, 57.
114. Burrus, *Begotten, Not Made*, 69.
115. Ibid., 72.

Augustine, another commentator on and alter ego of the rich young man, stands at the crossroads where the self-discipline of Christian ascetics increasingly comingles with another form of disciplinary power—that of empire. The catholic church would now be brought into a volatile cohesion with the empire, which moved church leaders positions uncomfortably close to that of imperial functionaries. One of the intellectuals and church leaders of the time was Augustine. About thirty years after Athanasius wrote the West's most influential hagiography, Augustine reported in his *Confessions* how, far away in Trier, the *Life of Antony* touched the lives of four young men in the services of the emperor. One function of empire is that it brings together people and ideas that might have never met otherwise. Thus, Ponticianus, a court official, fellow African and acquaintance of Augustine's in Milan, introduced him and his friends, for whom Antony and his monks were "total strangers at opposite ends of the Roman world," to Athanasius's text.[116] This episode occurs in the context of Augustine's deferred search, having "put off giving time for the quest for wisdom" though it should, as he writes, be "preferred even to the discovery of treasures and to ruling over nations and to the physical delights available to me at a nod" (*Conf.* 8.7.17). Spurred on by Augustine's rapt silence and ignorance about the monastic life, Ponticianus tells of an incident in Rome at which four "friends of the emperor," one of them Ponticianus, chanced upon Athanasius's book in a small local monastery while (futilely) waiting for an audience with the emperor, who was attending a circus spectacle. The text sparks several reactions in each of the four readers and listeners. The ensuing narrative shows them debating the power/knowledge formations within the *oikos* of the empire and how it constructs imperial theology, masculinity, and Christian ascetic subjectivity.

Deeply impressed by the text and tired of the enormous stress of life as imperial secret agents and informants in highly sensitive and dangerous positions, two of the young men debate the futility of their efforts to his colleague:

> What is the motive of our service to the state? Can we hope for any higher office in the palace than to be Friends of the Emperor? And in that position what is not fragile and full of dangers? How many hazards must one risk to attain to a position of even greater danger? And when will we arrive there? Whereas, if I wish to become God's friend, in an instant I may become that now.[117]

---

116. Peter Brown, *Augustine of Hippo* (Berkeley: University of California Press, 1967), 159.
117. The English translation of the *Confessions* follows Saint Augustine, *Confessions* (trans. Henry Chadwick; World's Classics; Oxford: Oxford University Press, 1992), 8.6.15.

As clients of the emperor, they immediately recognize the challenge Antony's story poses to empire and patronage, the specific form of power/knowledge grid they find themselves in. Both of them immediately join the monastery while the two others, including Ponticianus, decline the invitation to join them and remain within the imperial household (*Conf.* 8.6.15). Ponticianus and his colleague decide to reinvest into the imperial economy and weep for themselves (*Conf.* 8.6.15). While Ponticianus and his friend walk back toward the palace, the center of power, "dragging their hearts along the ground," the new monks have "fixed their hearts on heaven." For them, the *Life of Antony* provided a glimpse of a way out of the dangerous grid of high-powered brokering they were involved in. In Augustine's *Confessions,* Athanasius's rhetorical economy of the desert monk Antony engages four hearers—and thus, as though in response, Augustine's tale quadruples (four young men encounter the text) and doubles (both choices are made in the same story by two men each) Athanasius's version, refracting in part the Matthean young man, and in part Antony. Out of four young men, two can let go of the seductions of power and follow the example of Antony. The other two find themselves unable to, and they go "away grieving, for [they] had many possessions" (Matt 19:22). The surprise visit by Ponticianus, who recounts the previous story, precedes and prepares Augustine's own "final" conversion, not so much to Catholicism as to asceticism, to "Lady Continence." Augustine, while listening to his fellow African and fellow protegee of Symmachus,[118] finds his own reluctance to convert his assets into heavenly wealth unveiled by God through his account. "While he was speaking, Lord, you turned my attention back to myself," so that the story becomes a mirror in which "I did not want to observe myself, and you set me before your face so that I should see how vile I was" (*Conf.* 8.1.16–18). The *Life of Antony* facilitates a key confrontation with his own self, causing Augustine to be "overcome by a fearful sense of shame during the time that Ponticianus told the story"(*Conf.* 8.7.16–18). Augustine himself testifies to the great power, yet again of the story of the rich young man, even once or twice removed:

> For I had heard how Antony happened to be present at the gospel reading, and took it as an admonition addressed to himself when the words were read: "Go, sell all you have, give to the poor, and you shall have treasure in heaven; and come, follow me." By such an inspired utterance he was immediately "converted to you." (*Conf.* 8.12.29)

---

118. Brown, *Augustine of Hippo,* 71.

And likewise with Augustine: immediately preceding this recollection of Antony, Augustine is in the garden, and he hears the famous voice that encourages him to "pick up and read." Thus, like for Antony, a passage heard or read from the biblical text becomes the turning point. And with this, Augustine reports, "All the shadows of doubt were dispelled" (*Conf.* 8.12.29).

The club of young elite males that had gathered around Augustine in "intellectual friendship" experiences his final conversion to chastity as a group event that allows them to retain their "ideal of a shared life," their desire for male bonding that had been threatened by a potential marriage of their "brilliant friend." An elite clique like theirs, a homosocial learning community would be threatened by the libidinal distractions of women. This "collective decision," Brown avers, "pointed directly toward the little monastery Augustine would found" soon after his arrival back in Hippo; an all-male ascetic oasis that would form the "calm eye of the storm" in the forty tumultuous years to come.[119] Athanasius's *Life of Antony* and the soteriology expressed therein shines through, as if through the upper layer of a palimpsest, as part of the intertext for Augustine's *Confessions,* as both texts constitute palimpsests of Matthew 19.

Throughout the development of soteriology in the centuries after the death of Jesus and the development of an orthodox form of Christian faith, the economy of power increasingly shifted away from possible and necessary human contributions to the divine economy of redemption, to a theology wherein God and the Logos were imagined as solidly omnipotent and singularly efficient in bringing about redemption. Despite Augustine's later disillusionment, the Roman Empire came dangerously close to being identified with the reign of God, and the divine economy was brought close to the political economy of the Roman Empire. Elaine Pagels and Peter Brown stress that with Augustine we see a type of soteriology that strongly de-emphasizes the possibility of human participation in salvation as well as any "original capacity for self-government."[120] Furthermore, Pagels asserts that whereas for many converts the Christian proclamation of *autexousia* in the face of civil authorities had been synonymous with the gospel, the message changed with Augustine, who stressed human enslavement and

---

119. Brown, *Body and Society,* 395.
120. Robert Markus, Peter Brown, and Elaine Pagels are among those who have tracked Augustine's theological writings and written about how the North African bishop's texts have constructed Western attitudes toward political systems, sex, and salvation. Markus, *Saeculum,* 134ff; Brown, *Augustine of Hippo,* 369; Elaine Pagels, *Adam, Eve, and the Serpent* (New York: Vintage, 1988), 112, 117.

the need for obedience.[121] Differing strongly not only from Origen—and to a lesser degree from Athanasius—but from almost every patristic writer before him, Augustine identifies the human will as incurably "twisted" from the moment of conception. Whereas Antony successfully battled external demons that attempted to keep his soul from mythical ascent, Augustine shifted the problem inside the person.[122] When contemporaries such as Pelagius, Julian of Eclanum, and John Cassian complained that he "preaches despair" and blunts the "sword of the free will," Augustine, who, compared to Jerome and other ascetic contemporaries moved in an "all-male world," appeared possessed—or perhaps more adequately obsessed—by a strong awareness of his own unruly libidinal powers, sexual and otherwise.[123] Augustine primarily located the fall from grace exactly there, and proceeded to pass on to those who would come after him a strange hypermasculine notion of sin and human will mapped onto the observable "lust for mastery" exemplified in the urge for coitus as well as in the need to dominate others. This oddly gendered twist on soteriology effectively disabled men's efforts to participate in salvation while it served to obscure women's possibly different experience of sin. Augustine's own body and mind generously filled the space of his writing and disciplining economy as the libidinal consciousness of his readers was aroused. The *libido* for full erectile control of a man's member resembles the *libido dominandi*, the desire for power over others, especially the members of the church body Augustine later oversaw. Compromises around issues of power abounded in Augustine's life.[124] Tragically, as Robert Markus has eloquently pointed out, Augustine's awareness of the human "lust for mastery" resulted in a highly ambivalent involvement in power brokering rather than resistance to it.[125]

For fifteen years, Augustine remained mostly fascinated with the triumphant progress of Christianity and the establishment of a Christian empire. But eventually he became one of the few critics of imperial politics. Markus writes, "Outside dissenting or schismatic circles Augustine was the only thinker of any stature who was deeply disturbed by the developments

---

121. Pagels, *Adam, Eve, and the Serpent*, 99, 105, 118.
122. Brown, *Body and Society*, 404.
123. Ibid., 411–12, 396.
124. He was from early on familiar with and dependent on the attention of various patrons, such as Symmachus and Marcellinus, who allowed his education, and promoted him regarding his employment, politicking, and publications. The grid of patronage remained in place throughout Augustine's life subsequently, but became crucial to his success as a bishop and as a writer. See Brown, *Augustine of Hippo*, 302–3.
125. Thus, Augustine "invoked the idea of a changing *ordo temporum* to justify the use of coercive power against the Donatists" in a notorious letter to Boniface. See Markus, *Saeculum*, 35.

of the fourth century towards a sacral conception of the Empire."[126] Yet, though Markus asserts that Augustine was most emphatic in his identification of the Roman Empire with the Christian order in the years 399–400,[127] this period lies within the time during which he wrote the *Confessions*. This might well suggest that Augustine's discomfort with imperial powers and patronage was already underlying. As a bishop, however, despite his growing disillusionment with a "Christian empire," he kept invoking the Christian *ordo temporum* in the rhetoric that justified the use of coercive power against Donatists and other ecclesial opponents. The *tempora christiana*, a "distinct phase in the history not only of the Roman Empire, but of salvation,"[128] thus became a powerful tool for religious coercion. Augustine's ambivalent attitude toward the Roman Empire, which put him in a position of power as well as one of submission toward the empire and the catholic church, was significant to his social as well as theological stance. Aware of the ambivalence of power—imperial, episcopal, and clerical—he describes the hybridity of the church as a *corpus permixtum*,[129] neither at home in the Christian empire nor in a pure church of martyrs, as the Donatists continued to claim. Along with Augustine's soteriology, based on the premise that humanity and the world are incapable of improvement, his own position of power produced an uncomfortable acquiescence with imperial power structures and reduced his actions and hopes to the minimization of disorder and damage control. Though Augustine insisted that political authority is a result of the sinful condition of the *libido dominandi*, he accepted it as a necessary evil and even compared his use of dominative powers in ecclesial disputes with a divine *disciplina* his rhetorical economy constructed analogously. The Trierian moment represents an ambivalent act of defiance of imperial power as distinct from divine power. Here and in Augustine's own turn to asceticism, empire is contested and mocked, if not for a moment rendered expendable. The narrative and alternative of the *Life of Antony* relieves the pressures of clienthood on Augustine's young men so much that two of them decide to leave the services of the emperor, while the other two become even more aware of how compromised and tragic their co-optation and complicity with empire is.

Might we perhaps read Augustine as an ancient version of a "colonial intellectual," his hybridity inscribed in his body?[130] Educated by the

---

126. Ibid., 157.
127. Ibid., 33.
128. Ibid., 31.
129. See the preface of *De civitate Dei*.
130. This is Homi Bhabha's term. See also Lyman's reading of Justin and Irenaeus as colonial intellectuals, which I am here applying to Augustine. Lyman, "Politics of Passing," 44–45, 47.

standards of an empire that had long been present in his homeland, he was the offspring of a mixed marriage (his mother might have been of Berber descent). He was fluent in the linguistic, intellectual, and monetary currency of Rome, the newly Christian empire whose combined political and spiritual power he was both suspicious of and hopeful for. From the status of an impoverished rural elite in his homeland, he moved to Milan and up through various alleys of patronage. Though he remained ambivalent about the trafficking of power in the upper echelons of the empire, he wound up employing it himself to control partisan Donatist Christians. Yet Augustine's early enthusiasm about the *tempora christiana* was eventually replaced by a more complex notion of the divine economy.[131] Whereas Irenaeus spent five books in the rhetorical attempt to manage the church and to exorcise and excise dissenting heretics' counterfeiting accounts of divine investment, Augustine, if grudgingly, saw the church as a hybrid body, a *corpus permixtum*.[132] Compromised by his theological as well as political involvement in imperial power structures, Augustine became a suspicious observer of the empire and a reluctant if forceful broker of ecclesial power.[133] The young men's tears in Trier speak of a similar conflict between the imperial *oikonomia* and Antony's subversive ascetic householding as resistant to imperial power economies.

As Augustine's theological economy divests humans of a sense of the hopeful and constructive participation in deification, he devalues the currency of human investments in the divine economy. Human efforts can no longer form effective contributions to redemption. Thus, even the possibility of a coredemptive enterprise is deflated, unveiled as counterfeit capital, and the divine effort in salvation becomes singularly effective in procuring salvation. The sole true and effective investor is the divine capitalist. "His" profile, which uncannily mimicks the empire's central political and economic authority, serves to reinforce the omnipotence of empire and God. Augustine's remainder of resistance, exemplified in the Trier incident, whimpers off almost ineffectively. More effectively, though, Augustine's rewritten divine economy has served as an enabling structure to exploit and oppress other, differing economies and currencies of faith. His theology, wordy and brilliant, bolsters Western orthodoxy. Augustine's own special brand of hysteria is the fear of a lack of willpower over body functions, exemplified in male genitalia. The fear of his own chaotic sexuality, mixed

---

131. Thus, Markus writes, "Even though, in the years following 410–411, Augustine lost his earlier enthusiasm about the alliance between the Roman Empire and the Catholic Church, he could hardly have renounced it in practice." Markus, *Saeculum*, 154.
132. See *Doct. chr.* 3.32.45. See also Markus, *Saeculum*, 120.
133. Pagels, *Adam, Eve, and the Serpent*, 124.

with his homoerotic desires, results in the blaming of Eve for masculine impotence. Since women were generally considered even less able to control the use of their bodies or minds, a man's loss of control over his body through the power of sin rendered a man more effeminate and less distinct from women. Thus, Augustine effectively, though not literally, iterates the motif of hysterical lack in Matthew's narrative.

The Colonial Properties of Divine Economy

> For the epic intention of the civilizing mission, "human and not wholly human" ... "writ by the finger of the Divine" often produces a text rich in the traditions of *trompe-l'œil,* irony, mimicry, and repetition. ... [M]imicry emerges as one of the most elusive and effective strategies of colonial power and knowledge. ... [T]he discourse of mimicry is constructed around an ambivalence; in order to be effective it must continually produce its slippage, its excess, its difference.
>
> Homi Bhabha, *The Location of Culture*

The interpretations of the rich young man presented in this chapter were written by privileged men whose education and profession allowed them to know, explore, and shape a divine *oikonomia* that shows an uncanny resemblance to their own context and location. While Irenaeus's inscription of *oikonomia* still has subversive potentialities in his time in its attempt to create an alternative, resistant knowledge, it retains—and in the long run of its *Wirkungsgeschichte* catastrophically rebirths—the hierarchical shape of patterns of exclusion similar to those that drove our young Roman officials to tears. The fear of loss of life, livelihood, and patrimony if service to the emperor were denied, kept them in shackles. The Western Christian spread of the divine economy—materialized, for example, in the witnessing of both Christian missionaries and colonial businessmen to the natives of the Indian subcontinent—is revealed and mimicked by postcolonial writers. Homi Bhabha's descriptions of colonial mimicry, for example, add a divergent reading to the privileged narratives of ancient patristic writers and contemporary economists. In a text entitled "Signs Taken for Wonders: Questions of Ambivalence and Authority under a Tree outside Delhi, 1817," Bhabha recounts an incident from modern British colonialism in India. In the attempt not only to strengthen their own presence and power in the Indian subcontinent but to simultaneously convert Hindu "heathens" into Christian citizens of the empire, British officials and missionaries employed the Bible as a spiritual and political disciplining tool. They hoped that their dispersal of Hindi translations of the Bible would assist in the struggle for British control, "so that the natives may resist the Brahmins' 'monopoly of knowledge' and lessen their dependence on their own religious and cultural traditions."[134] The Christian canon was intended as the weapon of a disciplinary power/knowledge against native power/knowledge, not unlike Irenaeus's five books against heretical *pouvoir/savoir* (power/knowledge). Sure enough, some of the Hindu natives under the tree find its message subversive: "An indifference to the distinctions of Caste soon manifested itself; and the interference and tyrannical authority of the Brahmins became more offensive and contemptible," the Indian catechist present reports.[135] A subversive tool against hierarchies, the Bible here functions to deconstruct one hierarchy and—in the colonizers' intention—establishes another, better power structure, namely, the British Empire and its claim to identity with the government/household of God. Yet instead, a "double inscription" at once "disciplinary and disseminatory" occurs, as the readers of the Hindi Bible apply it within their own context and culture. Invariably, the symbol of missionary and Christian authority becomes hybridic and functions as the "sign of the productivity of colonial power, its shifting forces and fixities," describing the "strategic reversal of the process of domination through disavowal."[136] While the new (vegetarian) readers embrace the content of the gospel, they resist its connection with British carnivorous colonial rule: "'These books,' said Anund, 'teach the religion of the European Sahibs. It is THEIR book; and they printed it in our language, for our use.' The natives expel the copula, or middle term, of the Evangelical 'power = knowledge' equation, which then disarticulates the structure of the God = Englishman equivalence."[137] Thus the colonizer-God identification becomes deconstructible: "Ah! no,' replied the stranger, 'that cannot be, for they eat flesh.'"[138] During the ensuing conversation the native Bible readers insistently reject the provenance of the Bible from the British, which would limit its liberative economy, and adjust it to their own cultural taboos: "We are willing to be baptized, but we will never take the Sacrament." No meat will be served in this house of God! The miraculous exchange of the bread and wine into body and blood is not good housekeeping in the eyes of these readers. The Bible, detached from its British interpretive context, becomes a site where "the natives' questions contest the logical order of the discourse of authority" where "the words of the

---

134. Homi Bhabha, *The Location of Culture* (London: Routledge, 1994), 118.
135. Ibid., 103.
136. Ibid., 111–12.
137. Ibid., 119.
138. Ibid., 103.

master become the site of hybridity."¹³⁹ Hybridity and mimicry thus map the flow of colonizing powers, revealing the impossibility of gaining a sense of absolute power. Likewise, biblical and patristic texts function complexly in various intertexts, and remain elusive to all aspirations to control their meaning and use.

Contemporaneously with the religious mission to Christianize natives, the economic system of the West was carried into the colonies with missionary zeal. Yet the "great anonymous technique of capital" of the modern colonial "civilizing mission" has begun to elude the patronizing grip of Western economists.¹⁴⁰ Though as Arif Dirlik points out, "postcolonial critics have been largely silent on the relationship of the idea of postcolonialism to its context in contemporary capitalism," perhaps not the least because many postcolonial intellectuals profit from this location.¹⁴¹ Gayatri Spivak and Amitava Kumar have, more recently, begun to frame postcolonial issues more visibly in an economic context. Spivak, for example, points to the "explanatory power of economics" in colonial and neocolonial reasoning that continues to function as a legitimizing structure for imperialist projects.¹⁴² After the demise of socialist systems in the late twentieth century, Spivak regards Marxism as "at its best a speculative morphology" and warns of treating what is "powerfully speculative as predictive social engineering."¹⁴³ Still, her critique of postcolonial reason stresses the importance of specifically *economic* power/knowledge regimes in colonial and neocolonial settings and holds other postcolonial writers accountable for their lack of engagement of economic issues involved in colonialism as well as in postcolonial and neocolonial spaces.¹⁴⁴ Doubtlessly, the mercantile exploitation of colonies and the subsequent growth of wealth in colonizing societies have played a significant role in how power flows in and between societies. Since neocolonialism manifests itself largely through economic rather than territorial imperialism,

---

139. Ibid., 120, 119, 121.
140. Gayatri Spivak, *A Critique of Postcolonial Reason: Toward a History of the Vanishing Present* (Cambridge: Harvard University Press, 1999), 212.
141. Arif Dirlik, "The Postcolonial Aura: Third World Criticism in the Age of Global Capitalism," in *Dangerous Liaisons: Gender, Nation, and Postcolonial Perspectives* (ed. Anne McClintock, Aamir Mufti, and Ella Shohat; Minneapolis: University of Minnesota Press, 1997), 502.
142. Spivak, *Critique of Postcolonial Reason*, 221.
143. Ibid., 84.
144. Thus, she argues that "elite 'postcolonialism' seems to be as much a strategy of differentiating oneself from the racial underclass as it is to speak in its name." Spivak warns of a resurrection of a certain colonial hybrid, who had been "produced of indigenous functionary-intelligentsia who were not-quite-not-white and acted as buffer between the foreign rulers and the native ruled." In contrast, Spivak has increased her own efforts to speak for, to, or on behalf of the "subaltern" in the form of the invisible women employed and exploited by textile industries. Spivak, *Critique of Postcolonial Reason*, 358–59.

investigations into economic hybridities along with cultural ones increasingly enter into postcolonial discourse.[145] Thus, Spivak and Tani Barlow call for a distinction between various manifestations of capitalism, and in Spivak's case specifically between industrial capitalism and commercial capital.[146] Extending postcolonial analysis to a critique of the colonial and neocolonial structures of transnational migration and globalization, Kumar asks whether "the Third World and its peoples have a future different from Europe's. It seems that Western analysts, in declaring capitalism the chosen path for the Third World, are unprepared to grant the Third World any legitimate identity, an identity that need not be yoked to Europe's triumphs and failures."[147] Thus, Kumar takes the sales pitch back to where it came from: "I want to teach [my U.S. students] that multicultural education in the U.S. might be nothing more than propaganda—or worse, advertising—if it doesn't hear, and amplify, those voices all over the world who talk back to power."[148]

Dissenting from the orthodoxy of free market capitalism, questioning the truth claims of its salvation history, has often resulted in the accusation of economic heresy. Economism's neocolonial rhetoric is even somewhat reminiscent of Irenaeus's diatribes. The constructive contribution of the "heretics" who doubt the power of "the market as God" is effectively silenced by branding them as deeply immoral and destructive people, aside from their disbeliefs, mimicking an ancient strategy of marking those who think in a fashion contrary to society as destroyers of society's fabric.[149] The hysterical denunciations found in much of the rhetoric that supports the status quo seem as unproductive as the protesters' at times simplistic, if effective, demonizations of "TNCs" (transnational corporations) or "big money." Both strategies function to obscure the presence of economic

---

145. Thus Spivak: "(By neocolonialism I always mean the largely economic rather than the largely territorial enterprise of imperialism. The difference between colonialism and imperialism, crucial to historians, is not of the last importance here.) The post-Soviet situation has moved this narrative into the dynamics of the financialization of the globe." Spivak, *Critique of Postcolonial Reason*, 3.

146. Spivak observes that "industrial (and specifically postindustrial) capitalism is now in an interruptive *différance* with commercial capital" and has criticized Derrida for his "apparent ignorance (or ignoring) of the difference between industry and finance." Furthermore, she identifies a "difference between mercantile capitalism (dependent on exploration and conquest) and transnational financialization (the mode of production that determines 'postcolonial' new immigrant')." Spivak, *Critique of Postcolonial Reason*, 3n.4, 394. See also Tani E. Barlow, "'Green Blade in the Act of Being Grazed': Late Capital, Flexible Bodies, Critical Intelligibility," *Differences* 10, no. 3 (1998): 119–58.

147. Amitava Kumar, *Passport Photos* (Berkeley: University of California Press, 2000), 87.
148. Ibid., 127.
149. Wes Howard-Brook and Anthony Gwyther observe the same tendency. Howard-Brook and Gwyther, *Unveiling Empire: Reading Revelation Then and Now* (Maryknoll, N.Y.: Orbis, 1999), 239.

alternatives, which are already in danger of being crushed by the crudities of the rhetorical economies of "left" and "right." A countereconomic third place que(e)ries the properties and the gender of the figure of the *homo economicus*.

Insufficient Funds: Managing the Gendered Politics of Hysteria and Modern Economics

> *Legei auto ho neaniskos: Panta tauta ephulaxa. Ti eti hustero?*
> The young man said to him, "I have kept all these; what do I still lack? (Matt 19:20)

What might the rich young man have in common with the *homo economicus*? Exposing lack, Matthew's hysterical youth finds himself hollow and thereby feminized: *Ti eti hustero?* "What do I lack?" Indeed, "what does he lack?" exegetes have puzzled. Like Origen, some contemporary exegetes of Matt 19:16–30 comment on the oddity of the "lack" the young man expresses immediately after he states that he has fulfilled all the commandments. Has he not played by the rules such as Jesus specified? The audience is left in suspense. We are never quite sure what is amiss. "Would Matthew," ask Davies and Allison, "have supposed Zaccheus deficient because he gave away only half of his goods?"[150]

Roughly two millennia later, the axiomatic quality of "scarcity" in neoclassical economics seems to invert ancient notions of the persistence of human lack in perfection or essence, transferring them into the modern science of economics, where we find the fundamental concept of the scarcity of goods.[151]

Max Weber held that the Athenian man did not function as *homo economicus* but rather, due to his disengagement with the feminine realm of the household, as *homo politicus*.[152] Feminist economist Julie Nelson has identified the modern gendering of the traditional neoclassical academic study of economics not only as masculine but also as public.[153] Academic economics has thus been more steadily identified with the masculine and the public realm and not from what might then be defined as women's

---

150. Davies and Allison, *Matthew*, 47.
151. While the notion of scarcity is certainly not identical with lack, it does echo it, even while it reverses what is considered lacking. Thus, not salvation but goods are invested with redemptive value and become salvific in modern economics. Compare James B. Twitchell, *Lead Us into Temptation: The Triumph of American Materialism* (New York: Columbia University Press, 1999).
152. Humphreys, *Family, Women, and Death*, 10.
153. Julie A. Nelson, "The Masculine Mindset of Economics Analysis," *Chronicle of Higher Education* 42 (28 June 1996): B3.

realm, the private household: "[I]t is clear that the dominant cultural understanding in the modern United States associates men and masculinity with being public, active, and rational, and women and femininity with being private, passive, and emotional."[154] One shift seems to lie in the definition of what counts as "economy" and "economics," namely, no longer the management of a household that might look much like a small in-house business as described by Torjesen and Burrus,[155] but a modern public realm in which still predominantly male agents pursue growth and wealth. This may in part be due to the fact that with industrial capitalism the household itself was less and less the site of what was considered the "production" of goods, but became increasingly a reservoir for a (mostly male) workforce engaged in economic endeavors outside the home and in which the "homely" enterprises of women were not counted toward economic productivity.

Nelson and Ferber's collected volume *Beyond Economic Man* has begun to voice a specifically feminist critique of the *homo economicus* defined by scarcity elaborated by Susan Feiner's reading.[156] Feiner's essay "A Portrait of the *Homo Economicus* as a Young Man,"[157] evokes resemblances between Matthew's rich young man and the generic yet masculine agent of Western modern economics. Gendered as a "he" and imbued with an economic agency that was the domain of modern European men only, the *homo economicus* is described as a generic, corporate person. At the very least, we might wonder whether the rich young man is an ancestor of John Stuart Mill's "wealth maximizer," the *homo economicus* who, according to Carol Johnston, helped to shape what seems common sense at least in the West: the proliferation of growth as the sole goal of economic engagement.[158] Feiner's gendered expository reading reveals a masculine economic agent with the help of "clues strewn liberally through the didactic tales of *homo economicus*." As Feiner regards "textbook economics as autobiography," *homo economicus* appears as an "intensely romantic young man" who exhibits "sensitivities with which a great many people can identify" and who is fraught with the cultural and philosophical baggage of his time. He

---

154. Julie A. Nelson, *Feminism, Objectivity and Economics* (New York: Routledge, 1996), 23.
155. Torjesen, *When Women Were Priests*, 56 and passim.
156. For feminist critiques of *homo economicus*, see Ferber and Nelson, *Beyond Economic Man*, and Julie A. Nelson, "Economic Man," in *The Elgar Companion to Feminist Economics* (ed. Janice Peterson and Meg Lewis; Aldershot: Edward Elgar, 2000), 284–89.
157. Susan F. Feiner, "A Portrait of the *Homo Economicus* as a Young Man," in *The New Economic Criticism* (ed. Martha Woodmansee and Mark Osteen; New York: Routledge, 1999), 193–209.
158. Carol Johnston, *The Wealth or Health of Nations: Transforming Capitalism from Within* (Cleveland: Pilgrim, 1998), 49.

is the rhetorical embodiment of an androcentric economic culture.[159] As an enlightened man, self-interested, atomistic, omnipresent, and transparent, he occupies a generalized space that claims fully to explain the desires that drive all human behavior. Modern (and ancient?) economic man embodies the "self-invisibility" of Haraway's modern European scientific man masquerading as the "legitimate and authorized ventriloquist for the object world, claiming to add nothing from his mere opinions, from his biasing embodiment."[160] Feiner's exposition of *homo*'s masculinity reveals his gender, location, and particularity. On a quest for sensual satisfaction, he betrays a faintly Freudian longing for the retreating nipple of the motherly "perfect market" where "what households want, firms have; what firms have, households want." The *homo economicus*'s eternal desire, which aims to fill a hysterical lack, appears to be stretching toward these perfect markets and mothers that "meet all of our desires immediately, with no frustration and no anxiety." The vicissitudes of the market feel similar to the "vicissitudes of our mothers," as they "vacillate between generosity, availability, and affirmation" and "withholding, scarcity, and punishment," invoking "our earliest horrors and fears of total abandonment."[161]

The divine economy is imagined as the perfect maternal market, the perfect investment that satisfies all lack. The rich man's lack motivates his desire for fulfillment, yet the desire to be empowered in his society and context collides with the desire to fulfill his contribution to the divine economy: "If you wish to be perfect, go, sell your possessions, and give the money to the poor, and you will have treasure in heaven; then come, follow me" (Matt 19:21). Still, the power/knowledge formations in the young man's mind are too seamlessly constructed to accommodate a different understanding of wealth. Too strong is the belief in "our collective dependence on markets," on the "forces we cannot control."[162] Loosening control on his little patch of sovereignty, his household and possessions, then, is more than the youth can handle—too scary the loss, too remote the comforts of celestial dwellings. "When the young man heard this word, he went away grieving, for he had many possessions" (19:22). Scarcity scares him too much to let go.

The fear and rejection of lack (or scarcity) also extends to contemporary theological constructions of God. From among the group of theologians

---

159. Feiner, "Portrait of the *Homo Economicus*," 206.
160. Donna J. Haraway, *Modest_Witness@Second_Millennium. FemaleMan©_Meets_Onco-Mouse*™ (New York: Routledge, 1997), 23–24.
161. Feiner, "Portrait of the *Homo Economicus*," 195, 197.
162. Ibid., 195.

who claim access to a "radical orthodoxy," Stephen Long has offered a "comparison of theology with economics as theoretical disciplines."[163] Long's position angles triadically in relation to two other theological positions. His "third place" is positioned in a postliberal "residual tradition" that claims to overcome the "liberalist" fallacies of both a "dominant tradition" and an "emergent tradition."[164] The "dominant tradition," whose work, according to Long, "fits comfortably with the dominance of global capitalism,"[165] succumbs to "marginalism," a "form of rationality" that singularily prioritizes monetary profit in exchange relationships and affirms capitalism at large. In opposition to it he locates an "emergent tradition," largely identified with liberal and liberation theology, providing a critique of capitalism that favors a version of socialism. However, as Long observes, this tradition appears also based on a modernist notion of freedom and "does not provide a form of theology that can emerge out of and against modernity."[166] Long charges Latin American liberation theologians with opposing scarcity to divine plenitude, claiming that Rosemary Radford Ruether's feminist liberation theology, for example, "certainly assumes the metaphysics of scarcity that defines modernity."[167] Yet it remains unclear how his own approach might transcend this dualism of divine plenitude and need. Long's own critique of modernist notions of scarcity is a leitmotif throughout his account. Thus, he claims that theologians too "must deny this narrative of scarcity, for it forces our language and actions into the inevitable embrace of death." And just like the liberation theologians he intends to defy, he himself asserts an essential or foundational divine plenitude, which simply repeats what became orthodoxy, when he claims that "God is never defined by lack: God is an original plenitude never able to be exhausted."[168]

Douglas Meeks's approach to scarcity and "satiation" is more nuanced. He finds American society beleaguered by both a "sense of scarcity [that] makes the members of the household less accepting and compassionate," while "a pervasive sense of satiation . . . makes the household members drowsy and inattentive to their own and other's suffering."[169] Thoughtfully,

---

163. D. Stephen Long, *Divine Economy: Theology and the Market* (New York: Routledge, 2000), 6.

164. Long accords a "dominant tradition" to Michael Novak, Max Stackhouse, and Philip Wogaman, while the "emergent tradition" is represented, among others, by Gustavo Gutierrez, James Cone, Jon Sobrino, and Rosemary Radford Ruether. See Long's chapter on "Scarcity, orthodoxy, and heresy," in Long, *Divine Economy*, 143–74 and passim.

165. Ibid., 10.
166. Ibid., 2.
167. Ibid., 85, 148.
168. Ibid., 146.
169. Meeks, *God the Economist*, 17–18.

he distinguishes between the "lack of food[,] ... decent housing, potable water, adequate sanitation and health care" and the "deepest assumption of modern economics, namely, scarcity." While "lack is not an illusion," it is "not the same thing as the modern economic definition of scarcity." Meeks goes on to assert that nothing "is deeper in the spirit of capitalism, and of socialism as well, than the belief that there is not enough to go around."[170] McFague evokes Christian notions of abundance already in her title *Life Abundant*. Meeks and McFague have offered redefinitions of abundance as the "abundance of God's grace," to which a Christian might respond by changing how she relates to the world around her and by demystifying the dogmas of the market,[171] or as a life "not based on material good, but on those that really make people happy: the basic necessities of food, clothing, shelter for themselves and their children; medical care and educational opportunities; loving relationships; meaningful work; an enriching imaginative and spiritual life; and time spent with friends in the natural world."[172]

These redefinitions, helpful and hopeful, can serve as goals to strive for. Yet while to juxtapose lack and/or scarcity to Christian notions of abundance is an effective rhetorical tool, it hardly is enough to rest the argument.[173] By asking what kind of lack is being managed by the theological discourse of our wealthy men, we have discovered that the economies of power in their texts also manage fears of loss. Irenaeus reads the story of the rich young man within the context of the *oikonomia theou*, even as a touchstone for it: the dialogue with the Savior reveals that the divine economy of the Hebrew and the apostolic traditions match up perfectly. For Irenaeus, the divine economy of salvation unfurls as a progressive learning experience. The divine commandments form levels of this process of deification laid out for the faithful learner as steps on a ladder. Whereas Clement finds almsgiving sufficient for the rich, whose donations would be reimbursed by the prayer of the poor for their causes, Origen suggests

---

170. Ibid., 171. Though it is certainly worthwhile to mark the difference between lack and scarcity, this present book attempts to map how lack and scarcity have often colluded in rhetorical economies and what the effects thereof have been.

171. Ibid., 172.

172. Sallie McFague, *Life Abundant: Rethinking Theology and Economy for a Planet in Peril* (Minneapolis: Fortress, 2000), 209–10.

173. Meeks writes, "The Christian perspective on needs and consumption is that God the Holy Spirit is providing enough of what it takes for all to live and live abundantly." Meeks, *God the Economist*, 171. While McFague calls for a "cruciform life of sacrifice and sharing burdens," one might wonder if instead of trying to lift high the banner of sacrifice, it would be useful to develop what McFague does in the same text, namely, to reconstruct ancient notions of asceticism, or, as McFague prefers, "deification." McFague, *Life Abundant*, 209–10.

that the commandment to love one's neighbor cannot be fulfilled while a person still owns significant riches. Both would, however, agree that wealth is a problem that calls for some form of divestment; whether through alms or through asceticism is a matter of debate. As Clement's *Salvation of the Rich*, Athanasius's *Life of Antony* addresses wealthy young men of a certain stature and business sense. Athanasius's rendering of Antony's response to the rich young man's narrative attempts to redirect the business sense of his readers toward the usurious heavenly economy, where far larger profits can be incurred by only the most daring investors. In the context of the Christianization of the Roman Empire, Athanasius's rhetorical economy disciplines Antony for the purposes of anti-Arian discourse, harnessing him to an orthodox theological position. However, Antony's ascetic life, which might have implied for most of his contemporaries that perfection is attainable, if under great sacrifices, is only tenuously portrayed as an endorsement or expression of Athanasian ousianic theology. This function is more safely dispensed in Athanasius's doctrinal treatises, where singular agency in salvation is ascribed to Christ alone. Augustine's homosocial community of friends, under pressure through their involvements with patronage in the Roman Empire, encounter the rich young man's story as a challenge to and a way out of their own privileged oppressions. The story's protagonists multiply, and we see both responses to Jesus' call among four friends. Asceticism, for Augustine the condition of a full conversion, finally becomes possible, but even in the act, less significance is given to ascetic life. Augustine pushes the Athanasian de-emphasis of human coredemptive contributions even further, arguing that human self-improvement, even with the help of God's grace, is of little consequence. His theology instead emphasizes the omnipotence of both God and the empire, which leaves little for humans but to acquiesce to authority. His own collusion with these imperial images of divine economy occur in the form of church discipline that draws the line of kinship and household similar to the earlier vision of Irenaeus's *Adversus haereses*. Thus, the Lyonnese presbyter's rhetorical economy created the theological structure that later became the blueprint of church and imperial power/knowledge.

Our ancient men's hysterical fears manifest themselves in the subtexts of their economic tractates and strangely resemble the underlying fears of the notion of scarcity in neoclassical economics. Though their texts manage power, they also economize their fears of lack: Irenaeus's fear of disunity and disintegration of the carefully but fragilely mapped divine economy; Origen's fear of totally letting go of a certain sense of security and convenience, even though he appears less concerned about holding on to the conventions of physical masculinity of his culture or financial independence;

Clement's fear of losing his wealthy congregants, while trying to instill in them a sense of regard for the impoverished members of his congregation by rhetorically constructing a semblance of "economic" exchange between rich and poor Christians; Athanasius's need to assure his young male ascetics of the control over their own lives and bodies they would achieve by buying into the skyrocketing profit margins of the divine exchange rates, while asserting orthodoxy and limiting women's access to either a sense of self-control or possibility to theologize freely; Augustine's hysterical obsession with the lack of mastery over both will and body sees all of that control vanish away in a Christian empire whose mastery is asserted in its attempts to control doctrine; and Augustine's ambivalence toward power, expressed in his longing for an ascetic life as well as his "masterful" applications of power as a church official.

In the modern notion of the *homo economicus,* we have discerned a distant relative of the hysterical male, centered around the basic assumption of the scarcity of goods, always longing for an ever elusive abundance of them.

CHAPTER 3

Ms. Appropriating Properties: Hysterical Women and the Gendering of Redemption

> If there is a self proper to woman, paradoxically it is her capacity to depropriate herself without self-interest: endless body, without "end," without principal "parts"; if she is a whole, it is a whole made up of parts that are wholes, not simple, partial objects but varied entirety, moving and boundless change, a cosmos where eros never stops traveling, vast astral space.
>
> Hélène Cixous and Catherine Clément, *The Newly Born Woman*

Though hysteria has been much maligned and has served as a misogynist label for women who resisted the constraints of patriarchal culture, it has been retrieved by the second wave of feminism, in particular by French feminists Hèléne Cixous and Catherine Clément, as a tool of feminist resistance, intentionally—and mimetically—read and inhabited as a desperate way of voicing dissent through verbal and physical dissonance. In her introduction to Cixous and Clément's *The Newly Born Woman*, Sandra Gilbert writes of the hysteric's exemplary position: "[T]he hysteric is, after all, the creature whose wandering, even wondering, womb manifests the distinctively female bonding, or bondage, of mind and body, the inescapable female connection between creation and procreation, the destiny that is inexorably determined by anatomy."[1]

---

1. Sandra M. Gilbert, "Introduction: A Tarantella of Theory," in *The Newly Born Woman*, by Hélène Cixous and Catherine Clément (Theory and History of Literature; Minneapolis: University of Minnesota Press, 1975), xiii.

For Cixous and Clément, the hysteric constitutes a good example of "the typical woman in all her force."[2] Elaine Showalter has added a new layer of readings of hysteria that are critical of the second wave's fascination with the hysterical, instead emphasizing the need to find feminist "models rather than martyrs."[3] It is between and beyond these critical reappropriations that the present chapter traces women's "capacity to depropriate" throughout ancient Christian texts. This allegedly "feminine" quality is what sets the woman with two copper coins apart from the rich young man; it characterizes female martyrs and their erotic appropriations by male writers, and it is lifted up by patristic commentators in their management of ascetic "brides of Christ." This gender stereotype serves—mimetically rather than essentially—as a heuristic device for constructing a Harawayan "feminist figure" and denizen of the countereconomic sphere.

Certain early Christian texts function as economic tractates that inscribe a divine economy of redemption and portray women who give of their property abundantly and excessively. Thus, female lack emerges as abundant plenitude. We encounter varieties of mis/appropriated and depropriated women: women ambivalently remembered, dismembered, refashioned, naked, clothed, transgendered, queered, managed, and disciplined. The rhetorical economies of these texts attempt to manage the redemption of women's bodies by negotiating women's relationship to their natal *oikos*, their possible departure from and entry into a marital *oikos*, or their attachment to a—often similarly patriarchal—divine *oikos* and husband. The texts—household tractates of sorts, as they debate women's relationship to the natal and divine *oikos*—recommend a certain demeanor, a worthy way for women to suffer or be continent, to give or reserve their faith, bodies, and their money. The texts attempt to exclude and discipline women, to structure notions of women's libidinal, physical, and financial economies, and inscribe women's *soteria* within the divine economy. Jerome and Athanasius praise and decry the real, as well as imagined, actions of these women according to certain household norms. What comes to light in this dialogue between ancient texts and contemporary feminist theory, historical, postcolonial, and theological writings is how the Western intertext has distorted and constructed women, hysterical or not. The polyglossy of voices yields resources for a countereconomic theology, helps to reevaluate hysteria through its mystical connections, decodes the sometimes tragic, sometimes invigorating tricksterlike economies of women's

---

2. Cixous and Clément, *Newly Born Woman*, 154.
3. Elaine Showalter, *Hystories: Hysterical Epidemics and Modern Culture* (New York: Columbia University Press, 1997), 61.

dealings, and begins to map ways in which women may seek a different kind of redemption by incarnating queerly divine economic relations.

In a "cosmos where eros never stops traveling," the martyr Blandina is transgendered, Agnes's executor morphs into a phallic Christ, Eustochium's divine groom confines her to domestic decency, and her mother Paula emerges as a "joyful giver," which strikes her friend Jerome both with admiration and discomfort. Through the figures of these hysterical, deficient, and depropriated women we see a que(e)rying of female agency. Economic agency has functioned differently for women than for men. It is precisely women's earthly deficiency and lack that functions as an exemplary quality in the divine economy. Their scarcity, their lack of funds, of power, or virtues, their willingness to give money—even body and soul—to God is lifted up as the kind of libidinal economy that, paradoxically, gives them access to masculine qualities. They show self-possession that puts them beyond their social station as women, they explode the confines of the *oikos*, they emerge from its closets as que(e)red hysterics. They find that their feminine economies give them masculine properties. But their willingness to give and depropriate themselves and their bodies has also been deftly exploited, both in cultural and religious contexts. These women's honorary masculine qualities and privileges are anxiously economized by their male commentators and hagiographers. Lack of self-possession and the propensity to give and suffer have also held women in situations of domestic, patriarchal, theological, and colonial violence. It is this double bind that we will critically investigate for a more profound que(e)rying of female agency in a countereconomic context. The economy of gender roles fluctuates: these women are widows, virgins, martyrs; they emerge as "Saint Hysteria,"[4] are disowned yet self-possessed, or inappropriately wasteful with their wealth. The types they represent also resemble Haraway's "feminist figures," emerging as tricksterlike participants in the divine countereconomy, where neither perfect plenitude nor complete destitution but rather multiple "misappropriations" and exchanges take place.[5] Can this saintly mystic—if female mystics are under the suspicion of being hysterics, this Saint Hysteria—provide a model for living rather than an exemplary martyrdom? Might Thecla, the Christian trickster martyr who survived and then managed to crossdress and preach her way out of the patriarchal *oikos*, help point toward new ways at constructing divine economy?

---

4. See Christina Mazzoni, *Saint Hysteria: Neurosis, Mysticism, and Gender in European Culture* (Ithaca, N.Y.: Cornell University Press, 1996).

5. Donna J. Haraway, "Ecce Homo, Ain't (Ar'n't) I a Woman, and Inappropriate/d Others: The Human in a Post-Humanist Landscape," in *Feminists Theorize the Political* (ed. Judith Butler and Joan Scott; New York: Routledge, 1992), 86.

Bottoming Out: A Widow's Bio-Power[6]

> He sat down opposite the treasury, and watched the crowd putting money into the treasury. Many rich people put in large sums. A poor widow came and put in two small copper coins, which are worth a penny. Then he called his disciples and said to them, "Truly I tell you, this poor widow has put in more than all those who are contributing to the treasury. For all of them have contributed out of their abundance; but she out of her poverty has put in everything she had, all she had to live on." (Mark 12:41–44)

I've been lookin' 'round and watchin' things, and I know a little mite 'bout Woman's Rights, too.

> Sojourner Truth, "I Suppose I Am about the Only Colored Women That Goes about to Speak for the Rights of Colored Women"

Joel Williams has argued that the poor widow in Mark 12:41–44 is a figure that "like Bartimaeus and the scribe ... stands in contrast to the rich man."[7] Though there are parallels between the two pericopes—the topic of rich and poor and a context in which Jesus instructs his disciples—Williams observes that both figures differ in their economy of lack: "The poor widow gives all out of her lack (*hustereseos*, 12.44), while the rich man lacks (*husterei*, 10.21) one thing, a willingness to give all and follow Jesus."[8] She, the rich man's social inferior, a woman, a widow, and a person without her own income, throws away her life, her *bios*, and "gives all she has ... in contrast to the rich man who is commanded to give all that he has ... but refuses to do so."[9] A proverbial image of selfless giving and humility, she has been held up as an example in a Christian "gift economy," exemplifying the

---

6. Foucault describes "bio-power" as the notion of power over life and death that is exerted either by the paterfamilias or by the sovereign. In Mark's text, however, the widow—whose culture employs her biology as a pretext to deprive her of bio-power—takes charge of her own assets and asserts her own power over life and death. See Michel Foucault, *The History of Sexuality: An Introduction* (New York: Vintage, 1990), 1:135–36, 140.

7. Joel F. Williams, *Other Followers of Jesus: Minor Characters as Major Figures in Mark's Gospel* (Journal for the Study of the New Testament Supplement Series 102; Sheffield: JSOT Press, 1994), 178.

8. Ibid.

9. Ibid. Bonnie Thurston writes that the term "'widow' frequently connoted not only marital but also economic status. A widow was often 'left without' money or financial support as well as (or as a result of being) 'left without' a husband." Poor widows were frequently financially vulnerable and often needed and at times received specific care from the community or the church. Within the church, they also experienced the possibility of a certain status, as it appears that

"proper" investment in the heavenly economy, and her action, unlike that of the young man, is commended by Jesus. Cyprian's treatise on works and alms links the rich man tightly to the widow, who represents the poor he is refusing to give to. Thus, "the widow has cast in two farthings into the offerings of God, that it may be more abundantly evident that he who hath pity on the poor lendeth to God." But, more poignantly, the widow, a symbol of barren femininity—a woman without a man to provide seed—comes to stand for genitivity,[10] for property and wealth, since "the Lord" regarded "her work not for its abundance, but for its intention, and considering not how much, but *from* how much, she had given." Thus, Cyprian proclaims, "Let the rich be ashamed of their barrenness and unbelief. The widow, the widow needy in means, is found rich in works." Thus, she "gives, whom it behooved to receive, that we may know thence what punishment awaits the barren rich man."[11] Despite the obvious subversiveness of those readings, most traditional interpretations do not challenge but rather support potentially oppressive readings of the text. While the text inverts social convention by lifting up the lowest, it also reinscribes the hierarchies it seeks to subvert. Even so, the narrative might reveal an additional economic and redemptive subtext, a "hidden transcript" to the widow's gift, a "discourse that takes place 'offstage,' beyond direct observation by powerholders."[12] She may even function as an ancestor of what the transgendered economist Donald/Deirdre McCloskey has called a *"femina economica,"* an economic agent imbued with "feminine solidarity." She thus can be represented, in McCloskey's terms, as countering the image of the explicitly male *"vir economicus,"* whose character resembles that of a "cross between Rambo and an investment banker" with "certain boyish charms."[13] McCloskey further explains that

---

"widow" was a church office. In the third century, often depending on their financial status, widows at times occupied fairly high offices within the church, which was, however, likely replaced by the office of the "deaconess." Bonnie Bowman Thurston, *The Widows: A Women's Ministry in the Early Church* (Minneapolis: Fortress, 1989), 10, 35, 104–5.

10. Again, I am referring to Stephen Ross's use of the term "genitivity" as describing the connection between male ownership and the ability to generate, reproduce, procreate children, wealth, etc. from this *ousia*. See Stephen David Ross, *The Gift of Property: Having the Good: Betraying Genitivity, Economy, and Ecology: An Ethic of the Earth* (Albany, N.Y.: SUNY Press, 2001).

11. The English translation of Cyprian's *Works and Almsgiving* follows Alexander Roberts and James Donaldson, eds., *Fathers of the Third Century: Hippolytus, Cyprian, Caius, Novatian*, (vol. 5 of *Ante-Nicene Fathers*; Peabody, Mass.: Hendrickson, 1994).

12. James C. Scott, *Domination and the Arts of Resistance: Hidden Transcripts* (New Haven, Conn.: Yale University Press, 1990), 4.

13. McCloskey apparently did not only critique the masculinity of economic agency but he himself found the *femina economica* also physically more "inhabitable." Donald McCloskey is

neo-classical economics does not take solidarity seriously, except implicitly within the family and within the firm.... No wonder. *Vir economicus* sporting around the market place is stereotypically male: rule driven, simplemindedly selfish, uninterested in building relations for their own sake.... When it suits his convenience he routinely defects from social arrangements, dumping externalities on the neighbors. *Femina economica*, by contrast, would more often walk down the beach to dispose of her McDonald's carton in a trash bin—not because she reasons in the manner of Kant (and again of men) that one must test one's behavior by hypothetical universalization ... but because she feels solidarity with others. It is simply not done to dump trash on the beach; we do not treat our neighbors that way.[14]

Most feminist economists would probably challenge McCloskey's characterization, since they would hesitate to reinforce economic gender stereotypes. Likewise, my concern here is not to solidify patterns but to analyze how such gender stereotypes structure Christian figural imagery and produce reality. Might McCloskey's *femina economica* be uncovered in biblical and patristic texts? If the gospel narrative's widow lacks in the "virtues" of the *vir economicus*, if she is cast as the depropriated Other of the rich young man, might she offer hope for the deconstruction of the dualistic gender economies of her—and perhaps even our—culture? Might the queering of the sexually and economically stereotypical/hysterical female begin with her?

The widow and her copper coins are couched in a net of Markan stories that frame Jesus' observations about this "minor" female character in a sequence of texts on Jesus' tenuous relationship to the temple in Jerusalem (12:13–38) and a preview of his passion in chapter 13. In the eyes of Mark's Jesus, the widow represents a notable example of an investor in the divine economy or *basileia*—a woman lacking in resources but whose ability to give and to empty herself completely is a stark example of absolute giving, an embodiment of a feminine emptying self. Predictably enough, most exegetes interpret Jesus' words as a commendation of her exemplary giving: "Truly I tell you, this poor widow has put in more than all those who are contributing to the treasury. For all of them have given out of their abundance; but she out of her lack threw in all she had, her entire life *[bios]*." She gives out of her lack, her deficiency, *ek hustereseos autes* (Mark 12:44).

---

today Deirdre McCloskey, a transsexual economist. See her memoir about changing gender. Deirdre N. McCloskey, *Crossing* (Chicago: University of Chicago Press, 1999).

14. Donald N. McCloskey, "Some Consequences of a Conjective Economics," in *Beyond Economic Man* (ed. Julie A. Nelson and Marianne A. Ferber; Chicago: University of Chicago Press, 1993), 79.

As far as gender stereotypes are concerned, the physicality of women has often been held to be constructive of their economic gender, and thus women have been encased as "monuments of lack,"[15] not unlike the widow in Mark's account. The link between femininity, lack, and the phenomenon entitled "hysteria" is ancient and well documented in philosophical, medical, and religious sources. For Aristotle, as paraphrased by Keller, women are deviant "monsters," and their monstrosity is defined by a lack of physical and mental characteristics. They "lack 'active' intellectual souls, possessing only lower 'passive' intelligence. Inadequately informed, lacking the power to contribute form to the offspring of their bodies, women fall short of the full actuality of a substantial individual. . . . Women, lacking real ontological independence, remain exceptions to the norm."[16]

Similarly, we find hints of feminine "lack" or "deficiency" in a number of gnostic texts, such as the *Apocryphon of John*. When Sophia "conceived a thought of her own," the product, because it lacks the consent and approval of both the "Spirit" and her "consort," is "imperfect and different from her appearance," "dissimilar to the likeness of its mother." In short, Sophia by herself creates an inferior, degenerate monster, the "lion-faced serpent" Yaltabaoth.[17] Her creative act is inferior, deficient, and imperfect because it lacks the input, the consent, or the form that the male partner would provide. Paula Fredriksen ventures that "suffering, ignorance and evil" are the "leitmotifs" of gnostic cosmogonies, and that the Greek loan word *husterema* (deficiency), found in Coptic texts of Nag Hammadi, is one "minor source for these themes."[18] This *husterema*, a cognate of *hustera* (womb) and *hustero* (to lack something, to be deficient), signifies the inferior, defective quality of the gnostic Sophia's actions, and offspring in gnostic cosmogonies Thus, the womb was designated as a "void" category that embodied lack. In Greek medical science, "hurtful disorderly wombs and deficiencies of femaleness" occur with a certain frequency in texts by Galen, Soranus, Aretaeus, and Hippocrates, where they are seen as the "seat and cause of a disease peculiar to women, *husterike pnix*."[19] This female condition, "hysterical suffocation" or "wandering womb," is imagined to be restless for lack of seminal irrigation. This arid lack of intercourse was thought to send the womb itinerant within the body, where it would cause

---

15. Cixous and Clément, *Newly Born Woman*, 68.
16. Catherine Keller, *From a Broken Web: Separation, Sexism, and Self* (Boston: Beacon, 1986), 50.
17. James M. Robinson, gen. ed., *The Nag Hammadi Library in English* (3d ed.; San Francisco: Harper & Row, 1990), 110.
18. Paula Fredriksen, "Hysteria and the Gnostic Myths of Creation," *Vigiliae Christianae* 33 (1979): 287.
19. Ibid., 288.

suffocation, muteness, exhaustion, and other mysterious female conditions. Within a gnostic universe, the symptom of sleepiness ascribed to women in medical texts is attributed to the uninitiated "dweller in the lower realm."[20] Women's supposed weakness, their alleged lack of biopower, is thus partially inscribed in the body of Mark's widow, who becomes a prime example of giving, in part because her culture's framework constructs her as weak, deficient, needy, and empty.

All the more powerful is her excessive, "hysterical" giving, which elicits a certain discomfort. Yet her strangely excessive divestment signifies her appropriation of a place of wealth in the divine *oikonomia*. Economically vulnerable, without protection and attachment to a man, the widow lacks in wealth, in funds to sustain herself. This woman—after the death of her husband without an *oikos* and thus a hysterically wandering womb again—lacks economic as well as symbolic capital. Paradoxically, she becomes the perfect embodiment of abundance as well as of lack. She gives excessively, out of her lack, without regard for the trifling of economic capital or substance that remains her own. For Douglas Meeks, as for most biblical exegetes, the widow remains an unambiguous exemplary giver, "so that all people in the household may have property."[21] In fact, he argues that "even though she is one of the poor and under the protection of Yahweh, she holds nothing back. She shares unconditionally with the poor. For the sake of others she gives her livelihood and thereby enters into the new property claim on the livelihood of God's household."[22]

Her "whole-hearted" sacrifice will put to shame those men who have much and give little: "The poor widow also exemplifies for the disciples the type of complete giving that Jesus desires of his followers."[23] Yet her gift seems to confirm that selfless women can be counted on to be endless givers, emptying themselves out of their lack—which becomes abundance in the divine *oikos*. The widow thus, according to Meeks, is an exemplary member of "God's household" in which those who give their property, who empty themselves, enter into "the new property claim" of the new, divine *oikos*. Is the widow's currency perhaps misappropriated through her coinage as exemplary for investment in the divine *oikos*? Might her "gift" and her "deficiency" be re/appropriated differently, rather than, by way of idealization, running the danger of sanctioning the exploitation of the poorest?

---

20. Ibid., 287–89.
21. M. Douglas Meeks, *God the Economist: The Doctrine of God and Political Economy* (Minneapolis: Fortress, 1989), 119.
22. Ibid., 119.
23. Williams, *Other Followers of Jesus*, 177.

Women, "The Gift," and Property

> Gain your freedom, get rid of everything, vomit up everything, give up everything. Give up absolutely everything, do you hear me? *All of it!* Give up your goods. Done? Don't keep anything; whatever you value, give it up.
>
> Hélène Cixous, "Coming to Writing"

Héléne Cixous and Jacques Derrida have, independently of each other, critically engaged Marcel Mauss's classic anthropological monograph, *The Gift*. Derrida avers that though Mauss spends an entire essay trying to convince himself and his readers that a phenomenon such as the gift without strings attached exists, he fails miserably. All Mauss demonstrates in the end is that the gift in the anthropological research he has conducted appears always to already presuppose an exorbitant return that can ruin both the giver and eventually the receiver, who, in turn, will have to top the initial investment. Thus, the circle of return, of economy, is never broken or even challenged. From this, Derrida theorizes the "impossibility of the gift." He continues:

> One could go so far as to say that a work as monumental as Marcel Mauss's *The Gift* speaks of everything but the gift: It deals with economy, exchange, contract (*do ut des*), it speaks of raising the stakes, sacrifice, gift, and countergift—in short, everything that in the thing impels the gift *and* the annulment of the gift.[24]

Though Mauss may have had a somewhat romantic vision for a precapitalist and precolonial economy that he hoped to find preserved in a gift economy not based on the exchange of goods on a contractual or monetary basis, his research eventually unveiled a nonmonetary exchange that could hardly be described as a "gift" economy. Instead, Mauss effectively described how the giving of gifts indebted the recipient to give back with an increase. This potlatch economy of gift and return remains continuous and circular, as far as he could see, and was often more ruinous to the fortunes of the families and tribes involved than that of a less exorbitant monetary economy.[25]

---

24. Jacques Derrida, *Given Time: I. Counterfeit Money* (trans. Peggy Kamuf; Chicago: University of Chicago Press, 1992), 24.
25. Marcel Mauss, *The Gift: Forms and Functions of Exchange in Archaic Societies* (New York: W. W. Norton & Co., 1967), 6, 10; and Derrida, *Given Time*, 12, 24.

While Derrida deconstructs Mauss's romantic notions of a precapitalist gift, some feminist theorists have approached the topic differently and pursued the suggestion that a gift economy may allow women access to a freedom that originates from excessive divestment. Cixous relates the gift specifically to women's freedom: giving frees from the self, thus liberates, and announces loss of a woman's self through which her freedom comes.[26] But, beyond her attempt to reappropriate a problematic female gender stereotype for subversion, this strategy can help to "ms.appropriate" the problematic heritage of millennia of Christian theologies that have read the emptying and reserveless giving, especially of women, as the ultimate gain in the divine economy, both challenging and reinforcing the stereotypical male urge to cling to economic and phallic power.

Cixous at times suspiciously eyes the viability of the gift, and it appears as if "both Cixous, and perhaps to an even greater extent, Derrida, are struck by the 'impossibility' of the gift."[27] Yet both are more concerned with the possibility of giving a gift than they are with the problematic nature of giving when it is forced on the other who is supposed to give without return, often never to be reimbursed. Perhaps it is just as well that giving always seems to include an aspect of return, if often not one that would easily be recognized as "just."[28] Though Cixous recognizes the subversiveness of complete giving, as in the epigraph to this section, she argues that even outside the masculine economy, "really, there is no 'free' gift. You never give something for nothing. But all the difference lies in the why and how of the gift, in the values that the gesture of giving affirms, causes to circulate; in the type of profit the giver draws from the gift and the use to which he or she puts it."[29]

Irigaray likewise insists on the gift as a component of the "new feminine identity" and its specific economic relations, while insisting that women and intellectuals be paid for the kind of work they contribute: "It is thought to be normal, moral, a sign of good policy, for a woman to receive no payment, or low payment, to be asked to do charity work."[30] Therefore, she

---

26. Cixous and Clément point out that rather than restricting this gift economy to women in an essentializing move, they intend to "avoid the confusion man/masculine, woman/feminine: for there are some men who do not repress their femininity, some women who, more or less strongly, inscribe their masculinity.... We have to be careful not to lapse smugly or blindly into an essentialist interpretation, as both Freud and Jones, for example, risked doing in their different ways." This feminine economy does not, however, clearly forestall the danger of gender essentialism either. See Cixous and Clément, *Newly Born Woman*, 81.
27. Judith Still, *Feminine Economies: Thinking against the Market in the Enlightenment and the Late Twentieth Century* (Manchester: Manchester University Press, 1997), 169.
28. For a more theologically slanted discussion of the gift, see John D. Caputo and Michael J. Scanlon, *God, the Gift, and Postmodernism* (Bloomington: Indiana University Press, 1999).
29. Cixous and Clément, *Newly Born Woman*, 87.
30. Luce Irigaray, *Sexes and Genealogies* (New York: Columbia University Press, 1993), 82.

concludes, "it seems impossible to make any durable and deep impact on social relations, language, art in general, without modifying the economic system of exchanges. The one goes with the other."[31] Yet the ambivalence of such a "feminine" mode of giving, the difficulty of how to effect such a change, permeates the texts of the West.

The widow's self-emptying contribution, unlike the rich young man's inability to let go, seems to require no comment or discussion about a final payoff or various levels of gratification. Her "gift" appears to speak for itself; it is—as Derrida would say about the economy of *différance*—"an expenditure without reserve" that "apparently interrupts every economy."[32] But is her giving well described as an absolute gift, with no strings attached? Does she succeed? Is her divestment complete? And even if it is, should it be?

Being "designated donors" has furthered women's exploitation even as it has kept open a gap of subversion in an economy of "getting even": the "freedom to give" can become an instrument to enforce women's giving "passivity" in economic relationships by effectively idealizing it and turning it into a virtue diametrically juxtaposed to male economic activity. These well-known trappings forestall a wholesale embrace of woman as the subversive giver, the ideal giver. Cixous, while cautioning against the dangers of giving for women, refuses to give up on the subversive power of the gift, praising, so writes Judith Still, the "psychic benefit to the subject of superabundant generosity."[33]

Feminist theorists have long pointed to the conjunction between women as exchange objects between men and a masculine and hierarchical conception of God. Cixous has observed the tendency of patriarchal societies to categorize women as property even while gauging women's economic "value" by their lack of visible genitals, thus identifying them as hysterics. This lack is assigned to women by a certain kind of economy, a system of exchange exemplified by *le propre,* the notion of property that represents the "Empire of the Self-Same," where "the same masters dominate history from the beginning, inscribing on it the marks of their appropriating economy: history, as a story of phallocentrism, hasn't moved except to repeat itself."[34]

In this economy, this "history of propriation," it is "*sexual* difference with an *equality* of force" that "triggers desire, as a desire—for appropriation."[35]

---

31. Ibid.
32. Jacques Derrida, *Margins of Philosophy* (trans. Alan Bass; Chicago: University of Chicago Press, 1981), 19.
33. Still, *Feminine Economies,* 168.
34. Cixous and Clément, *Newly Born Woman,* 79.
35. Ibid.

"All history is inseparable from economy in the limited sense of the word, that of a certain kind of savings. Man's return—the relationship linking him profitably to man-being, conserving it. This economy, as a law of appropriation, is a phallocentric production."[36]

The greatest fears in this hom(m)o-sexual economy of appropriation are the usual Freudian fear of separation from and the lack of a phallus.[37] Gain is crucial, and not even a gift is given without profitable return through the phallocentric "law of appropriation."[38] Irigaray's work equally exposes the phallocentric structures of libidinal, relational, and monetary economies that either place women outside of exchange relations or use them solely as exchange objects: "In our social order, women are 'products' used and exchanged by men. Their status is that of merchandise, of 'commodities.'"[39] A hom(m)o-sexual economy, according to Irigaray, is "based on the exchange of women" (and other properties) between men.[40] Women themselves are not considered economic subjects and thus have no property, and no properties. As Levi-Strauss observes, furthermore, women not only lack property, but the men observed "lack" women *as* property. Thus, Irigaray continues, referring to the anthropologist Levi-Strauss's conjecture about polygamy as the origin of scarcity: "Why this characteristic of scarcity, given the biological equilibrium between male and female births? Because the 'deep polygamous tendency, which exists among all men, always makes the number of available women seem insufficient.'"[41] Thus, Levi-Strauss links economic scarcity to a low supply of women, whose lack of place in the hom(m)osexual economy marks them as rare properties.[42] The economic scarcity of women as products and sources of wealth seems an odd reversal and yet a confirmation of their bodies' lack of certain

---

36. Ibid., 80.
37. Ibid.
38. Ibid. See also the excellent use of Cixous in S. Brent Plate and Edna M. Rodriguez Mangual, "The Gift That Stops Giving: Hélène Cixous's 'Gift' and the Shunammite Woman," *Biblical Interpretation* 7, no. 2 (1999): 113–32.
39. Luce Irigaray, *This Sex Which Is Not One* (trans. Catherine Porter; Ithaca, N.Y.: Cornell University Press, 1985), 84.
40. Especially poignant is the collusion in modern America of slavery and misogyny, so that abolitionists and women's suffragists often found common cause in fighting the economic disenfranchisement of women and slaves. Until this day, women and African Americans are disproportionately poor, with Latinos increasingly taking the place of upwardly mobile African Americans. It seems that the upward mobility offered by late capitalism requires its currently weakest and newest members to continue giving excessively so that others can begin to or continue to enter the circle of appropriation. Can we overcome this economic *circulus vitiosus*, perhaps in part by deconstructing the ruinous gap between gift and economy?
41. Irigaray, *This Sex Which Is Not One*, 170.
42. Levi-Strauss argues this even though historical data would suggest that during times of war men become scarce.

organs and facilities. These "scarce" women, who themselves own nothing and who initially appear only as symbolic capital, subsequently become valued by a hom(m)osexual economy, which converts them into a product to be exchanged through the use of currency and sold for a profit.[43] The profit, however, always "refer[s] back to men . . . [women] always pass from one man to the another, from one group of men to another."[44] Thus, doubly lacking—both in physical attributes and in quantities to satisfy the desires of men—in a "hom(m)o-sexual monopoly," these impoverished women lack properties, propriety, and possessions. Irigaray, in a mimetic investment into this feminine economy of plenteous lack, has suggested the possibility of "exchange without property. The possibility of property, without being fixed in it. What is possible in 'proper' without being transfixed in it."[45]

A sustained critical inquiry into the possibility of a pure, absolute gift is part of a constructive theology of gift/ing. If feminist theorist Toril Moi were to consider the economic gender of Mark's widow, she might well read her as placed within a femininely gendered "Realm of the *Gift*," and she might assign a masculinely gendered "Realm of the *Proper*" to the economy of Matthew's young man.[46] Cixous's and Irigaray's construction of feminine economies thus critically questions notions of properties and property, going so far as to deny the very notion of the "propre."[47] Property, they argue, tends to be identified with a masculine economy, while a feminist realm may exist outside of such an economy, and in the absence of ownership. But is exchange without "property" possible? Is it thinkable or even desirable that a gift, according to Irigaray, has no object, has no "for," is entirely disinterested?[48] What "is" property, if it "is," and how is this notion caught up in constructions of gender properties and gendered properties? How can women relate to property, to what they still might have to name as their own psychic, material "substance"? Must we agree with Irigaray that "it seems impossible to make any durable and deep impact on social relations, language, art in general, without modifying the economic system of

---

43. Pierre Bourdieu writes the following about the convertibility of symbolic capital: "Thus we see that symbolic capital, which in the form of the prestige and renown attached to a family and a name is readily convertible back into economic capital, is perhaps the most valuable form of accumulation in a society in which the severity of the climate . . . and the limited technical resources . . . demand collective labour." Bourdieu, *Outline of a Theory of Practice* (Cambridge: Cambridge University Press, 1977), 179.
44. Irigaray, *This Sex Which Is Not One*, 171.
45. Luce Irigaray, *Elemental Passions* (New York: Routledge, 1992), 44.
46. Toril Moi, *Sexual/Textual Politics: Feminist Literary Theory* (London: Routledge, 1985), 110.
47. Still, *Feminine Economies*, 174.
48. So at least according to Justith Still's reading. Still, *Feminine Economies*, 174, 175, 177.

exchanges"?[49] And if so, what does that mean for language and for the form of the more or less artful wordings of theology?

Not all exegetes accept the traditional reading of women's gifting, or, in this case, the destitute widow's self-emptying. Addison Wright, for example, resists the classical commendation of the female giver. He has Jesus exclaim in shock and horror at the widow's destitution, expressing strong disapproval of the tradition's easy "acceptance" of her gift.[50] Wright argues, against the exegetical consensus, that the passage does not express a commendation but that Jesus' words decry the exploitation of widows, similar to the passage in Mark 12:40: "[The scribes] devour widow's houses and for the sake of appearance say long prayers." Thus, Jesus' words would represent a lament that relates back to the exhortation of the scribes. Wright suggests that "she had been taught and encouraged by religious leaders to donate as she does, and Jesus condemns the value system that motivates her action, and he condemns the people who conditioned her to do it."[51] Elizabeth Struthers Malbon, though largely in agreement with Wright, takes exception to reading the text exclusively in this manner. Agreeing with his contextualization—reading Jesus' remarks as part and parcel of how the gospel's author positions Jesus in relation to the Jerusalem temple cult—Malbon yet wants to retain the possibility of other interpretations and readings. Preferring the "wealth of readings" of the poor widow's hidden interpretive treasures, Malbon also considers the possibility of reading the widow as a foreshadowing of Jesus' kenotic life and death in the figure of a woman.[52]

But certainly the rich readings of the poor widow need not stop here! Might one even read the widow's donation as an oblique assertion of self-confidence? Insisting on the value and worth of her own property, small though it may be, the widow holds on to a sense of self-worth and of being able to make a difference, despite the large amounts given by other donors. The widow appropriates her own version of what Foucault called "biopower" as she throws in her entire life, *holon ton bion autes* (Mark 12:44). Convinced that her contribution is important and matters in the scale of things, she "owns" the temple as the house of God, asserting that she too is responsible for its upkeep. Perhaps her dignity is at stake here. By giving, she asserts her self-worth and her relation to a community of worshipers.

---

49. Irigaray, *Sexes and Genealogies*, 82.
50. For an enlightening account of Wright's approach, see Elizabeth Struthers Malbon, *In the Company of Jesus: Characters in Mark's Gospel* (Louisville, Ky.: Westminster John Knox, 2000), 173.
51. Addison G. Wright, "The Widow's Mites: Praise or Lament?—A Matter of Context," *Catholic Biblical Quarterly* 44 (1982): 262, quoted in Malbon, *Company of Jesus*, 172.
52. The widow as the emptying self thus might also offer a primary foil for a Christology that sees several of Jesus' words and actions as directly related to the ironic Markan interpretation of the abrogation and destruction of the temple cult. Malbon, *Company of Jesus*, 177, 188.

Within Mark's rhetorical economy her act of giving is written as the re-en-gendering of salvation and is eminently achievable through what seem to be feminine characteristics—lack and the excessive ability to give—redefined as wealth in the heavenly *oikonomia*. Subverting her economic status by giving the little she has as though it mattered, she, like other women in early Christianity, resists her economic marginalization as best she can from her own particular location, though it may not look like "correct" resistance to contemporary purist forms of feminism.

Tragically, and often ironically, images and acts of women's giving have contributed to the submission of women throughout the world as well as to the exploitation of other subaltern subjects through colonial and neocolonial enterprises. Inspired by the widow's story, American "females" pooled their mites to aid the colonial missionary quest, to spread Bibles and hymn books through groups such as the Cent and Mite societies.[53] In the early 1800s, the idea for the Cent Society was conceived at a dinner meeting that seems to echo themes from Jesus' first public miracle. The transformation of water into wine this time is played out in reverse, if you will, as a luxurious glass of wine is transformed into a widow's mite to be given for the growth of the kingdom of God. The scene is a guest meal in a white missionary's household in Boston in 1802. One of the male guests remarks that by saving a glass of wine a week, one could set aside a small amount of money that could be given to buy gospels and tracts for missionary purposes. This was reminiscent of the widow with the two copper coins and what American women of the time, who lacked ownership of funds but who at least had the power to divert some of the funds needed to oversee domestic affairs (by saving on "frivolous" and "extravagant" expenses) toward worthy "Christian" causes, could do. This context, of course, is vastly different from that of the *Sitz im Leben* we might assume for the gospel account. The small sum of money involved in this salvific exchange meant very different things in each of these contexts. From the beginning, the Cent Society did not ask for "her entire life," nor did it even conceive of any other form of female giving than the diversion of the funds allotted to women by fathers and husbands, the owners of substance/*ousia*. Thus, the mites in question accrued through the curbing of domestic consumption for missionary causes. For white middle-class citizens in support of missionary causes, the denial of a "little thing,"[54] then, was about saving a penny a week.[55] Still, women's pennies amassed to a

---

53. Robert Pierce Beaver, *American Protestant Women in World Mission: History of the First Feminist Movement in North America* (Grand Rapids: Eerdmans, 1980), 14.
54. Ibid.,14.
55. Membership dues in the Cent societies amounted to fifty-two cents a year. This simple practice may have helped the organizations to spread rapidly.

"collective purchasing power of thousands of pennies that made each single cent seem significant."[56] This particularly caught "the feminine imagination," perhaps because like the widow in Mark, these women did not have that much to give. These cents were all they had (power over).

Hence, we find an interesting contrast and similarity, a form of mimicry/mockery in the dis/connection between "a woman who might be able to give if she denied herself some little thing"[57] and the widow in Mark, whose gift of a little amounts to her whole life, all she can give. Nobody keeps the widow from giving, which turns out not to have been true for the women involved in Cent societies. The widow has neither a father nor a husband. No one, not even Jesus, keeps her from "throwing her life away." This proved far more complicated in the United States of the nineteenth century. There, women—whether married or not—were excluded from missionary activity, except for the collection of funds. Until the 1800s, there is no mention of women's activity in records of mission. Yet, many women were increasingly discontented with their limited role, especially since their religious zeal often exceeded that of men. Soon the Cent societies spread across New England, and these women find power and agency in (not surprisingly) helping others, in charitable works, that is, within the well-prescribed confines of male-sanctioned female activity. These societies remained, however, auxiliary to the work of "our fathers and brethren," though the collective funds amounted to quite a sum.[58] The fundraising abilities of the women involved soon opened the doors to at least token female members of the male-only missionary societies.[59] (Money seems invariably to open doors.) Women acquired and supplied capital; hence, they also obtained social capital that transposed them into people to reckon with—quasi-males, because of the substance/*ousia* they offered. Over time, more specific philanthropies and plans for social action arose once women were no longer content to give only pennies or a few dollars. For example, women began distributing coal to "the meritorious poor."[60] So, on the surface at least, women slowly gained more power and influence because they wanted to give more. Because some of these causes were controversial (the reform of prostitutes, for example), women's societies became more controversial.[61] Notwithstanding these partial endorsements

---

56. Beaver, *American Protestant Women*, 13–14.
57. Ibid., 14.
58. Ibid., 20.
59. Ibid., 24.
60. Ibid., 28.
61. R. P. Beaver mentions a sermon by one Walter Harris that refers to the women mentioned in Luke 8:1–3 as ministering to Christ from their substance/*ousia*. However, the Greek is *ek ton*

of giving, criticism of these societies and their supposed lack of "propriety" fueled ongoing controversies about the "improper" nature of these societies as their influence increased.

The collection of these trifles occurred within the colonialist setting of missionary enterprises of the day. Thus, the "mission statement" of the Boston Female Society for Missionary Purposes announces the quest for a membership of "females who are disposed to contribute their mite towards so noble a design as diffusion of the gospel light among the shades of darkness and superstition."[62] We might then ask where these funds were put to "mission," to "prosper" for the kingdom, and who the recipients of this mission were. Where in the British Empire or U.S. territories did these funds go? Main missionary targets were "Indians, heathens at the ends of the earth,"[63] and settlers on the American frontier moving rapidly toward the West. There was also a specific mission instituted in Boston to further Christianity among Jews, in response to the eschatological belief that there has to be an "ingathering" of Jews before the Second Coming of Christ could proceed. It was then only as missionary wives, and more slowly as single women missionaries, that women of European descent found their unfurling agency tragically intertwined with the projects of imperial colonialism.

The Rhetorical Economies of Martyrdom

> I will later place the mobilizing of woman into *Sati* with the place of the epic instance of "heroism"—suicide in the name of "nation," "martyrdom"—suicide in the name of "God"; and other species of self-"sacrifice." These are transcendental figurations of the (agent of the) gift of time. The feminist project is not simply to stage the woman as victim, but to ask: Why does "husband" become an appropriate name for *radical* alterity? Why is "to be" equal to "to be wife"?
>
> Gayatri Spivak, *A Critique of Postcolonial Reason: Toward a History of the Vanishing Present*

---

huparchonton autais, again pointing us back to that which the women had power to administer, which did not involve the owning of property, it would seem. Harris reiterates the assumption that the widow's contribution is only a small amount. He admonishes women against putting their "whole lives" into it, but reads the text in such a way that it appears to point toward the rich man who keeps power, who hangs on to his *ousia*. Women are kept from giving all they have to offer, so that men can keep the power they have. And Jesus is called on the witness stand as the (male) enforcer of this sexual economy. Beaver, *American Protestant Women*, 30.

62. Ibid., 14.

63. Beaver does not specify whether "Indians" here designated Native Americans. Beaver, *American Protestant Women*, 17.

Spivak's careful investigation of *sati* (sacrifice) and martyrdom links the gendered and theological economies of Christian colonizers with the distribution of gender and religion among the Indian colonized, observing how gender, religion, and power are negotiated along the fault lines of culture. Thus, she reminds us that the ambivalent nature of victimization, resistance, and martyrdom is hardly restricted to Christian texts. The networked oppressions that crisscross the bodies of women in places occupied by Western colonizers—whose motives were then, and are now, often economic—are highly complex. With little room to resist, some forms of resistance exhibited by women in postcolonial contexts might remain unrecognized by Western eyes, since they are embedded in subtexts of patriarchy, nationalism, and capitalism. Mary Daly, for example, denounces the inconsistency of Frantz Fanon's "righteous indignation . . . against the French, coupled with his obstinate refusal to see the dehumanizing conditions imposed on Algerian women by Algerian men for what they are."[64] Gayatri Spivak would maintain that "white women—from the nineteenth-century British Missionary Registers to Mary Daly—have not produced an alternative understanding" of *sati*, the self-immolation by some Indian widows on their husbands' funeral pyre.[65] Similarly, Marcella Althaus-Reid notes how liberation theology falls short of its "liberalist intent basically due to its colonialist stand and its stereotyped heterosexual principles."[66]

The nested oppressions that become visible at these intersections are some of the blind spots that those engaged in liberative theological struggles had better not ignore. Resistance to oppression might take many different forms and shapes, to the point of not being recognizable for those on the outside. James Scott argues that the strategy of the "hidden transcript" allows the masking of dissent: "[T]he greater the disparity in power between dominant and subordinate and the more arbitrarily it is exercised, the more the public transcript will take on a stereotyped, ritualistic cast."[67] Camouflaged, the "hidden transcript" works as subtext. The postcolonial concept of hyperbolic mimicry resembles a similarly covert, though effective, strategy to expose subtle, insidious power structures by mimicking them. Homi Bhabha has described mimicry as a strategy that "must continually produce its slippage, its excess, its difference," is "stricken with

---

64. Mary Daly, *Beyond God the Father: Toward a Philosophy of Women's Liberation* (Boston: Beacon, 1973), 53.
65. Gayatri Spivak, *A Critique of Postcolonial Reason: Toward a History of the Vanishing Present* (Cambridge: Harvard University Press, 1999), 287.
66. Marcella Althaus-Reid, *Indecent Theology: Theological Perversions in Sex, Gender, and Politics* (London: Routledge, 2001), 77.
67. Scott, *Domination and the Arts of Resistance*, 3.

indeterminacy," and consists of "at once resemblance and menace."[68] Mimicry can be applied by colonizers as a tool intended to produce submission—Bhabha uses the example of British colonists encouraging Native Americans to mimick the British "motherland"—and by the colonized whose mimic efforts may turn into mockery and thus acts as a menace to the empire, in a refusal to completely accept its power. In order to remain effective, mimicry cannot but remain within this ambivalence, this slippage, though, as is the case with slippery tools and two-edged swords: they can cut both ways. Here as elsewhere, the replication of oppression within liberative movements might manifest itself again, physically, textually, and otherwise.[69] Thus, the futile search for an elusive "politics of purity" in liberative concerns, of which Keller warns, might as well be abandoned.[70] The exercise of countereconomic strategies must rather emerge from the conflicting implications and complexities resembling Donna Haraway's "dirty ontology."[71]

Mark's widow, though abandoned to poverty by her community, continues to feel a certain loyalty to the temple and the God worshiped there. Indian widows can be similarly torn between concerns for their own safety and survival, on the one hand, and cultural forces such as loyalty to a family and nation, on the other. Practices such as the rare but recently resurgent *sati* and the less drastic but for Western feminists often still alienating insistence of many Muslim women to veil themselves continue to confound the expectations and dogmatism of some forms of Western feminism. Thus Amitava Kumar asks: "What would it mean . . . to view the veil as a sign of unstable identity—and, by implication, the feminine as engaged in a struggle, a gendered struggle, within the postcolonial context but also between the East and the West," rather than as a "*fixed* sign of oppression"?[72]

The practices of veiling and *sati* might not seem to incorporate resistance against oppression in the eyes of many Western women, and yet they may be consciously in opposition to Western ideologies, culture, and capitalism, positioned in a painful clutch between "victimage versus cultural heroism—in the rift of the failure of decolonization." *Sati* might, as Spivak

---

68. Homi Bhabha, *The Location of Culture* (London: Routledge, 1994), 86.

69. For the specific application of Bhabha's mimicry to ancient Christian texts, I am indebted to Rebecca Lyman, "The Politics of Passing: Justin Martyr's Conversion as a Problem of Hellenization," in *Conversion in Late Antiquity and the Middle Ages: Seeing and Believing* (ed. Kenneth Mills and Anthony Grafton; Rochester, N.Y.: University of Rochester Press, 2003), 36–60.

70. Catherine Keller, *Apocalypse Now and Then: A Feminist Guide to the End of the World* (Boston: Beacon, 1996), 259.

71. Donna J. Haraway, *Modest_Witness@Second_Millennium. FemaleMan©_Meets_OncoMouse™* (New York: Routledge, 1997), 142.

72. Amitava Kumar, *Passport Photos* (Berkeley: University of California Press, 2000), 205–6.

argues, constitute an ambivalent action for women who have no access to "correct resistance."[73]

For Muslim women, veiling themselves might at times function as an expression of indignation against the perceived overbearing attitudes of some Western feminists and their involvement in the so-called development of women in the global south and Asia.[74] But, as Spivak suggests, it may be that the secrets of these women shrouded in veils and mystery keep us out, "not the other way around." Indian widows who perform self-immolation appear as subaltern females lost in an even deeper shadow, potential performers of "anti-colonialist nationalism."[75] Resisting colonialism—and its economic system of capitalism—they yet succumb to patriarchal nationalism. To complicate matters of resistance against dominative sexual and material economies even more, Spivak draws the comparison of *sati* and "Christian female martyrdom, with the defunct husband standing in for the transcendental One . . . for whose sake an intoxicating ideology of self-sacrifice can be mobilized."[76] Loyalty to the husband, the dead master of the Indian house, or the *kurios* of the heavenly *oikos*, results in a willingness to self-sacrifice.

Many centuries earlier, Ambrose strung together images of virginity and of marriage that combine a justification of the church's right to remove virgins from Roman households with a supplementary marriage vow that raffirms, if mimetically, the patriarchal marriage vow. Ambrose's account of Agnes's martyrdom deftly employs bridal imagery as the girl, "not a bride," prepares for her execution as for a desired wedding. "Aglow for Christ,"[77] this "female suicide bomber"[78] seeks out death, and Ambrose dangerously melds executioner and Christ, torturer and redeemer, into one, invoking disturbing images of sexual violence and murder so that, as Burrus says, "martyrdom may be identified with rape."[79] The phallic terminator Christ, wielding a sword that penetrates the tender throat of the oh-so-eager victim, has replaced the devilish torturers of early martyr narratives. In the post-Constantinian period, "the story of female resistance and liberation is

---

73. Spivak, *Critique of Postcolonial Reason*, 306.
74. See, for example, Chandra T. Mohanty, "Women Workers and Capitalist Scripts: Ideologies of Domination, Common Interests, and the Politics of Solidarity," in *Feminist Genealogies, Colonial Legacies, Democratic Futures* (ed. Jaqui Alexander and Chandra Mohanty; New York: Routledge, 1997), 3–29.
75. Spivak, *Critique of Postcolonial Reason*, 291, 245n.73, 274.
76. Ibid., 297–98.
77. Virginia Burrus, "Reading Agnes: The Rhetoric of Gender in Ambrose and Prudentius," *Journal of Early Christian Studies* 3, no. 1 (1995): 30.
78. Spivak, *Critique of Postcolonial Reason*, 297.
79. Burrus, "Reading Agnes," 36.

inevitably encoded in the savagely violent terms of the virgin martyr's tale," and the "fierce virgin finally rushes to her own destruction." Nonetheless, the "flexible tale of the virgin martyr proves productive of multiple interpretations,"[80] and we can discern aspects of mimicry, menace, and the resulting ambivalence of the tale. If Agnes appears to subvert her violent death by reinterpreting it, she appropriates it as a precious lover's embrace. At the same time, however, she rejects marriage, preferring death and a symbolic entry into the libidinal economy of Christ, her heavenly *kurios*, to her place as property within the earthly hom(m)osexual exchanges between natal and marital *oikoi*.

Yet, while to the observer she may appear a mere victim, she mocks her death by redefining it as a victory to be sought after. Her mockery of death thus defeats those who would kill her. It is the dying martyr's subversive claim to bio-power, this resistance to the imperial assertion of power dynamics that proves so appealing in the martyr acts and makes them attractive to those who would desire access to such defiant daring. The martyr's self-dedication thus functions as yet another reappropriation of excessive giving that remains ambivalent. Yet Agnes is of course also a victim, who—one may argue—blindly follows an ideology of martyrdom that offers her up to the powers that be. Spivak writes of a related dynamic in Indian widows engaging in *sati*: "It is in terms of this profound ideology of the displaced place of the female subject that the paradox of free choice comes into play."[81]

Ambrose, Virginia Burrus suggests, borrows Agnes's clothes in his own "hysterical" rhetorical economy so that he might play "the woman," thereby both interrogating and reinserting the "inner man."[82] His hom(m)osexual economy appropriates the martyr's garb, reinscribing femininity in his own words, according to his image of the divine economy. Thus, says Burrus, "in the tale of the virgin martyr, categories of gender defined by relationships of sexual penetration are not so much discarded as disrupted, rearranged in an asceticized discourse that enables an ambiguously masculine Christian orthodoxy to deploy powerfully the dual rhetorics of empire and martyrdom."[83]

Penetrated by the bridegroom Christ, the executioner's sword, and Ambrose's "veiled virility,"[84] Agnes's physical and textual bodies appear to

---

80. Burrus, "Reading Agnes," 30–32, 37, 39, 43, 45–46.
81. Spivak, *Critique of Postcolonial Reason*, 293.
82. Virginia Burrus, *Begotten, Not Made: Conceiving Manhood in Late Antiquity* (Stanford, Calif.: Stanford University Press, 2000), 138–39.
83. Burrus, "Reading Agnes," 46.
84. Burrus, *Begotten, Not Made*, 140.

be cut up entirely, though yet, as martyrs' bodies commonly are portrayed, they are uncannily resilient, alive and kicking far beyond probability and the audience's expectations. Gender is disciplined through Ambrose's rhetorical economy and is linked to redemption. The virgin martyr's death remains ambivalent, irreducible in its dangerous mimicry of the martyrdom and the victimhood of Christ. Ideologically and culturally sanctioned within Western Christian societies, martyrdom has been part of the ambivalent heritage that has enabled women's tortured endurance in situations of rape and domestic violence—the violence hidden by and often sanctioned by the *domus*, or *oikos*—especially when complicated by racism, colonial heritages, and economic inequality. Thus, womanist ethicist Traci West has described the complex interface of domestic violence against black women in which "white supremacy, patriarchy, and intimate violence often represent simultaneous, heinous violations of the personal and communal becoming of African-American women."[85] Racist, patriarchal, and religious narratives can collude to obscure and hide the resistance expressed in merely living through these attacks. As West stresses, "When a woman survives, she accomplishes resistance."[86] Survivors represent one incarnation of tricksterdom, as Daniel Boyarin has observed in his investigation of tricksters and martyrs. Though he may end up overly stressing the distinctions between the Jewish "Brer Rabbi" trickster who fools the powers that be in order to get away with his life and the Christian martyr who dies defiant of Roman authorities, what may emerge is a more ambivalent space where martyrs can equally emerge as tricksters and rabbis as martyrs.[87]

Que(e)rying the Female Martyr

The martyrdom narratives of early Christianity depict lacking females appropriating vir-tues, and thus masculinity, while upsetting gender economies. Brent Shaw has observed that adult male citizens were expected to exercise "economical control of the self, a mastery over the slavery of the passions, a rule of control of the mind over the heat of the body," thus

---

85. Traci C. West, *Wounds of the Spirit: Black Women, Violence, and Resistance Ethics* (New York: New York University Press, 1999), 1.
86. Ibid., 151.
87. Thus, Boyarin writes, "The debate between tricksterism and martyrdom as the most honored and most valuable response to oppression was in the air as a living and active cross-confessional issue at the time that the talmudic literature was being composed." "Brer Rabbi" is a play on the African American trickster figure B'rer Rabbit. See Daniel Boyarin, *Dying for God: Martyrdom and the Making of Christianity and Judaism* (Figurae: Reading Medieval Culture; Stanford, Calif.: Stanford University Press, 1999), 55–56.

exerting a kind of power over their bodies of which women and slaves, both subject to the *kurios,* were not thought capable of.[88] The image of the Christian female martyr, however, incorporates characteristics of Greek novelistic heroines like Leukippe, as the reader is presented with a "miraculously resistant" female body, a "virile woman" triumphant over the strongest of men and animals.[89] Like the pagan philosophical martyrs, writes Tertullian, Christians are able to control their sense of self, identity, and destiny by asserting their Christian identity. Revealingly, this exertion of bio-power by women is not easily extended to their role as Christian preachers or clergy, so Tertullian elsewhere feels called to disqualify the *Acts of Thecla* as an illegitimate, if well-intended, counterfeit that had falsely led to women's claims to power and authority within the church. Yet, according to Dennis MacDonald, "Tertullian undoubtedly was wrong in claiming that the author concocted these stories from his own fantasies, for several of them clearly are traditional and probably extend back into the first century."[90]

In the redemptive economy of the body, masculinity and vir-tues become permeable. Masculinity had been structured as the "vertical" stereotype of a male body standing "erect," inflicting pain, and dying on the battlefield, while feminine vir-tues were located more "horizontally," resembling the position women were thought to be in at the "defining" moments in their lives: during sexual intercourse and the delivery of a child.[91] Feminine "virtues" were identified as endurance and suffering, visualized and positioned in a body lying prostrate and helpless. The ancients suspected, however, that such virtues were not only found in a woman's body. In fact, the fluctuation of gendered virtues between sexes was cause for fear, since endurance of pain and suffering was needful for a man but was considered to be infiltrating, and thus potentially dangerous, to masculinity. "Feminine virtues" or "properties" were particularly useful in martyrdom. Thus, women and slaves, contrary to their usual social

---

88. Brent D. Shaw, "Body/Power/Identity: Passions of the Martyrs," *Journal of Early Christian Studies* 4, no. 3 (1996): 272.

89. Ibid., 274.

90. Dennis Ronald MacDonald, *The Legend and the Apostle: The Battle for Paul in Story and Canon* (Philadelphia: Westminster, 1983), 17. Kate Cooper suspects the text's readers of opportunism: "[W]hen the text fell into the hands of female readers, however, some of them proposed a different reading of the heroine. Be it a lack of cultural sophistication or a deliberate, self-interested blind eye, something led at least some women to see the Christian heroine not as an icon of obedience to the apostolic word but as a precedent for women's clerical authority." Cooper, *The Virgin and the Bride: Idealized Womanhood in Late Antiquity* (Cambridge: Harvard University Press, 1996), 64.

91. How this would apply to a virgin martyr, who could not be imagined in these horizontal positions, remains unaddressed by Shaw.

positions, emerged as the eminently capable heroes of Christian faith, and the pain of childbirth became one of the central metaphors of martyrdom.[92] Subsequently, *patientia,* the Latin equivalent of the Greek *hypomone,* became a more positive term as the evaluation of the disciplinary economy of suffering shifted in connection with martyrdom.[93] Thus, women and slaves such as Blandina, Sanctus, and Felicitas became likely and prominent hero figures of martyrdom. Martyrdom appears to allow women to transcend their "lacking" physicality, as they mimic the male within the divine economy. Thus, they are constructed as sufficient rather than deficient, and even more than sufficient—as exemplary, exorbitant givers of their lives. The martyrdom narratives thus, as economic tractates, perform a mimicry, a queering of the gender of redemption, especially in its mimesis—or mimicry—of Jesus' martyrdom. Martyrs, male and female, participate in the economy of redemption, the *kenosis* of the gift.

Employing an image from an experience most ancient women underwent, the writer of the *Letter of the Martyrs of Lyons and Vienne* compares martyrdom to birth, a close encounter with death, even if the mother survives. The refusal of martyrdom, however, was construed as miscarriage or as the inability to "deliver" the gift of death that leads to eternal life: "[S]ome were manifestly ready for martyrdom, and fulfilled with all zeal the confession wherein they gave witness; but others were manifestly unready and untrained and still weak, unable to bear the strain of the mighty conflict: of which number some ten proved abortions."[94]

Birth also functions as an image in the *Martyrdom of Saints Perpetua and Felicitas.* Both women are mothers and thus linked to the context of childbirth. At the time they are taken to prison, Perpetua is still nursing a son, who is miraculously weaned so Perpetua's health and strength can be preserved for the ensuing martyrdom.[95] On the heels of her mistress, Perpetua's

---

92. Thus, Page DuBois writes about the metaphorical meaning of touchstone *(basanos),* a physical testing in torture: "The slave on the rack waits like the metal, pure or alloyed, to be tested. The test, the touchstone, is the process of torture.... The test assumes that its result will be truth. ... The truth is generated by torture." DuBois, *Torture and Truth* (New York: Routledge, 1991), 35–36. See also Virginia Burrus, "Torture and Travail: Producing the Christian Martyr," in *The Feminist Companion to the New Testament* (ed. Amy-Jill Levine; Sheffield: Sheffield Academic Press, forthcoming).

93. Shaw, "Body/Power/Identity," 285, 289–90, 297.

94. The English translation of the *Letter of the Churches in Lyons and Vienne* follows Ross Kraemer, ed., *Maenads, Martyrs, Matrons, Monastics: A Sourcebook on Women's Religions in the Greco-Roman World* (Philadelphia: Fortress, 1988), *Letters,* 11.

95. "But my baby had got [sic] used to being nursed at the breast and to staying with me in prison.... But as God willed, the baby had no further desire for the breast, nor did I suffer any inflammation; and so I was relieved of any anxiety for my child and of any discomfort in my breasts." The English translation of the *Martyrdom of Saints Perpetua and Felicitas* follows Ross

slave, Felicitas, experiences a miraculously premature birth, just in time for her martyrium.[96]

Felicitas delivers in excruciating pain that baffles the guards of her prison and foreshadows her own and her companions' "birth" as martyrs:

> Hence one of the assistants of the prison guard said to her: "You suffer so much now—what will you do when you are tossed to the beasts? Little did you think of them when you refused to sacrifice." "What I am suffering now," she replied, "I suffer by myself. But then another will be inside me who will suffer for me, just as I shall be suffering for him." (*Martyrdom*, 15)

In martyrdom, the seemingly weak, fragile, and lacking physical economies of women's bodies mysteriously supply in abundance the utmost excellence. The martyred women and slaves are used to suffering and submission. Their lack of economic "propriety" makes them "appear mean and unsightly and despicable in the eyes of men [but] worthy of great glory in the sight of God" (*Letters*, 17). This, however, serves only to stress their well-suitedness for martyrdom. Women's value in the hom(m)osexual economy as producers of children and thus future wealth is reinterpreted and placed into the context of the divine *oikos*, in which a birth produces a different kind of "offspring"—martyrdom—one that brings women equally close to the threshold of death and thus entry into the heavenly *oikos*.

Women's sexual and material economies of lack also enable them to imitate even more perfectly the death of Christ. Blandina, crucified like Christ as part of her tortures, becomes the perfect image of Christ, that is, her body and pain signify and function as valid currency. Even the "outward eyes" of her fellow martyrs behold "in the form of their sister Him who was crucified for them" (*Letters*, 41). Eventually, she figures as the mother not only of her own martyrdom but of the martyrdom of her companions, as the writer's vision depicts a reversal of her status within the *oikos*, perhaps even her status in mimesis of the *kyrios Iesous*.

Blandina is depicted as a matron rather than a slave, surpassing her mistress in a class reversal where she functions "like a highborn mother,

---

Kraemer, ed., *Maenads, Martyrs, Matrons, Monastics, Martyrdom*, 6.

96. Felicitas "had been pregnant when she was arrested, and was now in her eighth month. As the day of the spectacle drew near she was very distressed that her martyrdom would be postponed because of her pregnancy; for it is against the law for women with child to be executed. . . . And so, two days before the contest, they poured forth a prayer to the Lord in one torrent of common grief. And immediately after their prayer the birth pains came upon her." Kraemer, ed., *Maenads, Martyrs, Matrons, Monastics, Martyrdom*, 15.

exhorted her children and sent them forth victorious to the King" (*Letters,* 56). Slaves and women, economically in-appropriate (without ability to appropriate, or to manage, property) in Roman society, both fit the role of exploited and tortured creatures and subsequently signify the highest possible subversion of power and property in these narratives. Despite the potent danger of confusing victor with victim, torturer with slave, male status with female status, the subversion of material and physical configurations of bio-power, their mimicry turned into mockery. A menace to the *oikonomia* of society is present even in the description of the most cruel public shaming and torture. The slave becomes a mistress, the woman a man, and the trials of martyrdom allow them to transform the economy of their redemption toward one of empowerment that transgresses the boundaries of gender and social status. Thus, their "gift" pays off; their economic status changes both in the earthly and heavenly economy, where they appropriate salvation and wealth. The implications of confessing membership in the Christian *oikos* seem to be profoundly queering, mimicking, and defiant of gender and power hierarchies. Yet the textual bodies of these martyr acts and their refashioning seem to "enable the more direct appropriation of the truth-telling claim of the female and slave bodies by the male authors of an imperial orthodoxy that paradoxically invoked the privileges of both political power and persecuted witness."[97] The ambivalence of these stories—since they reaffirm the superiority of the male body, the status of the mistress, and the superiority of a masculinely gendered orthodoxy—may insult contemporary sensitivities. Yet they demonstrate the dynamics of any situation of subversion: the interplay of mimicry and resistance, of a liberating narrative that already bears within it the dangers of reverting to a more complex per/version of the previous oppression. Still, on a certain level, Blandina, Perpetua, and Felicitas become the symbol of "social," economic, and redemptive "reversal."[98] Blandina's contribution to the divine salvific economy is hinted at by positing her as a second Eve and by her depiction as the adversary of the dragon whose head both Blandina and Perpetua crush, exemplary in their endurance and persistence in torture.[99] Moreover, Perpetua's witness brings about the severance of ties to home and family as she refuses the pleas of her father to forego martyrdom. She gives up her newborn to the care of others, and envisions an altered sexual identity as she competes as a male gladiator fighting the Egyptian/dragon/devil and defeats him by stepping on his head:

---

97. Burrus, "Torture and Travail."
98. I am adding economic and redemptive traits to Burrus's description of "social reversal." Burrus, "Torture and Travail."
99. *Martyrdom,* 4; *Letters,* 42; and Burrus, "Torture and Travail."

My clothes were stripped and suddenly I was a man.... Then I saw the Egyptian on the other side rolling in the dust.... We drew close to one another and began to let our fists fly.... Then when I noticed there was a lull, I put my two hands together linking the fingers of one hand with those of the other and thus I got hold of his head. He fell flat on his face and I stepped on his head. (*Martyrdom*, 10).

Yet, far from indicating a "complete severance with, or even simple inversion of, classical configurations of masculinity," these "slippages" in gendering "a feminized virility" or "virilized femininity," Burrus observes, does not preclude the "chastizing resubjugation of the Christian woman."[100]

Most early martyrs and ascetics do not seem to have spent large amounts of time pondering under what circumstances Christ's death was redemptive for them; it does not seem central in the texts that describe their lives and deaths. Their own suffering and death seems equally or at least sufficiently redemptive in its similarity to Christ's suffering and death. Women's lack of power and lack of substance, far from a reason for their defeat, becomes a reason for their ability to surrender, to give; it becomes their exorbitant bio-power. This power can become attractive even to men, so that Ambrose invested himself in the virgin Agnes's garb. Burrus comments, "It is revealing that Ambrose's earliest showcased alter egos are world-rending girls who face the executioner's knife with a focused ferocity and an uncanny feel for the dangerous and exhilarating power of a repressed sexuality."[101]

Agnes's martyrdom thus became Ambrose's queerly gendered tool in the discourse of "his advocacy of a Nicene orthodoxy" and his "emergent zeal for a Christianized empire."[102] Ambrose, says Burrus, further appropriated the figure of the hysteric for his gender performance: "There is, finally, something of the hysterical ... in Ambrose's act: the man who, like Mary, so carefully guarded his own inner space seems beset by a version of the malady the ancients attributed to the displacement of an empty and hungering womb."[103]

Women's self-sacrifice and the complexities of its motivation exhibit striking differences as well as similarities in a more recent colonial context where gender and power are equally contested. Thus, Gayatri Spivak cryptically, but significantly, compares Freud's research on hysteria with British

---

100. Burrus, "Torture and Travail."
101. Burrus, *Begotten, Not Made,* 138.
102. Ibid., 137.
103. Ibid., 138.

colonialists' attitudes toward *sati*. According to Spivak, Freud's discourse desires to "give the hysteric a voice, to transform her into the *subject* of hysteria." Yet it simultaneously creates a generalizing stereotype of irrational femininity that obscures hysterical women. This discursive ambivalence might yet resemble the British colonizers' interference with *sati*, which was partly due to humanistic concerns. Might their reaction to *sati* perhaps unveil another instance of male hysteria? At the same time, however, according to Spivak's coinage, this colonial interference results in an act where "white men are saving brown women from brown men" and the "language of racism combines with the dark side of imperialism."[104] Under these circumstances, where women—the concern of men who appear to be their advocates—might yet again be silenced by doubly privileged male voices, how indeed "can the subaltern speak"?[105]

The apocryphal *Acts of Thecla*, perhaps because it especially fueled hopes of retrieving the voices of women and a women-specific discourse, has contributed to an ongoing debate within feminist historical scholarship.[106] Thecla, martyr and model ascetic to many later women, removes herself from her paternal *oikos*, refusing a role as daughter, future wife, and mistress of female servants. MacDonald writes:

> But according to the legends, the disruption of the household is not primarily related to the liberation of slaves but the liberation of women.... Christian women who left the household often formed households of their own.... The radical reordering of the lives of women who chose to live outside the *oikia* system is treated with great sensitivity in the depiction of Thecla's relationship with her mother, Theocleia, who demands Thecla's death, and to Tryphaena, who becomes like a mother to Thecla and tries to save her from death. Theocleia's violent response is understandable when we keep in mind the economically precarious status of single women in most ancient societies.[107]

---

104. Spivak, *Critique of Postcolonial Reason*, 134, 274.

105. The "subaltern" or, more recently, the "native informant," is Spivak's term for those persons who remain outside literary, political, and economic discourses, whose voices are not being heard, despite the fact that some privileged postcolonial intellectuals (such as Spivak) have found the ears of Western readers, though perhaps only because they have learned to communicate with them in Western languages and by help of Western philosophical constructions. See Spivak, *Critique of Postcolonial Reason*, 283–84.

106. Cf. the following participants in the discussion of how to retrieve ancient female martyrs and ascetics as it pertains to the figure of Thecla: MacDonald, *Legend and the Apostle*; Elizabeth Castelli, "Virginity and Its Meaning for Women's Sexuality in Early Christianity," *Journal of Feminist Studies in Religion* 2, no. 1, (1986): 75–76; Virginia Burrus, *Chastity as Autonomy: Women in the Stories of Apocryphal Acts* (Lewiston, N.Y.: Edwin Mellen Press, 1987); and Cooper, *Virgin and the Bride*.

107. MacDonald, *Legend and the Apostle*, 50.

Upon hearing the apostle Paul proclaim the need to acknowledge only one God, one who "longs for the salvation of humanity," which can be accomplished by drawing "away from corruption and impurity,"[108] Thecla refuses to enter into an arranged marriage with one of the foremost citizens of Iconium. Instead the text has her become celibate and join the apostle Paul in his missionary travels. Though portrayed in a very intimate, erotically charged relationship with the apostle, she remains vulnerable to the financial and sexual power of other males. Her fiancé accosts two listeners of Paul with a bribe, then with an apparently more tempting invitation to a fancy banquet, upon which they enter into a plot with him. Thecla's fiancé thus conspires:

> Gentlemen, tell me, who are you? And who is this man who is inside with you, the beguiling one who is inside with you, the beguiling one who deceives the souls of young men and virgins that they should not marry but remain as they are? I promise now to give you a lot of money if you will tell me about him, for I am the first man of the city. (*Acts of Thecla*, 11)

Thamyris subsequently brings Paul in front of the proconsul, who interrogates him and throws him in prison. Thecla, still endowed with some of her home's wealth, strikes a bargain herself and bribes the guard with her jewelry so he will bring her into Paul's cell. Later, when Paul and Thecla travel together, a wealthy urbanite takes a fancy to her and offers Paul money and gifts to gain sexual access to her. In a twist on a hom(m)osexual economy, the two men engage in an economic contest over who has the right of ownership with regard to Thecla:

> Alexander, the first man of the Antiochenes, seeing Thecla, desired her and sought to win over Paul with money and gifts. But Paul said, "I don't know the woman of whom you speak, nor is she mine." But he, being a powerful man, embraced her on the open street; she, however, would not put up with it but sought Paul and cried out bitterly.... And grabbing Alexander, she ripped his cloak, took the crown off his head, and made him a laughing stock. (*Acts of Thecla*, 26)

Surprisingly enough, given what we know of the canonical Pauline and deuteropauline traditions, this apocryphal Paul proclaims that he has no patriarchal or connubial power over her. This hands-off approach creates a

---

108. The English translation for the *Acts of (Paul and) Thecla* follows the *Acts of Thecla* in Kraemer, *Maenads*, 280-88, *Acts of Thecla*, 17.

scene in which "Paul not only fails to support Thecla, but actively betrays her." This abandonment encourages Alexander to try to rape the unprotected Thecla.[109] The maiden, however, gives him a good wallop, and Alexander huffs off to avenge the humiliation of his masculinity by having her cast to the beasts. At this point, the two offenses to *oikos* and *polis*, her sexual and religious independence, seem to contribute equally to her martyrdom. Disrupting the decency of patriarchal property claims, Thecla refuses rape and sexploitation, and deflates patriarchal expectations of women's fear and submission. Thecla's quasi-martyrdom resembles "a trickster-escape tale" rather than the "tale of a virgin martyr."[110] For Thecla, as resistant to male advances as the other martyrs and perhaps with an enhanced tricksterlike flair about her, serves to highlight the tricksterlike qualities and ambivalent readings of other martyrs as well. Thecla witnesses not through her death but rather by assuming redemptive biopower by baptizing herself in a ditch, proclaiming enslavement to the *oikos* of the father God ("I am a servant of the living God"), as well as unmediated access to and authority over her own salvation: "And when she had finished her prayer, she turned and saw a great ditch full of water and said, 'Now is the time for me to wash.' And she threw herself in, saying, 'In the name of Jesus Christ, I baptize myself on the last day!'" (*Acts of Thecla*, 34).

Here again is a story in which elements subversive as well as reinscriptive of gendered economic oppression become manifest. The tone of the story suggests Thecla's successful appropriation of some measure of control over her life, even if it continues to occur in the shadow of Paul's and later the divine paternal authority (which Thecla willfully submits to). Her embodied redemption is distinct from that of earlier martyr acts, such as those of Blandina, Perpetua, Felicitas, and Agnes, who find an ambivalent salvation through submission and death. Though the virgin Thecla is depicted as male-centered in her erotic attachments, we glimpse her leaving the pages of the *Acts of Thecla* as Paul sends her off to "go and teach the word of God" and as both the apostle and God relinquish paternal and

---

109. Again MacDonald brings Thecla's vulnerability into context: "Except for the wealthy, single women were likely to become destitute unless they could establish some relationship with an *oikia*, usually with their relatives.... Like orphans, they were anomalies to the basic socioeconomic arrangement." MacDonald, *Legend and the Apostle*, 51.

110. Boyarin distinguishes the Jewish trickster who escapes death through tricks from the Christian martyr narratives, but may end up overly stressing their differences, asserting: "This instance of the discourse of martyrdom turns out to be almost emblematic for the textual forces that eventually, in my view, would mark the greatest cultural difference between Judaism and the Church." At the same time, he admits trickster and martyr can be found to switch sides and should not too hastily be confined to one side: "One could conclude from this, too hastily, that the Rabbis always will opt for tricksterism, the Christians for defiance. The matter, however, is not quite that simple." Boyarin, *Dying for God*, 65, 52.

patriarchal authority.[111] Incidentally, her financial support originates from a new female-centered *oikos,* from that of her adopted mother Tryphena, who "sent her a lot of clothing and gold, so it could be left behind for Paul for the ministry of the poor" (*Acts of Thecla,* 34). Though society's hierarchies remain powerful, mimicry can menace them so as to unveil and reconstruct more redemptive glimpses of divine economy.

The *Acts of Thecla* may impress us in part as a midrash, taking the figure of Paul out of the context of his letters and tradition, and in part as a reinvention of the pagan novel with a few replacements and additions.[112] It is a revamped Paul we encounter through the lens of the young, wealthy Thecla, an apostle who preaches continence and seems to encourage young women to leave hom(m)osexual economy, where women's worth consists in their exchange value as potential mothers between fathers and future husbands and households. Naked in front of her male persecutors, Thecla produces an ancient version of indecent "theology without underwear"[113] in a rebellion against the law of the (dead) father and the (potential) husband. The *Acts of Thecla* expand on the ascetic traditions present in the Pauline corpus. Women renunciants, according to Peter Brown, were excluded from the priesthood and other ecclesial offices, but they could participate on somewhat more equal footing in ascetic life, so much so that married men felt themselves bested by ascetic widows and virgins.[114] Thus, women figure prominently in the ascetic texts of the early Christian period. Renunciation became an avenue to exert at least some influence through patronage and monastic leadership.[115] Over time, however, the economic and spiritual powers of women in the church increasingly prompted repressive reactions.

---

111. I differ from both MacDonald and Burrus who argue that Thecla does achieve a kind of independence from men, ensconced completely in a female household with her new mother Tryphena. See MacDonald, *Legend and the Apostle,* 51; and Burrus, *Chastity as Autonomy,* 89.

112. See MacDonald, *Legend and the Apostle,* 19; and Burrus, *Chastity as Autonomy,* 58 and passim.

113. See Althaus-Reid's encouragement to do "theology without underwear," that is theology in the presence and in awareness of ourselves and God as sexual beings. Althaus-Reid, *Indecent Theology,* 1.

114. Brown writes, "Married men trembled on the brink of being demoted to the position of women: their physiological involvement in sex made them ineligible for roles of leadership in the community. Some women, however, edged closer to the clergy: continence or widowhood set them free from the disqualifications associated with sexual activity." Peter Brown, *The Body and Society: Men, Women, and Sexual Renunciation in Early Christianity* (New York: Columbia University Press, 1988), 146.

115. Elizabeth Clark, *Ascetic Piety and Women's Faith: Essays on Late Ancient Christianity* (Lewiston, N.Y.: Edwin Mellen Press, 1986), 175 and passim; Elizabeth Clark, *Reading Renunciation: Asceticism and Scripture in Early Christianity* (Princeton, N.J.: Princeton University Press, 1999), 37.

The widow, giving her whole life, her entire *bios*, can be read as one of the ancestors of the female martyr and ascetic, equally willing to give all. Yet these exorbitant gestures of giving do not leave women lacking or empty. Furthermore, they emerge as eminently substantial in virtue and in wealth in the divine economy. This subversion of gender and material economies is, however, constantly in danger of being reappropriated by the powers that be, who camouflage themselves, invest themselves into the exorbitant investment of the tragic trickster martyr, who remains a volatile symbol and figure—endangered, yet enormously powerful in her seizure of biopower in the divine economy.[116]

Domesticating the Virgin and the Bride

> His desire, fragile and kept alive by lack, is maintained by absence: man pursues. As if he couldn't have what he has. Where is she, where is woman in all the spaces he surveys, in all the scenes he stages within the literary enclosure?. . . We know the answers and there are plenty: she is in the shadow. In the shadow he throws on her; the shadow she is.
>
> Hélène Cixous and Catherine Clément, *The Newly Born Woman*

Ascetics are the heirs of martyrs. Whereas martyrs give their life to witness to Christ, the ascetic's discipline witnesses to the power of redemptive transformation through living practice. When contemporary readers look for "holy women" in antiquity "none appear to function as the precise female counterpart to the 'holy men' described by [Peter] Brown."[117] The lives of ascetic women, such as those written by Jerome, depict educated, mostly "independently wealthy" high society virgins and widows, whose "status . . . derives from their vast inherited wealth and social position, whose prestige they carry into monastic life."[118] Women's ascetic lives take

---

116. Compare Burrus's discussion of how the figures of matron and virgin function within ancient discourses on economies of gender and Christian discourse. See Burrus, *Begotten, Not Made*, 182–83.

117. While the patronage of "holy men" appears to be rural, the life and patronage of "holy women" is centered around and "largely identified with cities and towns," and, in contrast to the men, they are "not generally reported to have worked miracles during their lifetimes." Elizabeth Clark, "Holy Women, Holy Words: Early Christian Women, Social History, and the 'Linguistic Turn,'" *Journal of Early Christian Studies* 6, no. 3 (1998): 413–15. For the case of Alexandria see also Susannah Elm, *"Virgins of God": The Making of Asceticism in Late Antiquity* (Oxford: Oxford University Press, 1996), 369; and David Brakke, *Athanasius and Asceticism* (Baltimore and London: Johns Hopkins University Press, 1998), 57ff.

118. Clark, "Holy Women, Holy Words," 414.

place in a more urban setting than those of their male counterparts. While holy men are generally depicted as leaving culture for nature, ascetic women are more often presented as household ascetics, even confined to their *oikoi* by the instructions of their teachers. Only rarely, if ever, do we see in them a complete breakaway from civilization. Their economic patronage appears to "follow older, urban models of patronage," such as raising money for church buildings and monasteries.

The ventriloquized voices and stories of the female ascetics have presented hermeneutical problems for feminist historians such as Elizabeth Clark, Kate Cooper, Patricia Cox-Miller, and Virginia Burrus. Efforts to "uncover" what might seem like the "real women" of Christian antiquity need to be made cautiously considering the particular disciplinary discourses in which these women's stories are embedded.[119] We lack much information about these women; though they may take up spaces in the texts of men, there are also resounding silences in the margins of the texts. The disciplining of women as virgins or brides of Christ has a double function: while treatises on virginity function as *Haustafeln,* or household tractates, that aim to discipline the bodies of women, the tropes of virgin and bride are also assumed and managed by patristic authors to more strongly inscribe masculine authority and their own claims to orthodoxy. Christianity had become notorious early on for its close association with women.[120] How were women, including virgins and widows, able to enter into such prominent roles? Was it largely their wealth, their social position and ancestry, always reverting to a "hom(m)onymic" association to a man, father, brother, or husband? Their influence seems to have gone significantly beyond their financial contributions, though the possibility of siphoning their money into a church fund, out of which the clergy sustained their own existence, most likely played a significant role.[121]

One of those marginal ascetics was Saint Antony's sister. This nameless girl appears only twice and only briefly in the *Life of Antony.* What we see of the "quite young sister" does not suggest she had the same options as Antony.[122] According to Athanasius's narrative, Antony was a well-behaved and wealthy, if orphaned, young man, and the *oikodespotes* or *kurios* of his household. When Antony gives up his estate to follow the Savior, we do not

---

119. Ibid., 413–15, 417–18.
120. Indeed, women appear to have been so involved in getting themselves religiously educated that Emperor Licinius found it necessary to keep them from attending sacred schools in the 320s, which implies that there must have been enough of them and enough people complaining to warrant such an action on his part. Brown, *Body and Society,* 140–41.
121. Ibid., 145.
122. Athanasius, *The Life of Antony and the Letter to Marcellinus* (trans. and ed. Robert C. Gregg; Classics of Western Spirituality; Mahwah, N.J.: Paulist Press, 1980), 2.

see him seek counsel with his younger sister, whose destiny would have been dependent on his decision. Rather, Athanasius's account seems to indicate that he efficiently disposed of the land that belonged both to him and his sister, as well as selling most of the other mobile goods and donating the proceeds to the poor (*Vit. Ant.* 2).

Though Athanasius retained several items for his sister, there is no mention of a dowry—making her an unsuitable, or at least unprotected, match for marriage and a secure attachment to a marital *oikos:* "Giving his sister in the charge of respected and trusted virgins, and giving her over to the convent for rearing, he devoted himself from then on to the discipline rather than the household, giving heed to himself and patiently training himself" (*Vit. Ant.* 3).

Antony places her in a cenobitic village convent of virgins, then goes on to exchange the economic duties of overseeing an estate for the economy of ascetic discipline, of "giving heed to himself and patiently training himself." His sibling remains obscure, lacks space, name, dimension, and decision in this narrative. We do not know what she may have felt about his decision to give up most of the family's belongings. Yet a careful reader might sense a slight discomfort with Antony's treatment of his sister throughout Athanasius's narrative, manifested in the temptations the Enemy visits upon Antony in the desert, "suggesting memories of his possessions, the guardianship of his sister, the bonds of kinship, love of money and of glory," and later in a brief remark about a visit Antony may have paid to his sister in the convent decades later: "He too rejoiced then, both seeing the ardor of the monks and seeing also that his sister had grown old preserving the life of virginity, and herself guided other virgins" (*Vit. Ant.* 54).

Virginia Burrus suggests that Antony's sister and the other virgins "function as a device of exclusion." The convent seems of little relevance; Athanasius's focus is on the monasteries and desert inhabited by male ascetics. Athanasius's rhetorical economy merely establishes that the virgins of Antony's sister's convent are the right kind of virgins—namely, orthodox—while "effectively eras[ing] the space for female asceticism in the world of this text."[123] Attempting to manage the orders of virgins in Alexandria was of critical importance to Athanasius's attempts to ascertain the power of his episcopacy and what would become Nicene creedal orthodoxy. Unlike Athanasius's recommendations for male monastics, whom he exhorted to become more involved in matters of public and

---

123. Burrus, *Begotten, Not Made*, 76.

clerical importance, the domestication and disciplining of women, whether they were married or virgins, was central.[124]

The Alexandrian virgins, who were wealthy and educated, had become involved and had taken sides in the struggles between Arians and the party of Athanasius in Alexandria.[125] David Brakke reports that they formed part of the study circles of an "academic Christianity" that encouraged theological debates centered around a teacher like Arius, while the "catholic" Athanasius tried to assert episcopal authority through a line of anti-intellectual and patriarchal strategies.[126] In order to shame the virgins of Alexandria into submission, Athanasius slandered gatherings of ascetic men and women, and subsequently exhorted virgins to keep sequestered either in their parental homes or in communities of other women under episcopal authority. The theological images used were those of the "bride of Christ." A virgin's marriage vow, according to Athanasius's authoritarian interpretation, was meant to restrict the virgin from theological, economic, social, or church political involvement—to keep her at home, in the *oikos*, and thus to literally "economize" her. But there were also other economic reasons for keeping virgins under wraps: "[C]hurch leaders were eager to redirect the inheritances of virgins into the Church. If virgins were to offer all their 'wealth' to Christ as Athanasius depicted it, they had little alternative but to live in one of the arrangements that the bishop endorsed: at home or in a community of other virgins."[127]

As a result of Athanasius's arguments that a virgin's only loyalty should be to her godly husband Christ and not to a teacher or any other male, except episcopal authorities such as himself, Alexandrian women's independence was diminished, especially over the course of the Arian controversies. Athanasius's instructions to virgins included seclusion, veiling in public, general modesty in clothing and food consumption, moderation of sleep, speaking as little as possible to a limited number of persons, avoiding all contact with the other sex, praying, keeping vigils, singing, and chanting psalms.[128] Not surprisingly, far more independence was granted to ascetic

---

124. Thus, David Brakke comments: "It is ironic that, in order to create a more unified Church, Athanasius considered it necessary to separate the virgins from the Church's public life more completely. The episcopal organization that the bishop was forming had no room for young women who engaged in independent commercial activities and undertook pilgrimages, who participated in study circles and their theological debates, and who formed alliances of mutual care with ascetic men. . . . Athanasius had a far different message for the men who lived as monks in the monasteries at the edges of the city or the desert. They were to become more actively involved in the life of local churches." Brakke, *Athanasius and Asceticism*, 78.
125. Cf. Elm, *Virgins of God*, 369.
126. Brakke, *Athanasius and Asceticism*, 58, 63.
127. Ibid., 33.
128. Ibid., 34.

men. In these controversies, bridal imagery and the title "bride of Christ" were employed in a rhetorical economy to reinforce the continued submission of a woman to a male. This strategy, as Brakke further observes, "had the double political function of exclusion and integration: on the one hand, Athanasius told the virgins to be secluded and exclusively devoted to their husband, like ordinary wives; on the other hand, he pointed to the virgins' fundamental kinship with Christian women who had chosen more earthly husbands."[129]

What might the various forms of ascetic life mean for the material, relational, and spiritual economies of early Christian women's lives? In what ways did it allow for withdrawal from certain male authorities, such as the paternal or conjugal household? Apart from some of the disciplining rhetoric of bishops like Athanasius, it seems that for women, "asceticism involved not so much a rejection of public life—from which they were always in theory excluded—as a rejection of the dominant ordering principles of the public sphere."[130] Thus, a "masculinization of the role of the women took place in so far as women resisted subordination and privatization." Burrus argues that both sexes "ultimately ... threatened to subvert the very distinction between public and private and to destabilize the gender roles and relations supporting that distinction."[131] Though initially women may not have been able to move out of their restricted sphere, the focus on monastic efforts on the part of both women and men served to question the primacy of the public sphere and thus the importance of the distinction between public and private.

This destabilization of gender roles and the distinctions between public and private seem to have become readily manifest in the *Acts of Thecla*. The image of Thecla had meanwhile become a fertile source for the ascetic imagination of women; indeed, it forms part of the intertext for the "holy women" of later centuries.[132] The (eventually not so) secret name of Gregory of Nyssa's sister Macrina was Thecla, a name given to her, so one would imagine, in hopes that she might aspire to the same qualities as the heroine herself.[133] Though Thecla's image is that of a rather indecent woman defying the city, her household, and her future household, male

---

129. Ibid., 57.
130. Virginia Burrus, *The Making of a Heretic: Gender, Authority, and the Pricillianist Controversy* (Transformation of the Classical Heritage; Berkeley: University of California Press, 1995), 14.
131. Ibid., 14–15.
132. Cf. Cooper, *Virgin and the Bride*, esp. 45–67 for an extensive investigation of the textual genre of apocryphal acts and its influence on the textual and disciplinary construction of later women ascetics.
133. Burrus, *Begotten, Not Made*, 120.

authors soon found ways to form her into the image of a modest virgin. Thus, Thecla's female imitators rarely took up traveling or teaching. Rather, as Paula and her daughter Eustochium, they appear to have been taught by authorities such as Ambrose and Jerome.[134] Jerome is familiar with the Thecla tradition and assures his teenage protégée in matters of virginity that the valiant heroine herself will expect and embrace her at heaven's gate if only she follows his instructions on how to attain the virginal ideal:[135] "Then shall Thecla fly with joy to embrace you" (*Epist.* 22.41). In the meantime, however, she should follow Thecla's example and "forget your people and your father's house[,] . . . scorn the flesh and cling to the bridegroom in a close embrace" (*Epist.* 22.1). Images of leaving the home, of renouncing relations and ties to the natal *oikos*, are worked through the entire letter. Sarah Pomeroy writes that "a wealthy heiress generated lively competition,"[136] and Eustochium, daughter of Paula of senatorial riches, would have had access to large holdings, at least before Paula gave them away, as we later learn. And so Jerome advances Christ as the most eligible husband. Though he claims not to write Eustochium about the "drawbacks of marriage," Jerome launches right into listing them with ironic gusto (*Epist.* 22.20).

At the same time as detachment from the patriarchal household is encouraged, as disobedience and even betrayal of family is justified, the new convent household closes its welcoming doors behind the "liberated" girl. Strict household rules are mapped out by Jerome's virginal economy, teaching the newlywed all the distinctions between "real virgins" and "evil virgins" and warning against keeping company with "those who only wish to seem and not to be virgins" (*Epist.* 22.5, 15). As Patricia Cox Miller writes, the alternative image Jerome casts of women who are unwilling to follow the same example might well constitute the "greatest slander of women since Juvenal's sixth satire," while Eustochium is portrayed as the perfect, yet endangered virgin.[137] Thus, Jerome sketches with erotic imagination and density the image of a tightly sequestered girl inscribing her virginal body with his own paranoia of any woman who would differ even the slightest from the living arrangements recommended to Eustochium inside

---

134. Cooper sees the "continent heroine" as a listener rather than a speaker or teacher, yet she neglects to consider Thecla and Macrina here. Cooper, *Virgin and the Bride*, 63.

135. The English translation of *Epist.* 22 follows *St. Jerome: Letters and Select Works* (trans. W. H. Fremantle; Nicene and Post-Nicene Fathers; 2nd ser.; vol. 6; repr. Grand Rapids, Mich.: Eerdmanns, 1989). Quoted in Cooper, *Virgin and the Bride*, 70.

136. Sarah Pomeroy, *Goddesses, Whores, Wives, and Slaves: Women in Classical Antiquity* (New York: Schocken, 1975), 61.

137. Patricia Cox Miller, "The Blazing Body: Ascetic Desire in Jerome's Letter to Eustochium," *Journal of Early Christian Studies* 1 (1993): 22–23.

the protective walls of her *oikos*. The founder and *kurios* of this new *oikonomia* is Eustochium's heavenly husband: "As soon as the Son of God set foot upon earth, He formed for Himself a new household there" (*Epist.* 22.21). This house will not be tainted by the impurities of the pecuniary world:

> For God is jealous and will not allow the father's house to be made into a den of robbers. Where money is counted, where doves are sold, where simplicity is stifled, where, that is, a virgin's breast glows with the cares of this world; straightway the veil of the temple is rent, the bridegroom rises in anger, he says: "Your household is left unto you desolate." (*Epist.* 22.24)

Jerome's economist God is portrayed as the paternal enforcer of virginity and decency. Rather than strolling around outside, a virgin should guard the home in hospitality and preserve herself for her husband. Likewise, new householding duties await her: "You must also avoid the sin of covetousness, and this not merely by refusing to seize upon what belongs to others, for that is punished by the laws of the state, but also by not keeping your own property, which has now become no longer yours" (*Epist.* 22.31).

Elsewhere Jerome discourages Eustochium's own management of her affairs by linking it with heresy and whoredom:

> Some women care for the flesh and reckon up their income and daily expenditure: such are no fit models for you. . . . Say not: "So-and-so enjoys her own property, she is honored of men, her brothers and sisters come to see her. Has she then ceased to be a virgin?" . . . Such virgins as there are said to be among the heretics and among the followers of the infamous Manes must be considered, not virgins, but prostitutes. (*Epist.* 22.38)

Ironically, Jerome appears to want to crush her body's physical yearnings even as he feeds her with explicitly erotic images about the heavenly bridegroom and his caresses in the bridal chamber: "When sleep overtakes you He will come behind and put his hand through the hold of the door, and your heart shall be moved for Him; and you will awake and rise up and say: 'I am sick of love'" (*Epist.* 22.25). And yet the union of her ascetic body with the beloved is continuously deferred. As in the Song of Songs, it remains ever elusive and becomes the driving force, the "theological desire" of her ascetic life.[138]

But even as she waits for the heavenly *kurios*, she cannot call the house of her confinement her own *oikos*:

---

138. Miller, "Blazing Body," 22, 28–30.

Not only is she the portion of strangeness—*inside* his universe where she revives his restlessness and desire. Within his economy, she is the strangeness he likes to appropriate.... She has been forbidden the possibility of the proud "inscription above my door" marking the threshold of The Gay Science. She could never have exclaimed:

    The house I live in is my own,
    I never copied anyone
She has not been able to live in her "own" house, her very body.[139]

Elizabeth Castelli, in a critical take on certain tendencies in feminist scholarship on ancient asceticism, has duly questioned more hopeful feminist reconstructions of ancient ascetic women. She argues that while the "theme of virginity as liberation was common in the treatises on virginity and occurs frequently in the traditions concerning particular holy women," their physicality was denied "because [as the fathers liked to argue] women who please God will be elevated to male ranks," while their lives were "orthodox attempts to frame and order experience and doctrine into a single, and monolithic image of Christian existence."[140] Thus, scholars have pondered whether female asceticism has often functioned as another, more transcendentalized—yet oddly embodied in masculine metaphors and images—version of a hom(m)osexual *oikonomia* tiringly enforcing the same rules and taboos as the nuptial and paternal economies.[141] Certainly the earlier untroubled liberative readings of female asceticism will need to be appropriately tempered.

Marriage to God has been one of the most powerful metaphors within Christian ascetic discourse. The function of the nuptial—and densely economic—image of the *conubium* in texts about female ascetics is invested with an ambivalence similar to that of the image of the virgin.[142] What is more, the image of the virgin and the bride are strangely merged with each other, in constant mimicry of the conventions of each state. Does Christ simply replace the woman's *kurios*, her human head of the household, with a divine husband? And does this new structure of hierarchy, of subordination, merely serve to reinforce with transcendent power the repression and control of men over women's economic status on both the metaphorical

---

139. Cixous and Clément, *Newly Born Woman*, 68.
140. Castelli, "Virginity and Its Meaning," 70, 75, 65.
141. Contrast the work of Clark, Ruether, MacDonald, and Burrus.
142. *Conubium* is the Roman legal term for the permission—required by both bride and groom—to enter into a marriage recognized by Roman law. Cf. "Conubium," in *Der Neue Pauly: Enzyklopädie der Antike* (ed. Hubert Cancik and Helmuth Schneider; Stuttgart: J. B. Metzler, 1996), 3:158.

and material level?[143] A divinized hom(m)osexual economy still stakes its claim on the virgins of God. Though they have not given their bodies to a man, their male advisers, standing in for the heavenly bridegroom and the heavenly father, continue to discipline the virgins' bodies and minds. God the economist remains circumscribed as masculine and as *kurios,* unless we rewrite the rhetorical economies of texts and households.

Other possible subtexts of female asceticism have been explored. Jerome might well have tried, as Clark points out, to preempt suspicions and criticisms of his own close ties to Paula and Eustochium.[144] Thus, we might, much more ambivalently, be witnessing another mimetic strategy, applied to the social strictures and structures of the Roman Empire, mimicking—whether with intent to subvert we may simply never know for sure—in form and structure the Roman *conubium.* According to Roman law, legitimate marriages were only possible between two partners who each had conferred upon them the *conubium.* It was only available to Roman citizens, but could, like the *commercium* (the right to trade with others who had the *commercium*), be given to persons who did not own it by birth. If the *conubium* was not available to each of the partners, the union was illegitimate, a *concubinage* or, among slaves, a *contubernium.*[145] The *conubium* as an ascetic, spiritualized image inhabited the metaphorical space of the honorable Roman union, thus claiming the same level of decency and respect. This strategy appears to have been used to justify winning wealthy Roman girls into asceticism, again a mimic strategy that mocked the traditional institution even while giving it credence. Thus, texts on women ascetics often replace the earthly bridegroom with a heavenly one—who is much more effective, because omnipotent and omniscient, at reinforcing order in the household—while at the same time ascetic living menaces the social order and gender systems of the Roman Empire.

Eustochium's mother, Paula, emerges as a householder of a somewhat less continent manner, at least as far as her finances are concerned. In a letter written to Eustochium on the occasion of Paula's recent death, Jerome praises Paula's "radical (and radically economic) asceticism."[146] Of high

---

143. As elaborated and discussed in Castelli, "Virginity and Its Meaning," 86, 88; and Burrus, *Begotten, Not Made,* 140, 147, 149.

144. Clark has pointed to the public honor and attention that came with the decision to remain a virgin. Virgins were also highly praised by their close male friends, the same patristic authors that would pen vitriolic misogynist rhetoric. See, for example, Clark, *Ascetic Piety and Women's Faith,* 43, 51, 175–76.

145. "Conubium," 158; J. P. V. D. Balsdon, *Roman Women: Their History and Habits* (New York: Barnes & Noble, 1962), 173–77; Eva Cantarella, *Pandora's Daughters: The Role and Status of Women in Greek and Roman Antiquity* (Baltimore: Johns Hopkins University Press, 1987), 114, 136–37.

146. Virginia Burrus, *The Sex Lives of the Saints* (Philadelphia: University of Pennsylvania Press, 2003), 60.

senatorial birth, Paula was heir to vast financial wealth as well as societal credit, which came in handy when she needed to borrow. "Noble in family, she was nobler still in holiness," Jerome writes and then continues to describe Paula's piety as excessive (*Epist.* 108.1). Paula, another widow, resembles Mark's widow, though her excess becomes visible in the quantities of wealth she is able to renounce. Thus, as Jerome is not sure how to speak of her "distinguished, and noble, and formerly wealthy house," since she left (as Eustochium, the recipient of the letter, would well know) "those dependent on her poor," though "not so poor as she was herself" (*Epist.* 108.5, 2). In a tone curiously critical of Paula's excessive giving, Jerome continues to make apologies for her while accusing her of lack of concern for her daughter. One wonders if such a thought would have ever befallen Athanasius, who gave precious little concern to Antony's little sister, who was equally dependent on him. Was it more acceptable for a rural male ascetic to abandon bothersome financial obligations to his family and community than for a wealthy urban woman to give all her inherited wealth and then some borrowed money to the poor? Thus, Jerome continues in a somewhat bewildered yet admiring voice: "So lavish was her charity that she robbed her children, and, when her relatives remonstrated her for doing so, she declared she was leaving to them a better inheritance in the mercy of Christ" (*Epist.* 108.5). Unlike the rich young man, "her liberality knew no bounds. Indeed so anxious was she to turn no needy person away that she borrowed money at interest and often contracted new loans to pay off old ones" (*Epist.* 108.15). At that point, even Jerome finds her too wasteful, admitting that "when I saw her too profuse in giving, I reproved her alleging the apostle's words" (*Epist.* 108.15). Yet Paula knows well the continuing powers of her social, if not financial, status, arguing, as Jerome quotes her, that "I, if I beg, shall find many to give me; but if this beggar does not obtain help from me who by borrowing can give it to him, he will die." Her excessive giving and exorbitant borrowing leads people to conclude she is not quite right in her head, that "owing to her great fervour in virtue some people thought her mad and declared that something should be done for her head" (*Epist.* 108.19). Jerome's report is ambivalent at best and, as Burrus writes, "is still pursuing the question of whether it is possible to make a virtue of excess—whether Paula in fact pulled it off."[147] Paula's hysterical financing habits, "marked as feminine by [their] very excess,"[148] outline the injunction to the disciples in the parable of the clever steward. Thus, she is reported as having defended the "conspicuous consumption"

---
147. Ibid., 16.
148. Ibid., 21.

of her fortune by quoting, among others, Luke 16:9: "make to yourselves friends of the mammon of unrighteousness" (*Epist.* 108.16). Paula is thus another incarnation of a giving woman, a wealthy widow whose excessive, wasteful giving might seem to emulate Mark's widow but who appears rather ambivalent to her contemporaries, leading to the suspicion of her insanity (perhaps hysteria?).

"Wasteful" and "Indecent" Women

> While he was at Bethany in the house of Simon the leper, as he sat at the table, a woman came with an alabaster jar of very costly ointment of nard, and she broke open the jar and poured the ointment on his head. But some were there who said to one another in anger, "Why was the ointment wasted in this way? For this ointment could have been sold for more than three hundred denarii, and the money given to the poor." And they scolded her. (Mark 14:3–5)

> There is waste in what we say. We need that waste. To write is always to make allowances for superabundances and uselessness while slashing the exchange value that keeps the spoken word on track.
>
> Hélène Cixous and Catherine Clément, *The Newly Born Woman*

A woman, due to her deficiency not considered a full participant in legal, religious and economic matters of Judean society, performs a mock inauguration of Jesus by pouring ointment on his head, making him, literally, the Christ—the Anointed One. Malbon finds that Mark's rendering of the anointing woman (Mark 14:3–9) and of the widow with the copper coins both exhibit the evangelist's sense of irony, showing how the least likely persons give exorbitantly. Malbon argues that as "one woman gives what little she has" and the other woman "gives a great deal, ointment of pure nard worth 300 denarii," each gift is given in a spirit of "self-denial."[149] The presumably wealthy woman is able to afford expensive luxury goods and gives, pours out, lets her physical and material substance overflow with plenty of fluid, crowning the head of God's chosen. Yet her gesture fails to secure the approval of the disciples standing by, and her outpouring is rejected—ejected, spat out. Is her gift richly given but sadly misdirected? Is her wealth wastefully spent? Is it a useless gift that does not ask for a useful

---

149. Malbon, *In the Company of Jesus,* 180–81; Elizabeth Struthers Malbon, "Fallible Followers: Women and Men in the Gospel of Mark," *Semeia* 28 (1983): 39.

return? Others present shame her, decry her investment as wasteful, since it deprives the poor of needed funds. The figure of the woman with the costly ointment frames the passion, signifying, perhaps, a version of a fluid "feminine economy" of outpouring. This feminine economy remains unrecognizable and unvalued within the economic conventions of those who would criticize the woman's generosity.

The women of the Cent societies, too, were treated to a reading of the woman with the alabaster jar that dispensed a distinctly gendered version of divine economy. Hence, a Reverend Green delivered a sermon on the anointing woman, arguing that "she did what she could," and subsequently proceeded to tell the women present what they themselves could and could not do: that, like the anointer, they were bound and limited by their sex and should therefore refrain from "things clearly improper for them to undertake."[150] In terms reminiscent of patristic treatises on women's apparel and hair, he argued that women's "shrinking delicacy" rendered women unfit for command (apparently a quintessentially male thing) and subjected them to the "rougher sex." And then he stated the painfully obvious: that it is not for women to offer anything "of substance," but that anything substantial comes from their husbands' and fathers' pockets, so they must first consult them.[151]

Several centuries later, Malbon's reading may seem to continue to commend women's self-denial, a phenomenon complicit with the "original sin" so effectively denounced by Mary Daly as women's tendency to the "internalization of blame and guilt" and the "enforced complicity" in their own oppression.[152] Women's redemption, at least according to the early Daly, would consist in the recognition of women's self-deprecation and self-sabotage, followed by a commitment to a process of change lived in the community of sisterhood:

> The first salvific moment for any woman comes when she perceives the reality of her "original sin" . . . Real insight implies commitment to changing this destructive situation, and the implications of this are not comfortable. . . . Recognition of this is redemptive and revelatory knowledge, pointing the way to "salvation" from the dehumanizing situation.[153]

How then can women be redeemed and redeem themselves from this original sin of self-denial and self-exhaustion? Remembering (putting the

---

150. Quoted in Beaver, *American Protestant Women*, 33.
151. Ibid.
152. Daly, *Beyond God the Father*, 49.
153. Ibid., 49–50.

pieces back together) women's contributions is already a challenge: though Jesus wants the unnamed woman remembered, as Schüssler Fiorenza famously observes, the text lacks her proper name.[154] Through a "wasteful" economy of anointing, Mark's anonymous woman engages in theological signification, yet she is accused of wasting precious materials. Bystanders try to shame her back into her giving role. How does she dare to give in order to empower herself and the one she gives to? Women's giving is sanctioned, but only if it does not threaten the constructs of economic gender and power. Perhaps it is not coincidental that a woman performing an economic action of her own is accused of waste, of being socially irresponsible. Is the offensiveness of her action perhaps not so much in what she has done but in to whom she has done it? Is her gift inappropriate because she appropriates economic as well as theological power, proclaiming redemption with a rich gesture of matter and spirit? Within the masculine economy of those that criticize the woman, the economic rationale would have been for her to invest her wealth in items more appropriate to her social position, into investments more gratifying to the hom(m)osexual economy. Thus, her investment is not wise; it is outside of the economic bounds of convention and thus is considered waste. The potent investment in the divine economy that is constituted by her seeming waste remains invisible.

Thus, the question of women's waste further explores the problematic opposition of gift and a circular economy. A reconstructed divine economy emerges as neither, but is compounded of multiple exchanges, composed of a network of countereconomies. These fluid ways of exchange resemble the subtle orders discovered in chaos and complexity theories; they defy perfect predictability of profit and return, but often invite risky investments. The grounding relationality of the universe and of our existence is part of these exchanges. They exhibit process and prehension, not absolute giving or taking. Yet they have qualities of the miraculous. Saint Mysteria, the figural embodiment of a construction of female economic agency, embodies one possible shape of redemptive exchange.

---

154. Elisabeth Schüssler Fiorenza, *In Memory of Her: A Feminist Theological Reconstruction of Christian Origins* (New York: Crossroad, 1994), xliii.

CHAPTER 4

Divine Commerce: A Countereconomic Reading of Redemption

O admirabile commercium: [1]
Creator generis humani, animatum corpus sumens,
De virgine nasci dignatus est:
Et procedens homo sine semine,
Largitus est nobis suam deitatem.

O wonderful exchange, wonderful trade:
The Creator of human kind, assuming an inspirited body,
Deigned to be born of a virgin;
And coming forth as a man without admixture of seed,
He bestowed upon us his godhead.

"O Admirabile Commercium," an antiphon for Lauds on the
Feast of the Circumcision (translation by Richard Allen Shoaf)

This chapter offers one possible reconstruction of the ancient theological motif of the *admirabile commercium,* a topos interpreting Christ's incarnation as a wonderful exchange. Building upon an ancient christological formula, among other images, it denotes the *kenosis,* the self-emptying of God from divine wealth to human poverty and enslavement. Christ, as Philippians 2:5–8 witnesses,

---

1. For a historical exploration of the term *commercium,* see Martin Herz, *Sacrum Commercium: Eine begriffsgeschichtliche Studie zur Theologie der römischen Liturgiesprache* (Munich: Kommissionsverlag, 1958).

though he was in the form of God,
did not regard equality with God
as something to be exploited,
but emptied himself,
taking the form of a slave,
being born in human likeness.
And being found in human form,
he humbled himself
and became obedient to the point of death—
even death on a cross.

The incarnation, thus, was associated early with a divine-human exchange of property and station, in the course of a redemptive transaction. Later, Gregory of Nyssa's *Oratio catechetica* portrays the figure of Christ as a shape-shifting trickster at the center of a crucial economic transaction in the divine economy between God and the devil. Posing as slave—a living currency—Christ becomes the counterfeit currency in a transaction in which an entrepreneur God deceives the devil, thus effecting redemption.[2] Other texts portray redemption as *conubium,* as the marriage between Christ, as the wealthy groom, and the church or believer, as a poor maiden or whore, whose redemption occurs through marriage into wealth. The redemptive economics of the *commercium* and *conubium* thus powerfully subvert yet reinscribe the economic power dynamics of slavery, ownership, and hierarchical gender relations in the theo-logic of the divine economy as well as its cultural inscriptions.

This chapter charts the development of the biblical ransom motif from its Hebrew context in sacrificial practice to the patristic *admirabile commercium* and subsequent iterations, meditating on the image's pervasive ambivalence and potential complicity with oppressive social and gender hierarchies. Relating the problematic motif of the *commercium* to that of the *conubium* (the image of the believer's marriage to the bridegroom Christ)—both of which can become linked, even identified in traditional theological discourse—the chapter then moves toward the reconstruction of a divine commerce. In awareness of the transactions of a globalizing economy as documented in current scholarly discussions on contemporary slavery, transnational racism, sexual exploitation, and feminist critiques of atonement, this reconstruction of redemption is contextualized in the complex economic fabric of our lives. The "divine deceiver" and "counterfeit

---

2. The term "living currency" is borrowed from Pierre Klossowski, *La Monnaie Vivande* (Paris: Rivages Poche Petite Bibliothèque, 1997).

Christ" emerging from this reconstruction can serve as models for subtle redemptive strategies of countereconomic tricksterdom. I do not claim recovery of the "original" topos of *admirabile commercium—s'il y en a* (if there is such a thing), as Derrida might murmur—but remain captive to the ambivalence of its interpretation and reception history. Yet my hope is that this strategic reconstruction offers a theological *kenosis* of a different kind—of tricksterlike instances of divine economy.

A "Miraculous" Exchange

> Curiously enough, the self-sacrifice of gods is sanctioned by natural ecology, useful for the working of the economy of Nature and the Universe, rather than by self-knowledge. In this logically anterior stage, inhabited by gods rather than human beings, of this particular chain of displacements, suicide and sacrifice (*atmaghata* and *atmadana*) seem as little distinct as an "interior" (self-knowledge) and "exterior" (ecology) sanction.
>
> > Gayatri Spivak, *A Critique of Postcolonial Reason: Toward a History of the Vanishing Present*

Contemporary Christian use of the term "redemption" is often oblivious to the economic undertones in early Christian interpretations of the work of Christ. Yet, on further investigation, it would be hard to ignore that the motif of redemption is deeply, if uncomfortably, embodied in the symbolism of economic deal making. The English word "redemption" is derived from the Latin term for "purchase" *(emptio)*, signifying an action of buying back, regaining, recovering.[3] The word "ransom" represents a contraction (through the stages of *rampcon* and *re(d)empcon*) of redemption and signifies the "action of procuring the release of a prisoner or captive by paying a certain sum."[4]

The ransom motif's social context within slavery provokes an engagement from liberation and postcolonial perspectives. As we map how redemption interacts in multitudinous ways with images of economic exploitation and oppression,[5] we find that the economic image of redemption became

---

3. See Stanislaus Lyonnet and Leopold Sabourin, *Sin, Redemption, and Sacrifice: A Biblical and Patristic Study* (Analecta Biblica 48; Rome: Biblical Institute, 1970), 98; and *Oxford English Dictionary*, s.v., "Redeem."

4. *Oxford English Dictionary*, s.v., "Ransom." "Redemption" most likely translates the Hebrew term *ga'al* and the Greek term *antallage*, and "ransom" finds a Greek equivalent in the term *lutron*. Lyonnet and Sabourin, *Sin, Redemption, and Sacrifice*, 98.

5. When we compare the *dogma* of Christ with the *kerygma* of Jesus' words and parables, we find two starkly different accounts of divine economy represented within the apostolic tradition.

part of an intertext—that of mimicry and subversion of enduring exploitative patterns such as slavery and patriarchy. The patristic motif of the *commercium*—as salutary exchange of divine power and human weakness brought about through a divine deal with the devil—is embedded in the historical as well as the more metaphorical conception of slavery and discipline, that is, in hierarchical relationships of power. When these texts are reconstructed in a contemporary context, issues of slavery, gender, and economic oppression in and through various forms of colonialism hover at the edges and clamor for hermeneutic admission. As the volatile and disturbing interpretive interface of slavery and its involvement in salvation unfurls before our eyes, a countereconomic reading of the motif of the *commercium* comes into view.[6] The sense of discomfort with which many contemporary interpreters have shied away from early Christian interpretations of salvation as an economic exchange—in part because these texts portray God as involved in exchange with created beings and thus have seemed to disregard the dogmatic expressions of God's sovereignty and omnipotence, or do not seem retrievable for liberationist or feminist readings—has regrettably kept most modern, and certainly postmodern and feminist interpreters, at a distance from a renewed engagement with this motif. A notable exception is Darby K. Ray, whose feminist recasting of Christ as a trickster defeating violence and abuse has helped to inspire the present reconstruction.[7]

The *admirabilis commercium*, or "wonderful exchange," represents a somewhat marginal tradition. Though several ancient writers employ it, it was effectively replaced by Anselm's doctrine of satisfaction and has since fallen into disrepute or even obscurity. Only a handful of studies of this

---

The parables of Jesus portray forgiveness through economic images of debt relief, displaying redemption and release without the notion of a ransom paid in return. In some strands of the Gospels, and certainly very starkly in Paul, we find Jesus' body and soul converted into an economic transaction that effects the release of an indebted creation within the divine economy. While the texts in which Jesus is described as a ransom occupy the interest of this chapter, it will remain of concern to this reconstruction that the *basileia* as portrayed in the parables does not seem to depend on a ransom paid by Jesus. The Bultmannian distinction of kerygma as the proclamation of the kingdom of God by Jesus and dogma as the proclamation about Jesus seems helpful to visualize the shift in interpretation. Adolf von Harnack called this gap *doppeltes Evangelium* whereas Jesus and Paul preached two different gospels. While Jesus proclaimed the *basileia,* Paul proclaimed Christ. See Gerhard Friedrich, *Die Verkündigung des Todes Jesu im Neuen Testament* (Neukirchen-Vluyn: Neukirchener Verlag, 1982), 9–10.

6. See Dale Martin's provocative and insightful reading of the Pauline notion of "slavery as salvation." Martin's text on the ambivalence of slavery as practice and theological metaphor has been instructive to this project. See Dale Martin, *Slavery as Salvation: The Metaphor of Slavery in Pauline Christianity* (New Haven, Conn.: Yale University Press, 1990).

7. Darby Kathleen Ray, *Deceiving the Devil: Atonement, Abuse, and Ransom* (Cleveland: Pilgrim, 1998).

motif have been published, most of which date from the 1950s or 1980s. The miraculous divine commerce in the texts of Irenaeus, Cyprian, Origen, Tertullian, and especially Gregory of Nyssa emerges as a potent location from which to interpret Christ's redemptive opus as tricksterlike economic work.[8] Such a countereconomic *commercium* does not represent a one-sided or "done deal."[9] It must instead function as a common—if hardly neatly reciprocal—investment of divine and human energies that constitute the increments of a *redemptio continua*.

A Ransom for Many? Slavery, Redemption, and Debt Relief

> At a time when slavery was still a current practice it is not surprising that redemption has been understood as a liberation from the servitude of the devil.
>
> Stanislaus Lyonnet and Leopold Sabourin, *Sin, Redemption, and Sacrifice: A Biblical and Patristic Study*

The metaphor of the ransom (Greek, *lutron*) must be situated within the larger context of ancient practices of slavery that undergird the motifs of early Christian writings. Soteriological motifs that envision economic transactions appear somewhat scattered throughout the biblical and patristic texts, and are often intermingled with other motifs such as sacrifice, the death of the just person, or the victorious Christ. In the apostolic writings, we find only a small number of phrases that involve the idea of redemption by ransom or payment. The notion of sacrifice is often concomitant with the slave/ransom image, partly because the term *lutron* can be used synonymously with *hilasterion* (expiation) but possibly also because the death on the cross was a slave's death.[10]

As Stephen Moore points out, *stigmata*—the wounds that mark the crucifixion of Christ—is the *terminus technicus* for the marks owners imprinted on their slaves and constitutes a form of labeling that would guarantee easy retrieval of one's property.[11] In his hermeneutical investigations, Moore has tracked through the blood puddles of the "slaughterhouse of

---

8. The *commercium* is a rather neglected soteriological motif in modern theology, though it can at times be found in Catholic theology (e.g., that of Erich Przywara, Hans Urs von Balthasar, and Raymund Schwager) as well as in Luther.

9. Ray, *Deceiving the Devil*, 128.

10. Adela Yarbro Collins, "The Signification of Mark 10:45 among Gentile Christians," *Harvard Theological Review* 90, no. 4 (1997): 381.

11. Stephen D. Moore, *God's Gym: Divine Male Bodies of the Bible* (New York: Routledge, 1996), 28.

soteriology," exposing the profuse hemorrhaging of the slain lamb of God. The "search for salvation through sacrifice" has been with us for a long time, as Derrida observes.[12] The "absolute gift" of the life of a son in Derrida's meditations on Jewish and Christian notions of an "economy of sacrifice" form the volatile yet unavoidable heritage of any constructive reinterpretation of divine economy.

One key biblical passage from which ransom and *commercium* theologies flow occurs in the context of an encounter between Jesus, the unnamed mother of John and James, and the circle of the twelve disciples. In Matt 20:20–28, we find the following exchange: two brothers, perhaps too cowardly to come forward with the request themselves, instruct their mother to ask Jesus to grant them the two foremost places of power in the coming *basileia* they imagine Jesus to rule.[13] Jesus, however, draws a confusing picture of power, one that involves suffering and enslavement:

> But Jesus called them to him and said, "You know that the rulers of the Gentiles lord it over them, and their great ones are tyrants over them. It will not be so among you; but whoever wishes to be great among you must be your servant, and whoever wishes to be first among you must be your slave; just as the Son of Man came not to be served but to serve, and to give his life a ransom for many." (Matt 20:25–28)

In what may represent a "hidden transcript"[14] of resistance against colonial Roman powers, Jesus' words mark the *différance* between the tyrannical hierarchies of the "Gentiles" and the alternative vision of power in the *basileia ton ouranon*.[15] In a significant departure from the persistent

---

12. Jacques Derrida, *The Gift of Death* (trans. David Wills; Chicago: University of Chicago Press, 1992), 94.

13. Mark's version does not interject the men's mother as a petitioner. Instead, the sons petition Jesus themselves. W. D. Davies and Dale C. Allison, *A Critical and Exegetical Commentary on the Gospel according to Matthew* (International Critical Commentary on the Holy Scriptures of the Old and New Testaments; Edinburgh: T&T Clark, 1988), 84. In Matthew, the introduction of the mother adds gendered complications. Luz hints that since Augustine and Jerome, the woman is read ambivalently. She is seen as the mere front for the ambitions of her sons, but often was attested both *affectus pietatis* and a specifically feminine *error mulieribus* (so Jerome). Many later authors follow this line. Ulrich Luz, *Das Evangelium nach Matthäus: Mt 18–25* (Evangelisch-Katholischer Kommentar Zum Neuen Testame; Zürich: Benziger Verlag; Düsseldorf: Neukirchener Verlag, 1997), 161 and n.9.

14. James C. Scott, *Domination and the Arts of Resistance: Hidden Transcripts* (New Haven, Conn.: Yale University Press, 1990).

15. Scholars such as Richard P. Saller and Bruce Malina have stressed the pervasiveness of patron-client relationships in Roman antiquity. See Saller, *Personal Patronage under the Early Empire* (Cambridge: Cambridge University Press, 1982); and Malina, *The Social Gospel of Jesus: The Kingdom of God in Mediterranean Perspective* (Minneapolis: Fortress, 2001).

patterns of patronage in Roman antiquity, Jesus asserts that within the heavenly household, positions of power or influence are not available through appeals to patronage, power positioning, or the exploitation of connections to persons perceived to be in some form of power. Matthew's Jesus, living within the Roman Empire, knows well that hierarchies and top-down power management penetrate most forms of human community. But rather than encourage those in his company to vie for positions at the top, he appears to reverse the map of power. The slave, the most unfree member of this society, whose work and life is a commodity, emerges as an agent of liberation. Through a form of divine commerce, the paying of a ransom for the redemption of others, the dominant economy of power is thrown into disarray. Furthermore, Jesus asks those in his company to mimic this economy of voluntary enslavement as a model for redemptive relationality.

But James and John as well as the other male disciples scatter quickly when the time of suffering and a slave's death approach for Jesus.[16] Davies and Allison remark on a thematic connection of this text to the pericope of the rich young man, since both involve the theme of a "reward." Matthew's rendering of the power mongering among male disciples and its context in Matt 20 reflects—unlike the pericope about the rich young man in Matt 19—considerable ambivalence toward the nature of any reward, and perhaps even denies its existence. At the very least, some questions about the nature of discipleship are raised.[17] Warren Carter includes the present pericope in his reading of Matt 19–20 as a household tractate.[18] In the particular sequence of Matt 20:20–28, the theme of slavery is related to the mimetic structure of discipleship. Jesus challenges his disciples to emulate the example of his leadership, which is exemplified not by being served by and lording it over others, but by reversing, perhaps even by abolishing, rank within his circle of friends. Carter observes, "Enslavement to God

---

16. The injunction to serve appears to be specifically directed at the male disciples and might be read as primarily addressing this outburst of masculine desire to rule, without thereby excluding female disciples from the secondary audience of these words. Victoria Phillips has argued for distinguishing audiences in the Gospel of Mark, thus highlighting the specific audience of Jesus' words. Drawing a parallel from her argument, the fact that in Mark 10:35–45 // Matt 20:20–28 the twelve male disciples are the only persons mentioned as present becomes significant. In Matthew, even with the disciples' mother present, Jesus immediately turns to the male disciples, not to her, to answer the request, recognizing, so one might argue, that it is they who have instigated it. Phillips, "Full Disclosure: Towards a Complete Characterization of the Women Who Followed Jesus in the Gospel according to Mark," in *Transformative Encounters: Jesus and Women Re-Viewed* (Leiden: E. J. Brill, 2000), 13–32.

17. Davies and Allison, *Gospel according to Matthew*, 84, 88.

18. Warren Carter, *Households and Discipleship: A Study of Matthew 19–20* (Supplement to the Journal of the Study of the New Testament; Sheffield: Sheffield Academic Press, 1994), 161.

rather than domination over others marks the anti-structure of the alternative household."[19]

Texts such as this constitute a form of "colonial discourse," that is, they express the formation of personal or national identity, resistant agency, and community under the influence of and with reference to colonial power. Most texts in the Bible were written within the context of ancient incarnations of empire, whether Assyrian, Babylonian, or Roman. Biblical images of human and divine power, liberation, resistance, and oppression express the various effects of forms of hegemonic power. Empires form and fall, peoples are governed, oppressed, enslaved, exiled, liberated. Within this context, the portrayal of Jesus as a slave separates the conceptual realm of the kingdom from the Roman Empire: as the text "presents Jesus as a slave and calls disciples to live a marginal existence as slaves," the "cultural pattern is subverted. The household or community of disciples is a community of slaves, of the marginal and of equals, which has no masters except God."[20] This image of an alternative society, playing on Hellenistic traditions of the king as servant of the people,[21] is marked by service, an account much echoed in church services, though ministers of church and society too often fall short of this ideal. Despite this egalitarian vision, the real similarity that disciples could feel to their own marginal association, and the honor that came with being a highly valued slave associated with a powerful master, "there was little questioning of the existence or normalcy of slavery," and "no matter how improved its conditions, slavery remained a system of domination and ownership of one human being by another."[22]

Several texts have been suggested as the possible source behind the notion of salvific ransom employed in Matt 20:28. Some of those found in Hebrew and Jewish traditions were laid out by Joachim Jeremias, who lists several persons or entities that have functioned as ransom in ancient Jewish literature. In Exod 30, for example, coins function as the payment YHWH—portrayed as an ancient Near East patron—receives to protect the male Israelites in his care who are over twenty years old:[23] "When you take a census of the Israelites to register them, at registration all of them shall give a ransom for their lives to the LORD, so that no plague may come upon them for being registered. This is what each one who is registered shall give: half a shekel according to the shekel of the sanctuary . . . , half a

---

19. Ibid., 191.
20. Warren Carter, *Matthew and the Margins* (Supplement to the Journal of the Study of the New Testament; Sheffield: Sheffield Academic Press, 2000), 399.
21. Ibid., 403.
22. Ibid., 404–5.
23. Joachim Jeremias, "Das Lösegeld für Viele (Mk. 10,45)," *Judaica* 3, no. 4 (1948): 250.

shekel as an offering to the LORD" (Exod 30:12–13). The contractual shape of the covenant with the masculine rite of circumcision and the exclusion of women from the payment of the ransom represent a hom(m)osexual economy between the Israelite males and a YHWH depicted as a male. Clearly this God is not in the habit of doing business with women.[24]

As if reassuring his perhaps somewhat nervous German Protestant readers—in whose mind medieval images of the selling of indulgences are prone to rise to the surface—that the early Hebrew practice of paying a ransom to God had been superseded, Jeremias explains that at the time of Jesus, this ransom would have been codified and institutionalized in the Jerusalem temple tax.[25] Though perhaps somewhat appeased by this factoid, ethical sensibilities remain alert as he further reports that good deeds can count as a ransom against debts incurred and, far more troubling for many contemporary readers, that the godless—whether goats, individuals, or an entire people—could take the place of Israel when it comes to divine punishment. Jeremias also finds texts that consider the wise a ransom for the godless, wherein the good and the wise function as a blessing to those around them.[26] The image of the *akedah*, the binding of Isaac, shares a close iconographic connection with the image of the Jewish martyr who can function as a ransom for the sins of Israel. Eventually, the *akedah* becomes associated with Passover, and then perhaps either as a source for, or reaction to, early Christologies, in what Daniel Boyarin calls a "recirculation between Christians and Jews that allows for no simple litany of origins and influence."[27]

Other scholars have contested Jeremias's examination in some respects, especially his attempt to nail down Isa 53 and its notion of the salvific economic power of the death of a just person as ransom, as the major source for Mark 10:45. At times his analysis displays a troubling, if unconscious, anti-Judaistic tinge in its passing off of the Jewish notion of the ransom as ethically questionable and as eventually ineffective in light of the ever so much more effective and ethically safe, once and for all, ransom of Christ. Even so, his text shows that the biblical and extrabiblical sources that form the intertext of passages such as Matt 20:28 display various opinions and

---

24. Warren Carter notes, however, that the plays of Euripides and Sophocles include women characters such as Antigone and Iphigenia, to name the two most well-known figures, who are associated with a substitutionary ransom for the sake of others and peoples. See Carter, *Matthew and the Margins*, 406.
25. Jeremias, "Das Lösegeld für Viele (Mk. 10,45)," 250.
26. Ibid., 252–53.
27. See Jeremias, "Das Lösegeld für Viele (Mk. 10,45)," 254; and Daniel Boyarin, *Dying for God: Martyrdom and the Making of Christianity and Judaism* (Figurae: Reading Medieval Culture; Stanford, Calif.: Stanford University Press, 1999), 117–18.

approaches to questions such as the possibility of vicarious restitution, the effectiveness of payment, the person or deity who pays the ransom, the exact conditions under which such a ransom might be valid (e.g., not for the final judgment), what or who might function as a ransom, and to whom the ransom is actually paid.

Regarding the question of who might stand in for a ransom, we should remember that in Hebrew tribal society, an individual had dense connections to the others in his or her community. At least in terms of a narrative device, one person can stand in for others, perform deeds, even live or die for others in the compound. Thus, the following passage from Isa 43:3–4—another debatable source for Mark 10:45/Matt 20:28—reveals how an entire people can function as a ransom for another:[28]

> For I am the LORD your God,
> the Holy One of Israel, your Savior.
> I give Egypt as your ransom,
> Ethiopia and Seba in exchange for you.
> Because you are precious in my sight,
> and honored, and I love you,
> I give people in return for you,
> nations in exchange for your life.

If a person or group were to serve as a ransom, ancient sources about slavery would suggest that only a slave, a person marked as property with a price, could function as a form of payment, as a monetary medium of exchange. Here, a personified nation depicted as a slave could be exchanged or taken as a ransom by YHWH. In eschatological traditions, these images are often connected to the final judgment, at which a ransom may be offered in payment for a person's or a people's transgressions.[29] However, as Matt 20:28 portrays Jesus as a "substitution" for sins, giving his life as a "ransom for many," many questions, as asked by Davies and Allison, yet remain unanswered: "What is the condition of 'the many'? Why do they need to be ransomed? To whom is the ransom paid—to God . . . to the

---

28. Dieter Vieweger and Annette Böckler consider both Isa 53 and 43 as sources for Mark 10:45 but remain unconvinced. Vieweger and Böckler, "'Ich Gebe Ägypten als Lösegeld für Dich': Mk 10,24 und die Jüdische Tradition zu Jes 43,3b.4," *Zeitschrift für die alttestamentliche Wissenschaft* 108 (1996): 607.

29. *Didache* 4.6 encourages believers to give part of their wealth as ransom: "Of whatsoever you have gained by thy hands you shall give ransom for your sins" (*doseis lutrosin hamartion sou*). The English translation of the *Didache* follows *The Apostolic Fathers I* (trans. Kirsopp Lake; Loeb Classical Library; Cambridge: Harvard University Press, 1950), 315–316.

devil . . . or to no one at all . . . ? Is forgiveness effected now or at the last judgement or both? How is it appropriated?"[30]

These are just some of the questions one might ask. Others may wonder in what relation the notion of a ransom given by the believer stands to the ransom paid by Christ. It would seem, then, that Jewish and Greco-Roman notions of ransom, slavery, and redemption intersect with each other in the texts of early Christian divine commerce. Though biblical precedents also suggest the influence of other contexts, the image of ransom appears strongly tied to the various practices of slavery.[31]

Philo, the Alexandrian, knows several connotations for *lutron*. One of these suggests that "every wise man is the *lutron* of a perverse man," evoking echoes both of extrabiblical Jewish literature and of the Stoics. For Philo, the Levites as a priestly people functioned as a ransom for the firstborn of Israel, as "the Levite is one who redeems, for a man of wisdom redeems the man who is foolish." Lyonnet comments, "*Lutron*, therefore, is nothing else, according to Philo, than that by which freedom is obtained."[32] The language of a slavelike ownership relation hinges on these words: "The Levites shall be mine, for all the firstborn are mine" (Num 3:12b–13a).

Slavery in antiquity was a rather complex phenomenon. In a recent collection of essays on slavery in ancient Jewish and Christian texts, Richard Horsley has suggested that previous scholarship of antiquity, particularly that of a modern German variety of classicists enamored with Greek antiquity, has remained unduly uncritical of the practices and policies of slavery.[33] While scholars such as Dale Martin have sketched a Pauline understanding of "slavery as salvation," partly on the basis of that arguably more complacent German tradition of research, Horsley and others have proceeded to reconsider the severity and ethical indefensibility of the practice of classical slavery. In this reconsideration, an important distinction is found between slavery in ancient Judea and the Greco-Roman practice of slavery. While chattel slavery played only a limited role in Israel as well as in

---

30. Davies and Allison, *Gospel according to Matthew*, 100.
31. Later readers of these texts may well have related them to the elusive phenomenon of manumission (that often did not result in what we today would recognize as freedom but rather in a state of *paramone*, that is, the former slave remained dependent upon the former master.) See Lyonnet and Sabourin, *Sin, Redemption, and Sacrifice*, 109. Both Wilfrid Haubeck and, more recently, Adela Yarbro Collins argue that even if the ransom motif was not directly inspired by the practice of slavery, for later interpreters the practice of secular (Haubeck) and sacral (Collins) manumission would have been evoked. Haubeck, *Loskauf durch Christus: Herkunft, Gestalt und Bedeutung des paulinischen Loskaufmotivs* (Witten: Bundes-Verlag, 1985), 294; and Collins, "Signification of Mark 10:45," 376–77.
32. Lyonnet and Sabourin, *Sin, Redemption, and Sacrifice*, 86.
33. Richard Horsley, "The Slave Systems of Classical Antiquity and Their Reluctant Recognition by Modern Scholars," *Semeia* 83/84 (1998): 22–28 and passim.

other ancient Near East societies, it was prevalent in the Roman Empire.[34] In Greco-Roman antiquity, slaves were under the "absolute control" of their owner, and could be "sold, mortgaged, taxed, leased, bequeathed, and insured."[35] Yet there were clearly many varieties of how an enslaved person lived and was embedded in society. Dissenting from Horsley's critique of Martin, Jennifer Glancy argues that Orlando Patterson's useful definition of slavery includes both menial slaves and elite slaves.[36] Thus, according to Patterson, "slavery is the permanent, violent domination of a natally alienated and generally dishonored person."[37]

The characterization of slaves in (Matthean) parables might then support Dale Martin's analogy of patron-client/master-slave relations, though Glancy argues that the difference between slave and client is that a slave's body is punishable while that of a client is not:[38] "Readers of Matthew recognize the disciplined flesh of parabolic slaves as an antitype, a model to avoid. Curiously, however, Matthew features another tortured body as a model to emulate, the battered and crucified body of Jesus."[39]

The context of this slave's punishment, as well as that of the *commercium*, is that of an ancient *oikonomia*, of the relationship between *kurios*, *diakonos*, and *doulos*, of master, servant, and slave. These relations function as the grounding of the image of the *lutron*, or ransom. Exegetes have expressed a certain discomfort with passages involving the *lutron*. Ulrich Luz, for example, finds various biblical applications of the term "very vague" and "indeterminate" and feels that within the context of the gospel, Matt 20:28 appears as an isolated verse, though the verse is found also in the Markan version of the pericope.[40] Though likely spoken specifically to men vying for power in a patriarchal system, authorities have recommended this injunction more often to those already with little power, as an instrument of power and knowledge that subjugates rather than encouraging self-discipline. Luz observes that for the most part this passage has been employed to effect the veiling of hierarchical power through the deceptive renaming of an unbroken continuation of ecclesial power pyramids as "ministries."[41] The synoptic Jesus' revision of power/knowledge as the ability to

---

34. Dexter E. Callender Jr., "Servants of God(s) and Servants of Kings in Israel and the Ancient Near East," *Semeia* 83/84 (1998): 67, 71.
35. Carter, *Households and Discipleship*, 179.
36. Jennifer A. Glancy, "Slaves and Slavery in the Matthean Parables," *Journal of Biblical Literature* 119, no. 1 (2000): 74.
37. Orlando Patterson, *Slavery and Social Death* (Cambridge: Harvard University Press, 1982), 13.
38. Glancy, "Slaves and Slavery in the Matthean Parables," 72, 74, 75.
39. Ibid., 90.
40. Luz, *Das Evangelium nach Matthäus*, 165n.40; my translation.
41. Ibid., 166.

serve and suffer has clearly produced its own problematic *Wirkungsgeschichte*. The feminist critique of Christian notions of atonement takes its departure from similar concerns, arguing that the ransom offered through servitude has been implemented less as a currency for liberation than as a counterfeit for it. But we will examine feminist concerns regarding soteriology below, and in the meantime further ponder the ransom offered by Jesus.

Matthew's notion of the ransom also invites another, different reading. It cannot be simply reduced to an expression of the Nietzschean notion of "Sklavenreligion," or even to a revolutionary reversal of power hierarchies, but it may function as the complex, ironic deconstruction of dichotomic positions of power. Jacques Derrida's intertextual meditations on sacrifice, gift, economy, and counterfeit will serve as a literary guide to the trading floor of soteriology, as we wade not through blood but through discarded slips of theological and economic writing. Derrida has suggested that all economic transactions by way of money already contain a counterfeit element, since money itself claims to stand for an absent substance or value, and thus supplements or represents an absence: "Money replaces things by their signs . . . from one economic organization to another. That is why the alphabet is commercial, a trader. . . . The critical description of money is the faithful reflection of the discourse on writing. In both cases an anonymous supplement is substituted for the thing."[42]

The symbol of the ransom paid by the slave and the Son Jesus might even function in a way similar to Derrida's *"Signsponge."* The Son—or S(p)on(ge)—can thus, "when applied to a surface, expunge, wipe, and efface." Moreover, it "is also the chance for purification, something which sponges away the stain, and even . . . expunges the debt ('the slate')."[43] This S(p)on(ge), not only accomplishes the erasure of the scribblings of sin but also becomes a writing himself. Moore comments further:

> At his baptism the Son is accepted for publication by his Father ("with you I am well pleased"—Mark 1:11), although he goes into production only as he dies. The event is announced in the *Gospel of Truth:* "Jesus appeared; he put on that book; . . . he published the edict of the Father on the cross."[44]

Moore observes the obvious parallel of this gospel text to another economic splinter in the deuteropauline corpus: "And when you were dead in

---

42. Jacques Derrida, *Of Grammatology* (corrected ed.; trans. Gayatri Spivak; Baltimore: Johns Hopkins University Press, 1997), 300.
43. Stephen D. Moore, *Mark and Luke in Poststructuralist Perspective: Jesus Begins to Write* (New Haven, Conn.: Yale University Press, 1992), 52.
44. Ibid., 47.

trespasses and the uncircumcision of your flesh, God made you alive together with him, when he forgave us all our trespasses, erasing the record that stood against us with its legal demands. He set this aside, nailing it to the cross" (Col 2:13–14). The record mentioned here is a *cheirograpson,* a handwritten record of a person's debts. Possibly the "crucifixion" of that record relates to the practice of nailing the offenses of the crucified to the cross with them.[45] Rereading the *Gospel of Truth* with that allusion in mind, the economic connotations of a slightly earlier pericope become amplified:

> Just as there lies hidden in a will, before it is opened, the fortune of the deceased master of the house, so (it is) with the totality, which lay hidden while the Father of the totality was invisible, being something which is from him, from whom every space comes forth. For this reason Jesus appeared; he put on that book; he published the edict of the Father on the cross. O such great teaching![46]

And, O such an *admirabile commercium!* The *Gospel of Truth* mixes its metaphors well, combining (like Derrida much later) the practice of writing with that of coining/trading. Trees of knowledge can be turned into leaves of paper for edicts, bills, and wills. The writing that is erased is at the same time published: writing/erasing, publishing/obliterating the record of debt. Jesus becomes the visible, written expression of an invisible divine economy. Might we read in this payment of ransom an instance of Derridean erasure, simultaneously writing and crossing out the debts incurred?

"O what sweet exchange" (*o tes glukeias antallages*), chants the *Letter to Diognetus.* "[God] himself took upon him the burden of our iniquities, He gave His own Son as a ransom for us, the holy One for transgressors."[47] The burdened slave becomes currency, and this currency becomes a tortured body. If the slave's body as the "locus of abuse" is the most consistent feature of the characterization of a slave in Matthew, as Glancy argues, one might wonder whether it is not the signification of Jesus as a slave that makes him punishable and subject to the death of a slave for Matthew, Philippians 2, and subsequent early Christian traditions.[48] Thus,

---

45. Moore, *Mark and Luke,* 47; Eduard Schweizer, *Der Brief an die Kolosser* (Evangelisch-Katholischer Kommentar Zum Neuen Testament; Neukirchen-Vluyn: Neukirchener Verlag, 1976), 115 and n.362.

46. James M. Robinson, gen. ed., *The Nag Hammadi Library in English* (3d ed.; San Francisco: Harper & Row, 1988), 41–42.

47. The English translation of the *Letter to Diognetus* follows Alexander Roberts and James Donaldson, eds. *The Apostolic Fathers, Justin Martyr, Irenaeus* (vol. 1 of *Ante-Nicene Fathers*; Peabody, Mass.: Hendrickson, 1994), 9.

48. Glancy, "Slaves and Slavery in the Matthean Parables," 72; Moore, *God's Gym,* 25.

the pre-Pauline christological hymn in Phil 2 suggests Christ's assumption of obedience and an enslaved incarnate body as the precondition for his salvific death—as if only an enslaved God could be punished, by taking on a punishable body:

> ... though he was in the form of God,
> did not regard equality with God
> as something to be exploited,
> but emptied himself,
> taking the form of a slave,
> being born in human likeness.
> And being found in human form,
> he humbled himself
> and become obedient to the point of death—
> even death on a cross. (Phil 2:6–8)

Does the *kenosis*—the divine emptying of privilege—function as a precondition of this image of the economy of salvation? What of the obedient death, the ensuing exaltation and the (somewhat troublingly vengeful) restitution of Christ to an even further enhanced mastery where "every knee" must bend in service (v. 10)? Several commentators read the reference to slavery and lordship in Phil 2 as a metaphorical or theological expression only, and de-emphasize potential authorial assumptions about the audience's knowledge of the conditions of slavery. Ulrich Müller interprets "slavery" here as a reference to becoming human, a metaphorical usage that might mirror a skeptical branch of Jewish wisdom. Within this understanding of wisdom, the human condition is by definition one of slavery, where a preemptive self-humbling must precede the honor given to one by a superior. In this scheme, the conclusion often drawn is that self-diminishment precedes a definitive divine promise of salvation.[49] Similarly, Dale Martin has described Paul's use of enslavement as "a metaphorical expression for social self-lowering and social advancement" that serves as a "scaffolding for Paul's soteriology."[50] Unfortunately, this scheme has—beyond any number of conceivably wise applications—served to enhance and exacerbate the programmatic and religiously institutionalized humiliation of women and others perceived as social inferiors. Master-slave and bridegroom-bride are some of Paul's preferred metaphors for reflections

---

49. Ulrich B. Müller, *Philipper* (Theologischer Handkommentar zum NT; Leipzig: Evangelische Verlagsanstalt, 1993), 100–101, 111.
50. Martin, *Slavery as Salvation*, 129.

on sin, law, and righteousness, images that will flow heavily into the intertext of the fathers.[51] These hierarchical household relations function as images of salvation, of divine economy.

In Phil 2, the image of slavery—though it resembles Patterson's definition of slavery in its inclusion of natal alienation and social death—also departs from its known circumstances. Presumably, at least according to Phil 2 and many traditional expressions of soteriological doctrine, Christ becomes a "slave" voluntarily, while slaves in Roman society never had a choice. Similarly, the final elevation of Christ—"God also highly exalted him, and gave him the name that is above every name"—does not refer to a manumission but rather to a restitution of prior honor, power, and wealth. The idealization of slavery in Phil 2—or at least its modified and specific image of Christ's voluntary economic bondage—is at best highly ambivalent, since it did not lead to a general revalorization of slaves.

Still, the image did most likely have a scandalizing effect on slaveholding societies, introducing the "irreducible tension of a God who becomes a slave." Thus, we may hold with Sheila Briggs that it becomes "possible to conceive of an inversion of the hierarchy of being and worth held in ancient society." Briggs concedes that it is likely that at least some degree of subversion occurred, since slaves were obliged to participate in the religion of their masters. But common religious practices did not result in shared interpretations of the relevant text and thus "do not necessarily defuse social conflict" as the modern analogue of U.S. forms of slavery shows.[52]

The Enlightenment, as defenders of modernity might argue, eventually and effectively did away with the inhumanities of slavery. But a wider perspective, beyond a Eurocentric bias, reveals lingering forms of feudalism and slavery in numerous parts of the world. The practices of slavery are not limited to the institutionalized racism of the United States, or in the continuing wealth of nations who continue to profit from the now more camouflaged neocolonial exploitation of other counties. It comes as no surprise to more attentive contemporary readers that some writers see a literal slave system still very much in our increasingly global trading connections.[53]

---

51. Sheila Briggs, "Can an Enslaved God Liberate? Hermeneutical Reflections on Philippians 2:6–11," *Semeia* 47 (1989): 142.

52. Ibid.,148–50.

53. See Kevin Bales, *Disposable People: New Slavery in the Global Economy* (Berkeley: University of California Press, 1999) on contemporary slavery. The "race to the bottom" will likely exacerbate the trend to debt and wage slavery in poorer counties, as well as of the poor in wealthy counties. In early 2001, the news of a ship full of child slaves off the coast of Africa was in the news around the world, making it hard to ignore the relevance of this matter. For the slavelike conditions of much of domestic labor in the United States and the accompanying ethnic discrimination and stereotyping of immigrants, see Grace Chang, *Disposable Domestics: Immigrant Women Workers in the Global Economy* (Cambridge, Mass.: South End Press, 2000).

These forms of economic slavery are often complicit with forms of physical torture. Thus, Page DuBois has contested Foucault's Eurocentric claim that torture no longer exists as a form of discipline. "Tell it to the El Salvadorans," she quips, critiquing Foucault's "description of the transition from spectacular torture and execution to internalized discipline" as "resolutely Eurocentric," and limited to "a local analysis."[54] Perhaps not only a local analysis but also a local anesthesia? Even in the West, torture has merely changed location. It is still with us in the *maquiladoras* and the brothels where poor women from the "third world" are indentured or virtually imprisoned. And not only humans continue to become enslaved. We find torture, rape, and destruction equally relocated to the chicken batteries and laboratories of the pharmaceutical industry as other "suffering servants" are stretched on the benches of Haraway's secular salvation history of "technobiopower."[55] Forms of human enslavement are often additionally expressed in terms of gender hierarchies that enable and produce climates conducive to domestic violence, at times with the support of a twisted interpretation of theological expressions of *commercium* and *conubium*.

The proclivity of certain forms of atonement to enable or at least not counteract abuse has led to crucial questions, such as the one formulated by Sheila Briggs: "Can an enslaved God liberate?"[56] How indeed can an enslaved God redeem? Is such an image of God, a God who may function as a model for submission to be emulated, not even conducive to the enslavement and the physical and mental oppression of humans? Is the divine economy one in which somebody has to suffer to accomplish redemption? What constitutes redemption? Whose redemption, and at what cost to others? Given the liabilities of so many bankrupt interpretations, how can the notion of the *commercium*, the miraculous exchange of salvation, help to reconstruct a redemption from contemporary forms of slavery?

Rethinking the *Admirabile Commercium*

Gustav Aulén's *Christus Victor* attempts to revive interest in and study of forgotten and marginalized readings of redemption. Aulén observed that a number of scholars exhibited discomfort around the soteriological motif of an economic exchange with the devil and other early Christian atonement

---

54. Page DuBois, *Torture and Truth* (New York: Routledge, 1991), 154. For this reference to DuBois I am indebted to Stephen Moore. See Moore, *God's Gym*, 10.
55. Donna J. Haraway, *Modest_Witness@Second_Millennium. FemaleMan©_Meets_OncoMouse™* (New York: Routledge, 1997), 2.
56. See her essay of the same name, cited on previous page.

motifs.[57] Many felt that patristic approaches to soteriology were simply a "rough draft" of Anselm's theory of satisfaction, which they saw as "a relic of Judaism surviving in Christianity."[58] What were then seen as merely rudimentary and unripe instances of soteriology in the earliest centuries were often neglected or given scant attention in a number of histories of dogma.[59] *Christus Victor* performs a revaluation of one patristic motif, that of the "idea of the atonement as a divine conflict and victory" in which Christ fights and triumphs over the evil powers of the world.[60] Aulén makes a case for the reconsideration of early patristic soteriologies, hoping to overcome some of the more unfortunate prejudices—beyond a number of well-founded criticisms—of modern theology. Yet he also tends to blend the multiplicity of images together, so that the economic images are subsumed under triumphal motif of the *Christus victor*, serving again to obscure the specificity of the *lutron* or *commercium*.[61] Still, his work allowed others to overcome the view of scholars of early redemption theories such as Rashdall, who considered the ransom theory of a transaction with the devil "hideous" and not to be "taken seriously," and Hitchcock, who rejected the ransom theory of the early church as "grotesque."[62]

Thus, Aulén writes of the "deals with the devil":

> No other aspect of the teaching of the Fathers ... has provoked such criticism as their treatment of the dealings of Christ with the devil; primarily on this ground, their teaching has been commonly regarded as unworthy of serious consideration.... Anselm ... is regarded as having overcome the idea of a transaction with the devil, as well as the grotesque idea of a deception of the devil. Nothing is more common than to find the patristic teaching dismissed with an impatient shrug of the shoulders, as mere puerilities, or sharply rated as ethically intolerable.[63]

---

57. For a taxonomy of patristic ransom motifs, see Eugene Te Selle, "The Cross as Ransom," *Journal of Early Christian Studies* 4, no. 2 (1996): 147–70. A traditional dogmatic, if potentially reductionist, distinction between the "staurozentrische Soteriologie des Westens" and an "inkarnationszentrische Soteriologie des Ostens" as related by Thomas Pröpper, might be helpful as we try to map where the economic locus of *soteria* appears to be placed. The implications of a difference between the incarnation and/or the cross as the location of the *commercium* will yet have to be pondered. See Pröpper, *Erlösungsglaube und Freiheitsgeschichte* (Munich: Kösel, 1988), 71–88.

58. Gustav Aulén, *Christus Victor: An Historical Study of the Three Main Types of the Idea of Atonement* (New York: Macmillan, 1969), 7–8.

59. See Gunther Wenz, *Geschichte der Versöhnungslehre in der evangelischen Theologie der Neuzeit* (Munich: Chr. Kaiser, 1984).

60. Aulén, *Christus Victor*, 20.

61. A detailed account of soteriological motifs is given in John McIntyre, *The Shape of Soteriology: Studies in the Doctrine of the Death of Christ* (Edinburgh: T&T Clark, 1992).

62. Quoted in Aulén, *Christus Victor*, 10.

63. Ibid., 47.

Though Aulén sympathizes with the "disgust" that these patristic intimations of "naive simplicity" and "grotesque realism" evoke, he urges theologians to study these images in order to proceed to the deeper values he suspects lie within. But modern theological impatience with the motif does not necessarily indicate only a cultural disgust at the involvement of the divine in monetary exchange. Rather, it also rejects a payment to the devil that might indicate that a God conceived as transcendent, unchanging, and independent owes another entity anything. Gregory of Nazianzus, for example, explicitly denied the idea of a payment to the devil as shameful.[64]

Irenaeus expands on the canonical texts regarding the notion of the ransom. The *commercium* is part of Irenaeus's larger rhetorical economy in *Adversus haereses*—that of creating a metanarrative of divine *oikonomia* that binds all history into the being of the preexistent Word—and emerges as a smaller *oikonomia* identified with the ransom through the incarnate Word's blood. The Lyonnese presbyter assures his readers that it was "in a manner consonant to reason" that the late-born humans "have received . . . [the blessings of salvation] according to the ministration of the Word . . . who, redeeming us by His own blood[,] . . . gave himself as a redemption for those who had been led into captivity." For Irenaeus, the power that enslaves humans is identified as the "apostasy, who tyrannized over us unjustly" though "we were by nature the property of the omnipotent God" (*Haer.* 5.1.1).[65] This enslavement occurs through a kind of alienation, in terms of both property and semiotics. Apostasy, having "alienated" humans "contrary to nature, rendering [them] its own disciples," is defeated by the

---

64. Raymund Schwager, *Der wunderbare Tausch: Zur Geschichte und Bedeutung der Erlösungslehre* (Munich: Kösel, 1986), 43. Besides Aulén's Protestant attempt at recovery, the only other body of literature that focuses on the *lutron/commercium* appears in the German and Austrian Catholic theologies of Martin Herz, Erich Przywara, Hans Urs von Balthasar, and, most recently, Reinhold Schwager. Other Catholic theologians, such as Friedrich Normann, recoil from the suspicion of impiety and reject the image as unfit because of its "speculative" nature and on the grounds of the Thomist notion of the *analogia entis*. See Friedrich Normann, *Teilhabe: Ein Schlüsselwort der Vätertheologie* (Münsterische Beiträge zur Theologie; Münster: Aschendorff, 1978), 90–92. To my knowledge, only one theologian, feminist liberationist Darby K. Ray, has followed up on Aulén's suggestion and proceeded to use the potential of the "deception of the devil" rather than the more martial imagery of the *Christus victor* to help reconstruct an understanding of doctrines of atonement in the face of their historical employment to silence victims of human violence, especially women who have become victims of domestic violence. Her reinvention of Jesus as a trickster who "deceives the devil," thus overcoming evil, will help to reconstruct the image of the *commercium* attempted below.

65. Basil Studer argues that Irenaeus's rendering "stands in the context of Marcionite polemics," and Te Selle finds Irenaeus's "chief contribution" in the restatement of the "ransom theme, no longer in terms of the cosmic dualism of the Gnostics and Marcionites, but in the language of apostasy from the One creator." See Studer, *Soteriologie in der Schrift und Patristik* (Handbuch der Dogmengeschichte; Freiburg: Herder, 1978), 72; and Te Selle, "Cross as Ransom," 159.

Word, who repossesses the formerly divine property through a process of reeducation. Semiotic and material economies become curiously interrelated in a divine "deal" where true money and true words buy out false currencies and heretical teachings. The Word—the true and single narrative of divine economy—becomes the genuine currency that replaces the counterfeit of the many apostate narratives. According to this trading strategy, the economic work of the Word consists in "righteously turn[ing] against that apostasy, and redeem[ing] from it His own property, not by violent means, as the [apostasy] had obtained dominion over us, when it insatiably snatched away what was not its own, but by means of persuasion, as became a God of counsel"(*Haer.* 5.1.1). The economics of redemption, the payment of a ransom to apostasy, so imagines Irenaeus, must be executed in a divinely just and nonviolent way. And justice is preserved, within this divine trade, by exchanging counterfeit doctrines with the true denomination of the divine Word. Apostasy is the counterfeit knowledge and currency system from which those enslaved are redeemed. As a consequence of this divine *oikonomia*, Irenaeus proclaims, "all the doctrines of the heretics fall to ruin" (*Haer.* 5.1.1).

Shortly after Irenaeus, we find images of divine dealing in Tertullian's texts. In debate with Marcion, who claims two different gods, the lawyer and theologian asserts that humans are in fact created according to the image of the one and same God of both creation and redemption. In a monetary analogy, Tertullian finds it sufficient to point out that the image on a coin states whose property it is and declares void all transactions that may have interfered with the divine ownership of the *imago Dei* imprinted on every human coin:

> "Render unto Caesar the things which be Caesar's, and unto God the things which be God's." What will be "the things which are God's"? Such things as are like Caesar's *denarius*—that is to say, His image and similitude. That, therefore, which he commands to be "rendered unto God," the Creator, is *man*, who has been stamped with His image, likeness, name, and substance. Let Marcion's god look after his own mint. Christ bids the *denarius* of man's imprint to be rendered to His Caesar[,] ... not the Caesar of a strange god. The truth, however, must be confessed, this god has not a *denarius* to call his own![66]

---

66. The English translation of *Contra Marcionem* (Against Marcion) follows Alexander Roberts and James Donaldson, eds, *Latin Christianity: Its Founder, Tertullian* (vol. 3 of *Ante-Nicene Fathers*; Peabody, Mass.: Hendrickson, 1994), 4.38.

Tertullian bristles at the notion that humans are the property of any other God but the God of Christ. The true substance/wealth/coin is owned by the God of both testaments. Bankruptcy is unthinkable for the true God of all capital who coins humans as coins in his image.[67] The insubstantial god of Marcion does not have a penny to his name; all the wealth lies with God the supreme Caesar who has imprinted his image on every human coin he has impressed.

In *Against Praxeas,* Tertullian attempts to negotiate the complexities of the incarnation and the puzzle of how the divine and human natures might coexist in Christ. His opponents appear to suggest that the god-man himself resembles a coin, molded together from two different metals and thus forming a *mixture,* a *tertium quid.*

> For if the Word became flesh by a transfiguration and chance of substance, it follows at once that Jesus must be a substance compounded of two substances—of flesh and spirit—a kind of mixture, like electrum, composed of gold and silver. . . . Being compounded, therefore, of both, He actually is neither; he rather is some third substance, very different from either.[68]

Tertullian, however, rejects the "confusion" and complete fusion of human with divine that assumes Christ as composed of neither spirit nor flesh but "confusedly of some third character," thus, if weakly, refuting his opponents' opinions about the matter of the Word's substance. In fact, he excused himself shortly after he made his somewhat shaky point: "Concerning Christ, indeed, I defer what I have to say" (*Prax.* 27). It will take centuries to get to even a semblance of conciliar unity on these issues. However, the image of the living coin, the "monnaie vivande," sticks around for other conceptualizations of ransom and redemption.[69] In the christological negotiations of the fourth century, the term *homoousios*—a monetary term describing several coins as having been made from the same metal, and thus genuine—comes to stand for the consubstantiality of Father and Son.[70]

---

67. This train of thought resembles that of the *ex nihilo* doctrine: "According to the logic of ex nihilo, one is either good or evil, corporeal or incorporeal, eternal or temporal, almighty or powerless, propertied or inferior." Catherine Keller, *Face of the Deep* (New York: Routledge, 2003), 49.

68. The English translation of *Contra Praxeam* (Against Praxeas) follows Alexander Roberts and James Donaldson, eds. *Latin Christianity: Its Founder, Tertullian* (vol. 3 of *Ante-Nicene Fathers*; Peabody, Mass.: Hendrickson, 1994), 27.

69. Klossowski, *La Monnaie Vivande.*

70. The concept *ousia* can signify the identity or being of the household, which consisted of both land and slaves. See Jean Danielou, *Geschichte der Kirche* (ed. L. J. Rogier, R. Aubert, and M. D. Knowles; Einsiedeln: Benziger Verlag, 1963), 1:266.

Thirty years after Tertullian, Cyprian of Carthage's *Works and Almsgiving* outlines a divine commerce that builds on a more shared understanding of both divine and human contributions to salvation. Both risk and investment, it appears, are shared by the economic contribution of Christ and by the believer. Christ's ransom, accordingly, is given so that "He might draw out to liberty those who were in bondage." But, says Cyprian, divine providence has put in place "a plan of salvation [that has] provided for us, that more abundant care should be taken for preserving man after he is already redeemed!" Preserving the initial divine redemptive investment, the believer is called to follow it up by other contributions. For this purpose, "divine mercy, coming once more in aid, [opened] some way of securing salvation by pointing out works of justice and mercy, so that by almsgiving we may wash away whatever foulness we subsequently contract" (*Eleem.* 1). Cyprian addresses those in his context who appear to have abandoned their investment in the divine economy and who instead fear for their family's property: "[Y]ou are a lover of mammon more than your own soul; and while you fear, lest for the sake of yourself, you should lose your patrimony, your yourself are perishing for the sake of your patrimony."[71] Thus, Cyprian argues, the ransom of Christ has been rendered void: "You are the captive and slave of your money; you are bound with the chains and bonds of covetousness; and you whom Christ had once loosed, are once more in chains." As spiritual broker, he encourages his investors to "divide your returns with the Lord your God; share your gains with Christ; make Christ a partner with you in your earthly possessions, that He also may make you a fellow heir with Him in his heavenly kingdom" (*Eleem.* 13). His advice is directed at both men and women:

> You therefore, who are rich and wealthy, buy for yourself of Christ gold tried by fire; that you may be pure gold; with your filth burnt out as if by fire, if you are purged by almsgiving and righteous works.... And you who are a wealthy and rich matron in Christ's Church, anoint your eyes, not with the collyrium of the devil, but with Christ's eye-salve, that you may be able to attain to see God. (*Eleem.* 14)

Not only would those Christian investors then be "lending to God" by giving alms to the poor, she or he would "commend [their] children to God," bring the "fruit of their salvation," "change ... their possessions for the better, into heavenly treasures," and finally "repay Christ for the price of

---

71. The English translation of the *Works and Almsgiving* follows Alexander Roberts and James Donaldson, eds., *Fathers of the Third Century: Hippolytus, Cyprian, Caius, Novatian* (vol. 5 of *Ante-Nicene Fathers*; Peabody, Mass.: Hendrickson, 1994), 476–84.

His passion and blood" (*Eleem.* 16, 18, 22, 23). Cyprian envisions the divine economy as a mutual investment. The initial divine endowment requires a reciprocal investment by those who benefited from it, one that—depending on its amount—might position them well in the divine "contest of charity" (*Eleem.* 26).

An Alexandrian investigation of divine transactions nearly contemporary with Cyprian's comes down to us from Origen. His commentary on Matt 20:28 connects the Matthean ransom with Phil 2, where Christ is described as having taken the form of a slave.[72] The Alexandrian teacher betrays his personal interest in deception as an educational and disciplining tool elsewhere, recommending it as a means justified by the final redemptive concern that motivates it. In Origen, deception can function as a divine or human educational strategy, employed by God or the human teacher. Joseph Trigg would have us believe that "Origen considered deliberate deception a part of God's strategy for winning back erring souls. We must also conclude that he considered such deception acceptable on the part of spiritual Christians in their dealings with simple believers and employed it himself."[73]

Origen's take on the *commercium* displays his strong interest in the person of Christ and specifically in what part of himself Christ did or did not give to the devil. He proceeds to make an argument that it is the soul of Jesus—his psyche and nothing more, not his spirit (which he had given to God) nor his body—that was given as ransom. The divine payment, so he argues, could only include the soul, but not the "supreme substance and the divinity." The recipient of that soul, says Origen, is "certainly not God" but the "Evil One," who had assumed power over humanity. The Evil One let himself be deceived, thus allowing this transaction to take place: "This one namely had the power over us, until the soul of Jesus was given to him as a ransom. In this he let himself be deceived, as if he could become Lord over it."[74] As in Cyprian's account, humans are bought back through the blood of the enslaved Jesus. In Origen, Jesus' soul/life[75] functions as the actual currency. A whiff of divine deception hangs in the air as the devil "let himself be deceived" but is not explicitly thematized as a divine action by Origen's account. It seems as if the Evil One was deceived in thinking that the

---

72. Origenes, "Mattäus," in *Der Kommentar zum Evangelium nach Mattäus* (trans. Herman J. Vogt; Bibliothek der griechischen Literatur; Stuttgart: Anton Hiersemann, 1990), 2:178.
73. Joseph Trigg, "Divine Deception and the Truthfulness of Scripture," in *Origen of Alexandria: His World and His Legacy* (ed. Charles Kannengiesser and William Petersen; Notre Dame, Ind.: University of Notre Dame Press, 1988), 162.
74. Origenes, "Mattäus," 179; my translation.
75. In Hebrew, the *nephesh* would be housed in the blood of an animate being.

soul of Jesus could be held in captivity and would not by his enormous power break free: "[T]he soul of Jesus was given to him as a ransom, whereby he let himself be deceived, as if he could become Lord over it, and did not see that he could not stand the torture of trying to hold it down."[76]

Gregory of Nyssa's version on the divine deception of the devil offers more on the specifics of such a ransom transaction. Of all the fathers, the Cappadocian delivers the most "developed" account of the divine deal. Gregory's narrative occurs in the context of explaining—for the purposes of training new believers through a catechism—the necessity of the incarnation. He wriggles and strains to explain how such divine trickery can represent godly justice. Eventually he cannot but admit the divine trickery is "in some measure a fraud and deception." Might Gregory, though offering this piece of theology in deadpan style, secretly enjoy this slightly naughty, tricksterlike economy? The divine ransom is paid to redeem those "who have bartered away their freedom for money." Humanity is in bondage to the powers of evil: "The captive sought for a ransomer, the fettered prisoner for some one to take his part, and for a deliverer he who was held in the bondage of slavery."[77]

Gregory unveils the serene justice and wisdom with which this supreme divine economy is executed. A considerably more pacifistic God than that portrayed as the *Christus victor* will not use force in the work of redemption. Instead, this divine economist respects the human deal with the "Enemy" and will not use unjust "violence against him who has bought [the slave]" (*Or. Cat.* 22). Liberation of the slave "by tearing us away by a violent exercise of force," so reasons Gregory, "will clearly be acting unjustly in thus arbitrarily rescuing one who has been legally purchased as a slave." A just God must thus respect even problematic business obligations, pay the price for the redemption of rightfully owned slaves, and "make over to the master of the slave whatever ransom he may agree to accept for the person in his possession"(*Or. Cat.* 22). Thus preempting any "complaint" by "him who enslaved man through sensual pleasure," God pursues alternative strategies. But what property, what commodity, can be procured that "he would accept in exchange"? The ransom must be more valuable, more desirable, must promise "a gain in the exchange." The "special features"— what one might call the MVP (Most Valuable Player) effect—of Christ offer superior value: conceived without "carnal connection" through a

---

76. Origenes, "Mattäus," 179; my translation.
77. The English translation of *Oratio catechetica* (Catechetical Oration, or The Great Catechism) follows Philip Schaff and Henry Wace, eds., *Gregory of Nyssa: Dogmatic Treatises* (A Select Library of the Christian Church: Nicene and Post-Nicene Fathers; Peabody, Mass.: Hendrickson, 1994), 15.

birth without impurity by a virgin mother and with "voices of the unseen testifying from above to a transcendent worth," Christ takes the prize. The Enemy "chooses Him as a ransom for those who were shut up in the prison of death" (*Or. Cat.* 23).

Likewise, Homi Bhabha writes that "mimicry is like camouflage[,] a form of resemblance, that differs from or defends presence by displaying it in part, metonymically."[78] Christ's incarnation as a slave "clouds" the true extent of divine power: "the Deity was invested with the flesh . . . to secure that he . . . might have no fears in approaching that supereminent power" (*Or. Cat.* 23). The devil, that colonizer of humanity, is tricked by divine mimicry. Mimic resemblance threatens the exploitative system as it mocks it. A camouflaged trickster Christ masks his divinity in order to be sold into slavery to free an enslaved humanity. This stealth investment explodes the diabolic bank, breaks the chains, and buys redemption for all.

Thus mobilized, the divine investment and advertising strategy successfully attracts the intended buyer and ensures the impeccability of the divine business reputation: "Thus, you see how goodness was conjoined with justice, and how wisdom was not divorced from them." All three qualities—goodness, wisdom, and justice—remain preserved: "[M]aking the redemption of the captive [is] a matter of justice, while the invention whereby He enabled the Enemy to apprehend [the previously ineffable power of Christ] is a manifestation of supreme wisdom" (*Or. Cat.* 24). After having safely established that the divine deal is beyond reproach, Gregory appears tempted to flaunt the cleverness of the divine tricksterishness involved. He reveals that the "Deity was hidden under the veil of our nature, that so, as with ravenous fish, the hook of the Deity might be gulped down along with the bait of flesh, and thus life being introduced into the household of death" (*Or. Cat.* 24).

Gregory realizes that "those who question this *[oikonomia]* of God" may not yet quite "buy into" this divine business scheme and may have a few more doubts about its "justice." While the fact that the Deity could be born in our nature "ought not reasonably to present any strangeness to the minds of those who do not take too narrow a view of things," he realizes, of course, that a person might in her "examination of the amount of justice and wisdom discoverable in this *[oikonomia]*" be "perhaps, induced to entertain the thought that it was by means of a certain amount of deceit that God carried out this scheme on our behalf." To those inclined to direct their thoughts this way, Gregory admits that the "Deity [was] veiled . . . without the knowledge of His enemy" and thus able to penetrate "within

---

78. Homi Bhabha, *The Location of Culture* (London: Routledge, 1994), 90.

the lines of him who had man in his power," a plot that might suggest "in some measure a fraud and surprise." Yet, Gregory argues, the divine veiling functions as a "due recompense," a "repayment, adequate to the debt, by which the deceiver was in return deceived," and exhibits the "justice of the dealing" when "He who first deceived man by the bait of sensual pleasure is himself deceived by the presentment of the human form" (*Or. Cat.* 24–26).

In Irenaeus, the motif is colored by his engagement with heretics. Thus, humans are enslaved not by any slave master but by those who have captured humans with their tales of apostasy. Enslavement for Irenaeus is a dogmatic as well as intellectual category. The true Word becomes the only reliable currency, whereas the doctrines of the heretics are counterfeit coins. The Word thus can function to buy back apostates from a personified apostasy.

Payback Time: Feminist Critiques of Atonement Theories

The image of Christ as martyr, slave, and victim has had numerous effects throughout the history of Christianity. For some, the interpretive effects may have been liberative, depending on location and context of interpretation, while for others—especially for women and for those enslaved for economic reasons, supported by ethnic prejudice—they have more often proved to support the oppression by the interpreters who wielded considerable hermeneutic clout in their societies and economies. Thus, in Western economic history, the *commercium* and the *conubium*, the economic and sexual exploitation of enslaved peoples and women, have often gone hand in hand. Feminist theologians have pointed out the ambivalence of Christian symbols and the need to be aware of the history and potential of abuse of symbols such as the cross for the purposes of keeping people, and especially women, silenced under oppression.[79] Similarly, Augustinian conceptions of what constitutes sin have more often than not highlighted as sin qualities that would help women to emerge from abusive relationships. Thus, if human experience and interpretation is gendered, localized, and specific—if, as Valerie Saiving has held, the shape of women's "sins" (a better word in the specific context of this study may be "debts") are differently experienced and manifested from those of men, we must also assume that redemption comes in various shapes. Saiving's classic article "The Human Situation: A Feminine View" provides helpful hints to this purpose. If there

---

79. See, for example, the important article by Joanne Carlson Brown and Rebecca Parker, "For God So Loved the World?" in *Violence against Women and Children: A Christian Theological Sourcebook* (ed. Carol J. Adams and Marie M. Fortune; New York: Continuum, 1995), 36–59.

are (at least) two gendered ways to experience the human condition, then explanatory schemes and divine strategies of healing must be appreciative of locations, economic and otherwise.[80] Many texts in the Western tradition describe an androcentric perspective on what the problem and what the solutions may be. Yet this grid has not met the experiences of women and has, in fact, led to their continued if not enhanced oppression. If our debts are specific to our specific embodiment, then we need also to identify a variety of soteriological approaches. The divine economy connects redemption's gendered and powered economies intimately with the material exchanges of our everyday lives. Countereconomic redemption should thus be appreciated in the myriad ways it occurs. Yet the ambivalence of the cross remains powerful only if not obscured by a zeal for purity, as if the effects of a certain image could only be either oppressive or harmful. Previous generations of feminist theologians have been primarily invested in the necessary deconstruction of christological images, and rightly so. Yet the creative reconstruction and repossession—or better yet, reappropriation— of the doctrine of atonement have not only not been a concern, but many feminist theologians have neglected this work altogether. While I am far from willing to defend the values of an Anselmian or even Abelardian model of atonement, it seems to me that the last words concerning the reinterpretation the *commercium* motif have not yet been spoken (or written).

In *Life Abundant,* a reconstruction of theology in the light of ecological economics, Sallie McFague's dismissal of atonement and certain shapes of soteriology for the reconstruction of the relationship between theology and economics remains unhelpful, since she does not consider the possibility of reappropriating biblical or patristic loci for her cause. A case in point is McFague's abandonment of traditional theological images:

> What is wrong with the conventional picture of a mythological savior who descends from heaven and, as the God-man, shows us how to live, forgives our sins, and wins eternal life for us? While this may sound like a caricature of Christology, it is the bare-bones version that is deep in Western Christianity and even in Western culture. . . . So, once again what is wrong with this story? I would suggest two things: it is not believable, and it is bad theology.[81]

---

80. See also the previous chapter, which deals specifically with gender and theological economies.
81. Sallie McFague, *Life Abundant: Rethinking Theology and Economy for a Planet in Peril* (Minneapolis: Fortress, 2000), 158.

McFague argues that traditional "Christology" is "bad" in the "context of the ecological economic paradigm." It is good only "from the perspective of the neo-classical economic worldview," and for three reasons: "it is a form of 'Jesulatry'; it is individualistic and anthropocentric; and it understands salvation in purely spiritual terms. These characteristics fit well with the conventional economic paradigm."[82]

Thus, McFague continues, "it is *right* to find this Christology *wrong*, because it puts the offense of Christ at the wrong place," namely, as "a scandal to the intellect, which Christology should not and need not be."[83] Yet, piggybacking on liberal theologians' rejection of ancient and medieval soteriologies as "grotesque" images of salvation, McFague's blanket dismissal of the "traditional story" as "not believable" and "bad theology" merely reinscribes the liberal subjectivity and "individualism" she intently rejects even as she moves on to recommend yet another version of an Abelardian and Bultmannian Christology that sees Jesus as a mere moral example and teacher: "Jesus invites us into a different way of seeing—a transformation of perception."[84] While McFague lists a number of inspiring models for "ecological Christologies," such as "prophetic Christology," "wisdom Christology," and "sacramental Christology," she appears to give up on a sustained engagement with traditional theories of atonement, leaving the field to those more conservative interpreters who would still address the topic.[85] Rightly wanting to move beyond a "Jesus does it all" version of a "contemporary Christianity" that is "psychologically oriented rather than politically or cosmologically," McFague stresses "cruciform living" and deification, rather than atonement, as crucial elements of her eco-spirituality.[86] For North American Christians, she argues, "deification" must become incarnate in the limitation of consumption and the transformation of exploitative structures in solidarity with the oppressed. McFague's "cruciform living" employs the cross as the identificatory symbol of this deification. Yet she problematically links the practice of renunciation and ascesis to Christ's experience on the cross. It seems disproportionate, if not obscene, to compare the restriction of Western consumption to experiences "involving sacrifice, pain, and diminishment" experienced on the cross.[87] Since ascetic practice is a practice of life, though it may include mortification in the form of renunciation, it seems more appropriate to me

---

82. Ibid., 159.
83. Ibid., 158. Emphasis in original.
84. Ibid., 159, 172.
85. Ibid., 162–63.
86. Ibid., 160, 179.
87. Ibid., 177.

to stress the life-affirming qualities of "eco-asceticism" by linking them to Jesus' living practices of hospitality as well as renunciation.

Thus, little effort has yet been made to attempt a feminist reconstruction of atonement and redemption that assigns salvific meaning to the narratives of the life, death, and resurrection of Jesus. While the protests against abusive readings are crucial and often necessary as they concern certain hegemonic Christologies, I wonder whether neglecting the critical reconstruction of certain doctrines or images is helpful. Not only are we implicated in what we outrightly reject, but we also give abusive readings so much power that they seem to render the theological locus irredeemable and mark it as polluted.[88] Serene Jones, on the other hand, has stressed how much context matters for the interpretation of doctrinal loci, how important it is to acknowledge that the same image works differently in different contexts and is interpreted differently:

> [F]eminist theologians need to be aware that images of the broken body of Jesus on the cross may be violent and abusive to a battered woman in the United States, whereas in Guatemala they may serve to remind a mother that God grieves the loss of a child to political torture and military repression.[89]

The retention of ambivalence for texts and images should allow multiple interpretations and hermeneutical approaches that respect location and context. Womanists and theologians writing from within liberation contexts have, with such exceptions as Delores Williams, often focused less on critiquing soteriological constructs and more on unearthing the hidden layers of economic oppression in a variety of other biblical contexts. Where Meeks and McFague can describe "God's economy" as "a household of freedom," Williams might interject that Hagar was oppressed in this household, which liberated some but not others.[90] Williams has directed attention to the figure of Hagar, the female slave of Abram and Sarai, who stands at the margins of both Jewish and Christian notions of election and salvation. She has compared her to the way in which black women are still pushed to the economic and spiritual margins both by traditional white

---

88. Catherine Keller has described the urge to purge as the pattern of "anti-apocalypse," attempting to eradicate what one is opposed to without realizing that one is implicated in the same pattern. Keller, *Apocalypse Now and Then: A Feminist Guide to the End of the World* (Boston: Beacon, 1996), 15.

89. Serene Jones, *Feminist Theory and Christian Theology: Cartographies of Grace* (Minneapolis: Fortress, 2000), 53.

90. M. Douglas Meeks, *God the Economist: The Doctrine of God and Political Economy* (Minneapolis: Fortress, 1989), 78.

theologies as well as black men's liberation theologies.[91] Feminist and womanist theologians have voiced strong objections to doctrines of atonement that work to sanctify the victimization of the gendered and economic other. Flora Keshgegian has pointed out that Williams's stress on a Hagar who was not liberated by God, but rather received strength to survive in the context of slavery and a forced marriage that resulted in pregnancy and then abandonment, is one of the few theologies of the oppressed where the "cross is not the site of salvation."[92] Keshgegian's strategy for "redeeming" the "memory" of the cross recommends remembering the trauma and coping with it as best as possible so that it finds expression in a way that heals rather than generating "distorted relationality and arrested living."[93] Thus, she writes, "[T]o be redeemed is to be human—to remember that we are human, made in God's image and reflecting the glory of divinity."[94] For Keshgegian as for Rebecca Parker and Rita Nakashima Brock, the church is a "community of remembrance and witness."[95] The Jesus they remember is, however, not born of an attempt to get rid of the cross or to wish it away but of a refusal to sanctify violence religiously. He is not a victim of "cosmic child abuse," but instead is a "prophet who confronted injustices and risked opposition rather than conform to an empire that enforced its oppressive will through violence."[96] This "refusal to cooperate with injustice" and the courageous confrontation of "oppressive systems that dehumanize life" is the mark of Jesus' ministry, "even at the risk of violence."[97]

Traditional theories of atonement have often served to twist resistance and subversion into self-sacrifice, and to domesticate the social witness of Jesus into a doctrine of proverbial opium that keeps the people quiet under the yoke of oppression.[98] Even so, these interpretations of the cross may represent a widespread trend, but they do not therefore need to exclude other interpretations. Giving one particular interpretation too much space and power does, I think, little to subvert or defeat its harmful consequences. A more constructive challenge might consist in delivering alternate interpretations that "mess with" oppressive readings. In this effort,

---

91. Delores Williams, *Sisters in the Wilderness: The Challenge of Womanist God-Talk* (Maryknoll, N.Y.: Orbis, 1993), 5, 161–67.
92. Flora Keshgegian, *Redeeming Memories: A Theology of Healing and Transformation* (Nashville: Abingdon, 2000), 172, 185.
93. Ibid., 173.
94. Ibid., 182.
95. Ibid., 201.
96. Rita Nakashima Brock and Rebecca Ann Parker, *Proverbs of Ashes: Violence, Redemptive Suffering, and the Search for What Saves Us* (Boston: Beacon, 2001), 31.
97. Ibid., 39, 40.
98. For a helpful account of these issues, see chapter 3 in Ray, *Deceiving the Devil*, esp. p. 60.

however, ambivalent texts remain complicated and complex and can never become "safe." It is the responsibility of the interpreting community to decide whether an image in a certain context becomes damaging or whether a theological locus, long neglected and dismissed, may not enrich the contemporary debate and add new insights. We need many images and many hermeneutical locations to read them from.

O Admirabile Commercium: Of Indecent Proposals and Ties That Bind

> You were bought with a price; do not become slaves of human masters. (1 Cor 7:23)

During the boom economy in the year 2000, the American media giant NBC aired a new show called "Who Wants to Marry a Multimillionaire?" One in a seemingly unending line of TV shows that involve the word "millionaire" or a version of a "get rich quick" fantasy, this particular one exhibited a bizarre transaction. As a "beauty pageant with a twist," it would match a male multimillionaire with one of fifty women, who would volunteer to marry an anonymous man should he chose her from the group.[99] Ratings went through the roof as this libidinal economy hitched a rich man to a woman willing to marry and sleep with a stranger. But some commentators thought it resembled more a slave auction than a romantic tying of the knot:[100] "This particular contest—where the prize was a wealthy husband—laid bare the business of marriage, slapped all three waves of feminists in the face, and brought new meaning to the term 'trophy wife.'"[101]

Though some might dismiss this show as just one bizarre expression of contemporary U.S. pop culture, it exemplifies hysterical consumption in a culture where sex and romance have become so tied to late capitalism that they are becoming ever more merged in popular culture. Thus, one might diagnose the "millionaire" aspect of TV culture as one expression of the

---

99. Deborah Shapiro, "Leave It to Fox," *FEEDmag*, 16 February 2000, http://www.feedmag.com/daily/dy021600.html.

100. The show unfolded as a hoax of bizarre proportions. The alleged millionaire, Rick Rockwell, turned out to be barely so, and was uncovered as a onetime stand-up comedian with a restraining order against his girlfriend. The woman he chose to marry filed for divorce almost immediately afterward and retreated into obscurity. Caryn James, "It's Her Turn, but Don't Call Her Heartbreaker," *New York Times*, 8 January 2003, http://www.nytimes.com/2003/01/08/arts/television/08NOTE.html.

101. Shapiro, "Leave It to Fox."

"histories of hysterias,"[102] as mimetic symptoms of cultural distress that comment on the penetration of commerce into sexual and libidinal exchanges.[103] This kind of "reality TV" exemplifies Dell deChant's postmodern myth as transmitted through a secondary or tertiary medium, through "interview shows with 'stars,' sitcoms and sitdrams, or TV commercials and print advertisements." The "multi-million dollar contract, the acquisition of a palatial estate, the costly divorce settlements, the corporate takeover," and here, the latest on-screen match-making show, construct "living narratives of . . . success" that invite us to "involve ourselves with the myths," and to seek "to replicate them in our own experiences."[104]

But libidinal economies such as these have long been resident in the intertext of Western Christianity.[105] The ancient Christian motifs of *conubium* and *commercium* are here recast in characteristically raunchy fashion by Martin Luther: "Who then can fully appreciate what this royal marriage means? Who can understand the riches of the glory of this grace? Here this rich, and divine bridegroom Christ marries this poor, wicked harlot, redeems her from all evil, and adorns her will all his goodness."[106]

Luther's *fröhlicher Wechsel und Streit* (happy exchange and conflict),[107] which the contemporary TV show iterates with a twist, replays the economic hierarchies and transactions involved in ancient concepts of marriage and slavery that are part of the same Western intertext. Thus, gender hierarchy and servitude are embedded in a central theological *interpretum*. More recently, the German Catholic theologian Erich Przywara describes this uncanny connection between *commercium* (economic exchange) and *conubium* (marriage contract) in the following way:

---

102. Roy Porter, "Body and Mind," in *Hysteria beyond Freud* (ed. Sander Gilman; Berkeley: University of California Press, 1993), 229.

103. Roy Porter, "Baudrillard: History, Hysteria, and Consumption," in *Forget Baudrillard?* (ed. Chris Rojek and Bryan Turner; New York: Routledge, 1993), 4.

104. Dell deChant, *The Sacred Santa: Religious Dimensions of Consumer Culture* (Cleveland: Pilgrim, 2002), 54.

105. A twist on this reality TV show approached a new low in January 2003, when Fox's "Joe Millionaire" made headlines in the business sections, airing as the highest-rated premiere of the season. Bill Carter, "Ersatz Eligible 'Joe Millionaire' Gives Fox a Needed Ratings Hit," *New York Times*, 8 January 2003, http://query.nytimes.com/gst/abstract.html?res=FB0F1FF8395A0C7B8 CDDA80894DB404482. This program features a pre-recorded, secretly taped crossbreed between a show that exposes contemporary excesses of greed in the participants who compete for the attention of a bachelor who is a counterfeit millionaire, and a covertly sexist shaming of the women who would be so greedy. Cunningly, viewers are invited to direct their artificially produced outrage against greed for quick money as well as nurse ancient stereotypes about women as money-grubbing sluts.

106. The English translation follows *Career of the Reformer I* (ed. Harold J. Grimm; Luther's Works 31; Philadelphia: Muhlenberg Press, 1957), 352.

107. For a deeper exploration of this metaphor, see Theobald Beer, *Der Fröhliche Wechsel und Streit: Grundzüge der Theologie Martin Luthers* (Einsiedeln: Johannes, 1980).

Commercium as the "exchange on the slave market" is at the same time the innermost secret of what is human and what is Christian and thus the scandalous sign one resists as a folly and "scandal." The "slave market" is set up throughout all of history, so that in this manner the marriage between God and Humanity might occur.[108]

The soteriological loci of slavery and marriage generally occur separately throughout the texts of Christian tradition. But Przywara's perhaps shocking analysis of the theological combination of both motifs represents a staple of Christian theology and Western thought where class and gender hierarchies have often been constitutive of each other. Sheila Briggs suggests that Paul routinely combines both themes in his letters, so that "his central reflection on sin, law and righteousness in Romans alternates between metaphors drawn from the master-slave relationship ... and those drawn from the social dyad of husband-wife."[109] Similarly, Page DuBois has found that in ancient Greek texts "the female is analogous to the slave. The slave's body and the woman's body are marked as the property of the master.... [T]he Greek male citizen ruled over his subordinates, animals, barbarian slaves, and women, who were seen as like one another in their subordination."[110]

In Roman law, the *conubium* and the *commercium* closely connected marital and business transactions enacted primarily by propertied male citizens of the Roman Empire.[111] Luce Irigaray's analysis of "women on the market" suggests that "the society we know, our own culture, is based on the exchange of women."[112] The "hom(m)osexual" economy of the *conubium* thus exhibits a patriarchal structure similar to that of the *commercium*, which, at least in the sense we encounter it in this particular context, finds its most poignant expression in the power to buy, sell, and own other persons of either sex.[113] Other literary incarnations are, among others, the economic undertones to love and marriage in the search of Jane Austen's impoverished young women for a manly, propertied groom who represents her financial and libidinal salvation, often funded by the spoils of British colonialism.[114]

---

108. Erich Przywara, *Logos: Logos—Abendland—Reich—Commercium* (Düsseldorf: Patmos, 1964), 164; my translation.
109. Briggs, "Enslaved God," 142.
110. DuBois, *Torture and Truth*, 90.
111. Herz, *Sacrum Commercium*, 9, 11–12.
112. Luce Irigaray, *This Sex Which Is Not One* (trans. Catherine Porter; Ithaca, N.Y.: Cornell University Press, 1985), 170.
113. Ibid., 171.
114. Edward Said has famously described the colonial subtext of Austen's novels, especially that of *Mansfield Park*, in which the wealth of the main character's benefactors derives from

The social and theological construct of marriage between a man and a woman has long functioned as the stabilizing discipline of a culture's definition of decency. Przywara, who finds the *commercium* of crucial importance in Irenaeus, Augustine, and Luther, has described the christological notion of the *conubium* entwined with the *commercium* as the tie that binds God and humans together. The *syndesmos* in Col 3:14 (tie, bond, bondage, fetter) becomes the central christological formula of bondage both in slavery and marriage, of the slave or the wife to God, the master, or the husband: "[S]yndesmos is at the same time the fetter (of the imprisoned slave), and ring (of marital unification)."[115] Przywara seems unaware of what he reveals to a contemporary reader: the tradition's—and perhaps his own—complicity of economic and gendered oppression with the theological "decencies" of submissive soteriological images.[116] Przywara acknowledges that the theological enwrapment of *commercium* and *conubium* constitutes a "scandal," an annoyance. In his analysis, the hierarchies of slavery and marriage remain intact; they are merely transferred onto the divine-human plane. The subversive possibilities of these motifs are redomesticated as they collude with exclusive hierarchical ecclesial power. In a contemporary analysis, the connection between a patriarchal *commercium* and *conubium* powerfully highlights the enwrapment of traditional orthodox theologies with the economic hierarchies of gender and class. But Przywara's assessment of what constitutes the nature of the scandal differs strikingly from a contemporary viewpoint informed—unlike Przywara's work in the early 1960s—by the discourses of feminism, feminist and liberation theologies, and postcolonial thought.

Althaus-Reid's "indecent theology" exposes (with the benefit of a quarter century of women's theologies) the oppressive uses of gendered metaphors and theological patterns: "Theology is a sexual act, a sexual doing, based on the construction of God and divine systems which are male and worked in opposition (and sexual opposition) to women."[117]

---

cruelly operated slave plantations. Edward W. Said, *Culture and Imperialism* (New York: Vintage, 1993), 84–97. Austen drops similar hints about the origin of the wealth of her heroine's intended in *Pride and Prejudice*, *Persuasion*, and *Sense and Sensibility*.

115. Przywara, *Logos*, 123; my translation.

116. A debt owed can become a legitimization for enslavement and the feminization of debtors. Althaus-Reid points out how this dynamic has functioned as a sexual story in the Argentinean enslavement through the International Monetary Fund's "structural adjustment" programs. The government's "fear of a shrinking penis," which the economic crisis signified, lived out its own kind of hysteria. The government's economic policies included harsh macho, heterosexist measures that openly pursued "indecent" women who dared to use their mental facilities, and plans to create a ghetto for gays and lesbians in Patagonia, thereby expelling them from society. Marcella Althaus-Reid, *Indecent Theology: Theological Perversions in Sex, Gender, and Politics* (London: Routledge, 2001), 184–85.

117. Ibid., 36.

Thus, the meaning of Christian salvation has been tightly linked in "heterosexual Systematic Theology" with a "heavy emphasis on salvation from sexual transgressions," a setting in which suffering becomes (á la Derrida) a necessary supplement to salvation.[118] For Althaus-Reid's Argentinean Catholic setting, then, "the narrative of punishment of the bodies of the saints was a divine pedagogy to understand reality. I saw people's hearts pierced by swords of hunger, political repression and economic injustice." This collusion between theological, economic and political exploitation resulted in the theologian's "resignation to the sadistic economic policies of my country which had the spiritual blessing and support of the institutional church. This was the spirituality of political sadism."[119] For Althaus-Reid, the hierarchies of power and salvation resemble "stories of sexual fetishism" as a "mimicry of salvation," where God the master and the Christian as the submissive slave subject, the top/bottom relationship of S/M people, is a master sketch of Christianity done in a moment."[120] The "decent" theological economic of Christ as slave can undergird and reinforce acquiescence and submission to postmodern forms of slavery.

Though she stresses that to simply equate sadomasochism and Christian soteriology proves problematic, Althaus-Reid puts her finger in the wound of theologies of vicarious suffering and atonement, inducing both pain and pleasure: the dangerous pleasures of linking consent to suffering and to the silencing of victims of oppression through a theology of redemption that renders their suffering necessary and right; the difficult acknowledgment that pain cannot always be escaped but that all resistance includes, potentially, the acceptance of suffering as a result of the struggle. Whether it is consent, as Althaus-Reid suggests, that gives meaning to both submission and salvation, one may want to question.[121] Yet her inquiry touches the relational complexities of power at the core of such miraculous exchanges.

On the northern side of the U.S. border with Mexico, Grace Chang has observed how structural adjustment policies globalize domestic violence in the lives of third world women, who come to the United States to staff nursing homes, sweatshops, and to work as nannies and maids in middle-class households.[122] Another instance of transnational trading in

---

118. Ibid., 152.
119. Ibid., 153.
120. Ibid.
121. Thus, she writes, "Without consent the act of submission is indeed meaningless, and so it is with salvation. A consensual salvation is always risqué, unsafe, unsettled, but meaningful because it recognizes the body as the space of salvation." Althaus-Reid, *Indecent Theology*, 154.
122. Chang, *Disposable Domestics*, 140, who observes that third world nations have to surrender their citizens, especially their women, to first world economies. Their families have to rely on the few dollars sent back home, while the same arrangement enables a much more comfortable lifestyle in the United States.

humans shows the "ethnicization inherent to the global commodification process."[123] Chinese American scholar Rey Chow unveils a trade in a complexly signifying exchange economy between China and the United States. Chow argues that humans are the currency of a *commercium*, a trade agreement that results in profit for both sides.[124] Whether it is the "egregious, abusive trading of organs from slaughtered Chinese prisoners" or the "'humane' release of famous dissidents," they stem, says Chow, "from the same cold-blooded logic of economic transactions." They form "a diversified but cohesive globalized financial order: when dead, humans are exchanged in the form of replaceable body parts; when still alive, they are exchanged whole—body and soul—for lucrative long-term trading arrangements that benefit the entire nation."[125] Another level of the transaction involves ethnicity, here understood as "an otherness, a foreignness that distinguishes it from the mainstream, normative society," which is identified with Western, U.S. values. In this cultural narrative, U.S. society comes to stand for a superior moral system that reenacts familiar colonial patterns: "[O]nly the Chinese . . . remain so barbaric as to be ready to violate human rights, trade human organs, and use their people as bargaining chips; only 'they' would do something that is so unthinkable among 'us' in the enlightened, law-bound nations of the West."[126]

Thus, the "commercial transactions of ethnic bodies . . . become not merely exploitative . . . but also a morally justified course of action that helps free the other and confirm our own moral superiority."[127] Ethnic existence thus is represented as existence in "captivity" in an ethnocentric version of a cultural "narrative of captivity," based on what Chow identifies as Enlightenment motifs with a problematic "binarist correlation" in which captivity serves as the "indispensable underside to the emancipatory meaning of modern civilization itself."[128]

As we have seen, captivity, slavery, and redemption motifs are woven deeply into Western cultural fabric, iterating ancient Hebrew and Christian

---

123. Rey Chow, *The Protestant Ethnic and the Spirit of Capitalism* (New York: Columbia University Press, 2002), 22.
124. Chow acknowledges that the imposition of Western humanitarian values onto an Asian society forms the often invisible neocolonial ideology that undergirds these exchanges. Thus, she observes, "[W]hereas the West asserts its moral claims on the basis of a universalist rhetoric traceable to the European Enlightenment, China is reduced to a reactive position." Despite this dynamic, however, she sees the West and China as "collaborative partners in an ongoing series of biopolitical transactions in global late capitalism." Chow, *Protestant Ethnic*, 20.
125. Ibid., 21–22.
126. Ibid., 22.
127. Ibid., 23.
128. Ibid., 42, 47, 39.

topoi and revealing further indecencies: the redeemed, a poor woman with an indecent sexuality, in *conubium* with a wealthy divine husband; a godly master acquiring and thus redeeming a slave added to his property. Wedlock and enslavement are the ties that bind, and a new kind of submission replaces the old. In Irigarayan terms, one might say that the hom(m)osexual divine economy's income is generated by the women and slaves that produce wealth for the godly owner, where woman and slave function as currency. They are in-appropriate because property-less, appropriated because property, for a price. The redeemed believer is a property-less submissive wife and slave.

The Christ of Phil 2:6–7 self-empties, defaulting to utter lack of paternal wealth and power *(kenosis)*, de-propriation and enslavement *(doulos)*. The Jesus of Mark 10:45 becomes divine currency, the *lutron* (ransom), that effects *lutrosis* (redemption). The patristic redeemer, gifted into a virgin's womb *(de virgine nasci dignatus est)*, emerges from a human being without the seminal investment of masculinity *(procedens homo sine semine)*. The Christ-slave himself yet becomes currency in a divine deal, perhaps even with the devil. Yet soon the ransom is cashed in as the hom(m)osexual reproduction in Nicene orthodoxy, where "begotten, not made," the Son is of the same substance and wealth as the Father, as "the logic of theology follows models of spermatic flow, of ideas of male reproduction that defy modern science but are established firmly in the sexual symbolics of theology."[129] Yet the ransom remains ambiguously tendered, a *mixtura,* an amalgamated coin, dangerously close to a counterfeit: a queer enough divine economy, or a simple reiteration of hom(m)osexual economies?

---

129. Althaus-Reid, *Indecent Theology,* 155.

CHAPTER 5

Divine Economy Refinanced

The third millennium began with seemingly countless revelations of counterfeit accounting, insider trading, artificial stock inflation, and other financial scandals that were hushed, if not encouraged by the economies of exchange in a market dominated by stockholder capitalism. As they continue to be exposed, the hucksters and shams of this age oddly resemble those of the 1830s, the Jacksonian robber barons and self-made financiers of the Gilded Age. Can a "confidence man," a U.S. specific version of the trickster, function as a useful figure for a countereconomic theology and practice? Lewis Hyde posits in his account of tricksterdom that we may often be tempted to sympathize with, even secretly admire, protagonists such as confidence men who defraud their victims, as we are drawn into the romance of gamblers and gangsters, of rebels without causes. Hyde suspects that "con men" such as these "embody things that are actually true about America but cannot be openly declared (as, for example the degree to which capitalism lets us steal from our neighbors, or the degree to which institutions like the stock market require the same kind of confidence that criminal con men need)."[1]

We may revel in our middle- or lower-class anonymity and feel a bit better about ourselves while pointing the fingers at corporate executives and faceless multinational corporations. But no one is without fault, as feminist economist Julie Nelson explains:

---

1. Lewis Hyde, *Trickster Makes This World: Mischief, Myth, and Art* (New York: Farrar, Straus & Giroux, 1998), 11.

> [T]here is complicity at all levels: the poor succumb to the same consumerist ideals; the middle class and the not-quite-rich focus on their perceived powerlessness against the very rich, rather than noticing their own relatively elite status; and everybody angles to find the best way to "work the system."[2]

If then, as Hyde suggests, "America" as the "land of opportunity and therefore of opportunists" produces and attracts "pandemic" incarnations of the confidence man (or woman),[3] is this agent too ambivalent for, too dangerous, too close for comfort to the construction and emulation of a subversive yet saintly trickster figure? However, the setting, location, conditions, characteristics, and hermeneutics of a trickster's action function in multiple ways and remain open to reinterpretation. Trickster figures may not always elicit emulation or aspire to model exemplary agency; they may also provide negative examples and serve to reinforce the status quo. Yet they may be just as likely to inspire us to conspire with the divine forces of creativity on the edge of chaos. Divine tricksters thus de-monstr-ate, show forth the monstrous, perform perfidy, hail the hysterical, provide a hermeneutic of hyperbole, a syntax of sarcasm, and invent idioms of irony. The challenges brought to society by such a divine trickster are exemplified by acts such as the clever unveiling of whitewashing and greenwashing maneuvers of corporate capitalism; the hysterical, hyperbolic performance of compulsive consumerism; ascetic acts of prolonged tree sitting; symbolic periods of shopping boycotts; and comedic explosions through the silence and the smooth lies, twisted stories, and omissions of mainstreamed media through sidesplitting, heartbreaking muckraking. In and through this, these "Holy Fools" and "Saint Mysterias" are motivated by hope for better economies and better worlds. Their miraculous exchanges often transgress the boundaries of decency.

Redemptive Trickery: Confidence Men, "Strategic Tricksters," and Countereconomic Mysteries

> Indecent proposals in economics could decolonise our spiritual souls, which are also economic souls.
>
> > Marcella Althaus-Reid, *Indecent Theology: Theological Perversions in Sex, Gender and Politics*

---

2. Julie A. Nelson, "Breaking the Dynamic of Control: A Feminist Approach to Economic Ethics," *Journal of Feminist Studies in Religion* 19 (Spring 2003): 41.
3. Hyde, *Trickster Makes This World*, 11.

The tricksters figures found in the margins of Christian texts—Holy Fool, Saint Mysteria, and the Divine Counterfeit—share characteristics that evidence a crucial difference from the hucksters. These trickster figures suffer deeply from an oppressive, exploitative economic status quo. Its madness marks their bodies and minds, and their hysteria allows them to articulate its craziness, if in a coded, ambivalent way. If creatively produced, their pain and frustration can be translated into a form of resistance, through words, performances, bodies, and actions. Thus, they disturb the dominant discourse rather than simply conceding to victimhood or co-optation. One of the main interpretive moves of Christian *historia*, of *oikonomia theou*, has been the linking of figures or *typoi* to inscribe a history of succession and relation. These tricksters mimic and thus iterate this traditional notion of divine economy, or divine commerce, by counterfeiting (that is, through a divergent remaking) redemption as they deceive the deceivers and engage in alternative accounting and exchange.[4]

In a variety of Christian texts, such figures, or *typoi*, have helped to "stage salvation history, which then became the model for world history in the secular heresies of the centuries of European colonialism with its civilizing missions and genocidal discourses on common humanity."[5] The previous chapters attempted to textually reincarnate these "economic" theological and gender "stereotypologies" by iterating them as Harawayan "feminist figures" en route to a "nongeneric humanity." Thus, holy fools and divine tricksters serve as cross-temporal iterations of ancient *typoi* such as Adam, Eve, and Christ, which previously served as the building blocks of typologies linking *Heilsgeschichte*—one way of rendering the term *oikonomia theou*. As hysterics, the Holy Fool and Saint Mysteria demonstrate and incarnate through their tortured psyche and subversive therapeutic creativity the craziness of the economics of scarcity, and have, in the tricksterlike fashion of hysterics, articulated voices that disturb the purported consensus of consumerism. Through their openness to instances of divine economy as well as to the economic complexes that constitute their location, these reconstructed figures represent instances of a coredemptive soteriology.[6]

---

4. "Counterfeiting," from the French *contre-faire*, can thus function as close to "reconstructing."
5. Donna J. Haraway, "Ecce Homo, Ain't (Ar'n't) I a Woman, and Inappropriate/d Others: The Human in a Post-Humanist Landscape," in *Feminists Theorize the Political* (ed. Judith Butler and Joan Scott; New York: Routledge, 1992), 89.
6. Elaine Showalter has argued that contemporary feminists should, rather than casting hysterics as martyrs, produce models that demonstrate the courage to think as well as the courage to heal. Her call thus resembles the kind of redemptive performance and agency I am suggesting here. See Showalter, *Hystories: Hysterical Epidemics and Modern Culture* (New York: Columbia University Press, 1997), 61.

A countereconomic theology suggests "consensual salvation." Marcella Althaus-Reid argues that "without consent, the act of submission is indeed meaningless, and so it is with salvation. A consensual salvation is always risqué, unsafe, unsettled but meaningful because it recognizes the body as the space of salvation."[7]

Our figures mean to counter-feit—to re-produce in a third space but always already falsifiable—redemptive human agency, mimicking and imitating Jesus, whose "figure of incarnation," says Haraway,

> can never be other than a trickster . . . the figure that upsets the clarity of the metaphysics of light [through] his odd sonship and odder kingship, because of his disguises and form-changing habits. Jesus makes of man a most promising mockery, but a mockery that cannot evade the terrible story of the broken body.[8]

The countereconomic trickster, far more complex than a fashionable icon of "subversion," is the incarnation of the ambivalences of countereconomies, of the "edge of chaos," where possibilities are fragile and multitude. Tricksters can be prophets of chaos, "showing the way in which creativity can overcome overwhelming odds. Tricksters see beyond the limits of the system and bend the rules."[9] They induce discomfort, if not anger, in those on whom they play their tricks, and they make those who rely on the rules of a system uneasy. They unveil our rigidities and complacencies through their actions. They can help to rattle the rigid cages of perception that underlie repressive social and economic systems by pointing to their weaknesses and blind spots.

The divine trickster, hysteric, and counterfeit do this by producing—in Derrida's terms—an excess of meaning, their figures are ex-orbitant, excessive, well . . . *différant*.[10] This excess of meaning, this hermeneutical overflow, resembles countereconomic exchanges that accommodate a variety of textual and physical economies.[11] Compare Karmen MacKendrick's exploration of counterpleasures, which describes a similar dynamic, differentiating between

---

7. Althaus-Reid, *Indecent Theology*, 154.
8. Haraway, "Ecce Homo," 90.
9. The well-known analogy of the "butterfly effect" serves to illustrate the trickster's possible effect. The small animal's wings create aerial movements that can result in a hurricane on the other side of the globe. John Briggs and F. David Peat, *Seven Life Lessons of Chaos: Timeless Wisdom from the Science of Change* (New York: HarperCollins, 1999), 46.
10. Jacques Derrida, *Of Grammatology* (corrected ed.; trans. Gayatri Spivak; Baltimore: Johns Hopkins University Press, 1997), 159 et passim.
11. I differ from Derrida's often pointed juxtaposition of economy to the gift, and read *différance*, perhaps at times against Derrida, as a pointing toward a multiplicity of possible

the "economy of productivity" and the "transgressive economy of excess" that marks counterpleasures:

> In the everyday (nonecstatic) economy of investment, expenditure is loss (and desire is lack, founded upon the need to fill what is empty, replace what is lost). This is precisely the economy of productivity, the teleological economy found in the security of the center. The transgressive economy of excess links joy to desire such that one cannot increase without the other, and joy becomes not gratification (the teleological artifact of the orgasm) but intensification.[12]

The excessive exchange, by a revaluation of desire not as lack but as a crucial growth component of joy, queries the need for conventional reciprocity in economies and begins to open up a space where, at least for MacKendrick, pleasure and desire are mutually enhancing. Similarly, within a countereconomic theology, conventional reciprocity is questioned. The complex nature of our relationalities in the cosmos often balances on the "edge of chaos," where notions of adequacy and reciprocity do not always calculate neatly but emerge as unpredictable, flexible, and at times excessive. A reconstructed divine economy here includes varying degrees and different shapes of reciprocity. Since most of the relationships we are involved in are asymmetrical (parent-child, teacher-student, supervisor-employee), even despite our best efforts, the potential for the abuse of power remains a constant companion. It would also be problematic to claim some idealized egalitarian relationship between God and creation, despite the ever greater dreams of some humans to out-create God.[13]

In addition, countereconomic strategies are multiply located. Rather than resting on one singular salvific economic event, this divine economy proves invested in a great variety of salvific processes. There is no one way to "make change," but there must be many. The divine economy is not positioned as simply oppositional or simply identical with economic movements of currency, exchange, or what is called capitalism. Rather, there

---

exchanges that do not easily fall into dualistic categories of gift or exchange. I note with Derrida that a gift always includes a version of exchange, but will postulate, in tension with Derrida, that an absolute gift is not a desirable category to strive for but remains caught in a Hegelian search for absolutes. For more detail on this argument, see Marion Grau, "Erasing 'Economy': Derrida and the Construction of Divine Economies," *Cross Currents* (Fall 2002): 350–60.

12. Karmen MacKendrick, *Counterpleasures* (Albany, N.Y.: SUNY Press, 1999), 126.

13. Such as those who would like to see a posthuman or transhuman future. See, for example, Ray Kurzweil, *The Age of Spiritual Machines: When Computers Exceed Human Intelligence* (New York: Viking, 1999).

exists a complex relationship of mimicry, of both resemblance and menace between them.

Countereconomic strategies will often strive to reimagine local communities within a planetary network of connections, as Cobb and Daly suggest. They would thus, as Donna Haraway has put it in an application of feminist theory, be self-critically and historically "situated," not in a conservative move to a parochial location but in an attempt to achieve "specificity and consequential, if variously mobile, embodiment" in a global context.[14] They will come in different shapes and sizes, as tactics and strategies, combining personal transformation and structural change in a "dynamic interdependence."[15]

Figurative fragments of hysteric, tricky, indecent, martyred, wasteful, giving, lacking, ascetic figures contribute to a countereconomic theology emerging from the manifold locations of Haraway's "critical reflexivity," communicant through the "resonant relations" of a "polyphonic epistemology."[16] The divine economy emerging from such a context remains ultimately unpredictable as the effects of giving and receiving, of profit and loss, continue to be incalculable, on the edge of countereconomic chaos. These countereconomic strategies carry the fingerprint of the trickster, along with the trickster's characteristic ambivalence. This redemptive divine economy thus also unfurls at the "edge of chaos," as the countereconomic creative space resembles the dynamic of chaotic systems as described by Briggs and Peat:

> Chaotic systems lie beyond all our attempts to predict, manipulate, and control them. Chaos suggests that instead of resisting life's uncertainties, we should embrace them.... Making a pact with chaos gives us the possibility of living not as controllers of nature but as creative participants.... The clown, trickster, or shape changer becomes the personification of chaos for cultures all over the world.[17]

The trickster God's divine economy combines "wisdom" and "skill," an "orderly series and sequence" as well as the chaotic turmoil of divine

---

14. Donna J. Haraway, *Modest_Witness@Second_Millennium. FemaleMan©_Meets_OncoMouse*™ (New York: Routledge, 1997), 199.
15. Feminist economist Julie Nelson highlights the need to see personal and structural change as necessarily interwoven. Nelson, "Breaking the Dynamic of Control," 28, 32.
16. Haraway, *Modest_Witness@Second_Millennium*, 37; Catherine Keller, *Apocalypse Now and Then: A Feminist Guide to the End of the World* (Boston: Beacon, 1996), 266.
17. Briggs and Peat, *Seven Life Lessons*, 8–9.

deception to achieve salvation.[18] Yet even as the divine economy upends conventions and upsets the laws of stagnant orders, it remains vulnerable to reinscriptions of the same old hierarchies of power. Western narratives of conquest and colonization, motivated by an unsavory mix of economic and theological motivations, have constituted and continue to engender the suffering of the poor and of women as part of an economic exchange in which theology remains complicit, as it has often served to maintain theologically and economically underwritten exploitative hierarchies.

This divine economy shares many concerns with Althaus-Reid's postcolonial "indecent theology," interrupting the "decencies" of traditional and patriarchal systematic and liberation theologies as it "uncovers sexuality and economy at the same time" in a "process of de-hegemonisation of theology as a sexual normative ideology."[19] The "strategic essentialism" of a Gayatri Spivak and the "eschatological essentialism" of a Serene Jones serve as reminders that any economic plot we may develop must remain flexible and undergo change if its effects become more detrimental than beneficial to the goals of empowering women, the poor, and the environment.[20] And we must remain aware that any "strategic Jesus" we might construct can be deconstructed. Chicano cultural theorist Chela Sandoval has identified the trickster as a figure that exemplifies what she considers the most promising approach for the "differential coalitional consciousness" that enables persons from many ethnic, class, and cultural backgrounds to contribute, learn from each other, and work toward a "methodology of the oppressed." Thus, she writes:

> The cruising mobilities required in this effort demand of the differential practitioner commitment to the process of metamorphosis itself: this is the activity of the trickster who practices subjectivity as masquerade, the oppositional agent who accesses differing identity, ideological, aesthetic, and political positions.[21]

Any theological account of the divine economy remains subject to a reinscription of previous oppressions even as power hierarchies are turned

---

18. Gregory of Nyssa, *Oratio catechetica*, in *Gregory of Nyssa: Dogmatic Treatises* (ed. Philip Schaff and Henry Wace; Select Library of the Christian Church: Nicene and Post-Nicene Fathers; Peabody, Mass.: Hendrickson, 1994), 20.
19. Althaus-Reid, *Indecent Theology*, 7, 19.
20. See Gayatri Spivak and Ellen Rooney, "In a Word. Interview," in *The Essential Difference* (ed. Naomi Schor and Elizabeth Weed; Bloomington: Indiana University Press, 1994), 151–84; and Serene Jones, *Feminist Theory and Christian Theology: Cartographies of Grace* (Minneapolis: Fortress, 2000), 64–65.
21. Chela Sandoval, *Methodology of the Oppressed* (Minneapolis: University of Minnesota Press, 2000), 62.

upside down. To keep that exchange in flux and from stagnation, it would seem the task of the divine trickster agent to remain in the uncomfortable, multivalent "third space," living "on the edge of chaos" or in various stages of "chaosmos."[22] A countereconomic theology considers oppressions and wisdom both ancient and contemporary in its hope to map a strategic rather than purely essentialist space for envisioning alternative trading routes of differential coalitions. Countereconomic tricksters remain in constant awareness of the devastating effects of industrial capitalism to humanity and the environment.[23] They observe that most dominant economic policies and practices in the national and global arenas are set up to benefit a small minority of privileged investors, often at the conscious or unconscious expense of those left out of the managing scheme to a point where purely bottom-line economic reasoning can have a totalizing effect on a society and endanger the planet. They give voice to the increasing number of citizens, investors, workers, and business people that are not only aware of these issues but are getting increasingly outraged at revelations of corporate misconduct that more and more seem like the tip of an iceberg of corruption and hucksterism. An overwhelming number of U.S. citizens do not approve or support the totalitarian tendencies of corporate financial strategies, as a survey done in the year 2000 shows, and they certainly are even less popular in a post-9/11, post-Enron, post-WorldCom climate.[24] Countereconomic strategizing does not underestimate the hegemonic and totalizing aspects of contemporary forms of industrial, "extreme,"[25] or "permissive"[26] capitalism, but while it might note utopian

---

22. Catherine Keller, *Face of the Deep* (New York: Routledge, 2003), 166.

23. As pointed out, for example, in David C. Korten, *When Corporations Rule the World* (San Francisco: Berrett-Koehler Publishers; West Hartford, Conn.: Kumarian Press, 1995); David C. Korten, *The Post-Corporate World: Life after Capitalism* (San Francisco: Berrett-Koehler Publishers; West Hartford, Conn.: Kumarian Press, 1999); John B. Cobb Jr., *The Earthist Challenge to Economism: A Theological Critique of the World Bank* (New York: Macmillan Press, 1999).

24. Compare an August 2000 survey in *Business Week*, which notes that large numbers of the population think that business interests infiltrate too many other areas of life: "*Business Week*'s poll shows that nearly three-quarters of Americans think business has gained too much power over too many aspects of their lives." From "Americans Have a Beef with Big Business," *Business Week*, 31 August 2000, http://www.businessweek.com/bwdaily/dnflash/aug2000/nf20000831_923.htm. The accounting scandals that have emerged in the wake of the California energy crisis, such as Arthur Anderson's accounting of Enron, and various cases of insider trading and accounting fraud scams have contributed to a collapse of faith in the stock market. In 2002, a *New York Times* columnist raised the question whether the United States has entered a new Gilded Age of plutocracy. Paul Krugman, "The Class Wars, Part I: For Richer: How the Permissive Capitalism of the Boom Destroyed American Equality," *New York Times Magazine* (20 October 2002): 62.

25. Thomas Frank, *One Market under God* (New York: Anchor Books, 2000).

26. Catherine Keller, "A Christian Response to the Population Apocalypse," in *Population, Consumption, and the Environment: Religious and Secular Responses* (ed. Howard Coward; Albany, N.Y.: SUNY Press, 1995), 117–18.

hopes for the abolition of capitalism and the subsequent establishment of alternative societies (as formulated by early liberation theologians and most recently by Milbank and Long), it prefers a certain realistic pragmatism that would argue that it is necessary for most of us to survive spiritually and economically while resisting these forms of economy in the location where we are. Since utopian hopes continue to be frustrated, we need the strength to act transgressively within the economic system we live in. We need to avoid the tendency toward extreme solutions that set us up to be frustrated and disappointed. As Catherine Keller reminds us:

> [W]ithin the U.S. context, there is a traditional tendency to get active, to get enraged, and then to give up, surrendering to the lull of the comforts and conveniences extracted from the rest of the planet. I do this too. We see ourselves (or perhaps others) as innocent victims, and hope for ultimate vindication, and are soon disillusioned with the prospects. We think we must "save the earth." Who can carry this? In other words, to the extent that we get uncritically hooked on apocalypse—not merely the situation but the habit—we contribute to it. We wish for messianic solutions and end up doing nothing, for we get locked into a particularly apocalyptic either/or logic—if we can't save the world, then to hell with it. Either salvation or damnation.[27]

A countereconomic position strives to avoid such see-saw dualisms, as does Keller's counterapocalypse, and instead engages in plotting strategies to unveil destructive hierarchies, to pervert policies and structures that reductionistically pursue the financial goals of a minority only. It plots barter economies that subvert consumer mentality and occasionally lavishes gifts upon others; it encourages reciprocity not as if there was ever a way to repay in essence what one receives, but in a way that does not exploit those who give. What might some models of such tricky salvific economies look like?

A Trickster's Strategically Essential Investments

> And his master commended the dishonest manager because he had acted shrewdly; for the children of this age are more shrewd in dealing with their own generation than are the children of light. And I tell you, make friends for yourselves by means of dishonest wealth so that when it is gone, they may welcome you into the eternal homes. (Luke 16:8–9)

---

27. Keller, *Apocalypse Now and Then*, 14.

When looking for biblical instances of trickery, we may find tricksters—as Haraway has—in the figure of Jesus himself and in Jesus' parables. These "*oikonomoi*" may offer us inspiration for the work of figuring out strategies of divine commerce.[28] One instance of tricksterlike countereconomy can be reconstructed from the parable of the "clever steward" in Luke 16, a text that portrays a cunning use of mimicry, a redemptive deal that can be read as a source for a strategic essentialism that—in the interest of justice—will take the liberty to trick the powers of oppression and domination to liberate life. In this, one of the most perplexing texts in the canonical apostolic writings, the ambivalent character of Luke 16:1–13 continues to surface in the ongoing attempts to name the elusive figure of the *oikonomos*—is he an unjust, dishonest, or rather a clever steward?—in the parable. One might imagine exegetes cursing under their breath as they describe the pericope as "notoriously one of the most difficult of all the parables to interpret," "the *crux interpretum* among the parables," the "problem child," the "prince among the difficult parables," and a "notorious puzzle."[29] But let us review the story briefly: a wealthy man hears that his manager (*oikonomos*), has been squandering his property (v. 1). He speaks to the man and asks him to deliver an accounting (*ton logon tes oikonomias sou*, v. 2) before his dismissal for fraudulent management. Subsequently, the *oikonomos* tries to manage his crisis by coming up with a scheme that will let him land softly—with a golden parachute—on his way out and will enable him to avoid enmity with those he might need in the process. So he devises a plan. He calls every person who is indebted to his master and has them mark down their IOUs by half. His *kurios* hears of this and commends him for his shrewdness. What follows is what gets the exegetes so flustered: the gospel adds a dominical interpretation that affirms the cleverness of this worldly generation and seems to lament the naiveté exhibited by the "children of light." Rather, Jesus advises his disciples to use resources accumulated by exploitation to "make friends for yourselves" in the right places.

Dennis Ireland has listed an impressive number of different interpretations and has set up a taxonomy specifying the most common routes of approach to this troubling text. He distinguishes between those who consider the actions of the *oikonomos* fraudulent and dishonest but who

---

28. Biblical texts teem with trickster figures, especially in the Hebrew Scriptures. Trickster figures can also be found, perhaps a bit less obviously, in apostolic writings. The above example represents a particularly poignant example of Jesus' use of irony and wit.
29. Quoted in Dennis J. Ireland, *Stewardship and the Kingdom of God: An Historical, Exegetical, and Contextual Study of the Parable of the Unjust Steward in Luke 16:1–13* (Supplements to Novum Testamentum 70; Leiden: E. J. Brill, 1992), 1.

nevertheless hold that this figure provides a useful lesson for the disciples, and those who consider the manager's devices just, honest, and commendable because—according to the standards of ancient honor/shame, master/slave hierarchies—the manager ends up restoring the tainted honor of his *kurios* by cutting the debts of his debtors in half. Though Ireland neglects to accommodate any further interpretations, some exegetes continue to feel more ambivalent about the text and remain unwilling to resolve its tensions just yet. John Dominic Crossan, Dan Via, and Bernard B. Scott have attempted—with varying degrees of success—to read the story as a "picaresque story"[30] in which the *oikonomos* functions as a trickster, picaro, or rogue.[31] Justin Upkong and Paul Trudinger have pushed similar interpretations further, including a strong contextualization, and in the case of Upkong, a reading from the context of peasant farmers in West Africa. Upkong argues that the parable may be told at the cost of the master, who "is not the benevolent grand personage he is often thought to be, but an exploiter." Thus, Upkong establishes the *oikonomos* not as the "villain he is often thought to be, but the hero of the story, for having acted on behalf of the exploited peasant farmers."[32] Similarly, Trudinger reads the *oikonomos* as "party to a totally unjust system" but argues that "his actions may not have been dishonest" since he and the hearers of the parable have become "mainly victims of the injustices perpetrated in the agrarian economy." Thus, as Trudinger imagines, the hearers would appreciate the irony, even the "funny side" of a tale in which the "filthy rich landlord was forced to forego a sizable gain in income through the shrewd action of his agent."[33] The *oikonomos*, himself implicated in the debt slavery of his society, enacts an instance of debt relief that causes a financial loss to his master, while it increases the economic well-being of the debtors.

I do not suggest that I can solve the riddles of a parable that has long puzzled scholars, yet I do want to further highlight Upkong's and Trudinger's reading of the *oikonomos* as trickster accomplishing—through deception and fraud—a clever economy of redemption. I want to suggest this not as the "correct" reading but as a possible one. Jesus' parables, I

---

30. Stanley Porter, "The Parable of the Unjust Steward (Luke 16.1–13): Irony Is the Key," in *The Bible in Three Dimensions: Essays in Celebration of Forty Years of Biblical Studies in the University of Sheffield* (Journal for the Study of the Old Testament Supplement Series 87; Sheffield: Sheffield Academic Press, 1990), 134.

31. David Landry and Ben May, "Honor Restored: New Light on the Parable of the Prudent Steward (Luke 16:1–8a)," *Journal of Biblical Literature* 119, no. 2 (2000): 290–91.

32. Justin S. Upkong, "The Parable of the Shrewd Manager (Luke 16:1–13): An Essay in Inculturation Biblical Hermeneutic," *Semeia* 76 (1996): 208.

33. Paul Trudinger, "Ire or Irony? The Enigmatic Character of the Parable of the Dishonest Steward (Luke 16:1–13)," *Downside Review* 116 (April 1998): 96.

would suggest, rather than describing an idealized world, ambivalently map, by way of mimicry, the *basileia* onto an existing reality, with distorting as well as reinforcing effects. Perhaps we should read far more lightly and playfully, in a way that nudges the parables a bit closer to the edge of chaos than they are often allowed.

I would like to suggest, then, that the *oikonomos* resembles African American trickster figures. Darby Ray has argued that this type of trickster demonstrates that "confronting power from the underside requires a gritty resourcefulness, a willingness to take what is at hand and turn it into a tool of subversion."[34] African American tricksters display a particular skill in subverting the mental and physical bondage to which deported Africans were subjected, by keeping humor, spirit, and hope of final emancipation alive. For our own reading of Luke 16, the figure of the "High John," a representative of the "black foreman class" produced by the slaveholding societies of the South, provides a similarly hybrid and liminal character, a hybrid of African and Anglo-American influence, an expression of the "transmuted values of African people shaped by situations and conditions in America."[35] A person both empowered and overpowered, both exploiter and exploited, the *oikonomos* High John is stuck in a moral dilemma with no way out. Thus, he plays his tricks to "make a way out of no way," as diasporic blacks may have taught their children.[36] With little food and close to starving, economic survival was constantly at stake for the African slaves, and often the only choice was to lie in order to live and to steal in order to survive. In distinction, the B'rer Rabbit trickster often steals food and outsmarts the master, but is at times also outsmarted by him. The tales of B'rer Rabbit function as part of a hidden transcript that allows the expression of suppressed desires and fears in a safe but ultimately stimulating and cautiously hopeful oral form. The High John figure, on the other hand, represents more ambivalent feelings. Here is one whose loyalty to the master endangers his own well-being as well as that of his fellow slaves.[37]

The *oikonomos* of Luke 16 resembles the High John as he, too, functions as a person both exploited and exploitative of others in the story. Luke's economist, in all the mess and complicated power dynamics, is far from innocent, and yet he is not guilty of all he is accused of. In this uncomfortable, liminal space, a network of divine economy emerges. In

---

34. Darby Kathleen Ray, *Deceiving the Devil: Atonement, Abuse, and Ransom* (Cleveland: Pilgrim, 1998), 139.
35. John W. Roberts, *From Trickster to Badman: The Black Folk Hero in Slavery and Freedom* (Philadelphia: University of Pennsylvania Press, 1989), 52, 14.
36. Hyde, *Trickster Makes This World*, 278.
37. Roberts, *From Trickster to Badman*, 69.

danger of losing his own livelihood, the *oikonomos* cleverly concocts another fraudulent but oddly just deal: the release of debt for those who are indebted to his master. The *commercium/conubium* of Christ and the *commercium*—the counterfeit—of the Lukan *oikonomos* might both be described as countereconomic instances of a tricksterdom of the subjugated that refuses to see them as victims only. Whereas the Lukan household slave writes a fraudulent debt statement, the patristic Christ as slave himself becomes the counterfeit writ, coin and body himself. Both transactions, involving complex forms of agency, are at least puzzling, if not troubling, to many readers, and have had a history of arousing exegetical and theological horror and distrust. But perhaps it is exactly their ambivalence that establishes their value for a reconstruction of divine economy. Bakhtin stresses the "deep ambivalence of the grotesque" in the fiction of Rabelais that transcends the mere destructive push of the text as it also symbolizes through the strategy of the hyperbole of what is true and observable and provides the moral satisfaction to having dealt a blow to the vices.[38] Meant as a dismissive slur by theological commentators on the ancient notion of the *commercium*, the term "grotesque" can be a fitting description for some models of divine commerce, as the grotesque and the picaresque are often found in close proximity to trickster tales, depicting a form of redemptive agency in a context of deep complicity.[39]

Increasingly and complexly entangled in global trade connections, more and more people realize that their own location is not as remote from the flow of economic power as their perceived inability to influence it might make it seem. Most of us experience some degree of exploitation as well as profit from our entangled place in transnational trading. Stockholders profit from soaring shares they have invested in, we buy clothes made cheaply by workers without rights in *maquiladoras* south of the border. Yet our choices to live more modestly, and more justly, are severely limited. Try living without a car in a society where car and oil companies hobble the infrastructure of public transportation and refuse to increase fuel efficiency, where rail systems and subways are chronically neglected and underfunded. Try buying what you need in a Midwest supermarket that is the only one in town while making sure that the way it is produced does not exploit workers or harm the environment. Try taking care of your

---

38. Mikhail Bakhtin, *Rabelais and His World* (trans. Helene Iswolsky; Cambridge: MIT Press, 1968), 304, 305–6.
39. Across cultures, many tricksters, fools, and picaros play their tricks in situations with a strong economic undercurrent. Cf. Hyde, *Trickster Makes This World;* and Lori Landay, *Madcaps, Screwballs, and Con Women: The Female Trickster in American Culture* (Feminist Cultural Studies, the Media, and Political Culture; Philadelphia: University of Pennsylvania Press, 1998).

health and the health of your loved ones in a health care system run to produce profits rather than to prevent disease, and in treatment situations that discriminate against women and minorities.

Caught in fraudulent transactions, the Lukan *oikonomos* is shrewd enough to know how to turn things around by making them better and not worse: he employs his good business sense by helping out others while helping himself at the same time. Our tangled locations uncomfortably resemble that of this "economist," and the puzzling praise the shrewd manager receives catches us exactly in the ambivalent spots of our daily interactions: "And his master commended the dishonest manager because he had acted shrewdly; for the children of this age are more shrewd in dealing with their own generation than are the children of light" (16:8).

The Lukan parable of the *oikonomos* reminds us that we cannot easily extract ourselves from the debts of the past and present, our own or those who have gone before us. We begin, lead, and end our lives in unjust economies. If our own investments are unlikely to be "pure," how can we think countereconomic agency in a way that heeds Keller's warning of the dangers of dualistic, apocalyptic schemes and our own tendencies toward either full-scale enthusiasm or cynicism? How do we figure this agency out? How can we invest ourselves in contemporary forms of divine economy? What does redemption as the release from debts mean in this context?

What if we, like Gregory's Christ, "deceived the deceiver"? What if the "unjust stewards" wised up and became clever *oikonomoi,* still implicated, always already indebted, and yet inserting redemptive countereconomies as tricksters into a deceptively complacent plutocracy? The figure of the trickster provides one model for a social activism that would be "less deliberate and more quirky," that would need "the energy of the trickster who uses lies to reveal truth, appetite to bait, vulgarity to appall, wit to entrap," as Jeanie Wylie-Kellermann suggests.[40] What might a divine economic tricksterism look like in the contexts we live in? Would it "stop trusting that if we just play by the rules it will all come out right and instead engage in periodic mischief"? Would it attempt to "crack open the absurdities of corporate crime and corporate welfare" and plot a "third way" where "Jesus accompanies us into trickster territory"?[41]

What follows is a small sampling of possible strategies for Holy Fools, Saint Mysterias, and Divine Counterfeiters, suggesting that actions and performances may vary according to the type of tricksterdom, and may be specific to gender, race, ethnicity, class, cultural context, degree of public exposure, and other factors. Some strategies may strive to achieve a

---

40. Jeanie Wylie-Kellermann, "Coyote Wants More," *The Witness* (July/August 1998): 5.
41. Ibid.

symbolic measure of resistance to raise awareness and interrupt public performances of hegemonic power/knowledge, such as Julia Butterfly Hill's two-year-long tree-sit to protest Maxxam's clear-cut logging practices. Others act ascetically through a refusal or at least avoidance to participate in certain exchanges. Projects such as the San Francisco nonprofits Transportation for a Livable City, Citycarshare, and San Francisco Bicycle Coalition seek for ways out of oil dependency by promoting city planning that supports walking, bike commuting, car sharing, and the extension of public transportation. Divine tricksterdom might also involve a strategy that Derrida has named "erasure," a process in which a word such as "economy" that has become an empty shell is crossed out—not to erase it but to put it under erasure, to mark it for a process of rethinking and renegotiation.[42] The nonprofit organization Redefining Progress does exactly that, mapping "progress"—a problematic term to begin with—not, as generally done, by monitoring a narrow segment of the business world for growth in share value or sales volume but by creating "policies and tools to encourage accurate market prices, to protect our common social and natural assets, and to foster social and economic sustainability."[43] Redefining Progress unveils the shortsighted economic "decencies" of a form of stakeholder capitalism that consumes, oppresses, and wastes away both earth and humanity. Divine tricksterdom can expose, for example, contemporary slaveholding practices so that slavery might become unprofitable.[44] Divine trickery attempts to demystify and devalue the cult of the "bottom line," to upset presumably "decent" economies of oppression, unveil the traitor in the trader, and generally get invested in seemingly paradox commerce, of a strange—*admirabilis*—and wondrous *commercium*. Thus, we may invent a cornucopia of divine economic strategies in varying degrees of adjacency to the economies they are already invested in. Possibilities abound.

Asceticism as Resistance: Then and Now

Asceticism has received much bad press.[45] Asceticism's critics have held it responsible for bankrupting women and the body, of destroying and

---

42. Gayatri Spivak, "Translator's Preface," in *Of Grammatology*, by Jacques Derrida (Baltimore: Johns Hopkins Press, 1998), xiii–xiv.
43. This quotation is from Redefining Progress's mission statement, which can be accessed at http://www.rprogress.org.
44. Kevin Bales, *Disposable People: New Slavery in the Global Economy* (Berkeley: University of California, 1999), 240.
45. Richard Valantasis and Vincent L. Wimbush, *Asceticism* (Oxford: Oxford University Press, 1995), xx; Elizabeth Clark, *Reading Renunciation: Asceticism and Scripture in Early Christianity* (Princeton, N.J.: Princeton University Press, 1999), 14–15.

exploiting materiality in the obsessive search for otherworldly bliss. Not only has asceticism been reduced to an ideology of denial, negativity, and alienation from body and matter, but Max Weber's classic work *The Protestant Work Ethic and the Spirit of Capitalism* has linked it explicitly—and perhaps indelibly—to capitalism, contending that asceticism is paradoxically conducive to the acquisition of riches.[46] The "Protestant work ethic" described by Weber emerges as an unconscious by-product or unwanted side effect of a certain kind of ascetic spirituality. The resemblance of a certain form of Christian asceticism to capitalist structures has fooled many descendants of the capitalist Protestants whose work ethic Weber observed. In addition, a mistrust of asceticism might be the remainder of modern Protestant scholarship's preoccupation with identifying Hellenistic "imports"—Platonic dualism was detected as a major culprit—as intrusive elements in a purely imagined early Christianity.[47] But in the wake of Foucault, a number of scholars of asceticism—among them Valantasis, Clark, Harpham, and Burrus—have highlighted the reciprocal payoffs ascetics receive from renunciation.

Harpham formulates at an extreme that "early asceticism is capitalism without money."[48] While Harpham's notion of early asceticism as a form of capitalism might leave us in a slightly hypereconomic overdrive, MacKendrick's theorizing about asceticism as counterpleasure that is not neatly reciprocal or teleologically primed toward gratification points toward the third space we are trying to inhabit. Thus, one might argue that the salvific economics of asceticism may well at times resemble what we now call capitalism but that they are never as tidy, stable, or predictable as Harpham's analysis might suggest. Rather, its losses and gains—to speak with the early Derrida—disseminate. The general economy of *différance* is always exorbitant and excessive, thus incalculable and ambivalent in its investments and its payoffs. While Derrida might seem to argue that monetary and semiotic symbols resemble each other in their structures, he is not thereby suggesting that they both can be reduced to—or that they can redeem—capitalism. Rather, his disseminative reading of both writing and currency or counterfeit reveals the extent to which both language and monetary exchanges are not at all tidy, neat, "restricted," or calculable. Though asceticism remains an ambivalent practice, neither purely subversive nor purely

---

46. See Max Weber, *Die protestantische Ethik I: Eine Aufsatzsammlung* (ed. Johannes Winckelmann; Gütersloh: GTB Siebenstern, 1991), 35; and, expanding Weber's controversial thesis to early Christian asceticism, Geoffrey Galt Harpham, *The Ascetic Imperative in Culture and Criticism* (Chicago: University of Chicago Press, 1987), 30 and passim.
47. Clark cites Harnack as a classic example. Clark, *Reading Renunciation*, 19–20.
48. Harpham, *Ascetic Imperative*, 30.

co-optable, it always accommodates countereconomic strategies ready to emerge and shift the dynamics of power.

It seems that even the boldest patristic economist would hesitate to argue that biblical texts (or even the Lord Christ himself, for that matter) would advise, or even straightforwardly model, the outright acquisition of wealth. Yet does ancient Christian asceticism function—as Geoffrey Galt Harpham points out—as a moneyless early form of ascetically managed Protestant capitalism after all? Is it perhaps even a premonition of industrial capitalism? As we track the figure of the rich young man through these texts, accounting for the exchanges of almsgiving, asceticism, and imperial divine economies, it may seem as if capitalism and Western Christianity might prove structurally continuous after all.

A number of contemporary descendants of Weber's Protestants continue to write, buy, and read texts that portray Jesus' "business-friendly attitude." When God and Mammon seem close to being identified, either consciously or unconsciously, we find images such as God as "my broker," a spoof about an ex-stockbroker gone monk gone monastic investor.[49] Or we find—less spoofy but rather spooky—financial guru Laurie Beth Jones' *Jesus, C.E.O: Using Ancient Wisdom for Visionary Leadership* and her most recent best-seller, *Jesus, Inc.: The Visionary Path: An Entrepreneur's Guide to True Success,* or Wade Cook's *Business Buy the Bible.*[50] Such writers have produced texts in the tradition of Bruce Barton's *The Man Nobody Knows,* where Jesus appears as the fullest incarnation of a "muscular" capitalism. James Twitchell wryly comments on Barton's (a Baptist preacher's kid) text:

> In the context of literary history Barton's book, *The Man Nobody Knows,* fits into a robust genre of "What if Jesus were alive today: how would He act?" . . . Barton's Jesus was an advertising executive busy at "my father's business," selling redemption by the newly named but ancient devices of advertising. . . . Jesus and his little band of twelve entrepreneurs are shown carrying the Word to the modern world. He is no passive "lamb of God," but a full-fledged salesman going about his business.[51]

---

49. Brother Ty, with Christopher Buckley and John Tierney, *God Is My Broker: A Monk-Tycoon Reveals the 7 1/2 Laws of Spiritual and Financial Growth* (New York: Random House, 1998).

50. Laurie Beth Jones, *Jesus, CEO: Using Ancient Wisdom for Visionary Leadership* (New York: Hyperion, 1995); Laurie Beth Jones, *Jesus, Inc.: The Visionary Path: An Entrepreneur's Guide to True Success* (New York: Crown, 2001); Wade Cook, *Business Buy the Bible: Financial Wisdom of the Ancients* (Seattle: Lighthouse, 1997).

51. James B. Twitchell, *Lead Us into Temptation: The Triumph of American Materialism* (New York: Columbia University Press, 1999), 64–65.

In the face of such commercialization of redemption, how can we retrieve different versions of ascetic divine economy? Can a reconstruction of ancient asceticism, a practice of power that seems so singularly congregated around personal salvation, contribute to a postmodern soteriology with a more inclusive—that is, social, ecological, and cosmological—notion of salvation? In contrast to Weber's identification of asceticism as a virtue that helped industrial capitalism to its success, other forms of asceticism, such as voluntary simplicity, attempt a resistance to a consumerist economy by reducing dependence on its products. Thus, Duane Elgin's classic text describes persons who live in voluntary simplicity as those

> who stand with a foot in two worlds—with one foot in an unraveling industrial civilization and another foot in a newly arising post-industrial civilization. These are the "in-betweeners"—people who are bridging two worlds and making the transition from one dominant way of living to another. Their way of living is an amalgam, a blending of the old and the new into a more workable and meaningful alternative to the deteriorating status quo.[52]

A new wave of research on ancient asceticism has provided alternative, perhaps more appreciative conceptions of ascetic practices as formations of power and knowledge (Foucault), a set of varied practices that neither simply deny, nor simply affirm body or world, but retain a certain ambivalence (Harpham). New readings portray more optimistic notions of early Christian ascetic anthropologies that argue humans can improve through ascetic practice and that such a transformation is a matter of close cooperation of mind and body, rather than a regime simply hostile to the body.[53] Orthodox attempts to efface Arian approaches to salvation have perhaps functioned to discredit the contribution ascetic practices might have to divinization. Yet, ascetic discipline is also deeply embedded in the Christian life of the disciple as the art of imitating Christ, and often appears, says Richard Valantasis, as "performances designed to inaugurate an alternative culture, to enable different social relations, and to create a new identity."[54] This mimesis "is never without the *theoretical* perception of resemblance or

---

52. Cf. Duane Elgin, *Voluntary Simplicity: Toward a Way of Life That Is Outwardly Simple and Inwardly Rich* (New York: William Morrow & Co., 1981), 2; see also Michael Lerner, *The Politics of Meaning: Restoring Hope and Responsibility in an Age of Cynicism* (Reading, Mass.: Addison-Wesley, 1996).
53. See Peter Brown, *The Body and Society: Men, Women, and Sexual Renunciation in Early Christianity* (New York: Columbia University Press, 1988); and Clark, *Reading Renunciation*, 17.
54. Richard Valantasis, "A Theory of the Social Function of Asceticism," in *Asceticism*, by Richard Valantasis and Vincent L. Wimbush (Oxford: Oxford University Press, 1995), 548.

similarity, that is, of that which always will be posited as the condition of metaphor."[55] I would suggest that Harpham's, Valantasis's, Burrus's, and others' rediscovery of the resistant qualities of asceticism points toward such a possibility. If we can affirm Harpham's claim that "asceticism provides us with an extraordinary useful concept, that of *resistance*,"[56] ascetic elements found in economies of salvation both ancient and post/modern can be employed to help elaborate on strategies of a "new eco-asceticism."[57] The resultant ascetic practice can incorporate a variety of disciplines that contribute to rethinking soteriological tropes as well as to reconstructing economic practices.

Among constructive theologians, we find those who consider "Jesus's counter-apocalyptic basileia"[58] impossible to harness for the promotion of personal and corporate gains. McFague, for example, excepts deification from her negative evaluation of asceticism and claims it as a necessary virtue for a "North-American Liberation Theology."[59] Her "ecological economic" theology explicitly recommends "deification in terms of cruciform living," as a practice critical to "our culture's current lifestyle," including alternative visions of "the good life."[60] This voluntary asceticism, however, is meant as a discipline for those who have more than enough, not for the destitution of those who are or were poor! Deification—*theosis*—is, however, also the deeply ascetic characteristic of the imitation of Christ. Catherine Keller exhibits even less fear of asceticism and recommends its iteration as a new or eco-asceticism,[61] while James Nash has engaged resident Christian ascetic traditions such as frugality and monasticism for a spirituality of loving nature.[62] Critics may argue that voluntary asceticism and environmentalism is a form of bourgeois agency, affordable only for some. But if a change of mind is to be effected, these voluntary restrictions can certainly be a part of limiting the impact and seduction of consumer goods and can prepare greater changes.

These and other contributions to a theology of coredemptive salvific agency stand in critical loyalty to conceptions of divine economy as experienced, formulated, and interpreted in early Christian writings.

---

55. Jacques Derrida, *Margins of Philosophy* (trans. Alan Bass; Chicago: University of Chicago Press, 1981), 237.
56. Harpham, *Ascetic Imperative*, xv.
57. Keller, "Christian Response to the Population Apocalypse," 118.
58. Keller, *Apocalypse Now and Then*, 290.
59. Sallie McFague, *Life Abundant: Rethinking Theology and Economy for a Planet in Peril* (Minneapolis: Fortress, 2000), 33, 177.
60. Ibid., 23.
61. Keller, "Christian Response to the Population Apocalypse," 117–18.
62. James Nash, *Loving Nature: Ecological Integrity and Christian Responsibility* (Nashville: Abingdon, 1991), 65.

Countereconomic reasoning hopes to avoid traditional reductionist, androcentric colonial and neocolonial trading, focusing instead on locations from which more complexly gendered economies resistant to continued imperialism can emerge.

Ascetic living for women today may include, as it did for Jerome's protégé Eustochium, the renunciation of procreation, the managing of their own bodily economy. Ascetic investments display a similar dynamic as sanctification, deconstruction, and *Parusieverzögerung*, (delay of the *parousia*) or what Derrida has sometimes termed the "supplement." Similarly, Irigaray's concept of virginity is not one of asexuality, necessarily, but consists in the renunciation of being used as a property or product in the masculine economy.

Thus, "virginity," as a form of asceticism, can include the decision to forego procreation. This ascetic "reform" of the womb may also contribute, for some, to the curbing of the population growth that threatens the planet. Keller envisions new forms of ascetic life especially for those women living in the affluent West and suggests that

> this new Christian asceticism, like the original, does not concern sex per se but its fruits. The new asceticism will focus on abstinence from inappropriate childbearing rather than from sex. If sex, apart from its procreative uses, is safe, mutually voluntary, and linked to a communally responsible, egalitarian ethos, it simply does not deserve much further discipline by Christian social ethicists.

Thus, Keller intends not to "decry the choice to parent as immoral" but to "discourage any parenting which is not based on responsible choices, made within the framework of not just private but familial, communal, and global responsibilities."[63] A related choice is that of many straight, gay, and lesbian couples to adopt children who are not welcome elsewhere, to parent those who are orphaned for one reason or another. Serene Jones finds that the doctrine of sanctification assumes women's agency, a property so often denied them, so that a woman can become "the embodied agent struggling to become the ever shifting essential woman of the future." This redemptive move toward perfection "resists falsely gendered versions of the self."[64] McFague and Jones affirm a reconstruction of sanctification, and I suggest doing the same for asceticism by retrieving ancient resources, while elaborating Keller's notion of "new eco-asceticism."[65] Jones insists on

---

63. Keller, "Christian Response to the Population Apocalypse," 117–18.
64. Serene Jones, *Feminist Theory and Christian Theology*, 64–65.
65. Keller, "Christian Response to the Population Apocalypse," 118.

the eschatological dimensions of sanctification "not as a process destined to be completed in this life."[66]

Biblical texts can only tenuously be claimed as guides to achieving wealth. Instead, the manifold layers of biblical tradition display a variety of approaches and incarnations of the relationship between God and Mammon. This ambivalence of the third space, of a countereconomic divine household, is a site admittedly complex and unruly, in which asceticism, too, is a fragile form of economic power management. The ascetic capitalism we have observed is also a mimetic capitalism that imitates, harnesses, and mocks the desire to gain wealth, resulting in a loss of earthly wealth, even as it promises eternal riches. Bhabha's analysis of mimicry and mockery helps read the intertextual interpretations of the metaphor of Jesus' *basileia* and subsequent ancient ascetic practices as performing a resistant sense of divine *oikonomia* in an ambivalent context of empire.[67] Asceticism thus emerges neither as purely subversive nor purely co-optable, but always carries the possibility of both within it. It also accommodates the possibility of—with MacKendrick—variously reciprocal counterpleasure and countereconomy within it.

Holy Wisdom, Holy Fools

A number of contemporary theologians have suggested a resort to trickery or wise folly. In 1969, Harvey Cox published *The Feast of Fools,* a passionate essay on the rediscovery of fantasy, festivity, fun, and clownery as part of Christian spiritual and political activity. Cox imagined Christ as a harlequin, a jester, his life full of subversive, ironic parables and actions. In the Middle Ages, the Feast of Fools would allow, like Carnival, the temporally restricted upending of cultural and social limitations, class and power differences, relieving pressure in a way that was not easily co-optable. It bothered the clerical and political authorities and eventually vanished with the rise of modernity. However, Cox argues that this foolery represents a way of connecting, of linking paradoxical and conflicting knowledge, that is needed direly in times of transition, in times where modernity has been severely questioned, in a "success- and money-oriented society, we need a

---

66. Serene Jones, *Feminist Theory and Christian Theology*, 65.
67. It is not clear how Bhabha's notion of colonial mimicry as "resemblance and menace" contributes to a subversive countereconomy. Here Spivak's critique of elite postcolonialism and its possible complicity in obscuring the oppression of the subaltern is useful as a corrective. Still, Bhabha's analysis can be used to map the permanently ambivalent matrix of colonial and postcolonial relationships. Homi Bhabha, *The Location of Culture* (London: Routledge, 1994), 86; and Gayatri Spivak, *A Critique of Postcolonial Reason: Toward a History of the Vanishing Present* (Cambridge: Harvard University Press, 1999), 358 and passim.

rebirth and patently unproductive festivity and expressive celebration" to express dissatisfaction, and to envision and facilitate change.[68]

Writing more than thirty years later, Peter Phan likewise perceives of the "wisdom of holy fools" as a way of un/knowing that remains as an alternative path to wisdom in an "in-between time," at the end of the Middle Ages, now at the end of modernity, in a postmodernity which has so deeply questioned traditional ways of knowing, such as *logos* and *mythos*.[69] Phan traces this "morosophia" back to Jesus and Paul's famous argument that the world's wisdom is foolishness for God, that God's wisdom seems foolish, with the cross as the utmost example of divine foolishness.[70] Phan finds this foolish wisdom related to apophatic theology and its *via negativa*, both distinguished from mere ignorance but rather manifest as *docta ignorantia*, a studied ignorance. Similar practices and epistemologies can be found in Sufism, Buddhism, and Eastern Orthodox Christianity.[71] Such foolish wisdom shuns convention and customs of society, as its nonconformity can turn into ideological (and theological) iconoclasm, social anarchy, literary satire. In many traditions, this foolish wisdom is perceived as being of divine provenance, not achieved by intelligence or learning but given, granted, revealed.[72] Through irony and the art of dissembling that which is assumed, holy folly is the witting or unwitting instrument of truth; it breaks the real and creates "not an alternative world, but an *other* world."[73] This alternate foolish vision and wisdom must be tempered, says Phan, by love, which must serve as the light of knowledge to keep this crazy wisdom from turning into insanity.[74] Like hysterics and tricksters, holy fools continually dance on the edge of chaos.

The countereconomic third space can be found in an unlikely and contested ascetic, a possible figural incarnation, the ancient holy fool Symeon as described by Derek Krueger.[75] Leontius's textual economy portrays

---

68. Harvey Cox, *The Feast of Fools: A Theological Essay on Festivity and Fantasy* (New York: Harper & Row, 1969), 5.
69. Peter C. Phan, "The Wisdom of Holy Fools in Postmodernity," *Theological Studies* 62 (2001): 730, 746.
70. First Corinthians 3:18; 4:10. Phan lays out that to be a "fool for Christ's sake" was later developed as a spiritual discipline with the desert fathers and other ascetics. Phan, "Wisdom of Holy Fools," 740.
71. Ibid., 739–40.
72. Ibid., 738.
73. Ibid., 749.
74. Ibid., 750–51. Liberation theologian Franz Hinkelammert calls for divine folly to counter "rational" *Verrücktheit*. For him, divine wisdom consists in the election of what is weak. Only if the weak can live, can all live. Hinkelammert, "Wider die Verfertigten Götzen der Macht: Zur Metaphysik der okzidentalen Unmenschlichkeit," in *Bilderverbot: Jahrbuch für politische Theologie* (ed. Michael J. Rainer and Hans-Gerd Janssen; Münster: LIT, 1997), 2:50, 51, 53.
75. Holy fools also appear as a crucial element in Russian culture, where they have been a staple of the social structures in villages and towns from at least the early Middle Ages to the October

Symeon, whose behavior is considered obscene and anything but saintly by most of his contemporaries, as more saintly and ascetic than any other previous saint. Symeon's story thus "challenge[s] our sometimes sanctimonious notions of early Christian piety," and contemporary readers might puzzle that the holy fools who were "clearly deviants . . . were held in high regard by clergy and laity."[76] While Symeon may seem to run with prostitutes, defecate in places of commerce, such as the marketplace, and run naked into a women's bath, these "miracles" are, to the knowing clerical eye, witness to Symeon's incredible restraint and control of his body and desires.[77] His asceticism is of a more secretive nature, and while he seems to the public a lecher and glutton, his true strength and restraint emerge even more starkly as he seeks out these temptations but stays miraculously untainted. Whether Leontius's somewhat strained sanitizing of a publicly defecating saint convinces us entirely or not, Symeon's public performance is certainly instructive. His concealed sanctity allows him to unveil the absurdities of urban life. Cast by Leontius in the garb of urban cynic philosophers, Symeon is a fool for Christ's sake, borrowing some cynical themes for his performance. Thus, he functions as a critic of his urban environment, mimicking, and thereby exposing, the excesses of the city. Thus, Krueger reports that "Symeon's profaning actions in the marketplace comment on society's hypocrisy, iniquity, and economic injustice."[78] Krueger stresses that while Leontius freely uses motifs of the life of Diogenes of Sinope, "Symeon is not a Cynic, nor does Leontius present a Cynic interpretation of Jesus. . . . Ultimately it is the life of Jesus which provides the guiding model for Symeon, the fool for Christ's sake, and for the Christian life toward which Leontius directs his readers."[79]

Leontius's Symeon is a holy fool who mimics Jesus—his model for holy foolishness—like a true disciple. The tricksterlike figure of the Holy Fool might provide space for reconstructing the figure of the ascetic hysterical males in countereconomic space, as he inhabits the ambivalence between earthly and divine economy. Krueger asks, "Is it possible that early Christians had a sense of humor? And to what use did they put this humor?"[80] We might ask ourselves what the countereconomic reconstruction of the figure of a holy fool contributes to the deconstruction of problematic

---

Revolution. See Ewa M. Thompson, *Understanding Russia: The Holy Fool in Russian Culture* (Lanham, Md.: University Press of America, 1987), 1–5.

76. Derek Krueger, *Symeon the Holy Fool: Leontius'* Life *and the Late Antique City* (Berkeley: University of California Press, 1996), 2.
77. Ibid., 47.
78. Ibid., 128.
79. Ibid., 129.
80. Ibid., 2

economic practices, tactics, and strategies, and to the construction of a tricksterlike countereconomic theology.[81]

Today, holy fools might be discerned in other "saints" who defy our expectations. One performance-oriented holy fool is Bill Talen's alter ego Rev. Billy of the "Church of Stop-Shopping." This New York improv group uses theater and play to highlight the "neighborhood destruction by transnational chain stores."[82] Trying to evade the powers that would keep him and the sheep of his flock of Stop-Shoppers from performing their renarration of Disney and Starbucks marketing techniques, Rev. Billy preaches a gospel that warns believers of the powers of satanic corporate practices. Exposing the economic and cultural violence involved in the "invasions of chain stores" in bombarding, or "mall-izing" urban neighborhoods with "fake communities like $tarbucks," their short episodes of "spat theater" attempt to reclaim public space from privatized corporate space. Posing as customers involved in an argument, Church of Stop-Shopping actors disrupt the quaint scenes of a local New York "sippery" and proceed to expose the involvement of the coffee giant in prison labor and neighborhood destruction, only to be quickly interrupted in their intent by the combined forces of baristas in green aprons and the blue uniforms of New York's finest. Rev. Billy advises, "Learn to be a fool. The transnational planners have no idea what to do with the politicized Fool," echoing Harvey Cox's words from thirty years earlier.[83]

Holy Fool and design trickster Kalle Lasn's magazine *Adbusters* includes a graphic designer's "vow of chastity" that describes the activist convictions of those that resist consumer culture by "jamming" it: "From now on I'll put truth and beauty in all my designs. If I have to lie, I'll lie for myself. No more grids, gimmicks, mindfucks, clients-haha."[84] Lasn's manifesto on "culture jamming" emerges from a "loose global network of media activists who see ourselves as the advance shock troops of the most significant social movement of the next twenty years."[85] These culture jammers regularly

---

81. I am borrowing the distinction between strategies and tactics from Vincent Miller's discussion of resistant agency in a consumer society. Following Bourdieu, he argues that tactics are more spontaneous, small-scale, and flexible, while strategies are often applied by and in organization and structures. In order to effect significant shifts in consciousness and practice, we will need both forms of change. Vincent J. Miller, *Consuming Religion: Christian Faith and Practice in a Consumer Culture* (New York: Continuum, 2003), 155.

82. Bill Talen, "Reverend Billy's Starbucks Invasion: The Church of Stop Shopping Takes a Stand," *Utne Reader* online, 14 April 2002, http://www.utne.com/web_special/web_specials_archives/articles/2761-1.html. Also see http://www.revbilly.com. See also Rev. Billy's book: William Talen, *What Should I Do if Reverend Billy is in My Store?* (New York: New Press, 2003).

83. Talen, "Reverend Billy's Starbucks Invasion."

84. See http://adbusters.org.

85. Kalle Lasn, *Culture Jam: The Uncooling of America*™ (New York: William Morrow & Co., 1999), ix.

mock and interfere with the slick trades of "daily business ... by getting consumer culture to bite its own tail."[86] Part of Lasn's thesis is that the separation of human consumers from their natural environment is related. Thus, Lasn writes, "Abandon nature and you abandon your sense of the divine. More than that, you lose track of who you are."[87] The holy foolery and a vow of public relations chastity—another, if unusual, form of neoasceticism—inhabit countereconomic space as it mocks and defies the form and function of advertising media. Within the "liturgical calendar" of consumerism,[88] culture jammers have begun celebrating a heretical feast day: the "Buy Nothing Day" on the day after Thanksgiving, traditionally one of the busiest shopping days of the year.[89]

Guillermo Gómez-Peña's border crossings take hybridity and tricksterdom to a liminal Mexican-American space of economic, political, and cultural exchange. The Mexican-born performance artist uses provocative forms of street theater, live installations that function as a mixture between museum and confessional to invite his audience, in the words of Roger Bartra, to "live on the border, to convert ourselves into permanent exiles, into nostalgic and melancholic beings, and to undergo the dangers that take us to the discovery of the infected wound."[90] Gómez-Peña's art wants to shock viewers and listeners into awareness of their own cultural stereotypes, and it invites confessions from viewers about their involvement in the cult of purist culture, racism, and nationalism. In the installation "Temple of Confessions," which combines the features of a museum exhibit with the sacral space of the confessional, the artist, decked out in a "Tex-Mex Aztec" outfit as the "hybrid saint" of San Pocho Aztlaneca, invites viewers to confess, orally or literally, their "racial bigotry" and their "South of border fantasies," thus examining public perceptions of Mexican and Mexican American culture. The gallery functions as a confessional, as a memory to the martyred of *la raza,* and allows people to reflect on their racist attitudes toward other cultures, to explore ambiguous spaces of race, ethnicity, and culture, to inhabit multiple interpretations of identity, border, hybridity. Through this "theater of mythos," set in a "melancholic, ceremonial space" that is at the same time sexually "seductive, yet threatening," Gómez-Peña's

---

86. Ibid., 111.
87. Ibid., 7.
88. Dell deChant interprets consumerism as a form of cosmological, postmodern religion, with its own set of high holidays and feasts, ritualizing consumption. He identifies a "postmodern liturgical year" with various subcycles. See deChant, *The Sacred Santa: Religious Dimensions of Consumer Culture* (Cleveland: Pilgrim, 2002), 38–39, 136ff., 159ff.
89. http://www.adbusters.org/metas/eco/bnd/
90. Roger Bartra, "Introduction," in *Warrior of Gringostroika,* by Guillermo Gómez-Peña (St. Paul: Graywolf Press, 1993), 7.

postcolonial exposures open a "Pandora's box" of "colonial demons" revealing America's "inability to deal with cultural otherness."[91] As a postcolonial fool of the border, Gómez-Peña exposes the economic, social, and cultural implications of border crossings. In a 1994 performance project entitled "cruci-fiction," Gómez-Peña and his collaborator, Roberto Sifuentes, crucified themselves at Rodeo Beach in the Marin Headlands facing San Francisco's Golden Gate Bridge. Thus renarrating a central Christian image in order to depict the crucifixion of Mexicans as political scapegoats for the socioeconomic problems of post-NAFTA California, they push the edges of the Christian narrative as it has been entwined with the economic forces of Western colonialism, displaying the cross as a subversive element of interpretation, of accusation, and refusing it any salvific, redeeming value. The image of the migrant, the border crosser, is central to Gómez-Peña's work also in the figure of the "Warrior of Gringostroika." This migrant hero, a quintessential trickster, provides a constant source of contamination and threat of identity as he embodies and prophesies the "borderization of the world," of *mestizaje*, of symbiosis, of hybridity.[92] Embodying various forms of border culture, he challenges nationalism and purist ideals on either side of the border. This "binational border diplomat," dressed as a combination of mariachi, low-rider, and disc jockey conveys a multiplicity of voices, hinting at the bifurcating differences among Latino cultures.[93] Among many other possible ways of reading these trickster performances, they may function to expose not only the stereotyping, racism, and exploitation of Mexicans depicted with the props of Christian imagery, but they also enjoy the mixing and matching of cultural and religious symbols to perform and embody a new way of crossing—and living—the border in the lives of all people.

Satirist and social critic Michael Moore, maker of *Bowling for Columbine*, author of *Downsize This!* the longtime but curiously ignored *New York Times* best-seller *Stupid White Men*, and the more recent *Dude, Where's My Country*[94] began his path into holy fooldom as a high school student.[95] Having been "religious" in his youth, and having attended "the seminary in high school to become a Catholic priest," Moore subsequently found his

---

91. Guillermo Gómez-Peña, *Temple of Confessions: Mexican Beasts and Living Santos* (New York: Powerhouse Books, 1996), 1, 6, 10, 19, 21–23.
92. Bartra, "Gringostroika," 11.
93. Gómez-Peña, *Warrior of Gringostroika*, 21–22.
94. Michael Moore, *Dude, Where's my Country* (New York: Warner Books, 2003).
95. See Michael Moore, *Downsize This! Random Threats from an Unarmed American* (New York: HarperPerennial, 1997); and Michael Moore, *Stupid White Men* (New York: Regan Books/HarperCollins, 2001).

calling in exposing the vices of corporate downsizing and its disastrous consequences on people and land.[96] A muckraker in the tradition of H. L. Mencken, he debunks "all this news about the 'great economic miracle' [as the] best propaganda that's been fed to the American people since Ronald Reagan declared ketchup a vegetable."[97]

A comic, clown, and trickster, Moore pokes fun at the dead-serious causes of public ignorance and apathy when it comes to economics and politics and the stunning and scandalous ignorance and arrogance of national leaders beholden to well-funded lobbyists. He laments the lack of political and policy alternatives available since the officials of both major parties "suck off the same corporate teat." Eventually, "Republican arsenic or Democratic arsenic, it really is the same damn crap being forced down your throat."[98] In the spirit of the merger mania of the 1990s, Moore sarcastically proposes to merge the two major political parties:

> And so I propose a course of action: the Democrats must merge with the Republican party. That way, they can keep doing what they both do very well—representing the rich—and save a lot of money by consolidating staff and headquarters into one tight, fit fighting machine for the top 10 percent.
>
> The good news of such a merger? The working people of this country will finally get to have their own party! What's so terribly wrong with that? It'll be the second party of the two-party system. Except it'll represent the other 90 percent of us.[99]

Relentlessly, Moore plies his trade by mixing hyperbole with shocking facts, inventing hoaxes to demonstrate the real poverty hidden from the public by a toothless media, and identifying "big welfare mamas" and "corporate crooks" among the CEOs of the Fortune 500 in the form of fake trading cards.[100] Engaging in his own ministry of the pastoral and prophetic tasks to comfort the afflicted and to afflict the comfortable, Moore comments on the surprising changes of mind—and subsequent changes in policy—found in public figures who encounter personal tragedy by formulating "A Prayer to Afflict the Comfortable with as Many Afflictions as Possible," thereby "asking God to smite every political leader and corporate executive with some form of deadly disease":

---

96. Moore, *Downsize This!* 10, 18–19.
97. Ibid., 2.
98. Moore, *Stupid White Men,* 220, 222.
99. Ibid., 225.
100. Moore, *Downsize This!* 50, 118.

I have decided that the only hope we have in this country to bring aid to the sick, protection to the victims of discrimination, and a better life to those who suffer is to pray like crazy that those in power are afflicted with the worst possible diseases, tragedies, and circumstances in life. Because I can guarantee you, as soon as it's their ass on the line, we're all on the way to being saved.[101]

Moore's publisher came close to shredding *Stupid White Men* before it ever reached the shelves. Even after it reached the shelves and became a major best-seller, it was virtually ignored by the major media and shunned by reviewers. Too dangerous? Too close to the truth, or at least too revealing of the motivations and practices of the powerful? Tricksters such as Symeon, Rev. Billy, Kalle Lasn, Gomez-Peña, and Michael Moore are dangerous because they threaten the silences and denials of the status quo.

Gendering the Trickster

The most recognizable, well-known, and well-described tricksters in many cultures are male. Female tricksters, if they exist and are recognized as such, often exhibit distinct practices and characteristics. There are a few tropes within feminist theory and scholarship that may lend themselves to a description of the female trickster, not in an attempt to describe an essentialist "female form of trickery" but rather to note a variety of differences in how trickery has been embodied partly due to the social restrictions that have circumscribed and limited women's agency. Eventually, it would seem not so much that there are "essentially" distinct male and distinct female tricksters but that tricksterdom can often appear as queer in that it is adaptable to a variety of genders and locations and engages in a mimicry of society's rules as well as those of gender in all kinds of settings.

Consider also the narrative of an anonymous slave who sees visions of her deceased master having been "his pet in his lifetime and he used to keep mistress from whipping me," and the ensuing ambivalence of power played out between the slave and that same mistress, whose power appears deeply challenged—we know not quite how—by the apparitions privy to the slave. The slave finds comfort in having become an "elect in the House of God." Fearless now, the illiterate woman rejoices that God has "taken me—a fool—for sometimes my head was so beat so I thought I was foolish—and hidden with me the secret of eternal life. He has made me to stand up on

---

101. Moore, *Stupid White Men*, 233.

my feet and teach the world-wise out of His wisdom that comes from on high."[102]

This black woman, a "fool" through the injury of her slaveholders, powerfully reinterprets the violence brought upon her head as holy fooldom that allows her access to a divine wisdom that transcends the knowledge of the learned. Donna Haraway reads Sojourner Truth as a trickster figure that challenges the white supremacist society's paradoxical definitions of womanhood as it intersects with race in her speech "Arn't I a Woman," unveiling the hypocrisy of a slaveholding society that recognizes Victorian womanhood only in white women.[103] In a speech at the Fourth National Woman's Rights Convention, Sojourner Truth inhabits another trickster space, casting herself as the widow with the two copper coins, who knows "a little mite 'bout Woman's Rights, too." Challenging assumptions about her supposed ignorance and low status assigned to her, she ironically surmises to only "throw in my little mite, to keep the scales a-movin'." But her mite, her contribution turns out to not be that small after all: she continues to argue that "in the old times the kings of the earth would hear a woman."[104] Referring to another female trickster figure, Queen Esther, she proposes to engage in similar prophetic actions, aimed at the redemption of her people: women, colored and white. With prophetic fervor she argues that "women want their rights as Esther. She only wanted to explain her rights." Met with hissing and booing, she continues: "The king ordered Haman to be hung on the gallows which he prepared to hang others; but I do not want any man to be killed, but I am sorry to see them so short-minded. But we'll have our rights; see if we don't; and you can't stop us from them; see if you can."[105]

Having put in her two cents, her mighty mites, she leaves the stage but reminds the audience of her ongoing watchfulness and prophetic presence: "I wanted to tell you a mite about Woman's Rights, and so I came out and said so. I am sittin' among you to watch; and every once and a while I will come out and tell you what time of night it is."[106]

More recently, feminist constructive theologian Darby Ray has linked the trickster figure's mimetic features to Irigaray's notion of mimicry:

---

102. George Rawick, ed., *The American Slave. Vol. 19* (Nashville: Fisk University Social Science Institute, 1945), as quoted in Patrick Allitt, *Major Problems in American Religious History* (Boston: Houghton Mifflin, 2000), 138–39.
103. Haraway, "Ecce Homo".
104. Sojourner Truth, "I Suppose I am About the Only Colored Woman That Goes About To Speak for the Rights of Colored Women," in *Freedom is a Dream* (ed. Sheryl Kujawa-Holbrook; New York: Church Publishing, 2002), 15.
105. Ibid., 16.
106. Ibid.

"According to Irigaray, the best strategy for resistance . . . is what she calls mimesis—a kind of playful imitation of the normative that exposes the absurdity, arbitrariness, and ruthlessness of its reduction of multiplicity and difference[.]"[107]

The present project expands Darby Ray's notion of the divine trickster by reading it as a redemptive motif within the divine economy. The connection between the trickster and feminist mimicry is elaborated further by feminist theologian Gisela Matthiae's reading of God as a female clown, a figure that links "theory and praxis, feminist theory and theology," so as to "break through dominant discourses."[108] Reconstructions of the female trickster have encountered problems similar to those that confront attempts to reconstruct the history of women within Christian history and theology. Lori Landay's study of the "missing female trickster" has demonstrated that female tricksters or clowns are far from identical with the predominantly male tricksters that most folkloric studies have focused on, and suggests that those tricksters should rather be understood as part of a "continuum of trickster figures as they change in response to historical and cultural conditions":[109]

> In a sexist society, the male trickster clearly has the advantages of masculinity: mobility, autonomy, power, safety. He is able to be a liminal figure who can move between the margins and centers of society as he deconstructs the power systems with his humor and trickery. . . . Obviously women have not had the same opportunities for such a high degree of mobility (physical as well as psychological, social, economic, artistic, and political.) Thus when scholars have looked for trickster figures using definitions based on the assumption of the trickster's masculinity, they haven't found female figures who fit. In order to identify female tricksters in American (or any) culture, therefore, we must turn from the margins of dominant society to the centers of women's spaces—the parlors, the kitchens, and bedrooms of domesticity.[110]

Gisela Matthiae offers one possible reconstruction of contemporary female tricksterdom: the "rediscovery of the Christian existence as clownesque." The clown, in distinction to the trickster, is a more everyday figure

---

107. Ray, *Deceiving the Devil*, 139.
108. Gisela Matthiae, *Clownin Gott: Eine feministische Dekonstruktion des Göttlichen* (Praktische Theologie Heute 48; Stuttgart: Kohlhammer, 1999), 20; my translation.
109. Landay, *Madcaps, Screwballs, and Con Women*, 17.
110. Ibid., 2–3.

that employs and invites mimicry.[111] Thereby, the "subject 'woman'" as determined by feminist attempts to inscribe a female subject represents a "mimetic or clownesque existence."[112]

Saint Mysteria: Women as Sacred Tricksters

> When I was born, my mother dressed me as a boy because she could not afford to feed any more daughters. By the mystic laws of gender and economics, it ruins a peasant to place half a bowl of figs in front of his daughters, while his son may gorge on the whole tree, burn it for firewood and piss on the stump, and still be reckoned a blessing to his father.
>
> When I was born, my father wanted to drown me, but my mother persuaded him to let me live in disguise, to see if I could bring any wealth to the household.
>
> I did.
>
> Jeanette Winterson, *The PowerBook*

One area in which the reinscription of neoliberal economics in the discourses of the gospel of prosperity continues relatively untroubled is the replication of the heterosexual, monogamous gender roles dictated by the normative capitalist household. Linda Kintz argues that "many of the tenets familiar from religious conservatism help shape market fundamentalism by sacrificing certain groups to the purity of the market while displacing attacks on workers, people of color, gays, and lesbians into the abstractions of economic theory."[113] Thus, the leaders of these churches promote patriarchal gender roles that stress the husband as the head of the family and as the sole breadwinner. Socially conservative gender roles and family values are also part of the curriculum and message of Bob Jackson's Acts Full Gospel Church in Oakland, where women are taught to respect the "headship" of their husbands.[114]

Many prosperity theologies thus share convictions with groups such as the Promise Keepers, whose appeals include the magic last-minute quick-fix

---

111. Matthiae, *Clownin Gott*, 22.
112. Matthiae here refers to Lauretis's "eccentric subject," Haraway's "multiple subject," Braidotti's "nomadic subject," and Thürmer-Rohr's "vagabonding subject." See Matthiae, *Clownin Gott*, 265.
113. Linda Kintz, *Between Jesus and the Market: The Emotions That Matter in Right-Wing America* (Durham, N.C.: Duke University Press, 1997), 4.
114. Chris Thompson, "Preaching Prosperity: Acts Full Gospel Became Oakland's Largest Church by Helping Its Parishioners Leave Town for the Suburbs," *East Bay Express* (24 April 2002): 18.

patching of several marriages on the brink of shattering.[115] In a similar vein, testosterone-enhanced muscular Christianity makes a comeback in the writing of George Gilder, an ultra-conservative yet cyberspace-age ideologist at the economically neoliberal Discovery Institute, a Seattle think tank with connections to Microsoft. Gilder has linked economic performance and masculine sexuality by arguing that the economic "frontier" allows the harnessed married male to play out his hypermasculine energy in the glorified role of the businessman, a Christ-like "cowboy entrepreneur as good shepherd," bulging the biceps of a new attempt to make Christianity more macho.[116] Gendered forms of economic power thus continue to inscribe and be inscribed by Christian traditions, ancient and contemporary.

The masculine rhetorical economies that functioned to domesticate early Christianity's female martyrs cannot but retain the stubborn ambivalence of their sacrifices. Narratives of female martyrs continue to challenge the gendered boundaries of masculine and feminine realms. Along with a theological reconceptualization of hysteria not as lack but as a quality that signifies an open relationship to God, such as in the lives of mystical women saints whose fervent devotions have often been described as located on the border between hysteria and san(ct)ity, Saint Mysteria's contesting of theological and economic genders offers a different approach to redemptive agency.[117] Women martyrs today may be equally hysterical—or "mysterical"[118]—in their witnessing as they voice their faith in a divine economy such that they speak out loudly and prophetically against the abuses of economic power, even if these include their own practices of consumption when they become complicit to hierarchical exploitation. The virgin martyr Thecla might serve as a trickster/clown figure for our countereconomic investments. Her "indecent exposure" before her accusers and intended torturers both resembles and is distinguished from the nakedness of other virgin martyrs such as Perpetua, who was concerned with keeping her hair and dress in order throughout her martyrdom and who, unlike Thecla, actually died. Thecla, though ready for death, gets away with life. On the fluid border between martyr and ascetic, Thecla remains an ambivalent figure, bridging and blurring both categories, willing to boldly

---

115. Bruce Wilkinson, *The Prayer of Jabez: Breaking Through to the Blessed Life* (Sisters, Ore.: Multnomah Publishers, 2000), 31, 81.
116. Kintz, *Between Jesus and the Market*, 201.
117. Christina Mazzoni, *Saint Hysteria: Neurosis, Mysticism, and Gender in European Culture* (Ithaca, N.Y.: Cornell University Press, 1996), 3.
118. Luce Irigaray, *Marine Lover of Friedrich Nietzsche* (New York: Columbia University Press, 1991), 171.

giver her life, but equally willing to take salvation into her own hands. Her witness occurs in part through her willingness to die but also through her queer, cross-dressing escape and survival. Through her own body's strength and resistance, she defends herself against the advances and abandonments of men.

The figure of tricksterlike Thecla resembles the equally tricksterlike "indecent" theologian so juicily exemplified by Marcella Althaus-Reid's lemon vendors. In her vision of theology, the subaltern women of Argentina, represented by Althaus-Reid, become an example of a postcolonial liberation theology that exposes the disciplining "decency" of colonial systematic theologies as well as of heterosexist, machismo liberation theologies.[119] With her indecent theological witness, she strains against the second millennium and the clutches of traditionally conceived salvation history from which Donna Haraway's "modest witness" wishes to escape.[120] Irigaray, Althaus-Reid, and many other women—increasingly indecent, uncanny women, or *unheimliche Frauen* (literally, "un-homely" as well as "not secret" women)—like Thecla, will not be confined to home and hearth (*Heim und Herd*). Homi Bhabha ventures that "for Freud, the *unheimlich* is 'the name for everything that ought to have remained . . . secret and hidden but has come to light.'"[121] Likewise, theologically indecent exposures unveil the *heimlichen*, the veiled, secret discriminatory economies of gender, race, ethnicity, and class. *Unheimliche*, or uncanny, exposures abound. Leaving the house to witness to indecent theologies, traveling, and crying out in the streets like wisdom, wise and strange, indecent women expose the perceived decencies of exploitative sexual and material economies.[122] Indecent theologians of all genders, races, ethnicities, and classes are working to uncover the "grandes medidas economicas," the presumed decencies of the neoclassical economic metanarratives to which too many of us are captive.[123]

Althaus-Reid's indecent women might resemble the "heretical women" shamed by Athanasius and Jerome and aptly retraced by Virginia Burrus. The countereconomic figures of the Giving Woman and her sidekick Saint Hysteria/Mysteria is part heretic, part orthodox, part virgin, part indecent woman. Heretical virgins, positioned as the feared Other of the orthodox virgin, ignore the physical restrictions and "corresponding social subordi-

---

119. Althaus-Reid, *Indecent Theology*, 1, 7.
120. Haraway, *Modest_Witness@Second_Millennium*, 2.
121. Bhabha, *Location of Culture*, 10.
122. For a reading of the Strange Woman in biblical texts as a trickster, see Claudia V. Camp, *Wise, Strange, and Holy: The Strange Woman and the Making of the Bible* (JSOT Supplement Series 320; Sheffield: Sheffield Academic Press, 2000).
123. Althaus-Reid, *Indecent Theology*, 165.

nation to the public sphere of men."[124] If the virgin's decent body symbolizes the orthodox boundaries of church and theological tradition, indecent women ironically function as a rhetorical tool employed to shame and accuse other dissenting male teachers in "redrawing the domestic space as the space of the normalizing, pastoralizing, and individuating techniques" of power where "the personal-*is*-the political; the world-*in*-the-home."[125] Heretical women thus come to stand as those who permeate and blur the perceived tight and tidy boundaries of faith and church where "hybridity is heresy."[126] The indecent women of the twentieth and twenty-first centuries, however, have begun to speak of and be heard in their difference.[127] Thus, indecent, improper female theologians have disrupted the purportedly "decent valuation of a situation" to expose the androcentrically located "ordering of properties (women, slaves)" and to express "women's longing for political and sexual transgression."[128]

The notion of strategic excess or waste plays on, inhabits, and mimicks a gender stereotype. Like the feminist hysteric, it mimicks a gender stereotype squarely inhabiting its hypertrophic self. Waste itself is clearly an ambivalent category, and to avoid a reinscription of wasteful behavior I am not interested in encouraging, it is useful to keep in mind the slippage of mimicry that is always already within. Thus, a general description of third space ambivalence seems crucial, serving as a reminder to strive to keep Irigarayan and Derridean mimicry from turning into a reinscription of the coercions it mimicks.

The strategies of hysteric inhabitation and appropriation of gender stereotypes that previously served to devalue women's experience form part of our countereconomic theology as they develop Irigaray's play on the hysterical as the "mysterical," linking mysticism and saintly emotional excess.[129] As a strategy, however, it is also always in imminent danger of flipping over into essentialism and reinscription and thus must remain critically flexible. Thus, "unfortunately, that crisis must be with us, otherwise the strategy freezes into something like . . . an essentialist position."[130] Mimicry as a strategy of resistance that attempts to destabilize dualisms and stereotypes by hypertrophically inhabiting them thus is a strategy with

---

124. Virginia Burrus, "The Heretical Woman as Symbol in Alexander, Athanasius, Epiphanius, and Jerome," *Harvard Theological Review* 84, no. 3 (1991): 232.
125. Bhabha, *Location of Culture*, 11.
126. Ibid., 225.
127. Luce Irigaray, *An Ethics of Sexual Difference* (trans. Carol Burke and Gillian C. Gill; Ithaca, N.Y.: Cornell University Press, 1984).
128. Althaus-Reid, *Indecent Theology*, 142.
129. See Irigaray, *Marine Lover of Friedrich Nietzsche*, 171; and Mazzoni, *Saint Hysteria*.
130. Spivak and Rooney, "In A Word. Interview," 154.

limited application but one that a countereconomic trickster would necessarily apply.[131] For the purpose of mapping a third space of countereconomy, Bhabha's use of the concepts of ambivalence and mimicry, which retain the consciousness of the enduring danger of reinscription, are helpful because they never cease warning of the temptation to think we have got resistance or subversion "figured out" by identifying it with/in a certain strategy.[132] Rather, both terms serve as a description of the third space and of points of resistance within that space—points of Irigarayan mimicry—that can open up possibilities for new strategies. Yet within Spivak's definition of a strategic essentialism, the challenge is to be both stable and flexible.[133]

Within the texts we have observed, widows, martyrs, and ascetics represent "at once resemblance and menace" to textual economies of gender and status as they visualize various theological estimates of divine economy.[134] Though remaining ambivalent and "available" for both subversion and reinscription, the de-essentializing of perceived gender stereotypes remains potent. This powerful dislocation and slippage found in early Christian texts has contributed to the emergence of feminist theological discourse. A countereconomic deconstruction of essentialized economic genders finds help in Catherine Keller's renunciation of the gendered stereotypes of a male "separative self" and female "soluble self," which stand for the essentialized gender stereotypes that can be overcome by a feminism that goes beyond the "naive glorification of connection" or "relationolatry" and weaves the ties of the "connective self" as from a broken spider's web, back and forth, in continuous repair and reconstruction.[135]

---

131. Robert Young argues that mimicry such as it is described here is found in the texts of Derrida and Irigaray, where it emerges as "a form of resistance as such." He distinguishes it from Bhabha's mimicry, which is far more ambivalent and endangered. See Robert Young, *White Mythologies: Writing History and the West* (New York: Routledge, 1990), 148.

132. Derrida's and Irigiaray's uses of mimicry can, says Young, can be more easily identified as structures of resistance. Bhabha's concepts of mimicry, however, stands close to his notion of ambivalence, which is distinguished by its ceaseless slippages. Young indicates that there obtains an even greater loss of control of either colonizer or colonized in ambivalence than in mimicry. Cf. Young, *White Mythologies*, 148.

133. Irigarayan mimicry can too easily freeze into a position, losing the flexibility it needs to remain subversive, while it then can defeat its purpose and instead serve to reinscribe gender stereotypes. Thus, Young writes, "This parodic doubling reinscribes the relation of alterity between the same and the other, woman as truth and as falsehood: it is the same as that which it simulates but necessarily also different from it, a doubling that can easily be mistaken for the real thing, leading to the accusations of essentialism." Young, *White Mythologies*, 209n.10.

134. Bhabha, *Location of Culture*, 86.

135. See Catherine Keller, *From a Broken Web: Separation, Sexism, and Self* (Boston: Beacon, 1986). Economist Julie Nelson has applied Keller's gender map to her investigations into the "gender of economics" and how neoclassical economic dogmas continue to perpetuate the public-private/culture-nature/male-female dichotomies to which the sexes are often still assigned.

Thus, the textual shapes of these women, though tragically redomesticated, remain always tragic tricksters of an ambivalently gendered divine economy. The widow gave excessively, with no concern to her own self. Did she therefore waste her living? Jesus saw her expenditure as an expression of infinite wealth, though it might seem small in monetary value: "Truly I tell you, this poor widow has put in more than all those who are contributing to the treasury" (Mark 12:43).

Today the widow might be a more critical investor, deciding to further the divine economy not by giving to the temple cult but by employing it to other causes, or to help her own family out of destitution, a purpose equally divine. Perhaps, with Wylie-Kellermann, she would seek out new allies for countereconomic investments rather than old ones, or even split her two copper coins for different purposes.[136] The divine economy is hardly furthered if the poor destitute themselves, but it might be expressed by those who engage in exchanges without an expectation of perfect reciprocity, where exorbitant losses and plentiful gains might not work out to immediate or longtime gratification.

The woman who anointed Jesus chose to spend a part of her particular wealth by investing it in a yet unknown divine theological economy. Her oil pours out like Cixous's wasteful writing, but at times we might "need that waste," even though it may come—as does speaking publicly for many women—with the "torture of beginning to speak aloud." We especially need women's economic witnessing if it can help "make allowances for superabundance and uselessness," thus providing another currency to counteract the phallocentric "spoken word."[137] Thus, we might want to develop a notion of "strategic excess," an excess that bargains on the future of the planet, not immediate gratification through cash crops and short-time, high-revenue investments. What might constitute "strategic excess" in distinction from "excess" or "waste"?

One figure embodying this excess is Julia Butterfly Hill, who found her own sense of divine calling through engaging in a contemporary version of an ancient ascetic practice most famously practiced by Saint Simon Stylites: prolonged sitting or standing on elevated heights widely visible. Stylites

---

Masculinely coined science and economics are understood as standing in a relationship of domination and exploitation of women and nature that is clearly gendered. The work of Nelson and other feminist economists whose work is perched on the heretical margins of neoliberal classical economics represents contemporary women's insistence to finally have their gifts and economic contributions valued. Julie A. Nelson, *Feminism, Objectivity, and Economics* (New York: Routledge, 1996), 23–24.

136. Wylie-Kellermann, "Coyote Wants More," 5.

137. Hélène Cixous and Catherine Clément, *The Newly Born Woman* (Theory and History of Literature; Minneapolis: University of Minnesota Press, 1975), 92–93.

became famous for his decade-long standing on the small platforms he inhabited. People would come from near and far to see these miraculous feats of physical control, eventually to make a pilgrimage to the site, feeling that the spectacle of the saint's divinely upheld physical endurance might provide pilgrims with access to healing and insight.

Risking her life as she survived helicopter intimidation, psychoterror by irate loggers, two winters, and many storms on the embattled northern Californian redwood tree named Luna, Hill imitated Christ in refusing to be a victim but willing to face death to stand up against powers of exploitation, economic injustice, and reckless overlogging. Having asked for guidance by intense prayer to be "made a vessel" for guidance and strength, the daughter of an itinerant preacher says that her childhood's itinerancy had prepared her well to live in a tree.[138] She describes the impact of her time in the tree as having been inspirational to others. Early on in her tree-sit, she knew that success was anything but guaranteed, and that whether or not the process of clear-cutting redwoods could be reversed or stopped, she could not give up but had to "do the right thing," regardless of the final outcome. Though entirely unschooled in public performances and dealing with the media, Hill's cell phone connection from that tree became a major way in which she began to "speak aloud" to puzzled, bewildered, admiring, and jeering audiences across the region, country, and globe. The "superabundance and uselessness" of her perch functioned as strategic excess, one that she used to speak to people about the causes for her action in a way that she hoped was positive and constructive. Her speech, transmitted through the fragile funnel of a cell-phone, made her a household name, resulting in *Good Housekeeping*'s nomination of Hill as "one of the most admired women in America."[139] The features of the hysteric, saintly trickster, often considered a laughing stock and comic figure and declared crazy and excessive in his or her action, also characterize Hill's stance on the tree-top. Her sanity and right mind were continually doubted by observers throughout her two years of perching, and duly tested by bad weather. Curses hauled at her from below, as well as coaxing, threats, attempts to curtail her free speech, and deceitful maneuvers to compel her to come down.[140] This woman, in some ways reminiscent of early Christian martyrs, relates her protest and witness to the death of trees to Jesus' death on the

---

138. Julia Butterfly Hill, *The Legacy of Luna: The Story of a Tree, a Woman, and the Struggle to Save the Redwoods* (San Francisco: HarperSanFrancisco, 2000), 198, 90.
139. Ibid., 163.
140. Ibid., 220, 229, 237–38. Part of these rhetorical maneuvers included the rather common dismissive feminization of environmental concerns in some instances of right-wing and economically conservative public discourse both in the United States and in Argentina. See Althaus-Reid,

cross, yet in a way that suggests a departure from traditional atonement theologies:

> To make a tree fall into a certain direction, they drive a wedge into it. Since I was raised in a Christian background, driving that wedge into the tree reminded me of the crucifixion. Jesus, an amazing prophet of love, was crucified by others driving spikes through him into a fallen tree.[141]

For Hill, the tree represents a prophetic presence of divine love. When felled, a tree's death resembles the deplorable and irredeemable loss of Jesus' life. Hill rejects interpretations that imply that the tree needs to be felled, or sacrificed to make way for lumber as if to fashion a stairway to the heavens of profit, as was incanted in a popular eighteenth-century hymn: "Allelujah to Jesus who died on the tree and who raised up a ladder of mercy for me."[142] Her reading of the death of Jesus mourns rather than celebrates the death of trees and those who are made to die "vicariously" for "our salvation." Thus, Hill provides one example of how one can redeem what is considered excess and waste in a neoclassical economy where profit is the bottom line, where every penny spent on community wellness, environment, and so forth is considered waste.

To counteract this ideology, a rethinking of excess is necessary. As in the narrative of the anointing woman, the punch line depends on who gets to define what waste or excess is, and what it is not. If we read with Derrida, then we might say that what is considered excess or supplementary in an economy that brackets social and economic costs turns out to be more than necessary. Thus, designated "supplements" represent in fact things required for a reasonably sustainable way of existing on this planet. Nature, considered a free-for-all that can be wasted away and consumed by greed, cannot be done without. It is not simply supplementary but rather functions like Derrida's supplement: the piece of writing, text, meaning, that emerges as more important than the main text. Designated as secondary, it is considered expendable, but without it life, writing, meaning is mortally truncated.[143] Rethinking excess must include focusing on what it is that truly wastes our life resources, what builds up their toxicity, uncovering the waste

---

Indecent Theology, 186. In the United States, however, groups such as the Evangelical Environmental Network have become active with their anti-SUV campaign "What Would Jesus Drive?" See http://whatwouldjesusdrive.org/.

141. Hill, *Legacy of Luna*, 63.
142. Anonymous, "As Jacob With Travel Was Weary One Day."
143. See part 2, "Nature, Culture, Writing," in Jacques Derrida, *Of Grammatology* (corrected ed.; trans. Gayatri Spivak; Baltimore: Johns Hopkins University Press, 1997).

of energy and natural resources that is expended because some want to continue expanding their profit margins.

Consider the unlawful policies Wal-Mart encouraged in its managers as it put an "intense focus on cost-cutting" to "keep payroll costs below a target that headquarters sets."[144] Wal-Mart's power/knowledge discourse transmits the message to managers—or *oikonomoi*—that paying workers overtime is a waste of resources and that this waste will be punished by demotion or dismissal. Thus, managers have been encouraged, whether explicitly or not, to "require off-the-clock work and avoid paying overtime," to "delete . . . hours from employee time cards," or even to "lock . . . doors and prevent . . . workers—even those who had clocked out—from leaving until everyone finished straightening the store." These practices "have helped Wal-Mart undersell the competition, push up profits and become the world's largest retailer."[145] What counts for waste here are adequate pay, humane treatment, and refraining from extortion and slave labor. In a bottom-line-oriented stockholder economy, only profits count, and expenses are waste. Enter a countereconomic strategy such as socially responsible investment funds (SRIs), such as those founded by Amy Domini. Domini Social Investment has long monitored Wal-Mart's employment practices and already in February 2001 removed the retailer from its Social Equity Fund for its "failure to implement an independent monitoring program of its overseas contract facilities, and various inadequacies in its code of conduct for overseas suppliers."[146]

Christian experiences of eschatological deferral can often resemble deconstruction, which questions the possibility of a pure presence, or *parousia*, of meaning—or in this case, of Christ or of redemption. Serene Jones's application of the notion of strategic essentialism to feminist theology might be enlisted to aid the move toward the sanctification of women, though she appears to stop short of Irigaray's notion of "divine women." We might further hope that "divine women" become invested in the construction of divine economies rather than merely reinscribing the ambivalent myth of the woman as the "designated giver." These economies might still seem wasteful to the logic of neoclassical economic theory, but not to the more inclusive economies exemplified in McFague's *Life Abundant*, which proposes that new approaches such as ecological economics may

---

144. Steven Greenhouse, "Suits Say Wal-Mart Forces Workers to Toil Off the Clock," *New York Times*, 25 June 2002, http://www.nytimes.com/2002/06/25/national/25WALM.html.
145. Greenhouse, "Suits Say Wal-Mart Forces Workers."
146. See http://domini.com/social-screening/non-us-operations/special-cases/international-labor-standards.doc_cvt.htm.

help to reconstruct a Christian theology that too long has portrayed God the economist in the image of classical economic theories.

The countereconomic space would describe a place in which divine women and mystery saints can participate in building divine economies of many shapes and colors. Both the notion of strategic essentialism and Jones's "eschatological essentialism" help complicate and solidify feminist theologies that move beyond liberationist rhetoric toward a more complex description and reaction to the lives of those left out of reductionist notions of "our economy." The "arachnean spirituality" of a deeply relational divine economy further invests in the reconstruction of redemption so as to avoid any "at-one-ment that would smash our many-ness" in danger of breaking the web of redemptive relations.[147]

Counterfeit/ing Christ

Has Jesus, CEO, been overpaid?[148] Have his stock options and Christmas bonuses impoverished the many different contributions to the success of the IPO of the Christian economic master plan? Christ, the ransom paid, by the formulations of orthodox divine economy became the ultimate price and gift. Christ was minted as the currency that explodes the terms of the old contract/testament, and became the new coin that bought out previous exchanges between God and humanity. But how does Christ function as currency? Currency represents that which makes current, enables exchange between gods, humans, and creation. It is what makes exchange, translation, relation possible. The answer to the question of how Christ can pay the debts incurred in the history of our planet has been a permanent deal breaker between Jews and Christians. Derrida, here perhaps functioning as a Jewish interlocutor, asks in *The Gift of Death* and other texts on forgiveness: Can we give, can we for-give, can we pay the debts we have incurred, ever? Or can Christ the ransom insert an edge of chaos into stifling economic orders, both divine and human?[149] Does the counterfeit currency Jesus unveil the fluctuations of the chaotic, meandering, tricky "edges of chaos" in the divine economy?[150] Or does the counterfeit/ed Christ reproduce redemption in a third space, always already falsifiable, relative, in the best sense of the word, that is, sensitive to its context and initial conditions?

---

147. Keller, *From a Broken Web*, 223, 233, 224–25.
148. Laurie Beth Jones, *Jesus, Inc.*
149. See Jacques Derrida, *The Gift of Death* (trans. David Wills; Chicago: University of Chicago Press, 1992).
150. For a theological treatment of chaos, order, and the edges of chaos, see Keller, *Face of the Deep*, 5.

Like Elisabeth Schüssler Fiorenza's reconstructive projects, this one does not aim at "getting the historical facts right" or try to defend a doctrinal locus.[151] Rather, it reevaluates certain queer places in the Christian tradition as part of a contemporary theological response to a situation of unprecedented economic globalization that harnesses old exploitative structures such as sexism and slavery with new speeds and technologies. This project reappropriates the ancient christological motif of the *commercium*, or the "deal with the devil," for a theology subversive to neoclassical economics and its links to continuing practices of forms of slavery that severely curtail the social, religious, and economic agency and integrity of individuals within communities. Furthermore, a countereconomic Christology finds ambivalent yet redemptive potential in interpretations of the life and death of Christ as well as in the ascetic practices of the church. It refuses to abandon biblical or patristic texts as mythological constructs and embarrassments to be hidden away, and aims to find locations in the textual tradition where the ambivalence of the text does not warrant a proclamation of its irredeemability but instead becomes a location for miraculous exchanges. The present coredemptive soteriology is not satisfied with portraying Jesus as an Abelardian/Bultmannian teacher of "enlightenment."[152] Instead, it attempts to see Jesus' life, death, and resurrection as having coredemptive meaning, resisting arguments that all atonement theory, if not soteriology in general, casts Jesus as a victim of the divine father. The constructive insights of feminist critiques of atonement suggest that Jesus emerges as an agent of divine economy whose verbal and physical transactions challenge and subvert the status quo rather than an obedient victim.

Postcolonial writers such as Homi Bhabha have mapped the often unpredictable and complex ways in which power is laced through human relationships, particularly in the context of empire. Bhabha's observations on the ambivalence of power and the practices of colonial mimicry contribute to a postcolonial hermeneutical lens that offers a poignant view at the chances and challenges of Christian tradition, its complicity with established power structures, and its subversiveness and resistance to them. Divine commerce reminds us that the spheres of God and Mammon are deeply related. Redemptive imagery within the Christian tradition shows signs of mimicry and ambivalence with the potential both for co-optation and resistance to exploitative economic hierarchies. Theology can reify,

---

151. Elisabeth Schüssler Fiorenza, *Jesus: Miriam's Child, Sophia's Prophet: Critical Issues in Feminist Christology* (New York: Continuum, 1994), 108–9.

152. For an overview of the development of theologies of redemption, see Gisbert Greshake, "Der Wandel der Erlösungsvorstellungen in der Theologiegeschichte," in *Erlösung und Emanzipation* (ed. Leo Scheffczyk; Quaestiones Disputatae; Freiburg: Herder, 1973), esp. 95.

challenge, unveil, call to conversion, subversion, or submission to the economic forces of our times.

Contemporary forms of neoimperialism continue to depend upon the resources of former colonies and economically dependent regions of the world to sustain governing power. New incarnations of slavery occur within these exchanges. Homi Bhabha's descriptions of ambivalence and mimicry in colonial discourse are eminently helpful in reconstructing a Christology of divine commerce that addresses the painful complexity of our economic ties to exploitation in a context of neoimperialism. A postcolonial reading of divine commerce describes then an exchange in which a tricksterlike Christ mimicks and mocks the boundaries of ownership and slavery.

Though the biblical images of divine *oikonomia* as transmitted through Jesus' parables resemble the form of Roman and Palestinian householding patterns of his context, they simultaneously menace them. Moreover, "in order to be effective, mimicry must continually produce its slippage, its excess, its difference."[153] Even so, the resemblance to known forms of power remains, and it remains with a vengeance. While images of divine economy do threaten and challenge certain forms of patronage, gender, and class hierarchies, they retain (ideologically loaded) certain power and knowledge formations. Thus, patriarchy and slavery are only partly contested in early Christian texts. Though the subversive power of an image opens up possibilities of change for more balanced powered relationships, and the edge of chaos that challenges social orders vibrates and rattles the cages, not all potential for subversion can be or will be effective in any given situation. Moreover, the image of subversion can, since it carries both mimesis and menace as possibilities within it, revert to new orders of oppression, thus subverting the subversiveness of what first was an image that threatened hierarchies. Oppressive images of heavenly hierarchy then become reinstituted with not only a resemblance to but as the superlative replacement of terrestrial hierarchies. Despite these dangers, the menace to oppression remains always present, continually threatening the power/knowledge regimes of domination. Biblical texts remain potent and effective challenges also in and for contemporary theology as they continue to threaten and menace the orders of domination, subtle though they may be. If it is true that we can never completely reverse but only mimetically inhabit present structures and inhabit them to subvert them from the inside, as well as create new structures that reinscribe those present, it would seem that Weber was at least in part correct in claiming asceticism can be complicit

---

153. Bhabha, *Location of Culture*, 86.

with what has been called capitalism. But it would also hold true that certain forms of asceticism can function to bring crystallized, stifling forms of order to the edge of chaos, where conversion into new, creative energy can occur. Though this energy is not automatically healing, inclusive, or tolerant, it has potentiality toward it. The edge of chaos or *différance* is not our new saviors or saving grace, yet they may emerge as useful locations of divinely economic saving grace for a while. An alternate reading of the *commercium* does not neglect past and present structures of oppression by focusing on a romanticized reading of redemption, but finds in the ambivalent traditions of the past texts that can produce new subversive plots of tricksterlike divine economy.

What sort of libidinal economy might a reconstructed *commercium* constitute? A more fully "indecent" theology disturbs the gender binaries and hierarchies of traditional soteriological loci, whether expressed as hierarchical dualisms between men and women or as hom(m)osexual economies that exclude women. A more deeply queered divine economy is neither a pure, feminine economy of the gift, nor a hom(m)osexual acquisition of wives and slaves, but a miraculous exchange, where a divine counterfeit acquires redemption. I offer a reconstructed *commercium* that further queries and queers God's economic gender and status as a tool to theologize redemptive departures from economic oppression and divine moves toward just trade.

Monetary economic exchange and writing always involve, according to Derrida, a counterfeit (from *contre-faire*). In the German, *Konterfei* denotes an image or picture of a person—a likeness, a facsimile. Yet every image and every coin or bill, every check and credit card, because it can never be identical with the "real thing" or person, fails to represent adequately and is therefore a counterfeit. A counterfeit "makes present," yet at the same time fails to do so. It is thus an instance of a Derridean "absent presence." Benedict Anderson argues that passports, designed to prove our identity and nationality, similarly make "high truth-claims" but actually represent "counterfeits in the sense that they are less attestations of citizenship, let alone of loyalty to a protective nation-state," than "claims to participation in labor markets."[154] The tradition of negative theology further suggests that any theology is always involved in counterfeiting God and, by extension, divine economy. Such God-talk is not a complete deception, but it is

---

154. Thus, Anderson concludes, "The segregated queues that all of us experience at airport immigration barricades mark economic status far more than any political attachments. In effect, they figure differential tariffs on human labor." Quoted in Amitava Kumar, *Passport Photos* (Berkeley: University of California Press, 2000), 40–41.

certainly never a "true" representation. Perhaps we must admit here to a theological counterfeit that portrays God as a divine trickster and economist. But, as Derrida ventures, "the circulation of the counterfeit money can engender, even for a 'little speculator,' the real interest of true wealth. Counterfeit money can become true capital."[155] Counterfeit money, *Falschgeld*, may be true money in an economy of oppression, and counterfeiting practices may also be tools of indecent divine tricksterdom.

Ruthann Knechel Johansen has argued that trickster narratives order, reorder, imaginatively invert, make, and remake language and literature as they participate in contests between good and evil, clarity and obscurity, truth and deception, leading and pushing hearers toward the interstices, the places in between.[156] Darby Ray's reconstruction of atonement as a tricksterlike deception reads the patristic model of the *commercium* as a clever scheme of "God in Christ,"[157] whose redemptive resistance aims to defeat the demonic schemes of domestic violence, abuse, and oppression. Ray has worked out this approach as a way to grapple with two conflicting theological positions, represented by feminist and liberationist concerns:

> How can I, on the one hand, agree with the conviction that traditional construals of the work of Christ constitute theological violence and, on the other hand, maintain that the life *and death* of Jesus have redemptive efficacy? Why do feminist theologians tend to dismiss all notions of atonement as irretrievably problematic, while most liberationists insist that some such notion is essential to Christian identity and community?[158]

In this quandary she works out a third space (she calls it a "middle ground"[159]) that is distinct from Anselmian satisfaction theory as well as from Abelardian and modern liberal notions of Jesus as a moral example and teacher. In a critical retrieval of Gustav Aulén's reconstruction of patristic Christology, Ray lifts the *Christus victor* up as a trickster. This notion of Christ, she argues, allows contemporary Christians to "confront evil in a decisive and redemptive manner" as it "rejects the tools of evil, but without glorifying passivity or suffering. It is based on the intuition of

---

155. Jacques Derrida, *Given Time: I. Counterfeit Money* (trans. Peggy Kamuf; Chicago: University of Chicago Press, 1992), 124.
156. Ruthann Knechel Johansen, *The Narrative Secret of Flannery O'Connor: The Trickster as Interpreter* (Tuscaloosa: University of Alabama Press, 1994), 151, 157, 159.
157. Ray, *Deceiving the Devil*, vii.
158. Ibid., viii.
159. Ibid., 7.

many church fathers that the power of evil cannot be easily or forcefully defeated but must be creatively and cunningly subverted."[160]

Beginning with the "sober recognition of the problem—the doctrine of atonement has had disastrous consequences," Ray moves, if only toward the end of her book and then only rudimentarily, to retrieve the deception model, because "this model's portrayal of evil as powerful and complex, though not invulnerable, has striking parallels with contemporary attempts to understand evil within a tragic context."[161] Though she introduces the image of the trickster that is crucial for the present approach, she does not develop it beyond noting how the "theme of the deception of the devil illuminates the nature and method of redemptive power" as pointing to the "reality that any struggle against oppression and injustice that seeks to avoid violent means or that emerges from a context of relative powerlessness must rely on cunning and ingenuity rather than ascribed authority or power."[162]

Similarly, I read Gregory's narrative of the *admirabile commercium* as a trickster narrative, and Gregory's Christ as a trickster with the capacity of a go-between, and, similar to Tertullian's amalgamated coin, as a currency that mediates between two different economies: the heavenly and the earthly one.[163] Gregory's Christ appears as an ambiguous combination of human and divine characteristics, acting as "deceiver" of the Enemy, a counterfeit and a "shape-shifter" who can at least partially hide his divine "essence" under a fleshy disguise. From this dangerously ambivalent transaction—a just and yet deceptive deal—the devil emerges having lost all his assets, a deceived deceiver. Christ here functions as a "situation inverter" who effects the release not only of an enslaved humanity but also averts his own enslavement by a trick, by reverting to his prior position in the divine household—that is, on top—having mastered his own enslavement.

The divine trickster slave is a "sacred bricoleur" who faces a seemingly hopeless situation by working with the means at hand in an oppressive situation to effect release. His "cosmic interplay engages unceasing sets of counterpoised sectors"; he is a border crosser and symbolizes multivalence.[164] It is with "cunning and creativity rather than force" that God "outsmarts evil."[165] As we have seen, the patristic instances are curiously intent on depicting a clever divine economist rather than a brutal bully with

---

160. Ibid., vii.
161. Ibid., 122.
162. Ibid., 138–39.
163. Johansen, *Narrative Secret of Flannery O'Connor*, 166.
164. William J. Hynes, "Mapping the Characteristics of Mythic Tricksters: A Heuristic Guide," in *Mythical Trickster Figures* (ed. William J. Hynes and William G. Doty; Tuscaloosa: University of Alabama Press, 1993), 34.
165. Ray, *Deceiving the Devil*, 140.

omnipotence. Power functions differently here; it is not the power of absolute dominance but the power of God's wisdom and justice, which—as we know from Paul—might at times be confused with folly. God's wisdom knows of the insatiable greed of the enemy, the unending desire for growth of property and wealth, and uses this "libidinal economy" to bait the enemy with a highly desired commodity—the spotless, sparklingly powerful Word as *commercium*. As Raymund Schwager observes, the *Tausch* (exchange) becomes a *Täuschung* (deception) that liberates the indebted and the enslaved.[166]

This highly unstable image of a slave's life defrauds the fraudulent basis of slave economies, ancient and contemporary. This divine commerce of incarnation or obliquely represents *"almost the same but not quite"* the contemporary economic context, while mocking embedded assumptions about power, hierarchy and gender. "Mimicry and mockery" thus produce a consistently ambivalent narrative.[167] "The ambivalence at the source of traditional discourses on authority enables a form of subversion, founded on the undecidability that turns the discursive conditions of dominance into the grounds of intervention."[168]

Bhabha argues that such a "discourse of mimicry" repeats *and* questions a dominant logic, since it cannot escape the inherent "ambivalence" of language and of economic relationships. The dangers and chances of ambivalence continue to be valid as we read the texts today. That means a text has the potential to interrogate structures of dominance but can at the same time function as the reinscription of the status quo. Thus, "mimicry is at once resemblance and menace."[169] Bhabha suggests that "mimicry marks those moments of civil disobedience within the discipline of civility: signs of spectacular resistance. Words of the master become the site of hybridity."[170]

Likewise, the image of divine commerce as described by Gregory of Nyssa engages the theme of liberation from slavery by the payment of a ransom. The motif iterates the terms of ancient slavery, while inquiring into its patterns of exchange. The ambivalence of these texts can result in at least two different readings—one reinforcing the dynamics of hierarchical exchange and one questioning it but without being able to envision a system beyond the status quo.[171]

---

166. Raymund Schwager, *Der wunderbare Tausch: Zur Geschichte und Bedeutung der Erlösungslehre* (Munich: Kösel, 1986), 34.
167. Bhabha, *Location of Culture*, 86.
168. Ibid., 112.
169. Ibid., 85, 86.
170. Ibid., 121.
171. One such example is the Magnificat. While the piece talks about an end to oppression by the mighty and powerful, it appears also to be replacing one form of hierarchical unilateralism with another. The structure of power thus remains unquestioned.

When we attempt to reconstruct the economy of the incarnation, how is it that we do not simply reiterate the rich/poor, male/female dichotomy that enslaves? How do we not become slaves of human masters but allow ourselves to experience the exorbitant edge of chaos in the divine economy with its nonteleological unpredictabilities—not as a technique to enhance our profits at the cost of those not as informed, skilled, or "with it" as us, but as an investment, an "en-clothing" into the great economy, the relationality in which we are embodied, which includes people and planet? Such a reconstruction cannot occur, I believe, without dealing with the heritage of a sacrificial economic logic and heterosexist gender hierarchy in theological imagery. Thus, it is crucial to note that the motif of divine commerce, though less explicitly termed as such in most of the literature, also occurs between "divine masculinity" and "human femininity."

A reconstructed image of divine commerce must then also "refinance" the gendered economic transactions and hierarchies that underlie redemption. If theology is a deeply "sexual act,"[172] then a reconstruction of divine commerce must challenge the heterosexist gender binaries of traditional images of redemption, where a divinized, male, propertied giver redeems a feminized, poor, or enslaved recipient. The patristic motif of redemption as divine commerce—the salutary exchange of divine power and human weakness brought about through a divine deal with the devil—has emerged from historical concepts of slavery and marriage—that is, from problematic imbalances of power.

It is in this volatile interpretive interface of slavery, marriage, and salvation that a postcolonial reading of redemptive commerce has to occur.[173] Thus, an ambiguously gendered divine trickster messes with the heterosexist notions of Althaus-Reid's "decent" theologies that continue to ignore the oppressive impact of a colonialist, masculine "*homo economicus*" on traditional notions of commerce and connubial life. Instead, this figure points toward a less dualistic, less essentially gendered, but rather "indecent" and queer, soteriology.[174] This queered divine commerce would neither represent a pure, feminine economy of the gift, nor a trading of wives and slaves

---

172. Althaus-Reid, *Indecent Theology*, 166.
173. Many interpreters have shied away from economic interpretations of salvation. Regrettably, this has kept many theologians at a distance from a renewed engagement with this motif. A notable exception is Darby K. Ray, whose feminist recasting of Christ as a trickster defeating violence and abuse has helped to inspire my reconstruction. The motif of the *admirabile commercium*, or "wonderful exchange," represents a somewhat marginal tradition. Though several ancient writers employ it, it was effectively replaced by Anselm's doctrine of satisfaction and has since fallen into disrepute or even obscurity. Only a handful of studies of this motif have been published, most of which date from the 1950s or 1980s.
174. Althaus-Reid, *Indecent Theology*, 36.

between males, but a miraculous exchange that aims to decolonize redemption and supports the search for more truly redemptive forms of divine and human economy.[175]

The counterfeit currency of Christ's ransom helps transform gendered exploitative economies. The counterfeiter can also be the countereconomist, resisting the dualistic structures of absolute gift versus idealistic notions of total circularity by speaking, identifying, inventing, and incarnating miraculous exchanges. We can counteract the gendered and economic power imbalances of *conubium* and *commercium* by reconstructing *commercium* as a joint venture, as a common investment in a mutual fund. Buying back might then represent Christ's liberative life, death, and resurrection as a down payment or a "matching grant" for redemption.

In distinction from Przywara, whose rendering of the enslaved Christ and the enslaved bride does not lead to their liberation but rather seems to proliferate and eventually sanction continued states of oppressive hierarchies in both class and gender relations, the current reconstruction focuses on tricksterlike divine interference with property, value, debt, and currency. Similarly, unlike Taylor's divine capitalist who speculates on the market of a stockholder society to achieve the wanted gain, the divine trickster respects then perverts, and thereby reveals as false, demonic claims to ownership of humanity. A countereconomic theology engages a divine counterfeit that undermines the sacrificial economy by taking seriously, despite Paul's ambivalent use of the concept of slavery, his proclamation that we should not become slaves of human masters again once we have been liberated (1 Cor 7:23).[176]

Przywara's text combines the libidinal economies or "mysteries" of *commercium* and *conubium* by melding enslavement and marriage together, as God acquires both slaves and brides in the "full circle of the *commercium* of the *conubium* in Christ."[177] His God buys up slaves and brides like a monopolist obsessed to own it all, an uncomfortably all-consuming

---

175. Critiques of Anselmian atonement theory began with Abelard, received new hearing in historical criticism, and then, heightened by the influence of gender analysis, propelled feminist theologians to critically interrogate soteriology. The classic article on this issue is Joanne Carlson Brown and Rebecca Parker, "For God So Loved the World?" in *Violence against Women and Children: A Christian Theological Sourcebook* (ed. Carol J. Adams and Marie M. Fortune; New York: Continuum, 1995), 36–59. Most recently, see Rita Nakashima Brock and Rebecca Ann Parker, *Proverbs of Ashes: Violence, Redemptive Suffering, and the Search for What Saves Us* (Boston: Beacon, 2001).

176. For an in-depth exploration of Paul's complex use of the category of slavery, see Dale Martin, *Slavery as Salvation: The Metaphor of Slavery in Pauline Christianity* (New Haven, Conn.: Yale University Press, 1990).

177. Erich Przywara, *Logos: Logos—Abendland—Reich—Commercium* (Düsseldorf: Patmos, 1964), 125.

version of God the economist, quite different from Meeks's far more humble trinitarian community of persons. Przywara's Christ has a ravenous mouth that gobbles up everything there is to own in his *"anakephalaiosis panthon,"* where he becomes a slave and bride merely to sweep everything up into the divine treasure troves in one huge final transaction that makes him "Haupt- und Inbegriff von allem gesamt" (the main concept and perfect example of all and everything). This omnipotent and omni-substantial, all-possessing deity hardly resembles the image of the trickster God of more modest countereconomies.[178]

A reconstructed divine commerce might then embody Christ's mimicry as something like an "ironic compromise" between "identity, stasis" and "change, difference," troubling the waters of assumptions of power.[179] Like a sacred trickster, he performs mimicry and incarnate ambivalence. This scandalously different Christ, a rather suspect and marginal "persona" or mask for divine agency, is here a holy fool, a divine trickster. Counterfeiting the counterfeiters, Christ the counterfeit ransom might help us invent ways to unveil and resist the deceivers of our own times, for the liberation of many.

Refinancing Theologies of Sacralized Slavery

In our reconstructive reading of Christ as salvific trickster, Christ does not appear as the messenger of divine omnipotence or all-possessiveness, but of a measured, wise, and just power that works in and through situations of oppression, assembling bits and pieces of a tricksterlike sacred bricolage of redemption. Thus, the divine economic trickster "mak[es] sure there is commerce," appearing to "suggest an amoral action, something right/wrong that will get life going again."[180] To trip up the grand deceptions of the powers that be, the divine trickster "trouble[s] conventional spaces" and in turn produces "ontologically dirty" and "provisional" instances of divine economy.[181] This countering, gender-ambivalent trickster would also attempt to mess with the heterosexist notions of "decent" theologies that continue to ignore the oppressive impact of *homo economicus* on nontraditional notions of commerce and connubial life and instead point toward a less dualistic, less essentially gendered, queered soteriology.[182] Althaus-Reid suggests that

---

178. Przywara, *Logos,* 125.
179. Bhabha, *Location of Culture,* 86.
180. Hyde, *Trickster Makes This World,* 7.
181. Haraway, *Modest_Witness@Second_Millennium,* 127, 275n.2.
182. Amy Gluckman and Betsy Reed, eds., *Homo Economics: Capitalism, Community, and Lesbian and Gay Life* (New York: Routledge, 1997).

Christian theology cannot match these new developments in socio-political and sexual understanding unless it can confront the limitations of heteronomy as a hegemonic system of organization and thought.... Indecenting Jesus and the tradition of his time is not always possible but in many cases such work could give a more positive ground for finding heterotopic visions in community.[183]

Though "deviancy as a methodological source" might be in danger to glorify deviance if taken to an extreme, countering trickster economies might have much in common with Althaus-Reid's "indecent proposals in economics [that] could decolonize our spiritual souls, which are also economic souls."[184] Trickster figures can be gender ambiguous, cross-dressing, even transgendered. Such a trickster can appear at a most unexpected site, such as in Jean-François Lyotard's text *Libidinal Economy*. Here, a transgendered incarnates a mimicry of redemption, an economy of desire as a capitalist whore, engaged in a divine business transaction involving the body as currency in a sexual, redemptive exchange. Lyotard writes of Jesus then as a "calculating prostitute," who says to God:

> You have me die, this is wrongdoing, but through this the whole world will be saved: the perverts or cretins ("they know not what they do") will be redeemed in the gracious body of creation, that is to say of capital. And God is a pimp, saying to Jesus, his woman... do this for me, do it for them. Would you say he wins Jesus over? And I answer: He wins a prostitute, who sells the most unexpected parts of his body.[185]

Lyotard's transgendered Christ enacts a transaction more akin to the *conubium* than the *commercium* as s/he "accepts prostitution in the name of a superior interest."[186] Lyotard reverses Luther's image of the sinner as whore by casting Christ as the prostitute in the divine deal, so that prostitution of the body functions as the incarnate ransom that effects the economic release of those enslaved. In this commerce, prostitution of the body—another form of *kenosis*, of incarnation—functions as the ransom that effects the release of those enslaved. Though Lyotard hardly would have anticipated this, to me his text unveils how trafficking in women mimicks/mocks features of Christian redemption and exposes the religio-

---

183. Althaus-Reid, *Indecent Theology*, 181.
184. Ibid., 194.
185. Jean-François Lyotard, *Libidinal Economy* (trans. Iain Hamilton Grant; Bloomington: University of Indiana Press, 1993), 65.
186. Ibid., 61.

economic undertones of the sexual exploitation of economically oppressed girls and women, whose bodies pay increments of redemptive ransom for the economic survival of their families.[187] At the same time, Christ the prostitute chooses this formal agency for the purposes of redemption.

The gender-ambiguous trickster can thus cross-dress or switch bodies.[188] One could read the two images—Christ the enslaved and Christ the prostituting trickster—as instances of divine *commercium* and *conubium* that recognize the reality and perversity of these patriarchal structures of bio-power and transform them by inhabiting and incarnating them. With Christ as a female prostitute, gender and libidinal economies become unsettled. Christ's body becomes, as in Gregory, a commodity that effects a salvific exchange, here through the whore's own initiative, even though she recognizes the falseness of the "wrongdoing" of the death she is given. Nonetheless, the deal seems worth it, the final profit exorbitant, as "the whole world will be saved."[189]

A transgendered trickster Christ marks the "elusive fluidity of Jesus."[190] S/he switches bodies, becomes real currency, and maps the trades of sexual economies. God as pimp and as customer symbolizes the powers of financial and sexual oppression. Christ the enslaved and Christ the prostituting trickster mimic instances of divine commerce that highlight the reality and perversity of patriarchal power structures. As we imagine Christ as a female prostitute—ambivalently inhabiting and mockingly unveiling hegemonic patriarchy—libidinal economies of gender and class come into view. Lyotard's Christ breaches the lines of decency as s/he offers her/his body as the commodity that seals the divine commerce. This divine commerce with its queerly gendered and ambivalently in/appropriate exchanges interrogates the patriarchal constructions of human and theological economies.

Lyotard's counterfeit Christ embodies the commercialization and commodification of women's bodies in the new global economic imperialism. The ransom they must pay for their own and their family's survival and integrity is perhaps not so much different after all from the ransom of Christ. What can we do if we are not willing to sacrifice others so we can

---

187. See Rita Nakashima Brock and Susan Brooks Thistlethwaite, *Casting Stones: Prostitution and Liberation in Asia and the United States* (Minneapolis: Fortress, 1996); and Sietske Altink, *Stolen Lives: Trading Women into Sex and Slavery* (London: Scarlet Press, 1995).

188. It is important to mention, however, that the act of cross-dressing alone is not necessarily "indecent," or countereconomic. Althaus-Reid finds little resistance to exploitative economic practices and gender politics represented in the example of the religious transvestite of the Aztec society. Since "women counted for little in their society" and were "overdetermined by roles and expectations of obedience," transgender representations did most likely not function as a "transgressive force in economic social relations." Althaus-Reid, *Indecent Theology*, 18.

189. Lyotard, *Libidinal Economy*, 65.

190. Althaus-Reid, *Indecent Theology*, 112.

remain in denial of the economic shackles we owe our own well-being to? What are ways beyond this denial? Will we sacralize their sacrifice, their enslavement, their commercialization the way we have sacralized (commercialized?) the enslavement of Christ? Or will we recognize the mockery represented by such commerce?

A reconstruction of divine economy cannot simply mean asserting that we belong to ourselves entirely, or to God entirely. Yet, as Foucault has observed, power is always a reality, and a certain kind of disciplining invariably occurs through our relations. The question is not eventually about whether or not we are undergoing discipline or disciplining ourselves and others, but what kind of discipline it is that we receive and pass on. Neither can we assert that God is the sole and absolute giver of all and that we are nothing but passive recipients. Rather, the divine economy is an exorbitant economy, ex-static beyond the given, *le don*, at times chaotic, tricksterlike.

This divine economy, with its queerly gendered and ambivalently appropriate exchanges, interrogates the patriarchal constructions of human and theological economies. Queer theology in itself is not by definition resistant to dominology, just as the "transgendered expression of the sacred" in Aztec worship was not necessarily "a transgressive force in economic social relations."[191] Queering gender may be deconstructive of patriarchal gender and theological narratives only as long as it does not become itself a product sold on the market.[192] Similarly, the progression of African Americans and Hispanics into the American middle class is only minimally subversive if the system itself that slices and dices economic class itself is not interrogated, questioned, and transformed. The grand narrative that a certain economic station in life is salvific and is somehow equivalent to theological salvation (see the discussion in chapter 1 on prosperity theology) is then simply retained. While in parts of the United States it might seem that new genders and colors of people increasingly profit from the structures of late capitalism, structures of exclusion and oppression worldwide, and even within the United States, are simultaneously confirmed. Though the "mighty mongrel," the bastard and hybrid that has so successfully adapted to the information age, seems to stand in some parts for the success of colonial integration, class barriers and economic boundaries remain as in place as ever, and become even more disparate. Furthermore, many immigrants cease to be subversive when their goal to fully participate in the "American dream," to integrate into the U.S. "mainstream" that profits from successive immigrant waves and cheap labor, becomes more and more tangible.

---

191. Ibid., 18.
192. See Gluckman and Reed, *Homo Economics*.

Whether counterfeiting theology or counterfeiting economic practices, fraudulent economies can occasionally generate countereconomic currencies of change. Yet despite Derrida's late and latent desire—despite his constant deconstruction of its possibility—for the absolute gift, according to which a man "is in a position of nonexchange with respect to God,"[193] I would suggest that the divine economy appears constantly involved, rather than absolute, absolved from the relations and transactions within the created world. Our bodies, whether as metaphor or, more specifically, incarnate, may become "inextricably involved with a divine economy," as the radical orthodox theologian Graham Ward argues. Yet I doubt Ward's notion of the christological transcorporeality as signified in the "transfiguration" represents grounds for "set[ting] Jesus outside any economy of exchange, any economy where the value of an object can be known and its exchange negotiated."[194] Rather, we have begun to realize that Christ's incarnation is an ongoing crucial expression of the divine economy and that a reconstructed typology such as in Haraway's feminist figuration allows us to continuously invent forms of resistant agency modestly witnessing to the liberating power of divine commerce. Thus, as Augustine writes, "This is the wonderful exchange, the divine business deal, the transaction effected in this world by the heavenly dealer" (*Enarrat Ps.* 30:3). Unlike Augustine, Graham Ward would seem to suggest a divine flight from a creaturely (fallen?) *oikonomia* and want to accomplish, if not to secure, another version of divine transcendence and omnipotence. The divine presence in creation, however, would suggest a constant, uninterrupted relation to the economy of creation. Meeks, in his aptly titled *God the Economist,* writes that God constantly "deals" with the world, is in a relationship of fluid exchange and reciprocity.

This divine economy does not remain apart from the various intricate, implicated, and messy economies of our world; rather, it is always already in-vested, wrapped up in, and incarnate in it. Likewise, the postcolonial concepts of ambivalence and mimicry remind us of how quickly a context, a reading, a practice can shift. The gift/poison (certainly not the "final" remedy) of ambivalence is that it encourages us to live in the presence of the complexities of life, love, and commerce and to resist the constant urge to simplify and erase the differences that make life a *chaosmos,*[195] a life moving through stages of order and chaos, and to see divine presence, creativity, and power within it.

---

193. Jacques Derrida, *The Gift of Death* (trans. David Wills; Chicago: University of Chicago Press, 1992), 96.
194. Graham Ward, *Cities of God* (New York: Routledge, 2000), 101.
195. For the use and definition of this term, see Keller, *Face of the Deep,* 12–13.

Our spiritual practices and our theologies should then be responsive to these rhythmic shuffles of order/chaos in that they are part of lived reality. Engaging in *redemptio continua* means to be, live, and speak out of a changing context that is tied into a responsive feedback loop constantly investigating the effectiveness and appropriateness of strategies of divine commerce. For the practice of theology, this suggests that we ponder doctrinal teachings in their ambivalence, without trying finally to resolve the paradoxes, as so much of theology is tempted to do. Such an attempt at a "postcolonial" theology would, with Marcella Althaus-Reid, allow that the "contradictions are many" rather than becoming the "art of erasing them,"[196] by selective readings and reductionism. Althaus-Reid thinks of Christ as of a tent or a tabernacle that "dwelt among us" (John 1:14). This image "conveys Christ's high mobility and lack of fixed spaces or definitive frontiers," as tents are "easily dismantled overnight and do not become ruins or monuments"; they "change shape in strong winds, and their adaptability rather than their stubbornness is one of their greatest assets."[197] Similarly, a tent is a form of dwelling, a more flexible form of a house, or *oikos*. In the *admirabile commercium,* the incarnation becomes a miraculous exchange, establishing an exchange rate between human and divine economies that marks a *common* investment. Thus Gregory of Nyssa asks, "For who is so simple as not to believe that there is Deity in everything, penetrating it, embracing it, and seated in it?"(*Oratio catechetica* 25).

Divine commerce refers to redemptive forms of agency not merely as understood through Christ's incarnation, death, and resurrection but as extended to the thoughts and acts of those who would mimick or imitate such acts of redemption in their own lives. We can counteract the gendered and economic power imbalances of *conubium* and *commercium* by reconstructing divine commerce as a joint venture, a *com-mercere*, as common investment. These theological decisions shape not only our understanding of Christ but also how we see ourselves as economic agents. It is my hope that this reconstructed image of divine commerce can inspire redemptive practices and currencies of change without denying the various intricate, implicated, and messy economies of our world. Living in the presence of ambivalence refuses to render stale, dogmatic, and unresponsive the liveliness of text and tradition, remaining open to the always unfolding qualities of all divine commerce. Thus, the ambivalence and mimicry embedded in divine commerce call us to experience the full reality of God, of life, beyond our attempts to domesticate divinity.

---

196. Althaus-Reid, *Indecent Theology,* 42.
197. Ibid., 120.

Works Cited

Abramowitz, Mimi. Introduction to *Disposable Domestics: Immigrant Women Workers in the Global Economy,* by Grace Chang. Cambridge, Mass.: South End Press, 2000.

Adair, Mark J. "Plato's View of the Wandering Uterus." *Classical Journal* 91, no. 2 (1996): 153–63.

Allitt, Patrick. *Major Problems in American Religious History.* Boston: Houghton Mifflin, 2000.

Althaus-Reid, Marcella. *Indecent Theology: Theological Perversions in Sex, Gender, and Politics.* London: Routledge, 2001.

Altink, Sietske. *Stolen Lives: Trading Women into Sex and Slavery.* London: Scarlet Press, 1995.

"Americans Have a Beef with Big Business." *Business Week,* 31 August 2000. http://www.businessweek.com/bwdaily/dnflash/aug2000/nf20000831_923.htm.

Athanasius. *The Life of Antony and the Letter to Marcellinus.* Translated and edited by Robert C. Gregg. Classics of Western Spirituality. Mahwah, N.J.: Paulist Press, 1980.

Augustine. *Confessions.* Translated by Henry Chadwick. World's Classics. Oxford: Oxford University Press, 1992.

Aulén, Gustav. *Christus Victor: An Historical Study of the Three Main Types of the Idea of Atonement.* New York: Macmillan, 1969.

Bakhtin, Mikhail. *Rabelais and His World.* Translated by Helene Iswolsky. Cambridge: MIT Press, 1968.

Bales, Kevin. *Disposable People: New Slavery in the Global Economy.* Berkeley: University of California Press, 1999.

Balsdon, J. P. V. D. *Roman Women: Their History and Habits.* New York: Barnes & Noble Books, 1962.

Barlow, Tani E. "'Green Blade in the Act of Being Grazed': Late Capital, Flexible Bodies, Critical Intelligibility." *Differences* 10, no. 3 (1998): 119–58.

Bartra, Roger. Introduction to *Warrior of Gringostroika*, by Guillermo Gómez-Peña. St. Paul: Graywolf Press, 1993.

Batstone, David, Eduardo Mendieta, Lois Ann Lorentzen, and Dwight N. Hopkins, eds. *Liberation Theologies, Postmodernity, and the Americas*. London: Routledge, 1997.

Baudrillard, Jean. *Jean Baudrillard: Selected Writings*. Edited by Mark Poster. Stanford, Calif.: Stanford University Press, 1988.

Beaver, Robert Pierce. *American Protestant Women in World Mission: History of the First Feminist Movement in North America*. Grand Rapids: Eerdmans, 1980.

Bedford, Nancy. "Little Moves against Destructiveness: Theology and the Practice of Discernment." In *Practicing Theology: Beliefs and Practices in Christian Life*. Edited by Miroslav Volf and Dorothy C. Bass. Grand Rapids: Eerdmans, 2002.

Beer, Theobald. *Der Fröhliche Wechsel und Streit: Grundzüge der Theologie Martin Luthers*. Einsiedeln: Johannes, 1980.

Bengsch, Alfred. *Heilsgeschichte und Heilswissen: Eine Untersuchung zur Struktur und Entfaltung des theologischen Denkens im Werk "Adversus Haereses" des Heiligen Irenaeus von Lyon*. Leipzig: St. Benno, 1957.

Bhabha, Homi. *The Location of Culture*. London: Routledge, 1994.

Bourdieu, Pierre. *Acts of Resistance: Against the Tyranny of the Market*. New York: New Press, 1998.

———. *Outline of a Theory of Practice*. Cambridge: Cambridge University Press, 1977.

Boyarin, Daniel. *Dying for God: Martyrdom and the Making of Christianity and Judaism*. Figurae: Reading Medieval Culture. Stanford, Calif.: Stanford University Press, 1999.

———. "Freud's Baby, Fliess's Maybe: Homophobia, Anti-Semitism, and the Invention of Oedipus." *Gay Lesbian Quarterly* 2 (1995): 115–47.

———. *Intertextuality and the Reading of Midrash*. Bloomington: Indiana University Press, 1990.

———. *Unheroic Conduct: The Rise of Heterosexuality and the Invention of the Jewish Man*. Berkeley: University of California Press, 1997.

Brakke, David. *Athanasius and Asceticism*. Baltimore: Johns Hopkins University Press, 1998.

Briggs, John, and F. David Peat. *Seven Life Lessons of Chaos: Timeless Wisdom from the Science of Change*. New York: HarperCollins, 1999.

Briggs, Sheila. "Can an Enslaved God Liberate? Hermeneutical Reflections on Philippians 2:6–11." *Semeia* 47 (1989): 137–53.

Brock, Rita Nakashima, and Rebecca Ann Parker. *Proverbs of Ashes: Violence, Redemptive Suffering, and the Search for What Saves Us*. Boston: Beacon, 2001.

Brock, Rita Nakashima, and Susan Brooks Thistlethwaite. *Casting Stones: Prostitution and Liberation in Asia and the United States.* Minneapolis: Fortress, 1996.

Bronfen, Elizabeth. *The Knotted Subject: Hysteria and Its Discontents.* Princeton, N.J.: Princeton University Press, 1998.

Brother Ty, with Christopher Buckley and John Tierney. *God Is My Broker: A Monk-Tycoon Reveals the 7 1/2 Laws of Spiritual and Financial Growth.* New York: Random House, 1998.

Brown, Joanne Carlson, and Rebecca Parker. "For God So Loved the World?" In *Violence against Women and Children: A Christian Theological Sourcebook.* Edited by Carol J. Adams and Marie M. Fortune. New York: Continuum, 1995.

Brown, Peter. *Augustine of Hippo.* Berkeley: University of California Press, 1967.

———. *The Body and Society: Men, Women, and Sexual Renunciation in Early Christianity.* New York: Columbia University Press, 1988.

Burrus, Virginia. *Begotten, Not Made: Conceiving Manhood in Late Antiquity.* Stanford, Calif.: Stanford University Press, 2000.

———. *Chastity as Autonomy: Women in the Stories of Apocryphal Acts.* Lewiston, N.Y.: Edwin Mellen Press, 1987.

———. "The Heretical Woman as Symbol in Alexander, Athanasius, Epiphanius, and Jerome." *Harvard Theological Review* 84, no. 3 (1991): 229–48.

———. *The Making of a Heretic: Gender, Authority, and the Pricillianist Controversy.* Transformation of the Classical Heritage. Berkeley: University of California Press, 1995.

———. "Reading Agnes: The Rhetoric of Gender in Ambrose and Prudentius." *Journal of Early Christian Studies* 3, no. 1 (1995): 25–46.

———. *The Sex Lives of the Saints.* Philadelphia: University of Pennsylvania Press, 2003.

———. "Torture and Travail: Producing the Christian Martyr." In *The Feminist Companion to the New Testament.* Edited by Amy-Jill Levine. Sheffield: Sheffield Academic Press, forthcoming.

Butler, Judith. *Gender Trouble: Feminism and the Subversion of Identity.* Thinking Gender. New York: Routledge, 1990.

Callender, Dexter E., Jr. "Servants of God(s) and Servants of Kings in Israel and the Ancient Near East." *Semeia* 83/84 (1998): 67–82.

Camp, Claudia V. *Wise, Strange, and Holy: The Strange Woman and the Making of the Bible.* JSOT Supplement Series 320. Sheffield: Sheffield Academic Press, 2000.

Cantarella, Eva. *Pandora's Daughters: The Role and Status of Women in Greek and Roman Antiquity.* Baltimore: Johns Hopkins University Press, 1987.

Caputo, John D., and Michael J. Scanlon. *God, the Gift, and Postmodernism.* Bloomington: Indiana University Press, 1999.

Carter, Bill. "Ersatz Eligible 'Joe Millionaire' Gives Fox a Needed Ratings Hit." *New York Times*, 8 January 2003. http://nytimes.com2003/01/08/business/media/08TUBE.html.

Carter, Warren. *Households and Discipleship: A Study of Matthew 19–20*. Supplement to the Journal of the Study of the New Testament. Sheffield: Sheffield Academic Press, 1994.

———. *Matthew and the Margins*. Supplement to the Journal of the Study of the New Testament. Sheffield: Sheffield Academic Press, 2000.

Castelli, Elizabeth. "Virginity and Its Meaning for Women's Sexuality in Early Christianity." *Journal of Feminist Studies in Religion* 2, no. 1 (1986): 61–88.

Chang, Grace. *Disposable Domestics: Immigrant Women Workers in the Global Economy*. Cambridge, Mass.: South End Press, 2000.

Chopp, Rebecca, and Mark Lewis Taylor. *Reconstructing Christian Theology*. Minneapolis: Fortress, 1994.

Chow, Rey. *The Protestant Ethnic and the Spirit of Capitalism*. New York: Columbia University Press, 2002.

Cixous, Hélène. *"Coming to Writing" and Other Essays*. Edited by Deborah Jenson. Cambridge, Mass.: Harvard University Press, 1991.

Cixous, Hélène, and Catherine Clément. *The Newly Born Woman*. Theory and History of Literature. Minneapolis: University of Minnesota Press, 1975.

Clark, Elizabeth. *Ascetic Piety and Women's Faith: Essays on Late Ancient Christianity*. Lewiston, N.Y.: Edwin Mellen Press, 1986.

———. "Holy Women, Holy Words: Early Christian Women, Social History, and the 'Linguistic Turn.'" *Journal of Early Christian Studies* 6, no. 3 (1998): 413–30.

———. *Reading Renunciation: Asceticism and Scripture in Early Christianity*. Princeton, N.J.: Princeton University Press, 1999.

Clement of Alexandria. *Salvation of the Rich*. Loeb Classical Library. New York: Putnam, 1919.

Cobb, John B., Jr. *The Earthist Challenge to Economism: A Theological Critique of the World Bank*. New York: Macmillan, 1999.

———. *Postmodernism and Public Policy: Reframing Religion, Culture, Education, Sexuality, Class, Race, and the Economy*. Albany, N.Y.: SUNY Press, 2002.

Coleman, Simon M. "America Loves Sweden: Prosperity Theology and the Cultures of Capitalism." In *Religion and the Transformation of Capitalism*. Edited by Richard Roberts. London: Routledge, 1995.

———. "Charismatic Christianity and the Dilemmas of Globalization." *Religion* 29 (1998): 245–56.

Collins, Adela Yarbro. "The Signification of Mark 10:45 among Gentile Christians." *Harvard Theological Review* 90, no. 4 (1997): 371–82.

"Conubium." Pages 158–59 in vol. 3 of *Der neue Pauly: Enzyklopädie der Antike*. Edited by Hubert Cancik and Helmuth Schneider. Stuttgart: J. B. Metzler, 1996.

Cook, Wade. *Business Buy the Bible: Financial Wisdom of the Ancients.* Seattle: Lighthouse, 1997.
Cooper, Kate. *The Virgin and the Bride: Idealized Womanhood in Late Antiquity.* Cambridge: Harvard University Press, 1996.
Countryman, L. William. *The Rich Christian in the Church of the Early Empire: Contradictions and Accommodations.* New York: Edwin Mellen Press, 1980.
Cox, Harvey. *The Feast of Fools: A Theological Essay on Festivity and Fantasy.* New York: Harper & Row, 1969.
———. "The Market as God: Living in the New Dispensation." *The Atlantic,* March 1999. http://www.TheAtlantic.com/issues/99mar/marketgod.htm.
Daly, Herman E., and John B. Cobb Jr. *For the Common Good: Redirecting the Economy toward Community, the Environment, and a Sustainable Future.* 2d ed. Boston: Beacon, 1989.
Daly, Mary. *Beyond God the Father: Toward a Philosophy of Women's Liberation.* Boston: Beacon, 1973.
Danielou, Jean. *Geschichte der Kirche.* Vol. 1. Edited by L. J. Rogier, R. Aubert, and M. D. Knowles. Einsiedeln: Benziger Verlag, 1963.
Davies, W. D., and Dale C. Allison. *A Critical and Exegetical Commentary on the Gospel according to Matthew.* International Critical Commentary on the Holy Scriptures of the Old and New Testaments. Edinburgh: T&T Clark, 1997.
DeChant, Dell. *The Sacred Santa: Religious Dimensions of Consumer Culture.* Cleveland: Pilgrim, 2002.
Derrida, Jacques. *Dissemination.* Translated by Barbara Johnson. Chicago: University of Chicago Press, 1981.
———. *The Gift of Death.* Translated by David Wills. Chicago: University of Chicago Press, 1992.
———. *Given Time: I. Counterfeit Money.* Translated by Peggy Kamuf. Chicago: University of Chicago Press, 1992.
———. *Margins of Philosophy.* Translated by Alan Bass. Chicago: University of Chicago Press, 1981.
———. *Of Grammatology.* Corrected ed. Translated by Gayatri Spivak. Baltimore: Johns Hopkins University Press, 1997.
———. *On the Name.* Translated by David Wood, et al. Stanford, Calif.: Stanford University Press, 1995.
———. *Writing and Difference.* Translated by Alan Bass. London: Routledge, 1978.
Dirlik, Arif. "The Postcolonial Aura: Third World Criticism in the Age of Global Capitalism." In *Dangerous Liaisons: Gender, Nation, and Postcolonial Perspectives.* Edited by Anne McClintock, Aamir Mufti, and Ella Shohat. Minneapolis: University of Minnesota Press, 1997.
Dobson, Edward G. "Prosperity Theology: Secular Humanism in Disguise." *Fundamentalist Journal* 4, no. 7 (October 1987): 12.

DuBois, Page. *Torture and Truth.* New York: Routledge, 1991.
Elgin, Duane. *Voluntary Simplicity: Toward a Way of Life That Is Outwardly Simple and Inwardly Rich.* New York: William Morrow & Co., 1981.
Elm, Susannah. *"Virgins of God": The Making of Asceticism in Late Antiquity.* Oxford: Oxford University Press, 1996.
Fanon, Frantz. *Black Skin, White Masks.* New York: Grove Press, 1967.
Feiner, Susan F. "A Portrait of the *Homo Economicus* as a Young Man." In *The New Economic Criticism.* Edited by Martha Woodmansee and Mark Osteen. New York: Routledge, 1999.
Ferber, Marianne, and Julie A. Nelson, eds. *Beyond Economic Man: Feminist Theory and Economics.* Chicago: University of Chicago Press, 1993.
Finley, Moses. *The Ancient Economy.* Berkeley: University of California Press, 1973.
Foucault, Michel. *The History of Sexuality: An Introduction.* Vol. 1. New York: Vintage, 1990.
———. "Nietzsche, Genealogy, History." In *The Foucault Reader.* Edited by Paul Rabinow. New York: Pantheon, 1984.
Frank, Thomas. *The Conquest of Cool: Business Culture, Counterculture, and the Rise of Hip Consumerism.* Chicago: University of Chicago Press, 1997.
———. *One Market under God.* New York: Anchor Books, 2000.
Fredriksen, Paula. "Hysteria and the Gnostic Myths of Creation." *Vigiliae Christianae* 33 (1979): 287–90.
Friedrich, Gerhard. *Die Verkündigung des Todes Jesu im Neuen Testament.* Neukirchen-Vluyn: Neukirchener Verlag, 1982.
Garrison, Roman. *Redemptive Almsgiving in Early Christianity.* Journal for the Study of the New Testament Supplement Series. Sheffield: Sheffield Academic Press, 1993.
Gifford, Paul. "Prosperity: A New and Foreign Element in African Christianity." *Religion* 20 (1990): 373–88.
Gilbert, Sandra M. "Introduction: A Tarantella of Theory." In *The Newly Born Woman,* by Hélène Cixous and Catherine Clément. Theory and History of Literature 24. Minneapolis: University of Minnesota Press, 1975.
Glancy, Jennifer A. "Slaves and Slavery in the Matthean Parables." *Journal of Biblical Literature* 119, no. 1 (2000): 67–90.
Gluckman, Amy, and Betsy Reed, eds. *Homo Economics: Capitalism, Community, and Lesbian and Gay Life.* New York: Routledge, 1997.
Gómez-Peña, Guillermo. *Temple of Confessions: Mexican Beasts and Living Santos.* New York: Powerhouse Books, 1996.
———. *Warrior of Gringostroika.* St. Paul: Graywolf Press, 1993.
Gonzalez, Justo. *Faith and Wealth: A History of Early Christian Ideas on the Origin, Significance, and Use of Money.* San Francisco: Harper & Row, 1990.

Grau, Marion. "Erasing 'Economy': Derrida and the Construction of Divine Economies." *Cross Currents* (Fall 2002): 360–70.
Greenhouse, Steven. "Suits Say Wal-Mart Forces Workers to Toil Off the Clock." *New York Times,* 25 June 2002. http://www.nytimes.com/2002/06/25/national/25WALM.html.
Gregg, Robert C., and Dennis E. Groh. *Early Arianism—A View of Salvation.* Philadelphia: Fortress, 1981.
Gregory of Nyssa. *Gregory of Nyssa: Dogmatic Treatises.* Edited by Philip Schaff and Henry Wace. Select Library of the Christian Church: Nicene and Post-Nicene Fathers. Peabody, Mass.: Hendrickson, 1994.
Greshake, Gisbert. "Der Wandel der Erlösungsvorstellungen in der Theologiegeschichte." In *Erlösung und Emanzipation.* Edited by Leo Scheffczyk. Quaestiones Disputatae. Freiburg: Herder, 1973.
Grim, Harold, ed. *Career of the Reformer I.* Luther's Works 31. Philadelphia: Muhlenberg Press, 1957.
Gutierrez, Gustavo. *A Theology of Liberation: History, Politics, and Salvation.* Maryknoll, N.Y.: Orbis, 1973.
Hackett, Rosalind I. J. "The Gospel of Prosperity in West Africa." In *Religion and the Transformation of Capitalism.* Edited by Richard H. Roberts. London: Routledge, 1995.
Haraway, Donna J. "Ecce Homo, Ain't (Ar'n't) I a Woman, and Inappropriate/d Others: The Human in a Post-Humanist Landscape." In *Feminists Theorize the Political.* Edited by Judith Butler and Joan Scott. New York: Routledge, 1992.
———. *Modest_Witness@Second_Millennium. FemaleMan©_Meets_OncoMouse™.* New York: Routledge, 1997.
———. *Simians, Cyborgs, and Women: The Reinvention of Nature.* New York: Routledge, 1991.
Harpham, Geoffrey Galt. *The Ascetic Imperative in Culture and Criticism.* Chicago: University of Chicago Press, 1987.
Haubeck, Wilfrid. *Loskauf durch Christus: Herkunft, Gestalt und Bedeutung des paulinischen Loskaufmotivs.* Witten: Bundes-Verlag, 1985.
Heinzelman, Kurt. *The Economics of the Imagination.* Amherst: University of Massachusetts Press, 1980.
Herz, Martin. *Sacrum Commercium: Eine begriffsgeschichtliche Studie zur Theologie der römischen Liturgiesprache.* Munich: Kommissionsverlag, 1958.
Hill, Julia Butterfly. *The Legacy of Luna: The Story of a Tree, a Woman, and the Struggle to Save the Redwoods.* San Francisco: HarperSanFrancisco, 2000.
Hinkelammert, Franz. "Liberation Theology in the Economic and Social Context of Latin America: Economy and Theology, or the Irrationality of the Rationalized." In *Liberation Theologies, Postmodernity, and the Americas.* Edited by David

Batstone, Eduardo Mendieta, Lois Ann Lorentzen, and Dwight N. Hopkins. London: Routledge, 1997.

———. "Wider die Verfertigten Götzen der Macht: Zur Metaphysik der okzidentalen Unmenschlichkeit." In *Bilderverbot: Jahrbuch für politische Theologie,* vol. 2. Edited by Michael J. Rainer and Hans-Gerd Janssen. Münster: LIT, 1997.

Hoare, Quintin, and Geoffrey Nowell Smith, eds. and trans. *Selections from the Prison Notebooks of Antonio Gramsci.* New York: International Publishers, 1971.

Hodgson, Peter C. *Winds of the Spirit: A Constructive Christian Theology.* Louisville, Ky.: Westminster John Knox, 1994.

Holman, Susan R. *The Hungry Are Dying.* Oxford: Oxford University Press, 2001.

Horsley, Richard. "The Slave Systems of Classical Antiquity and Their Reluctant Recognition by Modern Scholars." *Semeia* 83/84 (1998): 19–66.

Howard-Brook, Wes, and Anthony Gwyther. *Unveiling Empire: Reading Revelation Then and Now.* Maryknoll, N.Y.: Orbis, 1999.

Humphreys, S. C. *The Family, Women, and Death: Comparative Studies.* London: Routledge & Kegan Paul, 1983.

Hyde, Lewis. *Trickster Makes This World: Mischief, Myth, and Art.* New York: Farrar, Straus & Giroux, 1998.

Hynes, William J. "Mapping the Characteristics of Mythic Tricksters: A Heuristic Guide." In *Mythical Trickster Figures.* Edited by William J. Hynes and William G. Doty. Tuscaloosa: University of Alabama Press, 1993.

Ireland, Dennis J. *Stewardship and the Kingdom of God: An Historical, Exegetical, and Contextual Study of the Parable of the Unjust Steward in Luke 16:1–13.* Supplements to Novum Testamentum 70. Leiden: E. J. Brill, 1992.

Irigaray, Luce. *Elemental Passions.* New York: Routledge, 1992.

———. *An Ethics of Sexual Difference.* Translated by Carol Burke and Gillian C. Gill. Ithaca, N.Y.: Cornell University Press, 1984.

———. *Marine Lover of Friedrich Nietzsche.* New York: Columbia University Press, 1991.

———. *Sexes and Genealogies.* New York: Columbia University Press, 1993.

———. *Speculum of the Other Woman.* Translated by Gillian C. Gill. Ithaca, N.Y.: Cornell University Press, 1985.

———. *This Sex Which Is Not One.* Translated by Catherine Porter. Ithaca, N.Y.: Cornell University Press, 1985.

James, Caryn. "It's Her Turn, but Don't Call Her Heartbreaker." *New York Times,* 8 January 2003. http://www.nytimes.com/2003/01/08/arts/television/08NOTE.html.

Jameson, Fredric. *Postmodernism, or The Cultural Logic of Late Capitalism.* Durham, N.C.: Duke University Press, 1991.

Jeremias, Joachim. "Das Lösegeld für Viele (Mk. 10:45)." *Judaica* 3, no. 4 (1948): 249–64.

Johansen, Ruthann Knechel. *The Narrative Secret of Flannery O'Connor: The Trickster as Interpreter.* Tuscaloosa: University of Alabama Press, 1994.

Johnston, Carol. *The Wealth or Health of Nations: Transforming Capitalism from Within.* Cleveland: Pilgrim, 1998.

Jones, Laurie Beth. *Jesus, CEO: Using Ancient Wisdom for Visionary Leadership.* New York: Hyperion, 1995.

———. *Jesus, Inc.: The Visionary Path: An Entrepreneur's Guide to True Success.* New York: Crown, 2001.

Jones, Serene. *Feminist Theory and Christian Theology: Cartographies of Grace.* Minneapolis: Fortress, 2000.

Keller, Catherine. *Apocalypse Now and Then: A Feminist Guide to the End of the World.* Boston: Beacon, 1996.

———. "A Christian Response to the Population Apocalypse." In *Population, Consumption, and the Environment: Religious and Secular Responses.* Edited by Howard Coward. Albany, N.Y.: SUNY Press, 1995.

———. *Face of the Deep.* New York: Routledge, 2003.

———. *From a Broken Web: Separation, Sexism, and Self.* Boston: Beacon, 1986.

Kereszty, Roch. "The Unity of the Church in the Theology of Irenaeus." *Second Century* 4, no. 4 (1984): 202–18.

Keshgegian, Flora. *Redeeming Memories: A Theology of Healing and Transformation.* Nashville: Abingdon, 2000.

Kintz, Linda. *Between Jesus and the Market: The Emotions That Matter in Right-Wing America.* Durham, N.C.: Duke University Press, 1997.

Klein, Naomi. *No Logo: Taking Aim at the Brand Bullies.* New York: Picador, 1999.

Klossowski, Pierre. *La Monnaie Vivande.* Paris: Rivages Poche Petite Bibliothèque, 1997.

Korten, David C. *The Post-Corporate World: Life after Capitalism.* San Francisco: Berrett-Koehler Publishers; West Hartford, Conn.: Kumarian Press, 1999.

———. *When Corporations Rule the World.* San Francisco: Berrett-Koehler Publishers; West Hartford, Conn.: Kumarian Press, 1995.

Kraemer, Ross, ed. *Maenads, Martyrs, Matrons, Monastics: Sourcebook on Women's Religions in the Greco-Roman World.* Philadelphia: Fortress, 1988.

Krueger, Derek. *Symeon the Holy Fool: Leontius' Life and the Late Antique City.* Berkeley: University of California Press, 1996.

Krugman, Paul. "The Class Wars, Part I: For Richer: How the Permissive Capitalism of the Boom Destroyed American Equality." *New York Times Magazine* (20 October 2002): 62–69, 76–77, 141–42.

Kumar, Amitava. *Passport Photos.* Berkeley: University of California Press, 2000.

Kurzweil, Ray. *The Age of Spiritual Machines: When Computers Exceed Human Intelligence.* New York: Viking, 1999.

Lake, Kirsopp, trans. *The Apostolic Fathers I.* Loeb Classical Library. Cambridge: Harvard University Press, 1950.

Lakeland, Paul. *Postmodernity: Christian Identity in an Age of Fragmentation.* Guides to Theological Inquiry. Minneapolis: Fortress, 1997.

Lampe, G. W. H. *A Patristic Greek Lexicon.* Oxford: Clarendon Press, 1961.

Landay, Lori. *Madcaps, Screwballs, and Con Women: The Female Trickster in American Culture.* Feminist Cultural Studies, the Media, and Political Culture. Philadelphia: University of Pennsylvania Press, 1998.

Landry, David, and Ben May. "Honor Restored: New Light on the Parable of the Prudent Steward (Luke 16:1–8a)." *Journal of Biblical Literature* 119, no. 2 (2000): 287–309.

Lasn, Kalle. *Culture Jam: The Uncooling of America™.* New York: William Morrow & Co., 1999.

Lefkovitz, Mary R. *Heroines and Hysterics.* New York: St. Martin's Press, 1981.

Lerner, Michael. *The Politics of Meaning: Restoring Hope and Responsibility in an Age of Cynicism.* Reading, Mass.: Addison-Wesley, 1996.

Levine, Amy-Jill. *The Social and Ethnic Dimensions of Matthean Salvation History.* Lewiston, N.Y.: Edwin Mellen Press, 1988.

Liddell, Henry George, and Robert Scott. *A Greek-English Lexicon.* Oxford: Clarendon Press, 1996.

Long, D. Stephen. *Divine Economy: Theology and the Market.* New York: Routledge, 2000.

Loy, David R. "The Religion of the Market." *Journal of the American Academy of Religion* 65, no. 2 (1996): 275–90.

Luz, Ulrich. *Das Evangelium nach Matthäus: Mt 18–25.* Evangelisch-Katholischer Kommentar Zum Neuen Testament. Zürich: Benziger Verlag; Düsseldorf: Neukirchener Verlag, 1997.

Lyman, Rebecca. *Christology and Cosmology: Models of Divine Activity in Origen, Eusebius, and Athanasius.* Oxford: Clarendon, 1993.

———. "The Politics of Passing: Justin Martyr's Conversion as a Problem of Hellenization." In *Conversion in Late Antiquity and the Middle Ages: Seeing and Believing.* Edited by Anthony Grafton and Kenneth Mills. Rochester, N.Y.: University of Rochester Press, 2003.

Lyonnet, Stanislaus, and Leopold Sabourin. *Sin, Redemption, and Sacrifice: A Biblical and Patristic Study.* Analecta Biblica 48. Rome: Biblical Institute, 1970.

Lyotard, Jean-François. *Libidinal Economy.* Translated by Iain Hamilton Grant. Bloomington: University of Indiana Press, 1993.

MacDonald, Dennis Ronald. *The Legend and the Apostle: The Battle for Paul in Story and Canon.* Philadelphia: Westminster, 1983.

MacKendrick, Karmen. *Counterpleasures.* Albany, N.Y.: SUNY Press, 1999.

Malbon, Elizabeth Struthers. "Fallible Followers: Women and Men in the Gospel of Mark." *Semeia* 28 (1983): 29–48.

———. *In the Company of Jesus: Characters in Mark's Gospel.* Louisville, Ky.: Westminster John Knox, 2000.

Malina, Bruce. *The Social Gospel of Jesus: The Kingdom of God in Mediterranean Perspective.* Minneapolis: Fortress, 2001.

Markus, Robert A. *Saeculum: History and Society in the Theology of St. Augustine.* Cambridge: Cambridge University Press, 1970.

Martin, Dale. *Slavery as Salvation: The Metaphor of Slavery in Pauline Christianity.* New Haven, Conn.: Yale University Press, 1990.

Matthiae, Gisela. *Clownin Gott: Eine feministische Dekonstruktion des Göttlichen.* Praktische Theologie Heute 48. Stuttgart: Kohlhammer, 1999.

Mauss, Marcel. *The Gift: Forms and Functions of Exchange in Archaic Societies.* New York: W. W. Norton & Co., 1967.

Mazzoni, Christina. *Saint Hysteria: Neurosis, Mysticism, and Gender in European Culture.* Ithaca, N.Y.: Cornell University Press, 1996.

McCloskey, Deidre N. *Crossing.* Chicago: University of Chicago Press, 1999.

McCloskey, Donald N. "Some Consequences of a Conjective Economics." In *Beyond Economic Man.* Edited by Julie A. Nelson and Marianne A. Ferber. Chicago: University of Chicago Press, 1993.

McFague, Sallie. *Life Abundant: Rethinking Theology and Economy for a Planet in Peril.* Minneapolis: Fortress, 2000.

McIntyre, John. *The Shape of Soteriology: Studies in the Doctrine of the Death of Christ.* Edinburgh: T&T Clark, 1992.

Meeks, M. Douglas. *God the Economist: The Doctrine of God and Political Economy.* Minneapolis: Fortress, 1989.

Míguez, Néstor. "Globalization: A Challenge to Hear the Victim's Voice." *Jeevadhara* 1 (2000): 107–19.

Milbank, John. *Theology and Social Theory: Beyond Secular Reason.* Oxford: Blackwell, 1990.

Miller, Patricia Cox. "The Blazing Body: Ascetic Desire in Jerome's Letter to Eustochium." *Journal of Early Christian Studies* 1 (1993): 21–45.

Miller, Vincent J. *Consuming Religion: Christian Faith and Practice in a Consumer Culture.* New York: Continuum, 2003.

Mohanty, Chandra T. "Women Workers and Capitalist Scripts: Ideologies of Domination, Common Interests, and the Politics of Solidarity." In *Feminist Genealogies, Colonial Legacies, Democratic Futures.* Edited by Jaqui Alexander and Chandra Mohanty. New York: Routledge, 1997.

Moi, Toril. *Sexual/Textual Politics: Feminist Literary Theory.* London: Routledge, 1985.

Moltmann, Jürgen. *Der Geist des Lebens: Eine ganzheitliche Pneumatologie.* Gütersloh: Chr. Kaiser/Gütersloher Verlagshaus, 1991.

———. *Theology of Hope: On the Grounds and the Implications of a Christian Eschatology.* New York: Harper & Row, 1964.

Moore, Michael. *Downsize This! Random Threats from an Unarmed American.* New York: HarperPerennial, 1997.

———. *Dude, Where's My Country?* New York: Warner Books, 2003.
———. *Stupid White Men.* New York: Regan Books/HarperCollins, 2001.
Moore, Stephen D. *God's Gym: Divine Male Bodies of the Bible.* New York: Routledge, 1996.
———. *Mark and Luke in Poststructuralist Perspective: Jesus Begins to Write.* New Haven, Conn.: Yale University Press, 1992.
———. *Poststructuralism and the New Testament: Derrida and Foucault at the Foot of the Cross.* Minneapolis: Fortress, 1994.
Müller, Ulrich B. *Philipper.* Theologischer Handkommentar zum NT. Leipzig: Evangelische Verlagsanstalt, 1993.
Nash, James. *Loving Nature: Ecological Integrity and Christian Responsibility.* Nashville: Abingdon, 1991.
Nelson, Julie A. "Breaking the Dynamic of Control: A Feminist Approach to Economic Ethics." *Journal of Feminist Studies in Religion* 19 (Spring 2003): 155–62.
———. "Economic Man." In *The Elgar Companion to Feminist Economics.* Edited by Janice Peterson and Meg Lewis. Aldershot: Edward Elgar, 2000.
———. *Feminism, Objectivity, and Economics.* New York: Routledge, 1996.
———. "The Masculine Mindset of Economics Analysis." *Chronicle of Higher Education* 42 (28 June 1996): B3.
Normann, Friedrich. *Teilhabe: Ein Schlüsselwort der Vätertheologie.* Münsterische Beiträge zur Theologie. Münster: Aschendorff, 1978.
Origenes. "Mattäus." In *Der Kommentar zum Evangelium nach Mattäus,* vol. 2. Translated by Herman J. Vogt. Bibliothek der griechischen Literatur. Stuttgart: Anton Hiersemann, 1990.
Pagels, Elaine. *Adam, Eve, and the Serpent.* New York: Vintage, 1988.
Patterson, Orlando. *Slavery and Social Death.* Cambridge: Harvard University Press, 1982.
Phan, Peter C. *Culture and Eschatology: The Iconographic Vision of Paul Evdokimov.* American University Studies. Series 7, Theology and Religion. Vol. 1. New York: Peter Lang, 1985.
———. "The Wisdom of Holy Fools in Postmodernity." *Theological Studies* 62 (2001): 730–52.
Phillips, Victoria. "Full Disclosure: Towards a Complete Characterization of the Women Who Followed Jesus in the Gospel according to Mark." In *Transformative Encounters: Jesus and Women Re-Viewed.* Edited by Ingrid Rosa Kitzberger. Leiden: E. J. Brill, 2000.
Plaskow, Judith. *Standing Again at Sinai: Judaism from a Feminist Perspective.* San Francisco: HarperCollins, 1990.
Plate, S. Brent, and Edna M. Rodriguez Mangual. "The Gift That Stops Giving: Hélène Cixous's 'Gift' and the Shunammite Woman." *Biblical Interpretation* 7, no. 2 (1999): 113–32.

Plotnitsky, Arkady. "Re-: Re-Flecting, Re-Membering, Re-Collecting, Re-Selecting, Re-Warding, Re-Wording, Re-Iterating, Re-et-Cetra-Ing . . . (in) Hegel." *Postmodern Culture* 5, no. 2 (1995).

Pomeroy, Sarah. *Goddesses, Whores, Wives, and Slaves: Women in Classical Antiquity.* New York: Schocken, 1975.

Porter, Roy. "Baudrillard: History, Hysteria, and Consumption." In *Forget Baudrillard?* Edited by Chris Rojek and Bryan Turner. New York: Routledge, 1993.

———. "Body and Mind." In *Hysteria beyond Freud.* Edited by Sander Gilman. Berkeley: University of California Press, 1993.

Porter, Stanley. *The Bible in Three Dimensions: Essays in Celebration of Forty Years of Biblical Studies in the University of Sheffield.* Journal for the Study of the Old Testament Supplement Series 87. Sheffield: Sheffield Academic Press, 1990.

Pröpper, Thomas. *Erlösungsglaube und Freiheitsgeschichte.* Munich: Kösel, 1988.

Przywara, Erich. *Logos: Logos—Abendland—Reich—Commercium.* Düsseldorf: Patmos, 1964.

Rasmussen, Larry. *Earth Community, Earth Ethics.* Maryknoll, N.Y.: Orbis, 1996.

Rawick, George, ed. *The American Slave.* Vol. 19. Nashville: Fisk University Social Science Institute, 1945.

Ray, Darby Kathleen. *Deceiving the Devil: Atonement, Abuse, and Ransom.* Cleveland: Pilgrim, 1998.

Roberts, Alexander, and James Donaldson, eds. *The Apostolic Fathers, Justin Martyr, Irenaeus.* Vol. 1 of *Ante-Nicene Fathers.* Peabody, Mass.: Hendrickson, 1994.

———. *Fathers of the Third Century: Hippolytus, Cyprian, Caius, Novatian.* Vol. 5 of *Ante-Nicene Fathers.* Peabody, Mass.: Hendrickson, 1994.

———. *Latin Christianity: Its Founder, Tertullian.* Vol. 3 of *Ante-Nicene Fathers.* Peabody, Mass.: Hendrickson, 1994.

Roberts, John W. *From Trickster to Badman: The Black Folk Hero in Slavery and Freedom.* Philadelphia: University of Pennsylvania Press, 1989.

Robinson, James M., gen. ed. *The Nag Hammadi Library in English.* 3d ed. San Francisco: Harper & Row, 1988.

Ross, Stephen David. *The Gift of Property: Having the Good: Betraying Genitivity, Economy, and Ecology: An Ethic of the Earth.* Albany, N.Y.: SUNY Press, 2001.

Rousselle, Aline. *Porneia: On Desire and the Body in Antiquity.* Cambridge, Mass.: Blackwell, 1983.

Said, Edward W. *Culture and Imperialism.* New York: Vintage, 1993.

Saller, Richard P. *Personal Patronage under the Early Empire.* Cambridge: Cambridge University Press, 1982.

Sandoval, Chela. *Methodology of the Oppressed.* Minneapolis: University of Minnesota Press, 2000.

Scherzberg, Lucia. *Sünde und Gnade in der feministischen Theologie.* Mainz: Matthias Grünewald Verlag, 1992.
Schüssler Fiorenza, Elisabeth. *In Memory of Her: A Feminist Theological Reconstruction of Christian Origins.* New York: Crossroad, 1994.
———. *Jesus: Miriam's Child, Sophia's Prophet: Critical Issues in Feminist Christology.* New York: Continuum, 1994.
Schwager, Raymund. *Der wunderbare Tausch: Zur Geschichte und Bedeutung der Erlösungslehre.* Munich: Kösel, 1986.
Schweizer, Eduard. *Der Brief an die Kolosser.* Evangelische-Katholischer Kommentar Zum Neuen Testament. Neukirchen-Vluyn: Neukirchener Verlag, 1976.
———. *The Good News according to Matthew.* Atlanta: John Knox, 1975.
Scott, James C. *Domination and the Arts of Resistance: Hidden Transcripts.* New Haven, Conn.: Yale University Press, 1990.
Shapiro, Deborah. "Leave It to Fox." *FEEDmag,* 16 February 2000. http://www.feedmag.com/daily/dy021600.html.
Shaw, Brent D. "Body/Power/Identity: Passions of the Martyrs." *Journal of Early Christian Studies* 4, no. 3 (1996): 269–312.
Shoaf, Richard Allen. *The Poem as Green Girdle: Commercium in Sir Gawain and the Green Knight.* Gainesville: University of Florida Press, 1984.
Showalter, Elaine. *Hystories: Hysterical Epidemics and Modern Culture.* New York: Columbia University Press, 1997.
Spivak, Gayatri. *A Critique of Postcolonial Reason: Toward a History of the Vanishing Present.* Cambridge: Harvard University Press, 1999.
———. "Translator's Preface." In *Of Grammatology,* by Jacques Derrida. New York: Routledge, 1998.
Spivak, Gayatri, and Ellen Rooney. "In a Word. Interview." In *The Essential Difference.* Edited by Naomi Schor and Elizabeth Weed. Bloomington: Indiana University Press, 1994.
Still, Judith. *Feminine Economies: Thinking against the Market in the Enlightenment and the Late Twentieth Century.* Manchester: Manchester University Press, 1997.
Studer, Basil. *Soteriologie in der Schrift und Patristik.* Handbuch der Dogmengeschichte. Freiburg: Herder, 1978.
"Suits Say Wal-Mart Forces Workers to Toil Off the Clock." *New York Times,* 25 June 2002. http://www.nytimes.com/2002/06/25/national/25WALM.html.
Talen, Bill. "Reverend Billy's Starbucks Invasion: The Church of Stop Shopping Takes a Stand." *Utne* online, 14 April 2002. http://www.utne.com/web_special/web_specials_archives/articles/2761-1.html.
Talen, William. *What Should I Do If Reverend Billy Is in My Store?* New York: New Press, 2003.
Taylor, Mark C. *About Religion: Economies of Faith in Virtual Culture.* Religion and Postmodernism. Chicago: University of Chicago Press, 1999.

---. *Erring: A Postmodern A/Theology.* Chicago: University of Chicago Press, 1984.

Taylor, Mark McClain. "Vodou Resistance/Vodou Hope: Forging a Postmodernism That Liberates." In *Liberation Theologies, Postmodernity, and the Americas.* Edited by David Batstone, Eduardo Mendieta, Lois Ann Lorentzen, and Dwight N. Hopkins. London: Routledge, 1997.

Tertullian. *Tertullian, Part Fourth, Minucius Felix, Commodian; Origen Parts First and Second.* Edited by Alexander Roberts and James Donaldson. Vol. 1 of *Ante-Nicene Fathers.* Peabody, Mass.: Hendrickson, 1994.

Te Selle, Eugene. "The Cross as Ransom." *Journal of Early Christian Studies* 4, no. 2 (1996): 147–70.

Thompson, Chris. "Preaching Prosperity: Acts Full Gospel Became Oakland's Largest Church by Helping Its Parishioners Leave Town for the Suburbs." *East Bay Express,* 24 April 2002, 12–21.

Thompson, Ewa M. *Understanding Russia: The Holy Fool in Russian Culture.* Lanham, Md.: University Press of America, 1987.

Thurston, Bonnie Bowman. *The Widows: A Women's Ministry in the Early Church.* Minneapolis: Fortress, 1989.

Torjesen, Karen Jo. *When Women Were Priests: Women's Leadership in the Early Church and the Scandal of Their Subordination in the Rise of Christianity.* San Francisco: HarperSanFrancisco, 1995.

Trigg, Joseph. "Divine Deception and the Truthfulness of Scripture." In *Origen of Alexandria: His World and His Legacy.* Edited by Charles Kannengiesser and William Petersen. Notre Dame, Ind.: University of Notre Dame Press, 1988.

Troeltsch, Ernst. *Die Soziallehren der christlichen Kirchen und Gruppen.* Tübingen: J.C.B. Mohr, 1912.

Trudinger, Paul. "Ire or Irony? The Enigmatical Character of the Parable of the Dishonest Steward (Luke 16:1-13)." *Downside Review* 116 (April 1998): 85–102.

Truth, Sojourner. "I Suppose I Am about the Only Colored Woman That Goes about to Speak for the Rights of Colored Women." In *Freedom Is a Dream.* Edited by Sheryl Kujawa-Holbrook. New York: Church Publishing, 2002.

Twitchell, James B. *Lead Us into Temptation: The Triumph of American Materialism.* New York: Columbia University Press, 1999.

Upkong, Justin S. "The Parable of the Shrewd Manager (Luke 16:1–13): An Essay in Inculturation Biblical Hermeneutic." *Semeia* 76 (1996): 189–210.

Valantasis, Richard, and Vincent L. Wimbush. *Asceticism.* Oxford: Oxford University Press, 1995.

Veith, Ilza. *Hysteria: The History of a Disease.* Chicago: University of Chicago Press, 1965.

Vieweger, Dieter, and Annette Böckler. "'Ich Gebe Ägypten als Lösegeld für Dich' Mk 10,24 und die jüdische Tradition zu Jes 43,3b.4." *Zeitschrift für die alttestamentliche Wissenschaft* 108 (1996): 594–607.

Wagener, Ulrike. *Die Ordnung des "Hauses Gottes": Der Ort von Frauen in der Ekklesiologie und Ethik der Pastoralbriefe.* Wissenschaftliche Untersuchungen Zum Neuen Testament 2. Reihe 65. Tübingen: J.C.B. Mohr, 1994.

Wainwright, Elaine M. *Shall We Look for Another? A Feminist Rereading of the Matthean Jesus.* Maryknoll, N.Y.: Orbis, 1998.

Ward, Graham. *Cities of God.* New York: Routledge, 2000.

Weber, Max. *Die protestantische Ethik I: Eine Aufsatzsammlung.* Edited by Johannes Winckelmann. Gütersloh: GTB Siebenstern, 1991.

Wenz, Gunther. *Geschichte der Versöhnungslehre in der evangelischen Theologie der Neuzeit.* Munich: Chr. Kaiser, 1984.

West, Traci C. *Wounds of the Spirit: Black Women, Violence, and Resistance Ethics.* New York: NYU Press, 1999.

Whitehead, Alfred North. *Science and the Modern World.* New York: Free Press, 1925.

Wilkinson, Bruce. *The Prayer of Jabez: Breaking Through to the Blessed Life.* Sisters, Ore.: Multnomah Publishers, 2000.

Williams, Delores. *Sisters in the Wilderness: The Challenge of Womanist God-Talk.* Maryknoll, N.Y.: Orbis, 1993.

Williams, Joel F. *Other Followers of Jesus: Minor Characters as Major Figures in Mark's Gospel.* Journal for the Study of the New Testament Supplement Series 102. Sheffield: JSOT Press, 1994.

Willmington, Harold. "Prosperity Theology: A Slot-Machine Religion." *Fundamentalist Journal* (November 1987): 15–18.

Woodmansee, Martha, and Mark Osteen, eds. *The New Economic Criticism: Studies at the Intersection of Literature and Economics.* Economics as Social Theory. London: Routledge, 1999.

Wright, Addison G. "The Widow's Mites: Praise or Lament?—A Matter of Context." *Catholic Biblical Quarterly* 44 (1982): 256–65.

Wylie-Kellermann. "Coyote Wants More." *The Witness* (July/August 1998): 5.

Young, Robert. *Postcolonialism: An Historical Introduction.* Oxford: Blackwell, 2001.

———. *White Mythologies: Writing History and the West.* New York: Routledge, 1990.

Index

Acts Full Gospel Church of God, 28, 203
Acts of Thecla, 113, 118–21, 126
Adam, 57
Adbusters magazine, 196–97
admirabile commercium. See "miraculous" exchange
Africa, prosperity theology in, 3n.6, 28, 28–29n.23
African Americans, 28, 102n.40, 184, 224
   tricksters, 184, 200–201
   women, 112, 163–64, 200–201
Against Praxeas (Tertullian), 155
Agnes, 93, 110–12, 117
Alexandrian virgins, 124–26
Allen African Methodist Episcopal Church, 28
Allison, Dale C., 46, 83, 141, 144
almsgiving, 17–18, 87
   and the Cent Society, 105–6
   and the "poor widow," 95
   as redemptive practice, 63–65, 63n.74, 64n.78, 70, 70n.103, 156
Althaus-Reid, Marcella, 226
   "indecent theology" of, 1, 168–69, 174, 176, 179, 205, 219, 221–22
   and liberation theology of Latin America, 33–34, 37, 39, 108
Ambrose, and virgin martyr Agnes, 110–12, 117
Anselm, 138, 152, 161, 216, 219n.173, 220n.175

Antony, 123–24
   sister of, 123–24, 131
apocalypse, 13, 13n.35, 181, 186
Apocryphon of John, 97
Aretaeus of Cappadocia, 49
Arians, 70–71, 125
Aristotle, 31, 52, 97
Arius, 71, 125
asceticism
   and acquiring wealth in heaven, 17–18, 55, 69–70
   ancient and modern, 6, 87n.173, 162–63, 187–93
   in Athanasius' *Life of Antony,* 66–72, 88–89
   Augustine's conversion to, 73–76, 78–79
   in context of capitalism, 6, 43–44, 43n.5, 188, 214–15
   early Christian interpretations of, 62–66, 68–72
   eco-asceticism, 191, 192
   limitless quality of urge to, 45n.11
   of Thecla, 118–21
   and women, 92, 118–21, 121n.114, 122–32, 125n.124, 192–93
   See also wealth
Athanasius, 66, 68–72, 73–76, 88–89, 92, 123–24, 131, 205
   and the Alexandrian virgins, 124–26
a/theology, 25, 25n.9, 26
Augustine, 72, 75n.120, 76n.124–125, 78n.131, 160, 168, 225

243

commentary on "rich young man," 73–79, 88–89
divine economy vs. imperial economy, 56, 57
Aulén, Gustav, 151–53, 216
Austen, Jane, 167, 167–68n.114

Bakhtin, Mikhail, 185
Barlow, Tani, 82
Barton, Bruce, 189
Bartra, Roger, 197
Bataille, Georges, 9
Baudrillard, Jean, 41, 50–51
Bedford, Nancy, 29
Beyond Economic Man (Nelson and Ferber), 84
Bhabha, Homi, 205
    and hybridity, 16, 33, 81, 218
    and mimicry, 38, 59, 109n.69, 159, 193, 207, 207n.132, 218
    and mimicry as strategy of colonial power, 79–81, 108–9, 193n.67, 213, 214
Bible, as colonial instrument, 79–81
Bio-power, 94, 94n.6, 104, 113, 117, 120
Blandina, 93, 115–16
Bloch, E., 20
Boston Society for Missionary Purposes, 107
Bourdieu, Pierre, 39, 103n.43
Boyarin, Daniel, 49, 112, 143
Brakke, David, 68, 69, 125–26
Briggs, Sheila, 150, 151, 167, 178
Brock, Rita Nakashima, 164
Brown, Peter, 75, 121, 122
Burrus, Virginia, 38, 52, 84, 110, 111, 117, 124, 126, 191, 205
Business Buy the Bible (Cook), 189
"butterfly effect," 176n.9

capitalism
    and asceticism, 6, 43–44, 43n.5, 188, 214–15
    and Christianity, 3–4, 23, 23n.2
    and colonialism, 81–83, 81n.144, 82nn.145–146, 107–8
    as heresy, 30–32, 31n.31
    "late" capitalism, 14–15, 23–24, 26, 50, 180–81, 180n.24
    liberation theology as response to, 3, 26–27, 26n.14, 86
    and male hysteria, 41–42, 50–51
    vs. Marxism, 6, 6n.13
Carter, Warren, 51, 141–42
Castelli, Elizabeth, 129
castration anxiety, 60–61
Cent and Mite societies, 105–7, 105n.55, 133
Chang, Grace, 169
chaos, 5, 20, 42, 42n.2, 134, 174, 176–78, 180, 215, 225
Charcot, Jean-Martin, 50
Chow, Rey, 170
Christianity
    and capitalism, 3–4, 23, 23n.2
    and capitalism as heresy, 30–32, 31n.31
    early Christian attitudes, 3, 3n.5, 10–11, 16, 24, 24n.6, 52–55, 54n.51
    early Christian attitudes, towards wealth, 62, 62n.71, 64–65, 64n.79
    early Christian interpretations of asceticism, 62–66, 68–72
    early Christianity, women in, 18, 38–39, 52–54, 53n.45, 123, 123n.120
    Hebrew traditions influencing, 11
    and prosperity, 3, 27–30, 33, 51, 87, 203–4

Christology
    Arian, 70–71
    of economics and marriage, 168
    feminist critique of, 161–63
    and "poor widow" figure, 104, 104n.52
    reconstruction of, 213, 214, 216
Christus Victor (Aulén), 151–52, 158, 216
Church of Stop Shopping, 196
Cixous, Hèléne, 18, 91–92, 99, 100, 101, 103, 122, 132, 208
Clark, Elizabeth, 130
Clément, Catherine, 91–92, 122, 132
Clement of Alexandria, 62, 87, 88, 89
clowns, 202–3. *See also* tricksters
Cobb, John B., Jr., 10, 14, 14n.41, 34–35, 36–37, 178
Coleman, Simon M., 28
colonialism
    and Augustine, 77, 77n.130
    and capitalism, 27, 43, 81–82, 81n.144, 82nn.145–146, 107–8, 142, 198
    and Indian widows' acts of sati, 118, 118n.105
    and mimicry as strategy of, 79–81, 108–9, 193n.67, 213, 214
    and missionary work, 79–81, 105, 107, 108–10
    postcolonialism, 16–17, 32–33, 193n.67, 213–14, 226
    and spread of divine economy, 79–83
Colossians, The Letter of Paul to the
    2:13–14   47–48
commercium. See marriage: as economic exchange
Cone, James, 31
Confessions (Augustine), 73–75
conubium. See marriage

Cook, Wade, 189
Copeland, Gloria, 27, 51
Copeland, Kenneth, 27
Corinthians, The First Letter of Paul to the
    4:1   1
    7:23   165, 220
counterpleasures, 67, 67n.88, 70, 176–77, 188, 193
Countryman, L. William, 3n.5
Cox, Harvey, 23, 193, 196
creatio ex nihilo, doctrine of, 57
Crossan, John Dominic, 183
Cyprian of Carthage, 46, 63n.74, 64, 95, 139, 156–57

Daly, Herman E., 35, 36
Daly, Mary, 108, 133, 178
Davies, W. D., 46, 83, 141, 144
deChant, Dell, 24, 166
Derrida, Jacques, 5, 31, 52, 212
    and castration anxiety, 60
    commentary on Irenaeus, 59–60
    and consequences of giving the gift, 46–47, 99–100, 140, 225
    and counterfeiting, 215–16
    and *différance,* 7, 9, 55, 66–67, 101, 176–77n.11, 188
    and economic transactions, 147, 210
    and hysteria, 48
    postmodernism of, 32
    and tricksters, 176, 187
différance, 7, 9, 55, 66–67, 101, 176–77n.11, 188, 215
Diogenes of Sinope, 195
Dirlik, Arif, 81
divine economy, vision of, 5, 224–26
Domini, Amy, 211
Domini Social Investment, 211
Donatists, 76n.125, 77, 78

DuBois, Page, 151, 167

economics
  alternative approaches to, 35
  ancient discourses of, 6, 52–54, 57–60, 68–72
  comparison with theology as discipline, 86, 86n.164
  and countereconomic tricksters, 174–81, 182–86, 185n.39
  discourses of, resembling religious texts, 23–24
  ecological economics, 35–36, 36n.53, 161–62, 211–12
  femina economica, 95–96
  feminist, 1–2, 83–85, 84n.156, 103, 173–74
  and giving the gift, 99–107
  homo economicus, as figure of Western capitalism, 18, 41–43, 50, 83–84, 84n.156, 89
  influences of on theology, 23–25, 39
  "invisible hand" of, 8, 13
  and liberation theology, 4, 4n.7, 9–10, 30n.30
  linking with death of God, 25–26
  and male sexuality as symbol for economic power, 10–11, 47, 52, 60, 100, 204
  and marriage as economic exchange, 165–71
  modern trends in, 1–2, 2n.3, 13–14, 173, 180–81
  neoclassical, 4, 8, 24, 34, 36
  and scarcity, 83, 83n.151, 85–89, 102–3
  terminology and concepts, pervasiveness of, 7–9, 7n.18, 8–9n.22
  Tertullian's use of imagery of in theology, 154–55
  transsexual view of, 95–96n.13, 95–96
  voluntary simplicity in, 185–86, 190, 191
  and women, 18, 34, 42, 101–3, 102n.40, 207, 207–8n.135
  See also "third space" economic theory/theology; capitalism; divine economy, vision of; Marxism; *oikonomia* (household management)

Elgin, Duane, 190
Esther, Queen, 201
Eustochium, 93, 127–29, 130, 192
Exodus
  30:12   142–43

Fanon, Frantz, 108
Feast of Fools, The (Cox), 193
Feiner, Susan F., 84–85
Felicitas, 114–15, 115n.96
femina economica, 95–96. *See also homo economicus*, as figure of Western capitalism
feminism, 17n.49
  and consequences of giving the gift, 100–102, 100n.26
  and critiques of atonement theories, 160–65
  and economics, 1–2, 83–85, 84n.156, 103, 173–74
  and liberation theology, 86, 108
  and theology, 15, 20, 20n.53, 42, 211–12
  and view of holy women, 92–93
Ferber, Marianne A., 84
Flake, Floyd H., 28
fools. *See* Holy Fool; tricksters
For the Common Good (Daly and Cobb), 35

Foucault, Michel, 11, 104, 151, 188, 190, 224
Fredriksen, Paula, 97
Freud, Sigmund, 48–49, 117–18
"From Restricted to General Economy: A Hegelianism without Reserve" (Derrida), 9

Galen of Pergamon, 49
genitivity, 46, 46n.16, 95, 95n.10
Gifford, Paul, 28
Gift, The (Mauss), 99
Gift of Death, The (Derrida), 46–47, 212
Gilbert, Sandra, 91
Gilder, George, 204
Glancy, Jennifer A., 146, 148
God the Economist (Meek), 35, 225
gold, 25–26
Gómez-Peña, Guillermo, 197–98
Gospel of the Hebrews, 61
Gospel of Truth, 148
Gramsci, Antonio, 5
Gregg, Robert C., 71
Gregory of Nyssa, 126, 136, 139, 217, 218, 223, 226
  and Jesus as ransom, 158–60
Groh, Dennis E., 71
Gutierrez, Gustavo, 26–27

Hagar, 163
Hagin, Kenneth, 27
Haraway, Donna J., 8, 43, 85, 109, 151, 178, 205
  and Jesus as trickster, 12n.33, 176, 182
  and women tricksters, 12, 15, 16, 92, 93, 175, 201, 225
Harpham, Geoffrey Galt, 67–68, 70, 188, 189, 190, 191
Hegel, Georg Wilhelm Friedrich, 8

Heilsgeschichte. See salvation history
heretics, 59
Hill, Julia Butterfly, 187, 208–9, 209–10n.140
Hölderlin, J. C. Friedrich, 20
Holy Fool
  contemporary forms of, 19, 44, 174, 175, 186–87, 196–203, 196n.81
  in different cultures, 194, 194–95n.75
  as divine slave trickster, 3, 16, 18–19, 217–18
  Symeon, 194–95
  wisdom of, 193–94
  See also tricksters
homo economicus, as figure of Western capitalism, 18, 41–43, 50, 83–84, 84n.156, 89. *See also femina economica*
Horsley, Richard, 145–46
hospitality, ancient understanding of, 54
householders, early Christian
  vs. asceticism, 68–72
  vs. itinerants, 54–55, 54n.51
  men vs. women, 53–54
"Human Situation, The: A Feminine View" (Saiving), 161
hybridity, profiting from/ being exploited by a system, 16, 30, 32–33, 77–78, 80–82, 184, 197–98
Hyde, Lewis, 173, 174
hysteria
  ancient understanding of, 43, 43n.6, 48–49, 97–98
  defined, 48
  as experience of lack, 41–44, 46, 61, 83–89
  as feared and female quality, 42, 42n.2

as feminine lack, 48, 48n.23, 49, 93, 97–98, 101
Freud's commentary on, 48, 49, 117–18
in men, 17, 18, 46, 48–51, 60, 72, 78–79, 89, 117
as tool of feminist resistance, 91–93
tricksters exhibiting, 17, 51, 174–75, 194
as universal human response, 50
of women mystics, 204, 206
and women's excessive giving, 131–32, 209

India
colonialism in, 79–81
widows' *sati* in, 108–10, 111, 117–118
"invisible hand" regulating economy, 8, 13
Ireland, Dennis J., 182–83
Irenaeus of Lyon, 6n.13, 78, 79, 80, 88, 139, 168
commentary on "rich young man," 56–60, 87
and ransom, 153–54, 153n.65, 160
Irigaray, Luce, 7, 201–2, 205, 206, 207
commentary on women and economics, 18, 102, 103–4, 167, 192
and consequences of giving the gift, 100–101
Isaac, 143
Isaiah, The Book of the Prophet
43:3–4   144
53   143

Jackson, Bob, 28, 203
James and John, mother of, 140, 140n.13
Jameson, Fredric, 26
Jeremias, Joachim, 142–43

Jerome, 92, 93, 122, 130–31, 192, 205
and virgins, views on, 127–29
Jesus
basileia (kingdom) of, trying to reach, 18, 38, 54, 55, 56, 96, 137–38n.5, 140, 193
as Counterfeit(ing) Christ, 19, 136–37, 175, 186, 212–23
crucifixion of compared with felling a tree, 209–10
as divine trickster, 12n.34, 138, 176, 181–86, 193, 219n.173
kenosis of, 104, 104n.52, 135, 149, 171, 222
Paul's teaching vs. teaching of, 137–38n.5
as ransom, 18, 136, 139, 144–45, 147, 151–53, 157–60, 171, 212–13, 220
and resistance to qualities of Roman Empire, 140–42, 140n.15
as a slave, 140–42, 146–51, 157, 159, 171
as a slave, feminist critiques of, 160–65
and woman who anoints him, 132–34, 208
women vs. men with, 140–41, 141n.16
See also Christianity; Christology
Jesus, C.E.O. (Jones), 189
Jesus, Inc. (Jones), 189
"Joe Millionaire" (TV show), 166n.105
Johansen, Ruthann Knechel, 216
John, The Gospel according to
1:14   226
Johnston, Carol, 84
Jones, Laura Beth, 189
Jones, Serene, 163, 179, 192, 211, 212
Justin, 56, 56–57n.58, 63

Keller, Catherine, 5, 13, 97, 109, 181, 186, 191, 192, 207
kenosis, 104, 104n.52, 135, 149, 171, 222. *See also* Jesus
Keshgegian, Flora, 164
Kintz, Linda, 203
Krueger, Derek, 194–95
Kumar, Amitava, 81, 82, 109

Landay, Lori, 202
Lasn, Kalle, 196–97
Latin America, 30n.28, 37
 economics vs. theology in, 29–30, 86
Leontius, 44, 194–95
Letter of the Martyrs of Lyons and Vienne, 114
Letter to Diognetus, 148
Levi-Strauss, Claude, 102
Levites, 145
liberation theology
 and economic theory, 4, 4n.7, 9–10, 30n.30
 feminist, 86, 108
 of Latin America, 26–27, 26n.14, 29, 30n.28, 33–34, 37, 86, 205
 liberalism of, 31
 for North America, 35–36, 191
 as response to capitalism, 3, 26–27, 26n.14, 86
Libidinal Economy (Lyotard), 222
Life Abundant: Rethinking Theology and Economy for a Planet in Peril (McFague), 35–36, 87, 161–62, 211
Life of Antony (Athanasius), 66, 68–72, 73–75, 77, 88, 123–24
Long, D. Stephen, 10, 30–32, 30n.30, 86
Loy, David R., 23
Luke, Gospel according to
16	19
16:1	182
16:1–13	182–86
16:2	182
16:8	186
16:8–9	181
16:9	132

Luther, Martin, 166, 168, 222
lutron (ransom), 137n.4, 139, 145–46, 171
Luz, Ulrich, 146
Lyman, Rebecca, 56–57, 59
Lyonnet, Stanislaus, 139, 145
Lyotard, Jean-FranÁois, 7, 222, 223

MacDonald, Dennis, 113, 118
MacKendrick, Karmen, 67, 70, 176–77, 188, 193
Macrina, 126, 127n.134
Malbon, Elizabeth Struthers, 104, 132, 133
Mammon, God and, 10, 23, 24, 25, 42, 45, 189, 193, 213
Man Nobody Knows, The (Barton), 189
Marcion, 154–55
Mark, Gospel according to
10:17–31	42
10:21	62
10:45	143, 144, 171
12:13–38	96
12:40	104
12:41–44	94
12:43	208
12:43–44	16
12:44	96, 104
14:3–5	132
14:3–9	132

Markus, Robert, 76–77
marriage
 as economic exchange, 160, 165–71
 Roman *conubium,* 129n.142

as slavery for women, 165–68, 220–21
of virgins, to "bridegroom" Christ, 92, 110, 123–30, 136, 220–21
Martin, Dale, 145, 146, 149
martyrdom, 110–22, 114n.92, 204
  of Agnes, 110–12
  of Blandina, 115–16
  contemporary domestic violence as form of, 112
  of Felicitas, 114–15, 115n.96
  and female suffering, 114–15
  and feminine virtues, 113–14, 113n.91
  of Perpetua, 114–15
  Thecla as trickster martyr, 93, 118–21, 126–27, 204–5
  virgins as martyrs, 110–12, 117, 204–5
Martyrdom of Saints Perpetua and Felicitas, 114–15
Marxism, 4, 4n.7, 6, 6n.14, 9, 15, 26, 26n.14, 27, 33, 81
Matthew, Gospel according to
  6:24   45
  8:20   54
  11:19   54
  19–20   51, 141
  19:16–23   44–45
  19:16–30   16, 17–18, 42, 83
  19:19b   61
  19:20   41, 83
  19:21   85
  19:22   74, 85
  19:23–24   47
  19:26   47
  19:28–30   47
  19:29   51
  20:20–28   140, 141
  20:25–28   140
  20:28   142, 144, 146, 157
  22:2–14   54
Matthiae, Gisela, 202
Mauss, Marcel, 99–100
McCloskey Donald/Deirdre N., 95–96
McFague, Sallie, 10, 34, 87, 192
  and ecological economics, 35–36, 37, 161–63, 191, 211–12
Meeks, M. Douglas, 10, 34, 36, 37, 38, 86–87, 98, 163, 221, 225
Míguez, Néstor, 29–30, 30n.28
Milbank, John, 10, 31, 32
Mill, John Stuart, 84
Miller, Patricia Cox, 127
mimicry, 38, 59, 106, 138, 159, 182, 193, 206, 207, 226
  of Jesus in martyrdom, 111, 112, 114, 116
  as strategy of colonialism, 79–81, 108–9, 193n.67, 213, 214
  as strategy of tricksters, 18, 51, 200–203, 207nn.131–133, 218, 221, 222, 223
"miraculous" exchange, 5, 14, 16, 18, 44, 80, 137–38, 148, 174
  and Counterfeit(ing) Christ, 213, 215, 217, 220, 225–26
  incarnation as, 135–36
  tradition of writing of, 138–39, 219n.173
Mite society. *See* Cent and Mite societies
Moi, Toril, 103
Moltmann, Jürgen, 18–19n.51, 20–21, 35
Moore, Michael, 198–200
Moore, Stephen D., 139, 147–48
Müller, Ulrich, 149

Nag Hammadi, 97
Nash, James, 191
Nelson, Julie A., 1, 83, 173–74

Newly Born Woman, The (Cixous and Clément), 91
Numbers
   3:12b–13a   145

oikonomia (household management), 4, 8, 48, 54n.53, 64, 116, 129, 146
   defined, 6
   as God's actions within the cosmos, 56–57
   of heaven, 98, 105
   imperial vs. divine, 55–56, 78
   Irenaeus of Lyon's commentary on, 59–60, 79, 154
   origins of, 16
   place of men vs. women in, 52–54, 53n.45
   theology and, 9–15
   towards a countereconomic theology, 34–40, 153, 211
   and tricksters pointing to countereconomy, 182–86
   See also economics
oikonomia theou (divine agency), 5, 6, 6n.12, 10, 57, 60, 87, 175
oikos (house), 4, 15, 16, 37, 60, 72
   and almsgiving, 64
   of empire, 73
   patriarchal, 52–54, 53n.45, 92, 93, 118, 120
   renouncing, 55, 127
   and women, 38–39, 47, 92, 93, 98, 110, 115, 121–25
Oratio catechetica (Gregory of Nyssa), 136, 158–60, 226
Origen, 60–66, 76, 83, 87–88, 139
   and Jesus as ransom, 157
orthopraxis, 29, 29n.27
ousia (property/being of the household), 46, 52, 95n.10, 105, 106, 106–7n.61, 155n.70

Pagels, Elaine, 75
Parker, Rebecca Ann, 164
Patterson, Orlando, 146
Paul
   difference in teaching from Jesus, 137–38n.5
   and slavery as salvation, 145, 149–50, 220
   and slavery/marriage connection, 167
   and Thecla, 119–21
Paula, 93, 127, 130–32
Peat, F. David, 178
pentecostal movements, 28
performance art, 196–98
Perpetua, 114–15n.95, 114–15, 116–17, 204
Phan, Peter C., 194
Phenomenology of the Spirit, The (Hegel), 8
Philippians, The Letter of Paul to the
   2   157
   2:5–8   135–36
   2:6–7   171
   2:6–8   149
   2:9   150
   2:10   149
Philo, the Alexandrian, 145
Plato, 49
Plotnitsky, Arkady, 8–9
Politeia (Aristotle), 52
Ponticianus, 73–74
"poor widow" figure, 3, 16, 94–95n.9
   vs. black woman trickster, 201
   and consequences of giving the gift, 98, 99–107
   as foreshadowing of Jesus' life and death, 104, 104n.52
   vs. Paula, 131
   related to female martyrs, 122
   vs. "rich young man," 46, 94–98

and sacrifice or martyrdom, 107–12
and status as widows, 106, 106–7n.61
as "wasteful," 132–33, 208
vs. woman who anoints Jesus, 132–34
See also martyrdom
Porter, Roy, 50–51
"Portrait of the *homo economicus* as a Young Man" (Feiner), 84
power, 76–77, 76n.125, 218
   serving, rather than ruling, 140–47
prosperity theology, 3, 27–30, 29n.24, 33, 51, 65n.82, 203–4
   in Africa, 3n.6, 28, 28–29n.23
Protestant Work Ethic and the Spirit of Capitalism, The (Weber), 4, 188
Przywara, Erich, 166–67, 168, 220–21

Rabelais, François, 185
ransom, 171
   in ancient Jewish literature, 142–45
   and ancient practices of slavery, 139, 145, 145n.31
   Jesus as, in deal with devil, 18, 136, 139, 144–45, 147, 151–53, 157–60, 171, 212–13, 220
   as *lutron*, 137n.4, 139, 145–46, 171
   paid for redemption, 18, 137–38, 137n.4, 144–45, 147–48
   paid to apostasy, 153–54, 153n.65
   in soteriology, 151–53, 152n.57
Ray, Darby K., 138, 184, 201–2, 216–17
reality TV shows, 165–66
Redefining Progress, 187
redemption, economic undertones of, 137–38, 137n.4
"rich young man," 3, 16, 40, 141
   and Athanasius' *Life of Antony*, 68–72
   Augustine's commentary on, 73–79, 88–89
   Clement of Alexandria's commentary on, 62–66
   as example of male householder, 54–55, 56
   hysteria of, as symptom of lack, 41–48
   Irenaeus of Lyon's commentary on, 56–60, 87
   and modern economics, 83–89
   Origen's commentary on, 60–66
   vs. "poor widow" figure, 46, 94–98
Roman Empire, 75–77, 88, 130
   economics of marriage in, 167
   Jesus' resistance to qualities of, 140–42, 140n.15
   slavery practices in, 145–46
Romans, The Letter of Paul to the 5:12–15   57
Ruether, Rosemary Radford, 86

Sabourin, Leopold, 139
Saiving, Valerie, 160–61
salvation history, 6, 9, 9n.27, 12, 12n.33, 14, 14n.40, 16, 19–21, 56–57, 151
Salvation of the Rich (Clement of Alexandria), 62, 88
Sandoval, Chela, 17n.49, 179
sati, 108–10, 111, 117–118
Schüssler Fiorenza, Elisabeth, 38, 134, 213
Schwager, Raymund, 218
Scott, Bernard B., 183
Scott, James, 108
Shaw, Brent D., 112
Showalter, Elaine, 50, 92
Sifuentes, Roberto, 198
"Signs Taken for Wonders: Questions of Ambivalence and Authority under a Tree outside Delhi" (Bhabba), 79–81

slaves
    in antiquity, 145–46, 150
    being, as form of redemption, 137–38, 138n.6, 140–41, 148–51
    being, as Jesus' disciples, 141
    and contemporary forms of slavery, 150–51, 150n.53, 168n.116, 169–70, 169n.122, 170n.124, 198, 214
    as divine slave tricksters, 3, 16, 18–19, 217–18
    and Jesus as slave, 140–42, 146–51, 157, 159, 160–65, 171
    and similarity of status with women, 38, 101–3, 102n.40, 115–16, 167–68, 168n.116
    women as, in marriage, 165–68, 220–21
    and women tricksters, 200–201
Smith, Adam, 8, 13
socially responsible investment funds (SRIs), 211
soteriology, 6, 18, 18–19n.51, 20, 70–71
    and Augustine, 75–77
    and economic transactions with the devil, 151–53, 153n.64, 157–59
Spivak, Gayatri, 17, 33, 72, 137, 179, 207
    and colonialism/capitalism, 81–82, 81n.144, 82nn.145–146, 107–8
    and *sati*, 109–10, 111, 117–18, 118n.105
stigmata, 139
Still, Judith, 101–2
Stoics, 145
Stupid White Men (Moore), 198, 200
Stylites, Saint Simon, 208–9
Symachus, 74
Symeon, 194–95

Talen, Bill, 195

Taylor, Mark C., 10, 23, 25, 26, 220
Taylor, Mark McClain, 32
ten commandments, 44–46, 45n.12, 58
    love your neighbor as yourself, 61–63, 87–88
Tertullian, 113, 139, 154–56, 217
Thecla, 93, 118–21, 118n.106, 120n.109, 121n.111, 126–27, 127n.134, 204–5
theology
    a/theology, 25, 25n.9
    comparison with economics as discipline, 86, 86n.164
    constructive theology, 4, 4n.8
    and effects on of sexuality, 121, 121n.113, 168–69
    feminist, 15, 20, 20n.54, 42, 160–65, 211–12
    as form of counterfeiting God, 215–16
    gender issues in, 4, 19–20, 219
    images for dissent in modern world, 2, 2n.4, 5, 6–7
    influences of economics on, 23–25, 39
    and *oikonomia*, 9–15
    theological genealogies, 11–12, 15–16, 19
    Trinitarian theology, 35
    See also Christology; liberation theology; prosperity theology; soteriology
Theology of Liberation (Gutierrez), 26–27
"third space" economic theory/theology, 4–5, 6, 15, 30–32, 34, 36–37, 44, 177, 193, 194, 207, 216. See also economics; *oikonomia* (household management); theology
Torjesen, Karen, 38, 52, 84
torture, 151

tricksters
  African American, 184, 200–201
  as agents of transformative power, 2–3, 176, 176n.9
  B'rer Rabbit, 112, 184
  clowns, 202–3
  as "con" men, 173, 174
  countereconomic, 174–81, 182–86, 185n.39
  "figures," 16–19
  God the economist, 14–15, 18
  High John, 184
  hysteria, exhibited by, 17, 51, 174–75, 194
  Jesus as Counterfeit(ing) Christ, 19, 136–37, 175, 186, 212–23
  Jesus as divine trickster, 12n.33, 138, 176, 181–86, 193, 219n.173
  male vs. female, 200–203, 207
  martyrs as, 93, 112, 112n.87, 118–21, 120n.110, 122, 126–27, 204–5
  mimicry as strategy of, 18, 51, 200–203, 207nn.131–133, 218, 221, 222, 223
  "modest witness," 12–13, 12nn.32–33, 20, 205
  and performance art, 196–98
  Saint Mysteria, 19, 51, 134, 174, 175, 186, 203–12
  tactics and strategies of, 12–13, 12n.34
  transgendered, 223–24, 223n.188
  women, 200–203, 207
  See also "poor widow" figure; "rich young man;" Holy Fool; slaves
Trigg, Joseph, 157
Trudinger, Paul, 183
Truth, Sojourner, 94, 201
Twitchell, James B., 189

Upkong, Justin S., 183

Valantasis, Richard, 190, 191
Veith, Ilza, 49
Via, Dan, 183
virgins
  Alexandrian virgins, 124–26
  being, as form of asceticism, 118–21, 122–32, 125n.124, 192
  and feminine virtues, 113, 113n.91
  heretical, 205–6
  Jerome's views on, 127–29
  and marriage to "bridegroom" Christ, 92, 110, 123–30, 136, 220–21
  martyrdom of, 110–12, 117, 204–5

Wal–Mart, 211
Ward, Graham, 225
wealth
  detachment from, 65–66
  early Christian attitudes towards, 62, 62n.71, 64–65, 64n.79
  eternal wealth promised, through giving up, 17–18, 47–48, 51–55, 65, 69–70, 94–95
  fear of lack of, 41–44, 44n.8, 46–47
  giving up, as exemplified in *Life of Antony,* 68–72, 69n.95
  giving up, as form of loving one's neighbor, 61–62
  giving up, for purpose of salvation, 63–66
  See also asceticism; prosperity theology
Weber, Max, 4, 67, 83, 188–90, 214–15
West, Traci, 112
Whitehead, Alfred N., 2, 2n.3, 35
"Who Wants to Marry a Multimillionaire?" (TV show), 165–66, 165n.100

Williams, Delores, 163–64
Williams, Joel F., 94
Winterson, Jeanette, 203
women
    African Americans, 112, 163–64, 200–201
    as ascetics, 92, 118–21, 121n.114, 122–32, 125n.124, 192–93
    and conservative gender roles, 203–4
    in early Christianity, 18, 52–54, 53n.45, 123, 123n.120
    in early Christianity, as patrons, 38–39
    as economic property, 101–3, 102n.40
    and economics, 18, 34, 42, 207, 207–8n.135
    and feminine virtues, 113–14, 113n.90
    holy women, 92–93, 122, 122n.117
    and marriage as slavery for, 165–68, 220–21
    vs. men with Jesus, 140–41, 141n.16
    and Muslim practice of veiling, 109–10
    Saint Mysteria trickster, 19, 51, 134, 174, 175, 186, 203–12
    and similarity of status with slaves, 38, 101–3, 102n.40, 115–16, 167–68, 168n.116
    as symbolic capital, 103, 103n.43
    and the ten commandments, 45n.12
    tricksters, 200–203, 207
    "wasteful" and "indecent" women, 132–34, 205–11
    See also "poor widow" figure; feminism; hysteria; marriage; martyrdom; virgins
Works and Almsgiving (Cyprian of Carthage), 46, 64, 156–57
Wright, Addison, 104
Wylie-Kellermann, Jeanie, 186, 208